ZICKZACK

Bryan Goodman-Stephens, Paul Rogers, Lol Briggs.

Lehrerhandbuch 1

S. Nicholson, London, August 1992

Nelson

Zickzack Stage 1

Teacher's Book
Pupils' Book 1
Pupils' Book 1A
Pupils' Book 1B
Reproduction Masters
Cassettes
Flashcards

Assessment packs:
Was kannst du? 1A
Was kannst du? 1B

Thomas Nelson and Sons Ltd
Nelson House, Mayfield Road
Walton-on-Thames, Surrey
KT12 5PL, UK

51 York Place
Edinburgh
EH1 3JD, UK

Thomas Nelson (Hong Kong) Ltd
Toppan Building 10/F
22A Westlands Road
Quarry Bay, Hong Kong

Thomas Nelson Australia
102 Dodds Street
South Melbourne, Victoria 3205
Australia

Nelson Canada
1120 Birchmount Road
Scarborough, Ontario
M1K 5G4, Canada

© Bryan Goodman-Stephens, Paul Rogers & Lol Briggs
1987

First published by E. J. Arnold and Son Ltd 1987
ISBN 0-560-15000-8

This edition published by Thomas Nelson and Sons Ltd
1989
ISBN 0-17-439301-6
NPN 9876543

Printed in Great Britain by Bell & Bain Ltd, Glasgow

Tape Recordings

Speakers from:

Theater an der Marschnerstraße, Hamburg
(organiser: Frau I. Froh).

Walddörfergymnasium, Volksdorf
(organiser: Herr G. Frische).

Recorded at Studio Bardeleben, Hamburg.

Acknowledgements

We would like to thank the following people for their
valuable advice and assistance in the preparation of
Zickzack Stage 1:

Margaret Briggs
Diane Collett
Walter & Gülborg Gerecht
Ulrike Gersiek
Pamela Goodman-Stephens
Mike Hardy
Marianne Illi
Manfred Jungke and pupils of the Realschule, Bad Sachsa
Klaus May
Jeanne McCarthy
Herbert Nagel
Emma Rogers
Monika & Michael Schätzle
Christian Schweiger
Michael Spencer
Anna Timm
Jane Tuppen
Karen Woermer and pupils of the Gymnasium
Schwarzenberg, Harburg

We are particularly indebted to Gerold Deffner, formerly
Fachberater für Deutsch als Fremdsprache at the Goethe-
Institut, London, for his major contribution to all aspects
of the course over a period of two years.

We would like to thank the staff at the following
schools who class-tested draft material:

Mrs. M. Bennie, Inverkeithing High School, Fife
Mrs. A. Chaplin, Kineton High School, Warwickshire
Mr. P. H. Cox, Shireland High School, Warley
Mr. M. Foster, Campion School, Leamington Spa
Mr. O. Gray, Henry Beaufort School, Winchester
Mrs. L. Hagger-Vaughan, Shireland High School,
Warley
Mrs. E. Hinze, Chailey School, nr. Lewes
Mr. B. Lightman, Sondes Place School, Dorking
Mrs. J. Macrae, Armadale Academy, Lothian
Mrs. C. A. McKinven, Blantyre High School,
Lanarkshire
Mrs. H. Milnthorpe, Hayesfield School, Bath
Mr. J. D. C. Muir, Queen Anne High School,
Dunfermline
Mr. D. Neil, Monkseaton High School, Whitley Bay
Mr. D. Richardson, Woodkirk High School, Leeds
Mrs. R. Smith, Churcher's College, Petersfield
Ms. E. Williscroft, Bexhill High School, Bexhill-on-Sea
Mr. M. E. Wydall, Stratford-upon-Avon High School,
Warwickshire

Contents

Introduction .... page 3

Chapter 1:   Hallo! Wie heißt du? .... page 15

Chapter 2:   Meine Familie .... page 29

Chapter 3:   In der Schule .... page 42

Chapter 4:   Die Mahlzeiten .... page 53

Chapter 5:   ... und nach der Schule? .... page 63

Chapter 6:   Was kostet das? .... page 82

Chapter 7:   Willkommen in Osnabrück .... page 99

Chapter 8:   Beim Einkaufen .... page 117

Chapter 9:   Wie fährt man? .... page 140

Chapter 10: Wir feiern .... page 155

Chapter 11: Mir ist schlecht .... page 177

Chapter 12: Wo fährst du hin? .... page 192

Internationaler Treff .... page 205

Introduction

What is Zickzack?

Zickzack is a German course designed for beginners aged 11 to 13 and leading to examination at 16. It consists of three stages.

Stage 1 is suitable for a very wide range of ability, and is both a self-contained introduction and a firm basis for further study.

Stage 2 deals with topics chosen for their appeal to the age group. Topics determine the language and functions covered rather than vice versa. Points of grammar arising are dealt with clearly and concisely.

Stage 3 maintains the communicative and functional approach and completes coverage of the topics and functions of the various GCSE syllabuses.

Special features of the course

A   Authentic materials

Pupils learn to cope with authentic materials, to engage in purposeful verbal exchanges and to express their own feelings, interests and opinions.

B   Grammar

Presented at three different levels:

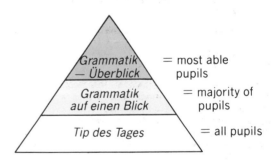

Level 1: *Tip des Tages* — new structures for productive use without formal, grammatical analysis. Provides help and support to pupils in pair and group-work and in writing.

Level 2: *Grammatik auf einen Blick* — summaries of all new structures. Functional presentation with occasional grammatical explanations.

Level 3: *Grammatik — Überblick* — section at the end of the book. Summary of main structures. Presentation both functional and formal.

C *Noch etwas mehr*

Includes substantial additional practice for both higher and lower ability pupils.

D **Colour**

Each Pupil's Book contains extensive use of full colour.

E **Teacher's Book**

Provides suggestions for the sequence and use of the material and the language necessary to conduct lessons in German.

F **Humour**

Many cartoons and entertaining games throughout.

G **Cassettes**

Produced from material generated from scenarios with unscripted dialogues. Voices featured are appropriate to the age group. Teachers can write in their own tape number for each item in the spaces provided in the cassette symbols by each tapescript. This will help them to find the start of each item more easily. A full index of recordings can be found on p.12.

H **Repromasters**

An **essential** part of the course. A large number of worksheets, information-gap activities, games, handouts and overhead transparency masters. (See the introduction to the Repromasters for hints on their use.) Reductions for all the worksheets are included for reference in the Teacher's Book. A full list can be found on p.11.

I **Flashcards**

112 in total, double-sided, in a range of colours. A full list appears in the Teacher's Book along with numerous hints and suggestions for their use.

How to use the Teacher's Book

The layout is clear for easy access. Symbols are used to show at a glance which components the teacher will require for each task.

As with the suggested sequence, practice sections are provided for use at the discretion of the teacher. Solutions to all major activities, including worksheets, appear at the end of the relevant sections.

For reference, German-English vocabulary lists are printed at the end of each chapter in the Teacher's Book. These are full lists of new items of both productive and receptive vocabulary within each chapter.

For testing productive vocabulary, the *Tip des Tages* should be used, but teachers may like to select items from the vocabulary lists for further testing of productive or receptive items, depending on the ability of their pupils.

A full *Wörterliste,* including all productive and receptive items, appears at the end of the Pupil's Book.

Recorded material: cassette recorder required

17 ← Worksheet number

Task to be found on Repromaster

144 (1B 46) ← Page number in appropriate editions

Task to be found in Pupil's Book

Blackboard or Overhead Projector required

Pair-Work task

6 **Area 2**

Chapter number and area

L, S, R, W

Skills being practised in a task: listening, speaking, reading, writing.

 nem 4

Task to be found in 'Noch etwas mehr' section

Suggested sequence of language for the teacher to use to introduce or explain the task

10-14 ← card numbers

Flashcards required

35

Symbol used again to mark the beginning of the tapescript. Box for the teacher to note down the tape reference for personal use

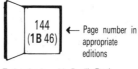

Group-Work task

{ Tapescript

Approach to grammar

All pupils will handle *Tip des Tages,* and the majority should be expected to handle *Grammatik auf einen Blick.* The *Grammatik — Überblick* is intended for reference only by the most able pupils.

An outline of Stage 1, including a breakdown of the grammar covered, can be found on p.14.

Assessment

In keeping with the GCSE communicative marking schemes, teachers may wish to devise simple symbols to replace numbers which are usually associated with accuracy rather than communication. A 0 - 1 - 2 scheme might, for example, convert thus:

Meaning not communicated

Partly communicated

Meaning clear

Or a 0 - 1 - 2 - 3 - 4 - 5 scheme thus:

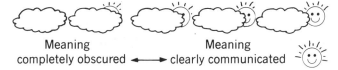

Meaning completely obscured ⟵⟶ Meaning clearly communicated

Many *Noch etwas mehr* items and the vast majority of Area 6 items may be used as they stand for classroom assessment.

Use of German in the classroom

Since the aim of any communicative course must be extensive use of the target language, English is only used or suggested for specific GCSE-type tests, usually at the back of the book, in *Noch etwas mehr,* or for the occasional complicated activity, where the German instructions might confuse some pupils and be much more difficult than the language required to perform the task.

Organisation of pair-work/ group-work

All pair-work and group-work tasks, of which there are a great number, must be well planned and the whole class must be clear about how the tasks are to be completed. The use of individual pupils to provide model dialogues with the teacher is the most successful way of presenting tasks to a group. Despite the undoubted noise they generate, they also generate an enormous amount of language and increase pupil motivation, provided they are kept brief and are incorporated into a variety of other activities. Pupils should not be placed in a situation for which their language is inadequate. The main aim should always be communication and teachers should take care not to place too much emphasis on absolute accuracy. Try to ensure that pupils do not always team up with the same partners, and keep an unobtrusive check on the level of communication.

Teaching to different abilities

Mixed ability classes should be able to deal with most activities, except some of the more demanding items in *Noch etwas mehr,* and they should thrive on the communicative oral tasks in the book. Pupils in lower ability sets will benefit from a gentler pace and will find that certain of the role-playing, listening and reading tasks will be more accessible if they are divided into two or three sections. The basic items in *Noch etwas mehr* will be particularly appropriate.

More able pupils should expect a brisk pace covering all aspects of the book, including the extended reading passages and more demanding items in *Noch etwas mehr.* They may not need intensive practice of some items.

All pupils will require support in written activities.

Teaching the different skills

Make sure, in all skill areas, that pupils make use of all available clues: setting/context; title; visuals; general knowledge; specific knowledge of Germany and German-speaking countries; features they recognise.

Listening

Encourage pupils initially to **skim** recorded items, i.e. elicit a general answer to the question: *,Worum geht es hier?'.* In order to achieve this, they will 'discard' language they find too difficult and focus on any recognisable vocabulary or structure. After skimming they should be expected to **scan,** again discarding language, which this time is redundant, in the light of the specific questions being asked.

The most difficult-looking texts can be made accessible, provided the tasks based on the text are graded, and pupils will feel they have achieved a great deal if they answer the specific questions asked of them.

Reading

Again pupils will be expected to skim and scan texts, but many pupils should also be able to go beyond mere scanning, and should read more intensively, extracting greater detail and beginning to draw their own conclusions about opinions expressed in texts, emotions and intentions. This will be moving them towards the higher level skill of **inferencing.**

Speaking

Great emphasis is placed upon accuracy of pronunciation, including activities on the alphabet and basic sound differences between key letters in German and English (z, w, v, j, plus umlauts, dipthongs and other letters at the end of words, -b (halb), -d (Geld), and so on). Pronunciation should always be corrected in a positive, supportive manner — it is not difficult to praise pupils for communicating messages successfully whilst suggesting improvements in accent and intonation. Reading aloud, used judiciously, can be particularly helpful.

Writing

Considerable patience will be required over pupils' failure to use capital letters correctly. Communication can still be praised, at the same time requiring a greater degree of accuracy from pupils. The differences in notation, such as ß, continental 7 and 1, should be drawn to the pupils' attention as they occur in the Teacher's Book.

Integrated skills approach

Despite the fact that GCSE requires that skills should be tested discretely, pupils should be given the benefit of an integrated approach, where German is used extensively to cue listening, speaking, reading and writing activities. In cases where English questions have been used (from *Noch etwas mehr,* for example), pupils should expect to answer the same questions again immediately in German, and could then record new vocabulary for homework.

List of Flashcards

The following flashcards are provided for use with Zickzack I. The numbers refer to the chapter and area to which they are most appropriate.

Pets 2/3
1 dog (with lead)
2 cat
3 budgie
4 horse (with saddle)
5 mouse
6 guinea pig
7 hamster
8 goldfish
9 rabbit
10 tortoise

Housing 2/5
11 *Wohnung*
12 *Reihenhaus*
13 *Einfamilienhaus*
14 *Doppelhaus*
15 *Bungalow*

Breakfast and other meals 4/1, 3, 4; 5/2; 8/2, 3; 9/5
16 Rolls; *Schwarzbrot;* loaf of bread
17 jar of marmelade/jam; jar of *Nutella;* jar of honey
18 packet of cornflakes; muesli packet
19 glass of milk; packet
20 cup of coffee; cup of tea; cup of cocoa
21 carton of orange juice; apple juice
22 cheeses
23 platter of cold meats
24 butter (packet); margarine (tub)
25 boiled egg; box of eggs
26 *Quark;* yoghurt
27 chips; mayonnaise
28 sugar (granules + cubes)
29 onions; red/green peppers
30 salt; pepper
31 cut of beef; any other meat
32 bottle of cooking oil
33 noodles; spaghetti
34 (cooked) chicken
35 bottle of coca cola; bottle of lemonade
36 rissoles
37 potatoes
38 tomatoes (tinned + fresh)

Activities 5/1, 2
39 watching TV
40 computer
41 record player; radio; cassette player
42 football; basketball
43 friends meeting/greeting
44 tennis; table tennis
45 cycling; rollerskates
46 going shopping
47 eating at table at home
48 homework
49 guitar; flute; clarinet; recorder; piano
50 comic; book
51 chess board + pieces
52 *Jugendzentrum*
53 *Disko;* gymnastics/dance
54 cooking
55 cinema
56 strolling
57 slouching on a sofa
58 stamp collection

More food and quantities 6/5; 8/2, 3; 9/5
59 *Hamburger*
60 *(Brat) wurst;* tube of mustard; curry sauce
61 *ein belegtes Brot;* (cheese + ham)
62 crisps
63 *Schaschlik*
64 crate of beer; litre of wine
65 carton/box (of chocolates); bag of sweets; (Mars) bar
66 *100 Gramm/200 Gramm/500 Gramm/1 Pfund*

In town 7/1, 2
67 *Dom*
68 *Rathaus*
69 *Schloß; Stadtmauer*
70 *Restaurant; Café*
71 *Stadthalle*

72 office blocks; high-rise flats
73 swimming pool (indoor + outdoor)
74 sports stadium
75 post office (main)
76 campsite
77 *Verkehrsamt*
78 harbour
79 railway station
80 hospital
81 car park
82 bank
83 museum

Shops 8/1

84 *Metzgerei* (backed with meats: *Wurst, Schinken* etc.)
85 *Bäckerei* (backed with bread)
86 *Drogerie* (backed with toothpaste, cosmetics etc.)
87 *Apotheke* (backed with medicines)
88 *Konditorei* (backed with pastries)
89 *Buchhandlung* (backed with books)
90 *Sportgeschäft* (backed with sports equipment)
91 *Schuhgeschäft* (backed with footwear)
92 *Kleidergeschäft* (backed with clothes on rails)
93 *Warenhaus* (backed with floor plan, records, consumer goods etc.)
94 *Supermarkt* (backed with tins, washing powder, biscuits etc.)
95 *Markt* (backed with fruit and vegetables etc.)

Purchases 8/4

96 postcard; stamps
97 t-shirt
98 souvenirs (doll, beer mug etc.)
99 writing block; writing paper; envelopes
100 purse/wallet
101 rubber; pencil; pen; ink
102 flowers; plants

Means of transport 9/1

103 on foot
104 bicycle
105 mofa; motorbike; moped
106 car
107 bus
108 tram
109 train *(S-Bahn)*
110 underground
111 ferry
112 aeroplane

Many flashcards can be used to represent several constructions.

e.g. No. 1: *der Hund/das ist ein Hund/ich habe einen Hund/ich führe den Hund an der Leine/der Hund läuft schnell/usw.*

You may also find it very useful to make the following cards and keep them with the rest.

— blank card for covering all or part of a flashcard

— to prompt a question: to signify any missing part of a set or sequence

— for *richtig* or *falsch* activities.

Making and using flashcards

Pupils generally respond well to visuals, and home-made flashcards can inject humour and increase motivation and comprehension. Cut-outs from magazines, simple line drawings, symbols, photographs etc. can all make good flashcards.

Various types of flashcard design

a) Picture on one side only
b) Related pictures on both sides, for example: *glücklich/unglücklich; hat einen Hund/hat keinen Hund; normalerweise trägt/heute trägt ...* (pictures b).
c) Related pictures on one or more flashcards, for example, a sequence of events. The Present Tense is used in describing them. (Later the Past Tenses can be used in recalling the sequence of events when the cards are removed.) (Pictures c).
d) Folded cards with one part hidden when folded, e.g. *Warum läuft er so schnell? Der Schulbus fährt los.* (Pictures d).
e) Card with a flap. The flap can be used to change the picture, e.g. *Normalerweise geht sie zu Fuß (zum Büro). Heute läuft sie Rollschuh.* (Pictures e).
f) A concertina of pictures can be used to tell a story. (Pictures f).

b

c

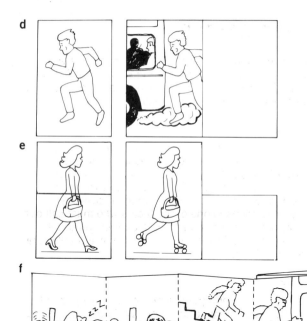

d

e

f

Some flashcard activities:

Half the class knows (Class/group/pair-work)

The pupils ask the questions. Once all the pupils know which cards you have in your hands, select one of them and show it to half of the class. The other half of the class must then ask questions to find out what it is (using questions forms and the Present Tense).

Kim's game (Class/group/pair-work)

Show about ten cards from one set (e.g. foods) and then ask the class to try and tell you what they remember. When they can remember all of them, remove one and ask them which they think is missing. Alternatively, change the order of two of them.

20 questions (Class/group-work)

(Or any number of questions.)

Hold a card so that the class cannot see it. Give a clue, e.g.:

Teacher: Ich habe ein Haustier
Class: Haben Sie eine Katze?

Miming (Class/group-work)

Show a picture of an object and ask a pupil to mime what is on the card so that the others can guess what it is.

Odd man out (Class/group-work)

Show four cards. Ask pupils to decide which they think does not fit with the others. Useful for revision of earlier flashcards.

Hast du das gesehen? (Class)

Challenge the pupils: flash the card for a split second only. Ask them to describe the picture, e.g.:

Q: Was hast du gesehen? (Was war drauf?)
A: Einen Mann (Ein Mann)
Q: War das ein Mann, John? Oder zwei?
A: Nein, das war eine Frau.

Allow pupils to cherish their illusions and encourage them to converse/speculate or even disagree before eventually showing them the card at length.

Such speculation can also be engendered by blurring slides or overhead transparency drawings and inviting pupils to work out what is depicted. The image should only be brought into sharper focus when each stage of questioning has been exhausted.

Was ist das? (To be played with any groups of flashcards depicting nouns)

The pile of flashcards is shuffled and a plain piece of paper placed on top to hide the picture. The caller looks under the paper to see what the top card is and says:

,Was ist das?'

Other pupils ask: ,Ist das ein(e) + noun?' and the person who guesses correctly comes out and acts as caller. He removes the top card and looks at the next before asking: ,Was ist das?'.

Was machst du?

This game is similar to the above, but with flashcards depicting actions.

Ich möchte ...

This game is played by two groups or small teams competing and several variations on the basic theme are possible (e.g. using different shops and combinations of cards).

1   Das Lebensmittelgeschäft (1). (Cards for butter, coffee, milk, wine, biscuits, etc.)

2   Das Lebensmittelgeschäft (2). (Cards for other foods and drinks).

The cards are given out to the pupils in each group who hide the pictures. Someone from group I asks group 2:

,Ich möchte ... + noun.'

If it is in stock, the second group must hand it over saying:

,Bitte schön.'

The group receiving keeps the card but does not look at it again.

Next someone from group 2 says:

,Ich möchte ... + noun'

If the product is not in stock the grocer says:

,Es tut mir leid.'

The object of the game is to see which group buys out the other first, and the problem is to remember which things have been sold and which remain.

A complication of the game is for the shoppers to ask a particular individual in each group if (s)he has a specific product and only to receive it if it is held by that person. Of course, the game lasts much longer when played like this.

Flashcard Bingo

Pupils could make their own sets of Bingo cards with four divisions and draw on them (or cut out and stick on) pictures of four of the things depicted on the flashcards. Each group of pupils could make sets of cards dealing with a different vocabulary area and then change them round for vocabulary revision games. (For eight vocabulary items provide eight cards.)

e.g.

1 bike	2 moped	2 moped	3 car	3 car	4 bus	4 bus	5 plane
3 car	4 bus	4 bus	5 plane	5 plane	6 train	6 train	7 boat
5 plane	6 train	6 train	7 boat	7 boat	8 motorbike	8 motorbike	1 bike
7 boat	8 motorbike	8 motorbike	1 bike	1 bike	2 moped	2 moped	3 car

Players need four counters or buttons each. The caller should shuffle the pile of relevant flashcards and turn them up one at a time saying:-

,*Das ist ein Zug'* (or ,*Ich fahre mit dem Zug'*).

The winner (who must shout ,*Lotto')* is the player whose card is full first and who can also say the names of the four nouns depicted in German. If the first to finish is unable to do this, he is out and the caller continues until the next card is full.

Richtig oder falsch? (Played in groups)

This is a version of 'Simon Says'. The leader has a pile of flashcards. He picks one up and shows the group, making a statement about it in German. If the statement is *richtig* everyone repeats it, but if it is *falsch,* they keep quiet. Anyone speaking in the wrong place or failing to repeat a true statement is out. The winner becomes the new leader.

Other games

There are many games which can be used to motivate practice of numbers, vocabulary and structures. Some are suggested at various places in the teacher's book, others which may be useful are listed below:

Und dann?

The teacher, (or later a pupil), counts aloud stopping at intervals and pointing at a pupil who must say the next number, or he is out. A more complicated version of this is *Dirigent.* For this the class is divided into two teams (*vorwärts* and *rückwärts*). The 'conductor' says any number and points to one of the teams who must call out the next or the previous number, depending on which team is indicated. Here again, a pupil can eventually take the place of *Dirigent.*

Zählt mal so!

The teacher (or later a pupil) starts off by saying ,*Zählt mal so!'* and beginning to count in a particular way, either forwards or backwards or alternate numbers or later in multiples of 2, 3 etc. Pupils join in as soon as they can with the right sequence and are out if they count a wrong number. The caller changes the sequence at intervals by saying ,*Zählt mal so!'* and beginning again. A group version of this can be played, in which only the group the teacher points at counts in the sequence which he begins and a group which makes a mistake or fails to grasp the sequence and join in after the first three or four numbers is out.

Bist du wach?

Each pupil in the class is given a number or a word at the beginning of a week and a full list is written on a notice or at the side of the blackboard. At any odd time during the German lessons for that week the teacher will call out a number and word and the correct pupil should stand up. If not, he is out and crossed off the list. At the end of the week those left on the list could perhaps be given a team point.

Abwischen!

The numbers are written on the blackboard in random order. When the caller says a number a pupil must rush out and rub the number off. This can be played by the teacher just pointing at the next pupil, or in groups or in teams. In the latter case it is advisable to write two sets of numbers on each half of the blackboard and provide two board rubbers. If the teacher wants the numbers left on for further practice they could be ringed in coloured chalk instead of being rubbed off.

This game can also be played with other vocabulary, in which case the teacher either draws a set of objects or writes a series of words on the blackboard.

Number square

Draw a square like the one below on the board or OHP. Pupils have to say the numbers against the clock, incurring a five second penalty for any incorrect number. This could be played individually or in teams. This, too, can be played with pictures or symbols to practise other vocabulary.

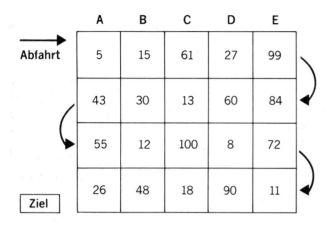

Mehr oder weniger? (or Höher oder niedriger?)

For this game you need a set of flashcards plus ten cards showing each of the numbers 10 — 20 — 30 — 40 — 50 — 60 — 70 — 80 — 90 — 100.

Divide the class into teams and display any of the flashcards, asking an appropriate question, e.g. ,Was ist das?'; ,Was machst du?'; ,Stelle eine Frage'; ,Entschuldigung, wo ist hier der/die/das ... ?'.

The first pupil to answer correctly wins for his/her team the right to work through a maximum of five of the numbered cards, (which have been shuffled). Each time the team must identify the number shown and then, if the answer was correct, decide whether the next (hidden) number card is higher or lower.

e.g. Card no. 70 is displayed by the teacher:

Pupil: Siebzig.
Teacher: Richtig. Mehr oder weniger (die nächste?)? or Höher oder niedriger?
Pupil: Weniger (niedriger).
Teacher: (Revealing card no. 20.) Richtig. Wieviel ist das?
Pupil: Zwanzig ...

Any pupil from the team may answer. If the team guesses the correct sequence (higher or lower), and gives the number correctly, the point for the original flashcard answer is given, plus a bonus for each extra number guessed correctly. If they guess incorrectly or make a mistake on any of the numbers the game starts again with another flashcard.

Würfelspiele

Some games require dice. These can be bought in sufficient quantities for a class or simple alternatives can be made:

e.g.   Six sided pencil with numbers written on.

Spinner made of card to go over a matchstick or (if big enough) a pencil.

Child's building brick.

Was macht das?

Players throw the dice and say aloud the appropriate numbers, or add up in German a sequence of numbers and see who has the most after six throws.

Die Leiter

Two or more 6-rung ladders can be drawn on the blackboard with a number (or word, part of verb, etc.) for each rung. Each team or group throws the dice and reads out the number or word and if it is the next on the ladder, it is crossed off and the team moves up to the next rung. No number or word must be crossed off until that rung is reached and the first team to reach the top of the ladder wins.

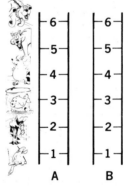

Ja/Nein Spiel

A pupil comes to the front of the class and the teacher asks him/her questions. The pupil has to answer without using the words Ja or Nein. If (s)he does, (s)he is out. A score can be kept of the number of questions each pupil answers 'correctly'. As well as being fun, this game helps familiarise pupils with phrases like ,Ich glaube schon', ,das stimmt', ,genau', ,natürlich', ,richtig', and so on. Questions like ,Trinkst du gern Wein?' can be answered with ,Ich trinke sehr gern Wein', etc.

From the teacher's point of view a good way of catching pupils out is to ask a question that requires a factual answer, and then to repeat their answer for confirmation.

e.g   T: Wann ist dein Geburtstag?
      P: Am 14. Juli.
      T: Am 14?
      P: Ja.

Kannst du einen Satz bilden?

A particularly good game for practice of word order and/or conjugation of verbs. Divide the class into two equal teams. Write a selection of words (see below for examples) on plain paper, making two copies of each — one for each team. Before the game begins these can be used to demonstrate the word order/conjugation point being practised, by sticking them in various combinations to the board and pegging them to a line or by getting pupils to stand in front of the class holding them.

| Ich | gehe | Morgen | gehe | Ich |

The physical **changing places of pupils** when a new component forces a change to the word order helps to make the point graphically. Similarly with inversion for questions. To play the game, distribute one set of word-cards to each team. A good, clear space will be needed in the classroom. Say a sentence in English. The aim is for each team to compose the sentence in German by getting pupils with the appropriate word-cards to stand in a line in front of the class. The first team to compose the sentence correctly gets a point. The game can become rather frantic, of course, but in order to arouse in pupils a passionate desire to get word order right this seems a fair price.

Below is an example of 15 word-cards (two sets of which would serve a class of 30) that could be used to practise both conjugation and word order. The teacher can quickly manufacture sets of his/her own word-cards to suit the occasion.

ich	wir	morgen	gehe	ins Kino
du	ihr	heute	gehst	schwimmen
er			geht	in die Stadt
sie			gehen	

N.B. In order to get all pupils involved, it is advisable to write a list of the words used and tick them off as they are required.

A variation of this is to have two-sided work-cards, thus increasing the possibilities — and the panic.

Useful addresses

Austrian Government Tourist Office: 30 St. George St., London W1R 9FA
German Government Tourist Office: 61 Conduit St., London W1R 0EN
Swiss Government Tourist Office: 1 New Coventry St., London W1V 8EE
Austrian Embassy: 18 Belgrave Mews, London SW1X 8HU
German Federal Republic Embassy: 23 Belgrave Square, London SW1X 8HW
Swiss Embassy: 16-18 Montagu Place, London W1H 2BQ
Lufthansa: 23/28 Piccadilly, London W1V 0EJ
CILT (Centre for Information on Language Teaching and Research): Regent's College, Inner Circle, Regent's Park, London NW1 4NS
Goethe Institut: 50 Princes Gate, Exhibition Road, London SW7 2PH
CBEVE (Central Bureau for Educational Visits and Exchanges): Seymour Mews House, Seymour Mews, London W1H 9PE

List of Reproduction Masters

No		Chapter/Area
1	Europa	1/3
2	Hier spricht man Deutsch	1/3
3A	Wie heißt dein Partner?	1/6
3B	Wie heißt dein Partner?	1/6
4	Und du? Wie heißt du?	2/1
5A	Wie heißen sie?	2/1
5B	Wie heißen sie?	2/1
6	Tiere	2/3
7	Wo wohnen sie?	2/5
8	Welches Zimmer ist das?	2/5
9	Was sind die Unterschiede?	2/5
10	Wo wohne ich?	2/6
11	Die Uhrzeit	3/2
12	Welches Fach ist das?	3/3
13	Kreuzworträtsel/Stundenplan-Lotto	3/3
14	Die Klasse 7c	3/3
15	Fünf Unterschiede	3/4
16	Was ißt man zum Frühstück?	4/1
17	Zum Frühstück ...	4/1
18	Ißt du gern Süßes?	4/3
19	Interviews/Kreuzworträtsel	4/3
20	Was machen sie nach der Schule?	5/1
21	Was machst du gern? Was machst du nicht gern?	5/2
22	Wer ist dein Computerpartner? Wer ist deine Computerpartnerin?	5/2
23	Jugendzentrum Pinneberg	5/2
24	Was spielst du?	5/3
25	Wann ist die Sesamstraße?	5/5
26	Dienstag, 18. Februar	5/5
27	Hans-Werners Tagebuch	5/6
28	Lückentext — Freizeit	5/6
29	Gern, nicht gern	5/6
30	Treffpunkt	5/6
31	Haben Sie mein Portemonnaie?	6/1
32	Acht junge Leute	6/3
33	Was kostet das?	6/4
34	Wir gehen einkaufen	6/4

35	Zwölf Unterschiede	6/4
36	Am Schnellimbiß	6/5
37	Was ißt du gern?	6/5
38	Die Achterbahn	6/6
39	Die Post? Das ist ganz einfach	7/3
40	Ist es weit von hier?	7/3
41	Was gibt es hier zu sehen?	7/4
42	Ein Brief an David	7/6
43	Wo ist die Post?	7/6
44	Unsere Stadt	7/6
45	Stadtrundgang	7/6
46	Ausflug/Jörgs Einkaufsliste	8/1
47A	Was kauft ihr für das Picknick?	8/2
47B	Was kauft ihr für das Picknick?	8/2
48	Einkaufszettel	8/2
49	Obst- und Gemüsespiele	8/2
50	Was darf's sein?	8/3
51	In der Stadt	8/3
52	Ladendieb	8/3
53	Wo kann ich das hier bekommen?	8/4
54	Wo kaufst du das?/Zu Weihnachten im Warenhaus	8/6
55	Wie kommst du dahin?	9/1
56	Abfahrt — Ankunft	9/2
57	Auskunft	9/2
58	Was paßt am besten?	9/4
59	Was hast du gemacht?	9/5
60	Jens-Peters Tagebuch	9/6
61	Geburtstagsumfrage	10/1
62	So eine Woche!	10/2
63	Wann denn?	10/3
64	Wer kommt mit zur Party?	10/3
65	Zehn Unterschiede	10/4
66	Geburtstagsfeier	10/5
67	Wie hast du sie gefunden?	10/5
68	Teenager	10/6
69	Austauschpartner	10/6
70	Was hast du gesehen?	10/6
71	Wo tut es ihm weh?	11/2
72A	Englandaustausch	11/3
72B	Englandaustausch	11/3
73	Was hat Monika geschrieben?	11/4
74	Was fehlt dir?	11/6
75	Was macht die Zähne kaputt?	11/6
76	Aua!	11/6
77	Eine Umfrage	12/1
78	Der ideale Urlaub	12/3
79	Im Reisebüro	12/3
80	Was machst du dieses Jahr?	12/3
81A	Welcher Campingplatz?	12/4
81B	Welcher Campingplatz?	12/4
82	Wie ist das Wetter?	12/5
83	Treffen im Urlaub	12/6
84	Ferienkrimskrams	12/6
85	Findet Jürgen das Essen gut?	I.T.
86	Kreuzworträtsel	I.T.
87	Ein Brief an Michael	I.T.

Index of tape recordings

Chapter 1

Area 1
1 Hallo!
2 Guten Tag!
3 Fotoquiz

Area 2
4 Feuer!
5 Wollen wir ins Kino gehen?
6 Die Hitparade
7 Wie alt bist du?

Area 3
8 Interviews mit Touristen in der Bundesrepublik

Area 4
9 Ich wohne in Hamburg
10 Richtig oder falsch?

Area 5
11 Internationales Leichtathletikfest

Area 6
12 Kannst du ein Formular ausfüllen?

Chapter 2

Area 1
1 Wie heißen sie?
2 Wieviel Geschwister hast du?
3 Jürgens Fotoalbum

Area 2
4 Wieviel Grad ist es?
5 Wer gewinnt?
6 Kennst du die Zahlen?
7 Telefonnummern und Adressen

Area 3
8 Wie alt sind sie

Area 5
9 Hast du ein Haustier?

Area 6
10 Wo wohnen sie?
11 Computerliste

Chapter 3

Area 1
1 Veronica kommt in Hamburg an
2 Bei Kirsten zu Hause
3 Pläne fur die Woche
4 Wieviel Uhr ist es?

Area 2
5 Was machen Veronica und Kirsten heute?
6 In der Schule

Area 3
7 Sechs Schüler und Schülerinnen

Area 4
8 Eine schlechte Note

Area 5
9 Wann beginnt der Film?

Chapter 4

Area 1
1 Interviews mit Teenagern

Area 2
2 Was ist Großmutters Problem?
3 Wie heißt die Frage?

Area 3
4 Das Mittagessen. Drei Interviews

Area 4
5 Janet Hurst bei Familie Bromma

Area 5
6 Um wieviel Uhr ist die Party?

Chapter 5

Area 1
1 Was machen sie nach der Schule?
2 Richtig oder falsch?

Area 2
3 Interviews mit Teenagern
4 Interviews nach der Schule
5 Wer ist dein Computerpartner? Wer ist deine Computerpartnerin?

Area 3
6 Spielst du ein Instrument?
7 Welches Instrument ist das?
8 Wie oft üben sie?
9 Orchester und Bands

Area 4
10 Sonja und Max
11 Lieblingsfächer

Area 5
12 Streit

Area 6	13	Interviews über Schulaufgaben
	14	Herbert Meyer und Band auf Tournee
	15	Ein Interview mit Herbert Meyer
	16	Was machst du am liebsten in der Freizeit?

Chapter 6

Area 1	1	Wo sind sie?
Area 2	2	Auf der Bank
Area 3	3	Wieviel Taschengeld bekommst du?
	4	Acht junge Leute
Area 4	5	Was kaufen die Leute?
	6	Billig oder teuer?
Area 5	7	An der Eisbude
	8	Mit Sahne?
	9	Was nimmst du?
Area 6	10	Wieviel Geld haben sie dabei?
	11	Was gibt es auf dem Jahrmarkt zu essen?

Chapter 7

Area 1	1	Osnabrück — meine Stadt
Area 2	2	Wo ist hier die nächste Post, bitte?
	3	Stadtplan — richtig oder falsch?
Area 3	4	Stadtrundfahrt
	5	Wegbeschreibungen
	6	Die Post? Das ist ganz einfach
	7	Ich suche die Post
Area 4	8	Im Verkehrsamt
	9	Was kann ich heute nachmittag machen?
	10	Wo ist das, bitte?
Area 5	11	Wer spricht?
Area 6	12	Welche Linie ist das?
	13	Was gibt's da für junge Leute?
	14	Ist hier ein Tisch frei?
	15	Stadtrundgang

Chapter 8

Area 1	1	Was kann man hier kaufen?
	2	Ingrid geht einkaufen
	3	Wo sind sie? Wo gehen sie hin?
Area 2	4	Was kaufen die Leute im Geschäft?
	5	Vollautomatik
Area 3	6	Beim Einkaufen
	7	Wo kommen diese Kisten hin?
	8	Ladendieb!
Area 4	9	Wegweiser
	10	Ich hätte gern ...
	11	Im Warenhaus verkauft man fast alles ... aber keine Briefmarken
	12	Auf der Post
Area 5	13	Was hast du heute gekauft?
	14	David kommt nach Hamburg
	15	Was hat David für seine Familie in England gekauft?
Area 6	16	Zu Weihnachten im Warenhaus
	17	Was kaufen sie auf der Post?
	18	Radiorezepte
	19	Frank und Erika im Warenhaus

Chapter 9

Area 1	1	Wie kommst du dahin?
	2	Gespräche
Area 2	3	Entschuldigung ...
	4	Ich bin hier fremd
	5	Zurückbleiben, bitte

	6	Auskunft
	7	Einmal nach Pfarrkirchen, bitte
Area 3	8	Welche Linie ist das?
	9	Vergessen Sie nicht, Ihre Fahrkarte zu entwerten!
	10	Zuggespräche
Area 4	11	Wie kommt man nach Helgoland?
	12	Wie fahren wir dorthin?
	13	Wie kommt die Familie Timm nach Spanien?
	14	Wir fahren nach England
Area 5	15	Telefongespräch
Area 6	16	Jens-Peters Tagebuch

Chapter 10

Area 1	1	Wann ist das?
	2	Wann hast du Geburtstag?
Area 2	3	Kommst du?
	4	Anjas Tagebuch
Area 3	5	Telefongespräch
	6	Tut mir leid!
	7	Wenn, wenn, wenn
	8	Die Clique am Samstagabend
Area 4	9	Gruppenfoto
	10	Kleidung
Area 5	11	Gestern abend
	12	Geburtstagsfeier
	13	Was paßt zu wem?
	14	Was hältst du von Elke?
	15	Hast du die Berti kennengelernt?
Area 6	16	Teenager

Chapter 11

Area 1	1	Ich habe Kopfschmerzen
	2	Ich kann nicht kommen
Area 2	3	Was wird hier gespielt?
	4	Die neue Turnhalle
	5	Im Jugendzentrum
Area 3	6	In der Imbißstube
	7	Ich darf nicht ... ich bin allergisch dagegen
	8	Krank im Urlaub
Area 4	9	Probleme beim Skifahren
	10	Renate ruft ihre Mutter an
	11	Interlaken, den 2. Februar
	12	Was ist in diesem Haus passiert?
Area 5	13	Ist am Freitag noch ein Termin frei?
	14	In der Sprechstunde
	15	Haben Sie etwas gegen Kopfschmerzen?
Area 6	16	Wundermittel
	17	Was meinen Sie, Herr Doktor Schweiger?

Chapter 12

Area 1	1	Wo fährst du hin?
Area 3	2	Was machst du gern im Urlaub?
Area 4	3	Camping ist billig ... oder?
Area 5	4	Drei Telefonate aus den Ferien
	5	Wie war denn dein Urlaub?
Area 6	6	Treffen im Urlaub

Internationaler Treff

	1	Die Schule in Großbritannien
	2	Kleidung und Make-up
	3	Radio und Fernesehen in Großbritannien
	4	Deutsche Teenager auf Urlaub in Großbritannien

13

		Pupil's Book Chapter introductions	Topics/Functions	Grammatical Points
1A	**1**	**Hallo!** **Wie heißt du?**	• Greetings • Counting to 20 • Saying how old you are • Geography of Central Europe (+ Britain) • Giving nationality • Saying where you live and describing briefly where it is • Using the German alphabet	• *ich/du* • *sein, heißen, kommen, wohnen* • *aus* + country • Polite *Sie* (receptive only) • *man*
	2	**Meine** **Familie**	• Describing and introducing the family • Counting from 21 to 100 • Giving ages • Talking about pets • Describing in more detail where you live • Describing accommodation	• *haben* • *er/sie* + verb • *der/die/das* • *einen/eine/ein* • *keinen/keine/kein* • *mein/meine* • Who?, What?, What kind of?
	3	**In der** **Schule**	• Staying with a family • Days of the week • Telling the time • Describing the school day (subjects, timetables, etc.) • Subjects — likes and dislikes • Classroom vocabulary	• *wir, sie* + verb • Separable verbs (*aufstehen, anfangen* etc.) • First, second etc. • *möchte*
	4	**Die** **Mahlzeiten**	• Food and mealtimes • Likes and dislikes • Having a meal with a family • Polite conversation • Enquiring about times of meals (revision of time)	• Question forms • Word order (inversion of the verb, e.g. *Abends esse ich* etc.) • Vowel change in verbs *essen* + *sprechen* • *mit, oder* • *in, auf, an*
	5	**. . . und nach** **der Schule?**	• Saying what you do in your spare time and what you like doing (most of all) • Sport • Music • Events (sporting, musical etc.) • Talking about television • 24 hour clock	• Expressions of time • Saying and writing the date • Use of *gern* • Structure with modals: *will* + infinitive • Word order • Nouns with different masculine and feminine forms
	6	**Was kostet das?**	• Revision of numbers and extension to 1000 + • Currency in German-speaking countries • Banks + changing money • Talking about pocket money • Prices — asking and saying what things cost (snacks, drinks, souvenirs) • Spending money at the fun fair	• Plural nouns • The definite and indefinite article • Nominative + accusative (an overview) • *mir (ich kaufe mir)* • *einmal, zweimal* etc.
1B	**7**	**Willkommen in** **Osnabrück**	• Finding out what there is to see in a town • Obtaining information from a tourist office • Main landmarks and destinations in a town • Understanding and giving directions • Describing the relative positions of things • Saying how far somewhere is • Tour of town • Finding out about the people in a town	• *Es gibt* + accusative • More prepositions (with dative) • Ordinal numbers • *können* • *haben* paradigm
	8	**Beim** **Einkaufen**	• Names of shops • Buying provisions • Expressions of quantity • Buying stamps • Buying other items • Telling someone what you have bought, what it cost, who it's for	• *in* + accusative/dative • Perfect Tense with *haben* (regular verbs) • *gefallen*
	9	**Wie fährt man?**	• Describing means of transport • Using public transport: bus/tram/underground • Understanding timetables • Finding out information, buying tickets etc. • Planning a journey • Describing a journey (to or from Britain to Germany)	• More separable verbs • More practice of the Perfect Tense *(haben/sein)*
	10	**Wir feiern**	• Talking about events • Revision of days of the week • Describing people and giving an opinion of them • Giving/accepting/declining an invitation • Getting to know people (revision of Unit 1)	• Perfect Tense of irregular and separable verbs with *haben* • Word order after *wenn* • Agreement of adjectives • Accusative pronouns *(ihn, sie)*
	11	**Mir ist schlecht**	• Describing parts of the body and symptoms of illness • At the doctor's/chemist's/dentist's • Describing a skiing/sporting accident/injury	• Dative reflexive pronouns • *dürfen*
	12	**Wo fährst du hin?**	• Talking about holiday plans and destinations • Revision of countries of Europe • East and West Germany • The Germans on holiday • Staying at a campsite • Talking about past holidays	• Present Tense with Future meaning
		Internationaler Treff	• Understanding opinions expressed about Britain and the British; schools, houses, clothes and make-up, spare time, radio and TV, traffic and food. In magazine format	
1A/1B		**Noch etwas mehr**	• Extra practice and consolidation exercises for each unit	
		Grammatik — Überblick	• Grammar survey of whole stage	
		Wörterliste	• German/English vocabulary section	

Area 1

> • Greetings - saying what your name is

L, S

Welcoming the class

Use German with the class from the very beginning. Initially this will require a lot of mime and gesture.

T: *Kommt bitte 'rein.*
Setzt euch.
Guten Morgen/Guten Tag.

Encourage pupils to repeat the greetings chorally and then individually.

L, S

Introductions

T: (speaking to individual pupils):
Guten Morgen/Tag. Ich bin Frau/Herr ...
(N.B. All women teachers in Germany are addressed as Frau, irrespective of marital status.)
T: *... Und du?*
(whisper): *Ich bin ...*
P: *Ich bin John.*

L, S

Pair-work

Encourage pairs to greet each other and give their names. This could be done as a chain activity, with the pupil who answers the first question asking the next question and so on.

L, S

Pronunciation

Practise *ich, guten* (chorally and individually).

L, S

Performing in front of the class

Observe pairs who perform well, call them to the front of the class to perform the dialogue.

T: *Kommt nach vorne.*
Ja, du Ann, und du, Andrew.
Du und du, kommt!
Gut/Sehr gut/Fein/Prima/(Fantastisch!)
Use *Sch/Ruhe* if required.

L, S

Hallo!

Hört gut zu.

Play the recording straight through. Elicit that it is a group of German children introducing themselves. Repeat section by section.

T: *Ist das Anne? Ja oder nein?*
P: *Ja.*
T: *Ja richtig. Das ist Anne. Sehr gut.*

Play the recording again, using the pause button.

T: *Sagt Anne ,guten Morgen'? Ja oder nein?*
P: *Nein.*
T: *Richtig. Was sagt Anne?*
P: *Hallo.*
T: *Prima!*

Hallo!

— Hallo. Ich bin Anne.
— Hallo. Ich bin Renate.
— Grüß dich. Ich bin Paul.
— Hallo. Ich heiße Uschi.
— Grüß dich. Ich heiße Andrea.
— Guten Tag. Ich bin Martin.
— Hallo. Ich bin Oliver.
— Guten Tag. Ich bin Frau Meyer.
— Guten Morgen. Ich heiße Stefan.
— Grüß dich. Ich bin Florian.

L, S

Pronunciation

Grüß dich. Guten Tag. Guten Morgen. Ich bin, ich heiße.

L, S

Saying your name

Ask: *,Wie heißt du?'*
Encourage pupils to take over the teacher's role.
Avoid *Sie heißen* for the time being, but teach it rather than being addressed as *du*.

L

Hier ist dein Deutschbuch

Hand out pupils' books in preparation for the following activities.

T: (mainly): *John, hier ist dein Deutschbuch.*
(occasionally): *Susan, bitte schön. Mark, hier bitte.*

Teach *Danke.*

Give pupils time to look through the book.

T: *Schlagt das Buch auf. Seite ...*
(Demonstrate; stress *Buch* and *Seite*, write page number on the board.)

4
(1A 4)

Hallo!

Play the recording once more. Ask pupils to look at the speech bubbles.

T: Hört gut zu. Lest Seite 4 (Point to speech bubbles)

Then ask: *'Was sagt Anne?'* etc.

Pupils can then read from the book.

4
(1A 4)

Guten Tag!

Members of the *Pinneberger Sportverein* introduce themselves. Ask pupils to look at the pictures and listen to the recording. They must decide the order in which people speak and make a note in their books.

Solution: **1**g; **2**f; **3**b; **4**a; **5**c; **6**h; **7**d; **8**i; **9**e; **10**j.

T: Seite 4 (write on board). *Seht euch die Bilder an. Das sind Jungen und Mädchen aus dem Pinneberger Sportverein. Andrea ist ein Mädchen, Boris ist ein Junge. Hört gut zu.*
Play the first person then ask:-
Ist das Andrea? Ja oder nein?
P: Nein.
T: Ist das Boris? Ja oder nein?
P: Ja.
*T: Richtig. Das ist Boris. Schreibt **1**g in euer Heft.* (Demonstrate on the board). *Hört jetzt gut zu und macht weiter!*

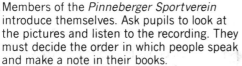

Guten Tag!

1 — Guten Tag! Ich heiße Boris. Ich spiele gern Tennis.
2 — Ich bin Andrea. Grüß dich. Ja, der PSV ist toll!
3 — Guten Morgen. Mein Name ist Schmidt. Ich bin der Tennistrainer.
4 — Hallo. Ich heiße Ute. Der PSV ist Klasse.
5 — Guten Tag. Ich bin Sven. Ich bin Schwimmer.
6 — Hallo. Ich heiße Martin. Ich spiele Fußball.
7 — Guten Tag. Krull ist mein Name. Ich bin der Fußballtrainer.
8 — Grüß dich. Ich heiße Elke. Ich spiele Fußball, aber ich bin nicht sehr gut!
9 — Hallo. Ich bin Barbara. Ich mache Leichtathletik im PSV.
10 — Guten Tag. Ich heiße Gaby. Ich spiele Tischtennis.

5
(1A 5)

Was sagen Sie?

Tell pupils to try to work out what the people are saying, and then write the sentences in their book. Practise orally first, if required.

T: Was sagt Paul?
P: Grüß dich. Ich bin Paul.
T: Richtig. Schreibt es in euer Heft. (Demonstrate on the board). *Jetzt macht weiter.*

5
(1A 5)

Fotoquiz

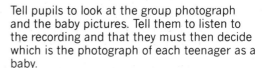

Tell pupils to look at the group photograph and the baby pictures. Tell them to listen to the recording and that they must then decide which is the photograph of each teenager as a baby.

Seite 5 Seht euch die Fotos an. Hier sind sechs Teenager: Christa, Bernd etc. Und hier sind Babyfotos von Christa, Bernd etc. Wer ist das? (point). *Hört gut zu.*

Fotoquiz
— Ich heiße Christa.
— Ich heiße Susi.
— Ich bin Lutz.
 Das ist Sven.
 Das ist Brigitte.
 Das hier ist Bernd.

— Wer ist das?
 Ist das Lutz?
— Nein, das ist Bernd.
— Ist das Susi?
— Nein, das ist Sven.

— Ist das Lutz?
— Ja, das ist Lutz.
— Nein, das ist Christa.
— Ja, das ist Christa.

— Ist das Sven?
— Nein, das ist Susi, oder?
— Nein, das ist Bernd.

— Jetzt bist du dran.
 Wer ist das?

Solution:

1 = Susi	**4** = Lutz
2 = Brigitte	**5** = Sven
3 = Bernd	**6** = Christa

Area 2

- Learning to count to 20
- Asking how many
- Saying how old you are
- Asking someone's name and age

L, S

Numbers 1 - 20

Introduce orally the numbers 1 - 20. Teach the numbers in groups of three with pupils repeating after you. Only move on to the next three when the previous three have been learnt. Since many of the numbers have sounds which pupils may find difficult to pronounce, it may be worthwhile at this stage to spend some time on pronunciation work, e.g. *zwei, drei, fünf, acht, zehn, elf, zwölf*. Differentiate between *vierzehn* and *fünfzehn* when spoken at normal speed.

Some classes may find it easier to learn the numbers 1 - 10 and 11 - 20 in two stages.

L

Numbers game

Write two sets of the numbers 1-20 in random order on a divided blackboard. Choose two teams and give each team member a number. Then call out a number from the board **twice** before nominating, by number, the two pupils who must rush to the board and cross out the number you first called out. Thus:-

T: Siebzehn - siebzehn ... Nummer drei.

The number 3 member of each team rushes to the board to cross out number 17.

L, S

Feuer!

Play the recording *Feuer!*, then ask pupils to count backwards, using the visual on page 6.

Real countdowns are sometimes stopped because of failures. Here a mistake in pronunciation has the same effect.

If the countdown is successfully completed, pupils can shout *'Feuer!'*.

Feuer!
ZEHN
NEUN
ACHT
SIEBEN
SECHS
FÜNF
VIER

DREI
ZWEI
EINS
NULL
FEUER!

The continental 1 and 7

Write numbers on OHP/board (ensure 1 and 7 look German). Ask pupils to spot the differences.

Practise numbers at random.

L, R

Wollen wir ins Kino gehen?

Tell pupils to listen to the conversation and to write down, in figures, in their exercise books, the order in which the films are mentioned. Write a-i on the board, and complete the first one with pupils.

Schlagt euer Buch auf Seite 6 auf. Schreibt a bis i und dann die richtige Saalnummer hinter den Buchstaben. Hört gut zu.

Wollen wir ins Kino gehen?
— Gehen wir ins Kino?
— Ja, gerne. Was läuft, denn?
— Also, im Kinocenter läuft ‚Schneewittchen und die sieben Zwerge' im Saal sieben.
— Hmm, was gibt's sonst?
— ‚Der Tunnel' im Saal zwei. Das ist ein Krimi.
— Lieber nicht.,
— Was läuft denn im Saal fünf? ... ‚Ede Funk in New York.' Oder wie wäre es mit ‚Superman' im Saal sechs?
— Nee.
— 'Feuer'?
— Was!?
— ‚Feuer' im Saal acht.
— Und im Saal eins?
— ‚Bambi' — toll, nicht?
— ‚Bambi'! Wahnsinn! Was gibt's sonst noch?
— ‚Tom und Jerry' oder ‚Tarzan' im Saal vier.
— Tja. Was meinst du? ‚Tom und Jerry'?
— OK. Gehen wir in Saal drei.

Solution: **a** 7; **b** 2; **c** 5; **d** 6; **e** 8; **f** 1; **g** 3; **h** 4; **i** 3.

N.B. This could be adapted as a communicative activity at the end of the chapter, with one pupil allowed to have the book open giving film titles and the other having to remember the studio number.

Die Hitparade

L, R

Refer pupils to *Hits der Woche*, on page 7 and play the recording of the disc jockey announcing the week's Top 20.

Schlagt eure Bücher auf Seite 7 auf. Hört gut zu!

Die Hitparade

- Nummer zwanzig: Sieben Narzissen von Feuerwerk.
- Nummer neunzehn: JoJo von Lola Lace.
- Nummer achtzehn: Einmal ist keinmal von Frei.
- Nummer siebzehn: Broken Dreams von Insomniacs.
- Nummer sechzehn: Susi ist erst siebzehn von Hbf.
- Nummer fünfzehn: Blitz von Evi Bamm.
- Nummer vierzehn: Die Sonne scheint von Karussell.
- Nummer dreizehn: Queen of Hearts von The Gamblers.
- Nummer zwölf: Toll Toll Toll von Punker Rockers.
- Nummer elf: Grüß dich von Hanno H.
- Nummer zehn: Komm mit von Schaukelschiffe.
- Nummer neun: Teenage Rock von Head Bangers Inc.
- Nummer acht: Anne von Vier Jahreszeiten.
- Nummer sieben: Mann oh Mann von Ozean.
- Nummer sechs: Lost in Dreams von Serpentine.
- Nummer fünf: Telefonliebe von Britta Tell.
- Nummer vier: He du da von Ede Funk.
- Nummer drei: So Easy von Simon Sez.
- Nummer zwei: Oh, Jane von Elegy ...
- Nummer eins ist diese Woche: Hallo, wie heißt du? von Polizei.

Die Hitparade

L, S, R

Practise both the **German** titles in the pop chart and the dialogue, before asking pupils to conduct their own dialogues using the chart. This activity becomes a memory test/communicative game if you tell one of each pair to close his/her book and then continue with the dialogues, either working from memory to answer questions or asking genuine questions.

Wiederholt, bitte: Hallo, wie heißt du? von Polizei ...
Partnerarbeit. Du sagst: Was ist Nummer sechs? Und du antwortest ...

Umfrage

L, S, R

If possible, obtain a recent Top 20 singles chart from a German magazine and practise the language used in the previous activity. Compare the German chart with the British Top 20, then conduct your own survey by asking pupils to name 20 singles and then vote for their 3 favourite titles.

nem 1 Wieviel ist das?

R, W

226
(1A 104)

Refer pupils to the visuals **a-j** on page 226 (**1A** 104) and ask the question: *'Wieviel ist das?'* Then, using concealed dominoes or cards, ask pupils to guess the totals in any combinations up to twenty.

Wie viele Eier? Wie viele Blumen?

Comment on the German custom of buying eggs in 6s, 10s or 15s and giving flowers in odd numbers.

Zahlenpuzzle

L, S, R

Tell pupils to look at the grid and try to work out which numbers are represented. Start at 'o' (=11) then work through the teens until pupils have sufficient clues to enable them to complete the task on their own. Finally check their answers in a reporting back session.

N.B. This grid also provides an opportunity to use the letters of the alphabet a-t, in advance of Area 5.

Solution:
a = 10	**e** = 1	**i** = 18	**m** = 5	**q** = 19
b = 6	**f** = 4	**j** = 15	**n** = 2	**r** = 17
c = 14	**g** = 7	**k** = 9	**o** = 11	**s** = 13
d = 12	**h** = 20	**l** = 8	**p** = 3	**t** = 16

T: Welche Nummer ist das (point to the letter on the board)?
P: Elf.
T: Prima! Elf. Und welche Nummer ist das ..?
P: Siebzehn.

Wie alt bist du?

L, S, W

Mini dialogues - name and age

Play the recording and ask pupils to note down the names in the correct order. Then play the recording again and ask them to add the ages.

T: *Hört gut zu und schreibt die Namen.* (Play first dialogue). *Ist das Anja oder Andrea?*
P: *Anja.* (Write on board).
T: *Gut. Wie alt ist sie? Ist sie zehn oder elf?*
P: *Zehn* (Write 10 on board next to Anja).
T: *Richtig. Jetzt hört zu und schreibt den Namen* (point) *und das Alter* (point) *in euer Heft. Ich spiele das zweimal.*

Wie alt bist du?

1 — Wie heißt du?
— Anja.
— Und wie alt bist du?
— Zehn.

2 — Und du? Wie heißt du?
— Sven.
— Ja, und wie alt bist du?
— Ich bin zwölf.

3 — Wer bist du denn?
— Ich bin Martin.
— Wie alt bist du, Martin?
— Ich bin vierzehn Jahre alt.

4 — Wie heißt du?
— Ich heiße Oliver.
— Und wie alt bist du?
— Ich bin gerade dreizehn geworden.

5 — Du bist Anne, ja?
— Ja, ich heiße Anne.
— Und wie alt bist du?
— Ich bin siebzehn.

6 — Und du? Wie heißt du denn?
— Andrea. Ich bin neun Jahre alt.

7 — Bist du Peter?
— Ja, ich heiße Peter.
— Wie alt bist du?
— Fünfzehn.

8 — Heißt du Uschi oder Gaby?
— Ich heiße Gaby.
— Und wie alt bist du?
— Ich bin sechzehn Jahre alt.

9 — Du bist die Heike, nicht?
— Ja, richtig!
— Und wie alt bist du, Heike?
— Ich bin elf Jahre alt.

10 — Wie heißt du?
— Ich heiße Florian.
— Und wie alt bist du?
— Ich bin acht Jahre alt.

Collate the names and ages on the board.

T: *Nummer eins. Wie heißt sie?* (receptive only).
Wie alt ist sie? (receptive only).

8
(1A 8)

Wie heißt du? Wie alt bist du?

Refer pupils to the photographs and captions. Practise reading the dialogue out loud. Then ask individuals: *'Wie heißt du?'* and *'Wie alt bist du?'* Practise the expanded forms: *'Ich bin zwölf'* and *'Ich bin zwölf Jahre alt.'* Encourage pupils to ask the questions as soon as possible. Practise in a chain game, or as pair-work giving pupils' own names and ages.

---

1 Area 3

- **Geography of central Europe**
- **Giving nationality**
- **Using the polite form *Sie***

1

The countries surrounding Germany

It is preferable to present the class with an OHT copy outline map of the countries to present and practise their names.

See also

11
(1A 11)

i. *Das ist (die) ...*
(Pupils do not see the written forms at this stage).
ii. *Ist das (die) ...?*
This question makes sense only when the names are not shown, i.e. as a kind of memory game.
iii. Point to a country and ask *'Ist das (die) (name the wrong country)?'* to elicit a negative reply. Accept the answer *'nein'* initially, but encourage: *'Nein, die Schweiz'* or *'Nein, das ist die Schweiz'.*

1

Names of countries

Use an overlay on the outline map to present the written forms of the countries. Alternatively, list these on the board. Pupils should practise reading the names out loud.

T: *Lest die Namen, bitte.*

Europa

nem 2

226
(1A 104)

Tell pupils to complete a blank map of Europe using the names of countries presented above.

Hier spricht man Deutsch

A map of Germany, Austria and Switzerland is provided on Repromaster for presentation at whatever stage the teacher thinks suitable.

Language games

L, S, W

1 Was hast du geschrieben?

Demonstrate with individual pupils in front of the class before asking them to work in pairs.

T: Andrew, schreibe etwa drei Länder in dein Heft, zum Beispiel: England, Frankreich, Belgien. (Demonstrate on board.) Zeig mir nicht, was du schreibst! (Cover up eyes.) Fertig? Gut. Was hast du geschrieben? Holland? Ja oder nein?
P: Nein.
T: Frankreich?
P: Ja.

2 Ich denke an ein Land

Tell pupils to guess the country you are thinking of as quickly as possible. Encourage them to take over the teacher's role as soon as possible.

T: Ich denke an ein Land. Welches Land ist es?
P: (Ist es) die Schweiz?

3 Play Länderlotto

Pupils write down 3-5 names of countries which are ticked when the teacher calls them out. The first pupil to tick all the countries on his paper calls out *'Lotto!'*

4 Call out a number and ask pupils to say a country which has that number of letters

England hat sieben Buchstaben. (Write England on the board, pronounce E-N-G-L-A-N-D and count each letter.) *Welches Land hat ... Buchstaben?*

5 Matching the language to the country

Welches Land ist das? Man spricht dort Englisch.

6 Matching the capital to the country

Die Hauptstadt ist Paris. Wie heißt das Land?

---

nem 3

L, S, W

226
(1A 104)

Länderquiz: Welches Land ist das?

A game for practising the names of countries. This could be consolidated in writing, if required.

T: Hier sind die Länder. Nummer eins: Welches Land ist das? Ist das Italien? Das ist Frankreich, oder?

Solution:

1 Dänemark	10 Italien
2 Österreich	11 Schweiz
3 Wales	12 Niederlande
4 Portugal	13 Belgien
5 Schottland	14 Luxemburg
6 Polen	15 Frankreich
7 Bundesrepublik	16 Spanien
8 England	17 Tschechoslowakei
9 BRD	18 Irland

L, W

9
(1A 9)

Interviews mit Touristen in der Bundesrepublik

Ask pupils to copy the grid into their exercise books. Play the recording and tell pupils to complete the details.

Tragt die Tabelle in eure Hefte ein.
Hört gut zu und schreibt den Namen, die Stadt und das Land.

Interviews mit Touristen in der Bundesrepublik

1 — Guten Tag. Wie heißen Sie, bitte?
  — Guten Tag. Ich heiße Marie Dupont.
  — Sind Sie Deutsche?
  — Nein, ich bin Französin. Ich komme aus Paris.
  — Sie sprechen aber gut Deutsch.
  — Danke.

2
— Guten Tag. Wie heißen Sie, bitte?
— Mein Name ist Brown.
— Sind Sie Engländer?
— Nein, Schotte! Ich komme aus Glasgow.
— Oh, Pardon.

3
— Guten Morgen. Wie ist Ihr Name, bitte?
— Ich heiße Frau Krull.
— Sind Sie Österreicherin?
— Nein, ich komme aus der Schweiz. Ich bin Schweizerin. Ich komme aus Zürich.

4
— Guten Morgen. Wie heißen Sie, bitte?
— Ich?
— Ja, Sie.
— Polizei?
— Nein, ich bin Reporter.
— Ach so. Ich heiße ..... Schmidt, ja Schmidt.
— Sind Sie Deutscher?
— Nein, Österreicher.

5
— Guten Morgen.
— Guten Morgen.
— Wie heißen Sie, bitte?
— Ich heiße Alison, Alison Short.
— Das ist ein englischer Name, nicht wahr?
— Ja, richtig. Ich bin Engländerin. Ich komme aus London.
— Danke.

6
— Guten Tag. Wie ist Ihr Name, bitte?
— Kumposcht.
— Sind Sie Schweizerin?
— Nein, Engländerin.
— Was?! Eine Engländerin mit dem Namen Kumposcht!
— Ja, richtig. Mein Mann ist Österreicher.

7
— Guten Morgen. Wie heißen Sie, bitte?
— Ich heiße André Schwarz.
— Sie sind kein Deutscher, oder?
— Nein, ich bin Franzose, ich komme aus Dieppe.

8
— Guten Tag. Wie ist Ihr Name, bitte?
— Ich heiße Sean Fergussen.
— Ach, Sie sind Engländer.
— Nein, ich bin Ire. Ich komme aus Dublin.

L, S, R

9
(1A 9)
Nationalitäten

Read through these extracts from *Touristen in der Bundesrepublik* and stress the way in which the people give their nationality. Interview pupils in the same way to elicit: *Ich bin Engländer/Engländerin*. Play the tape if necessary.

Lest die Dialoge auf Seite 9.

L, S, R, W

Touristen in der Bundesrepublik

Practise the dialogues (*Nationalitäten* and *Interviews mit Touristen*) orally with the whole class. Encourage further practice in pairs and then consolidate in written form.

L, S

9
(1A 9)
Nationalitäten

Tell pupils to practise the dialogues in rotation before playing a guessing game: Pupil A must guess the identity of Pupil B using the written dialogues, but without asking the question: ,*Wie heißen Sie?'*

Pupil A: Sind Sie Engländer?
Pupil B: Nein.
Pupil A: Sind Sie Französin?
Pupil B: Nein ...
Pupil A: Sind Sie ... ?
Pupil B: Ja.
Pupil A: Sie heißen Krull.
Pupil B: Richtig!

L, S, R, W

10
(1A 10)
Das Auto kommt aus ...

Pupils have to guess which country the various cars come from.

Some of the signs will be known. Ask pupils to guess the others.

Aus should cause no problem in this context.

Practise pronunciation of *au*, however.

This activity is also a good opportunity to practise the pronunciation of some of the German alphabet.

The incomplete sentences are intended primarily as a prompt for oral work, but the activity could be consolidated in writing if required.

R, W

10
(1A 10)
Länder: Sprachen und Hauptstädte

This provides information about capital cities and languages of English and German-speaking countries in Europe.

Pupils should be encouraged to read the text silently for information. Some of the language has not been introduced before, but most pupils should be able to understand what it is about. Learning to cope with unknown language is an important skill to be developed. Nevertheless, the teacher could ease the task by introducing the first example orally. Pupils can then copy out and complete the table.

---

nem 4
226
(1A 104)

R

Richtig oder falsch?

A simpler activity to consolidate *Hauptstädte* and *Sprachen*.

---

nem 5
227
(1A 105)

R, W

Purzelwörter

Jumbled words to practise the spelling of towns and countries.

Solution:

Länder:		
1	Luxemburg	5 Polen
2	Schweiz	6 Dänemark
3	Bundesrepublik	7 Frankreich
4	Belgien	

Städte:		
1	Hamburg	5 Bern
2	Wien	6 Bonn
3	Linz	7 Berlin
4	Zürich	

---

1 Area 4

- Saying where you live (town)
- and describing briefly where it is

L, S

Talking about where people live

Introduce the topic using examples from the local area.

T: *Ich wohne in Manchester. Es liegt im Norden. X wohnt in Sale. Das ist in der Nähe von Manchester.*

Introduce other points of the compass by asking where various towns in the UK are situated. A simple outline map on the board or OHP will make this explicit.

T: *Schaut auf die Karte. Manchester liegt hier.* (Write in the name.) *Im Norden. Was liegt hier im Süden?* (Point.)
P: *London.*
T: *Ja, richtig. London liegt im Süden. Was liegt hier im Osten?*
P: *Harwich.*
T: *Gut. Das ist Harwich. Es liegt im Südosten. Was liegt hier im Südwesten?*
P: *Bristol.*
T: *Richtig.*
    etc.

Encourage pupils to take over the questioning role as soon as possible.

12
(1A 12)

L, R, W

Ich wohne in Hamburg

Tell pupils that you are going to play a recording of some German speakers talking about where they live and that they must find the places on the map in their book and write down the name of the town.

Schlagt die Bücher auf Seite 12 auf. Schaut euch die Landkarte an. Jetzt hört ihr zehn Personen. Sie sagen, wo sie wohnen. Findet die Stadt auf der Karte und schreibt den Namen in euer Heft.

Do the first question with the class as an example.

Ich wohne in Hamburg

1 — Ich heiße Annette, und ich komme aus der Bundesrepublik. Ich wohne in Hamburg. Das liegt im Norden.
2 — Ich bin Peter. Ich wohne in Deutschland - in München. Das liegt im Süden.
3 — Mein Name ist Krall. Ich wohne in Wien. Das ist die Hauptstadt von Österreich und liegt im Norden
4 — Ich heiße Martin. Ich wohne seit einem Jahr in Bern, im Nordwesten der Schweiz.
5 — Ich bin Heidi. Ich wohne in der DDR. In Berlin. Das liegt im Osten.
6 — Hallo. Ich heiße Ralf. Ich wohne in Bonn. Das ist die Hauptstadt der Bundesrepublik.
7 — Wo ich wohne? Ja, ich bin Kölner. Ich wohne in Köln, im Westen der Bundesrepublik. Ich heiße Udo.
8 — Ich komme aus Österreich. Ich wohne im Süden in der Nähe von Graz. Schulz ist mein Name.
9 — Ich bin Jutta. Ich bin Schweizerin. Ich wohne im Norden - in Zürich.
10 — Ich komme aus der DDR und zwar aus Rostock. Das liegt im Norden. Ich heiße Erika.

Solution:

	Name	Land	Stadt	liegt im ...
1	Annette	BRD	Hamburg	Norden
2	Peter	BRD	München	Süden
3	Herr Krull	Österreich	Wien	Norden
4	Martin	Schweiz	Bern	Nordwesten
5	Heidi	DDR	Berlin	Osten
6	Ralf	BRD	Bonn	Westen
7	Udo	BRD	Köln	Westen
8	Frau Schulz	Österreich	Graz	Süden
9	Jutta	Schweiz	Zürich	Norden
10	Erika	DDR	Rostock	Norden

Wo wohnst du?

Ask pupils if they can recall how the people (in the recording) said where they live.

If necessary, play part of it again and elicit ,*Ich wohne in ...*'

Say where you live and encourage pupils to do the same.

66
99
T: *Ich wohne in Brighton. Das liegt im Süden. Und du, wo wohnst du?*

Pronunciation practice:

Concentrate on long o and glottal stop.

In addition, pupils could pretend that they live in various towns.

Du wohnst im Norden, oder?

Ask pupils to write up the details of *Ich wohne in Hamburg* using the (corrected) grid on page 12. Practise orally first.

66
99
Was sagt Annette?
,*Ich heiße . . .*'

13
(1A 13)

Richtig oder falsch?

Tell pupils to look at the map and to listen to the tape. They must decide who is telling the truth and who is lying and write *richtig* or *falsch* accordingly.

66
99
Schlagt euer Buch auf und seht euch die Karte an.

Richtig oder falsch?

1 — Hallo! Ich heiße Rudi. Ich wohne im Norden der Bundesrepublik. Ich komme aus Rellingen, das liegt in der Nähe von Hamburg.
2 — Guten Tag! Ich komme aus der DDR. Ich wohne im Süden, in der Nähe von Dresden. Freital heißt der Ort. Mein Name ist Dirk.
3 — Grüß Gott. Ich bin Österreicherin. Ich heiße Ulli und ich wohne in Graz, im Süden.
4 — Aus der Schweiz komme ich, und zwar aus Baden. Das liegt im Südwesten. Krull ist mein Name.
5 — Hallo! Mein Name ist Britta. Ich bin Deutsche. Ich wohne in Florisdorf im Norden, in der Nähe von Wien.
6 — Also, ich heiße Stefan, ich wohne in Siegburg. Das liegt in der Nähe von Bonn, im Westen natürlich.

7 — Grüß dich. Ich bin Uschi. Ich bin Deutsche. Ich wohne in der Nähe von Magdeburg, in Gommern.
8 — Guten Morgen. Ich bin Schweizerin und heiße Frau Zimmermann. Ich wohne im Südwesten, in der Nähe von Genf. In Korbach.
9 — Ich wohne in Bergheim in der Nähe von Köln im Norden. Ich wohne gern in der DDR. Wie ich heiße? Ach ja, ich heiße Jörg.
10 — Wo ich wohne? Ja, ich komme aus der Bundesrepublik, ich bin Deutsche, und ich wohne im Osten, in Korbach. Das liegt ganz in der Nähe von Kassel. Mein Name ist Petra.

Solution:

1 richtig	**6** richtig
2 falsch	**7** richtig
3 richtig	**8** falsch
4 falsch	**9** falsch
5 falsch	**10** richtig

12
(1A 12)

Was sagen sie?

Tell pupils to match the shapes in order to work out what each is saying. Do the first one with the pupils and write it on the board as a model. Explain the *Rattenfänger von Hameln* (no. 7). Pupils could research the story in English.

66
99
T: *Schlagt euer Buch auf Seite 12 auf. Schaut euch die Fotos und Bilder an. Was sagen die Jungen und Mädchen? Nummer eins. ,Ich heiße Michael. Ich komme aus der Bundesrepublik. Ich wohne in ...?*'
P: *Köln.*
T: *Gut. ,Ich heiße Michael. Ich komme aus der Bundesrepublik. Ich wohne in Köln'.* (Write sentence on board). *Nummer zwei.*
P1: *Ich heiße ...*
P2: *Ich komme aus ...*

12
(1A 12)

Was sagen sie?

Tell pupils to write up all the information from the previous exercise.

66
99
Und jetzt schreibt alles in euer Heft. Nummer eins: (point to the first answer already on the board). *Nummer zwei ...* (write no. 2 in margin and mime writing the answer in front of the group.) *Jetzt kommt ihr an die Reihe.*

1 Area 5

• Using the German alphabet

The German alphabet

Present the German alphabet in blocks of 3 letters and tell pupils to repeat.

" "

T:	*Hört gut zu. Wiederholt: A - B - C.*
Pupils:	*A - B - C.*
T:	*D - E - F ...*
Pupils:	*D - E - F ...*

L, S

Chain game: Das Alphabet

See how far the pupils can get on their own, taking it in turns to pronounce successive blocks of 3 letters.

" "

T:	*Und jetzt ein Kettenspiel. Du sagst: A - B - C* (pointing to the first pupil).
P1:	*A - B - C*
T:	*Und du sagst: D - E - F* (pointing to second pupil)
P2:	*D - E - F*
T:	*Und so weiter* (pointing to third pupil) *G - H ... Jetzt fangen wir an. Also, du* (pointing to first pupil), *A ...*
P1:	*A - B - C*
P2:	*D - E ...*

L, W

14 (1A 14)

Internationales Leichtathletikfest

Tell pupils to look at the pictures of the athletes giving their names to the Recorder before the 100 metres event, and to listen to the recording. Pupils could try to write down some of these names themselves.

" "

Hört gut zu!

Internationales Leichtathletikfest

Recorder: — Also. Nummer eins. Ihr Name, bitte.
Athlete 1: — Meier.
Recorder: — M - E - I - ...?
Athlete 1: — Nein, M - A - Y - E - R.
Recorder: — Also, M - A - Y - E - R, Mayer. Danke.

Recorder: — Nummer zwei. Ihr Name, bitte.
Athlete 2: — Smith.
Recorder: — Wie schreibt man das, bitte?
Athlete 2: — S - M - I - T - H.
Recorder: — Also, S - M - I - T - H, Smith. Danke.

Recorder: — Nummer drei. Ihr Name, bitte.
Athlete 3: — Jacquemart.

Recorder: — Wie schreibt man das, bitte?
Athlete 3: — J - A - C - Q - U - E - M - A - R - T.
Recorder: — Also, J - A - C - Q - U - E - M - A - R - T, Jacquemart. Danke.

Recorder: — Nummer vier. Ihr Name, bitte.
Athlete 4: — Nixon.
Recorder: — N - I - X - O - N?
Athlete 4: — Richtig.

Recorder: — Nummer fünf. Ihr Name, bitte.
Athlete 5: — Lundqvist.
Recorder: — Wie schreibt man das, bitte?
Athlete 5: — L - U - N - D - Q - V - I - S - T.
Recorder: — Also, L - U - N - D - Q - V - I - S - T, Lundqvist. Danke.

Recorder: — Nummer sechs. Ihr Name, bitte.
Athlete 6: — Piaget.
Recorder: — Wie schreibt man das, bitte?
Athlete 6: — P - I - A - G - E - T.
Recorder: — Also, P - I - A - G - E - T. Danke.

Recorder: — Nummer sieben. Ihr Name, bitte.,
Athlete 7: — Becker.
Recorder: — B - E - C - K - E - R?
Athlete 7: — Richtig.

Recorder: — Nummer acht. Ihr Name, bitte.
Athlete 8: — Waldorff.
Recorder: — Wie schreibt man das, bitte?
Athlete 8: — W - A - L - D - O - R - F - F.
Recorder: — Also, W - A - L - D - O - R - F - F. Danke.

L, S

14 (1A 14)

Welcher Buchstabe fehlt?

Tell pupils to work out the only letter of the alphabet which does not feature in the athletes' names. Conduct the exercise in the form of a chain game, in which successive pupils ask their neighbour if it is letter A, B, C etc.

" "

T: *Welcher Buchstabe fehlt? Du - ist es A?*
P: *Nein.* (Turns to neighbour.) *Ist es B? ...*

Solution: Z

L, S

14 (1A 14)

Wie schreibt man das?

Read the dialogue and then ask pupils to spell out their names in German, as in the Pupil's Book. Write letters on the board.

Game

L, S

Wer oder wo ist das?

Play this guessing game with the whole class until pupils can take over the teacher's role.

Begin spelling out the name of a pupil or a place and see how quickly pupils can guess the name.

T: *Hört gut zu. Wer ist das? J - O - H?*
P: *John.*
T: *Gut. Jetzt kommst du an die Reihe.*

L, S

Städte und Länder (Galgenspiel)

Play hangman with the class using towns and countries. Encourage pupils to take over the teacher's role as soon as they guess the correct answer.

T: *Jetzt spielen wir das Galgenspiel.*
P: *A (kommt ein A darin vor?)*
T: *Nein.*
P: *Kommt ein E darin vor?*
T: Writes in E on board.

---

nem 6

L, R, W

227
(1A 105)

Alphabetpuzzle

An exercise in logic, mainly for enjoyment. Fill in the first letter with the pupils.

T: *Schlagt euer Buch auf Seite 227 (105) auf. Dort seht ihr ein Alphabetpuzzle. Was ist der erste Buchstabe? Ist es 'i'?* (write 'i' on board).
P: *Nein.*
T: *Richtig. Belgien - Wien* (write on board). *Ist es 'e'? usw.*

Solution: *Wie schreibt man das?*

---

nem 7

W

227
(1A 105)

An der Party

An exercise to practise giving personal details.

---

nem 8

R, W

227
(1A 105)

Hörst du?

An activity focusing on question forms.

S

Wie sagt man das?

Some pupils may find the suggested transcription useful as a guide to pronunciation:

A	ah	N	en
B	bay	O	oh
C	tsay	P	pay

D	day	Q	koo
E	ay (rhymes with day)	R	air
F	ef	S	ess
G	gay	T	tay
H	hah	U	ooh
I	ee	V	fow (rhymes with now)
J	yot	W	vay
K	kah	X	eeks
L	ell	Y	oopsi-lon
M	em	Z	tset

---

1 Area 6

• Consolidation

15
(1A 15)

L, R, W

Kannst du ein Formular ausfüllen?

Tell pupils to listen to the recording and correct the relevant details for each person.

Schlagt euer Buch auf Seite 15 auf. Hört gut zu.

Go through the first example with the class, writing the details up on the board as pupils supply them. Then wipe the board clean and start again.

Kannst du ein Formular ausfüllen?

1 — Wie heißt du?
— Rellstab, Lutz Rellstab.
— Wie alt bist du, Lutz?
— Ich bin sechzehn.
— Wohnst du hier in Hamburg?
— Ja, meine Adresse ist Kleine Straße 13c.

2 — Guten Tag.
— Guten Tag.
— Wie heißen Sie?
— Helen Andrews.
— Sind Sie Deutsche?
— Nein, ich bin Engländerin.
— Ach so, Sie kommen aus England. Und wo wohnen Sie?
— Ich wohne in Hailsham, in der Nähe von Brighton im Südosten.
— Und Ihre Adresse?
— 20 Battle Road.
— Battle Road?
— Tja, das wäre Battle Straße.
— Ach natürlich, ja. Und Sie sind fünfzehn, oder?
— Genau. Fünfzehn Jahre alt.

3 **Im Hotel**
— Guten Tag. Ich habe ein Zimmer reserviert.
— Ihr Name, bitte.
— Jones.
— Wie schreibt man das, bitte?
— J - O - N - E - S.

— Also, Familienname Jones, und Ihr
Vorname?
— John: J - O - H - N.
— John Jones. Adresse?
— Wie bitte?
— Wo wohnen Sie?
— Ach ja. Ich komme aus England. Ich
wohne in Leeds, das wäre
L - E - E - D - S, im Norden, wissen Sie.
Und die Adresse: I9 Elland Road.
E - L - L - A - N - D, dann kommt Road:
R - O - A - D.

4 Am Telefon
— Campingplatz Sonneneck.
— Guten Tag. Ich möchte Ende August auf
dem Campingplatz zelten. Ist noch
Platz frei?
— Ja, sicher. Wie heißen Sie?
— Duclerc.
— Wie, bitte? Wie schreibt man das?
— D - U - C - L - E - R - C. Elisabeth. Ich bin
Französin, und ich wohne in Bordeaux,
im Südwesten.
— Und die Adresse?
— Zwölf rue Teulère. Das heißt rue:
R - U - E, Teulère: T - E - U - L - E - R - E.
— Danke. Wie lange wollen Sie bleiben?
— Acht Tage. Vom I5. bis 22. August.
— OK. Alles klar. Bis dann. Auf
Wiederhören.
— Auf Wiederhören.

R, W

15
(1A 15) **Englandaustausch**

Tell pupils to study the two documents before
completing their own details in the same
format in their exercise books.

*Schlagt euer Buch auf Seite 15 auf. Schaut
euch die Formulare an. Darauf sind die
Personalien zweier deutscher Schüler
eingetragen, die mit der Klasse nach England
kommen.* (After documents have been read
and understood:) *Und jetzt macht ihr einen
Austausch. Hier ist das Formular. Trage die
Tabelle in dein Heft ein und fülle das Formular
aus.* (Point to instructions in Pupil's Book.)

L, S, R

3A
3B

Wie heißt dein Partner?

In this communicative activity the aim is for
pupils to find out the name of their
correspondent. Each pupil is given a card
bearing his/her own name and the place
he/she comes from, plus the name of the town
his/her correspondent comes from. By asking
one person after another where they come
from, each pupil should eventually find their
own partner and so discover his/her name.

Deliberately false hopes are raised by having
usually two or more people coming from each
town.

Cut off the number of 'cards' you need for the
class. Altogether there are enough for
eighteen boys and eighteen girls. The boys'
cards are in the top half, the girls' in the lower
half of each sheet. One half of the sheet is for
the Germans, one for their British or Irish
partners. The 'real' partners are in the same
place on each sheet, so count the number of
boys you have, cut up **half** that number of
cards from one half of the sheet and then the
corresponding cards from the other half. Do
the same for the girls. This will ensure that
everyone finds a partner. Distribute randomly.

Check that pupils understand what
information they have on their cards and tell
them that they are going to have to work out
who their correspondent is by where he/she
comes from and so find out his/her name.
When a pair has found each other, they
should report to the teacher.

Go through a few typical dialogues with pairs
in front of the class as an example.

A: Woher kommst du?
B: Aus Bremen in Deutschland. Und du?
A: Aus Newcastle in England.
B: Dann bist du nicht mein Partner. Tschüs!

Checklist on pairs:
Boys

English:	German:
Andrew Gray	Dieter Braun
Nick Adams	Michael Dau
Mike Thomas	Jörg Mehde
Ian Scott	Peter Vogel
Martin Wilde	Bernd Hollweg
Anthony Farrell	Lars Kröner
David MacBride	Lutz Meier
Simon O'Brien	Thomas Weber

Girls

English:	German:
Sarah Pope	Gabriele Gellhorn
Mandy Grace	Renate Bauer
Catherine Fuller	Sabine Müller
Susan Burke	Kirsten Langer
Maureen Haddon	Monika Klein
Kate Murray	Barbara Fischer
Tina Fletcher	Merle Schwarz
Julia Lyle	Stefanie Adenauer

nem 9

227
(1A 105)

Abkürzungen

Tell pupils to look at the illustrations and then refer them to the table.

 Schlagt euer Buch auf Seite 227 (105) auf. Seht euch die Bilder an und dann die Tabelle.

Discuss briefly, in English, what the signs mean, as listed in the table, then use the questions in English (n.e.m. no. 9) as a follow-up activity.

R

16-17
(1A
16-17)

L, S, R

Abkürzungen

Test pupils on the pronunciation of the abbreviations.

 T: Was ist die Abkürzung für Volkswagen?
P: V-W.

nem 10

227
(1A 105)

R, W

Spelling quiz

Capital letters for nouns and the distinction between -ss- and ß.

Vocabulary

aber *but*
die Abkürzung(en) *abbreviation*
acht *eight*
achtzehn *eighteen*
die Adresse(n) *address*
alles *everything*
alles klar *fine, I've got it!*
das Alphabet *alphabet*
also *well*
alt *old*
Wie * bist du? *How old are you?*
das Alter(-) *age*
die Anschrift(en) *address*
anfangen *to start*
sich ansehen *to look at*
seht euch Seite 30 an! *look at page 30!*
antworten *to answer*
auf + Acc/Dat *onto, on*
* Wiedersehen *goodbye*
* Wiederhören *goodbye (on phone)*
aufschauen + Acc *to look at*
aufschlagen *to open*
schlagt das Buch auf! *open your book!*
August *August*
aus + Dat *out of, from*
ausfüllen *to fill in, complete*
der Austausch *exchange*
das Auto(s) *car*
das Baby(s) *baby*
das Beispiel(e) *example*
zum * *for example*
Belgien *Belgium*
das Bild(er) *picture*

bis *until*
bitte *please*
* schön *don't mention it, here you are*
bleiben *to stay, remain*
die Blume(n) *flower*
das Buch(¨er) *book*
der Buchstabe(n) *letter (of alphabet)*
die Bundesrepublik *Federal Republic (of Germany)*
die Bushaltestelle(n) *bus stop*
der Campingplatz(¨e) *campsite*
Dänemark *Denmark*
danke *thank you; no*
dann *then, next*
dran sein *to be one's turn*
du bist * *It's your turn*
dein *your*
mit deinem Partner *with your partner*
denn *then*
der/die/das *the*
deutsch *German*
Deutsch *German (lang)*
Deutsche *German person (f)*
Deutscher *German person (m)*
Deutschland *Germany*
die Deutschen *the Germans*
die DDR (Deutsche Demokratische Republik) *German Democratic Republic*
dort *there*
drei *three*
dreizehn *thirteen*

der Druckbuchstabe(n) *printed letter*
du *you (informal form, sing)*
das Ei(er) *egg*
ein(e) *a, an*
eins *one*
eintragen (in + Acc) *to copy (into)*
einundzwanzig *twenty-one*
elf *eleven*
das Ende(n) *end*
England *England*
Engländer *English person (m)*
Engländerin *English person (f)*
die Engländer *the English*
englisch *English*
Englisch *English (lang)*
etwa *approximately, about*
euer *your (pl)*
Europa *Europe*
falsch *wrong, incorrect*
der Familienname(n) *surname*
fehlen *to be missing*
Was fehlt? *What's missing?*
das Feuer(-) *fire*
*! *Lift off!*
finden *to find*
das Formular(e) *form*
das Foto(s) *photo*
Frankreich *France*
Franzose *French person (m)*
Französin *French person (f)*
die Franzosen *the French*

französisch *French*
Französisch *French (lang)*
Frau X *Mrs X*
frei *free, vacant, available*
fünf *five*
fünfzehn *fifteen*
für + Acc *for*
Fußball spielen *to play football*
das Galgenspiel(e) *hangman*
ganz *quite; whole*
geben *to give*
es gibt + Acc *there is/are*
gehen *to go, walk*
es geht *it's O.K.*
mir geht es gut *I'm fine*
gemischt *mixed*
genau *exact, exactly*
gerade *just*
gern(e) *with pleasure*
ich esse * *I like eating*
das Gleis(e) *platform*
die Größe(n) *height, size*
sich grüßen *to say hello*
grüß dich! *hello!*
gut *good*
guten Tag! *hello, good day*
guten Morgen! *good morning, hello*
das Gymnasium (Gymnasien) *grammar school*
hallo! *hello!*
die Hauptstadt(¨e) *capital city*
das Heft(e) *exercise book*
Herr X *Mr X*
heißen *to be called*
ich heiße Uschi *I'm called Uschi*

27

hier *here*
hinter + Acc/Dat *behind, after*
der Hit(s) *hit (in music)*
die Hitparade(n) *hit parade, charts*
hören *to hear*
ich *I*
ihr *you (informal, pl)*
in + Acc/Dat *into, in*
inclusive *including*
die Information(en) *information*
international *international*
das Interview(s) *interview*
Ire *Irish person (m)*
irisch *Irish*
Irland *Ireland*
Italien *Italy*
italienisch *Italian*
ja *yes*
das Jahr(e) *year*
  ich bin 13 Jahre alt *I'm 13 years old*
  jetzt *now*
die Jugendherberge(n) *youth hostel*
der Junge(n) *boy*
die Karte(n) *map*
  kein *not a, no*
  ich habe keine Ahnung *I haven't got a clue*
das Kettenspiel(e) *chain game*
das Kino(s) *cinema*
  klasse! *excellent, first class*
die Klasse(n) *class*
  kommen *to come*
  ich komme aus der Schweiz *I come from Switzerland*
  kommt 'rein! *come in!*
  können *to be able, can*
das Land(⁼er) *country, federal state*
  lang *long*
  Wie lange? *For how long?*
  laufen *to run*
  Was läuft? *What's on? (T.V., cinema, etc.)*
der Lehrer(-) *teacher (m)*
die Lehrerin(nen) *teacher (f)*
die Leichtathletik *athletics*
  lesen *to read*
  liegen (in + Dat) *to lie, be in*
das Lotto *bingo*
die Lücke(n) *gap*
  Luxemburg *Luxembourg*
  machen *to do, make*

das Mädchen(-) *girl*
  man *one, they, people*
  In Österreich spricht man Deutsch *they speak German in Austria*
der Mann(⁼er) *man; husband*
die Mark(-) *German mark*
  mein(e) *my*
  meinen *to think*
  Was meinst du? *What do you think?*
  mit + Dat *with*
der Morgen(-) *morning*
  nach + Dat *to, after*
  * vorne *to the front*
  in der Nähe von *near*
der Name(n) *name*
die Nationalität(en) *nationality*
  natürlich *of course*
  nein *no*
  neun *nine*
  neunzehn *nineteen*
  nicht *not*
  *(wahr)? *isn't it? aren't you? aren't they? etc.*
die Niederlande *Netherlands*
  noch *another; still*
  Was *? *What else?*
  ist * Platz frei? *is there room?*
der Norden *north*
  im Norden *in the north*
die Nummer(n) *number*
  oder *or*
  ... *? *isn't it?*
der Ort(e) *place*
der Osten *east*
  im Osten *in the east*
  Österreich *Austria*
  Österreicher *Austrian person (m)*
  Österreicherin *Austrian person (f)*
  Pardon *sorry*
die Partnerarbeit *pair-work*
die Person(en) *person*
die Personalien *details, particulars*
der Platz(⁼e) *place*
  Polen *Poland*
  polnisch *Polish*
die Polizei *police*
  Portugal *Portugal*
die Post *post office*
  Prima! *great, fantastic*
das Puzzle(s) *puzzle*
das Quiz *quiz*
das Radio(s) *radio*
die Reihe(n) *row*

  an die * kommen *to be one's turn*
der Reporter(-) *reporter*
  reservieren *to reserve, book*
das Restaurant(s) *restaurant*
  richtig *correct, right*
die Ruhe *quiet, silence*
  *! *Be quiet!*
der Saal *room*
  sagen *to say, tell*
der Salat(-) *salad*
das Schnitzel(-) *cutlet*
  Schotte *Scottish person (m)*
  Schottin *Scottish person (f)*
  Schottland *Scotland*
  schreiben *to write*
die Schreibmaschine(n) *typewriter*
die Schweiz *Switzerland*
  Schweizer *Swiss person (m)*
  Schweizerin *Swiss person (f)*
der Schwimmer(-) *swimmer*
  sechs *six*
  sechzehn *sixteen*
  sehr *very*
  sein *to be*
  seit + Dat *since*
  * einem Jahr wohne ich hier *I've been living here for one year*
die Seite(n) *page; side*
sich setzen *to sit down*
  setzt euch! *sit down!*
  sicher *certainly*
  sie *she; her*
  Sie *you (polite form)*
  sieben *seven*
  siebzehn *seventeen*
  sonst *otherwise, as well*
  Spanien *Spain*
die Speisekarte(n) *menu*
  spielen *to play*
der Sportverein(e) *sports club*
die Sprache(n) *language*
  sprechen *to speak*
die Stadt(⁼e) *town*
die Stadtmitte(n) *town centre*
die Straße(n) *road*
der Süden *south*
  im Süden *in the south*
die Tabelle(n) *chart, table*
der Tag(e) *day*
  Teenager(-) *teenager*
der Tennistrainer(-) *tennis coach*

  Tischtennis spielen *to play table tennis*
  toll *great, super*
der Tourist(en) *tourist (m)*
die Touristin(nen) *tourist (f)*
die Tschechoslowakei *Czechoslovakia*
  tschüs! *'bye!*
  und *and*
  und so weiter (usw.) *etc.*
die Untergrundbahn (U-Bahn) *tube*
  verstehen *to understand*
  vier *four*
  vierzehn *fourteen*
  von + Dat *from*
der Vorname(n) *first name*
der Wahnsinn *madness*
  *! *That's ridiculous!*
  Wales *Wales*
  Walisisch *Welsh (lang)*
  was? *what?*
  weiter *further*
  weitermachen *to continue, carry on*
  welche(r, s)? *which?*
  wer? *who?*
der Westen *west*
  im Westen *in the west*
  wie? *how?*
  wiederholen *to repeat*
  wieviel? *how much?*
  * ist das? *how much does it cost?*
  wir *we*
  wissen *to know*
  wo? *where?*
die Woche(n) *week*
  woher? *from where?*
  * kommst du? *Where are you from?*
  wohnen (in) *to live (in)*
  zählen *to count*
  zehn *ten*
  zeigen *to show*
  zeig mir! *show me!*
  zelten *to camp*
das Zimmer(-) *room*
  zu + Dat *to*
  zuhören *to listen*
  hört gut zu! *listen carefully!*
  zwanzig *twenty*
  zwar *more specifically, to be exact*
  zwei *two*
  zweimal *twice*
  zwölf *twelve*

CHAPTER 2 Meine Familie

Area 1

> • Introducing your family
> • Revision of Unit 1

L, R, W

Wie heißen sie?

Tell pupils that you are going to play a recording and ask them to say what they think is being said. Try to elicit the new element of brothers and sisters. Then tell them to look at the Pupil's Book and listen to the recording again, in order to work out the name of each person talking.

T: Hört gut zu. Worum geht es hier? Was sagt David? Schlagt jetzt Seite 19 auf. Lest den Text. Hier sind die Namen, und hier sind die Personen. Wie heißt Nummer 1? Ute? Oder Maria? Hört gut zu und schreibt hinter Nummer 1 Ute oder Maria (demonstrate on the board). *Und so weiter.*

Wie heißen sie?

1 — Ich heiße David und bin zwölf Jahre alt. Ich habe einen Bruder und eine Schwester.
2 — Ich bin Ute. Ich komme aus der Schweiz. Ich habe zwei Schwestern.
3 — Mein Name ist Oliver. Ich bin Österreicher. Ich komme aus Linz. Ich habe drei Brüder und zwei Schwestern.
4 — Ich heiße Maria. Ich wohne in Norddeutschland, und ich habe einen Bruder.
5 — Mein Name ist Raphael. Ich komme aus der DDR. Ich bin Einzelkind.
6 — Ich heiße Peter. Ich bin dreizehn. Ich habe zwei Brüder und eine Schwester. Ich komme aus Frankfurt.
7 — Ich bin Andrea und komme aus Halle. Ich bin vierzehn und habe einen Bruder.
8 — Ich heiße Maren. Ich bin fünfzehn Jahre alt und komme aus Köln. Ich habe eine Schwester.
9 — Ich heiße Kurt. Ich bin Schweizer. Ich komme aus Zürich. Ich bin Einzelkind.
10 — Ich bin Dorit. Ich komme aus München in Süddeutschland. Ich habe keine Geschwister. Ich bin Einzelkind.

Solution:

1 D	2 H	3 J	4 A	5 B
6 G	7 F	8 C	9 E	10 I

L, S

Hast du Geschwister?

Draw stick figures of one boy and one girl.

Write numbers next to them, e.g.

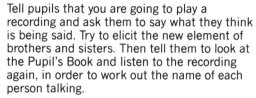

Ask the question ‚*Hast du Geschwister?*'. Then point to a stick figure and a number to elicit ‚*Ich habe zwei Schwestern*' etc.

Once the forms have been mastered, encourage pupils to take over the teacher's role.

Pronunciation: Avoid over-emphasising pronunciation of -**er**, i.e. make sure that there is no 'r' sound at the end of the word.

Insist on the long '**u**' in *Bruder* and the correct '**ü**' in the plural form.

L, W

Wieviel Geschwister hast du?

Further listening material on the theme of brothers and sisters. Get pupils to copy the grid on page 19. Tell them to listen to the recording and to write down the number of brothers and sisters each person has.

Hier sind acht Personen. Schreibt die Tabelle in euer Heft und hört gut zu. Wieviel Geschwister haben sie?

Wieviel Geschwister hast du?

1 — Ich heiße Andrea Hamann. Ich bin elf Jahre alt und wohne in Kassel. Ich habe einen Bruder, Michael, und zwei Schwestern, Regina und Carola.
2 — Ich heiße Peter Müller, und ich wohne in Köln. Ich habe eine Schwester. Sie heißt Birgit.
3 — Ich bin Sabine Brümmer. Ich habe zwei Brüder, Paul - der ist sechzehn - und Hans - der ist dreizehn.
4 — Ich heiße Kurt Hansen. Ich komme aus Stuttgart. Ich habe einen Bruder und eine Schwester.
5 — Mein Name ist Wolf Lichtenauer. Ich bin fünfzehn Jahre alt, und ich wohne in Österreich. Ich hab' keine Geschwister.
6 — Ich bin Katrin Winter. Ich habe drei Brüder. Leider habe ich keine Schwester.
7 — Ja, mein Name ist Sven Rellstab. Ich komme aus Lingen. Ich habe nur einen Bruder. Der heißt Torsten.
8 — Ich heiße Kirsten Stefan. Ich bin elf Jahre alt. Ich habe zwei Schwestern, Trudi und Jutta. Ich wohne in Halle.

Solution:

	Brüder	Schwestern
Andrea Hamann	1	2
Peter Müller	0	1
Sabine Brümmer	2	0
Kurt Hanseñ	1	1
Wolf Lichtenauer	0	0
Katrin Winter	3	0
Sven Rellstab	1	0
Kirsten Stefan	0	2

L, S, W

Talking about your own family

Tell pupils to interview five or six others about their own families using as many questions as possible. Tell them to take notes. Call upon individual pupils to report back to the whole class. They will probably have to use the first person: *Peter (sagt): ,Ich habe einen Bruder ...'* This can then be verified by the pupil mentioned.

Macht jetzt fünf Interviews.
Schreibt die Antworten auf. (Demonstrate with one pupil.)

L, S, R

Und du?

Refer pupils to the model dialogue in the book and practise it by replacing Lutz's and Jens' details with their own.

Schlagt die Bücher auf Seite 20 auf. Übt in Partnerarbeit:
(Speaking to one pair:)
Du sagst: ,Hallo! Wie heißt du?'
Und du sagst: ,Ich heiße Arthur. Und du?'
Du sagst: ,Jennifer'.
Und so weiter. Klar?

L, S, R, W

Und du? Wie heißt du?

Cut up part B of Worksheet number 4 and give one completed form to each pupil. Then distribute one sheet of blank forms (part A of the worksheet) to each pupil. They can now gather different sets of personal details from five other pupils in the class using the language of the model dialogue *Und du?*.

Allow pupils time to find the five different people and to record their details. (Make it clear that all the people have different names and that they should write down their own details first).

Collate pupils' results on the board.

(Pointing at a completed form from part B:)
Das bist du.

(Pointing at parts of the worksheet:) *Suche fünf andere Leute und schreibe alles auf.* (Help one pupil on the way, if necessary.)

R

Drei Briefe

This is the first encounter with German handwriting (see note on handwriting, TN p. 6). The language is familiar, except for the beginning and ending of the letters and the two references to birthdays, which should, however, be understood in context.

Draw pupils attention to the capital D in *Du* and *Dein/Deine*. The questions in English can be used to test comprehension. These letters also serve as models for the following activity.

W

Schreibe einen Brief auf Deutsch!

Ask pupils to write a similar letter about themselves. This may need further guidance, especially for the less able, perhaps by writing up questions or gapped sentences.

L, S

Jürgens Fotoalbum

Tell pupils to look at *Jürgens Fotoalbum* and to guess what it is about. Then play the recording of Jürgen talking about his family. Tell pupils to find out the order in which he introduces them.

Jürgens Fotoalbum

— Dies ist meine Familie:
 Das ist mein Vater.
 Das ist Tante Liesel. Sie wohnt in Bonn.
 Das hier ist meine Schwester Heike. Sie ist vierzehn.
 Hier ist meine Katze. Sie heißt Mitzi.
 Das ist meine Mutter.
 Das ist meine Großmutter. Sie ist schon alt.
 Und dies ist Erich, mein Bruder. Er ist acht.
 Dies ist mein Onkel. Onkel Kurt. Er wohnt nicht hier. Er wohnt in Wien. Das ist in Österreich.
 Das ist mein Hund. Er heißt Rowdy.
 Und hier, das ist mein Großvater. Er ist sehr alt.

Explain the familiar and formal forms of *Vati/Vater, Mutti/Mutter, Oma/Großmutter, Opa/Großvater*. Play the part of the previous recording referring to *Vater*. Encourage pupils to draw parallels with English.

> *Im Fotoalbum steht ‚Vati'.*
> *Aber Jürgen sagt nicht ‚Vati'.*
> *Er sagt ... ?/Was sagt er?*

Only the formal variants are intended for productive use at this stage.

L, S, R, W

21
(1A 21)

Fülle die Lücken aus

Practise the task orally with the whole class. Then write *mein/meine; er/sie* on the board and tell pupils to write out the complete sentences.

W

Mein Fotoalbum

Pupils could prepare a similar page from an imaginary photo album, using either real photographs or drawings, pictures from magazines etc.

nem 1

R, W

228
(1A 106)

Er heißt Oliver

An exercise consolidating the use of the third person in personal details.

L, S, R, W

5A
5B

Wie heißen sie?

One partner has a set of ten family trees, indicating number of parents and names and ages of children. The other partner has a set of ten family portraits, giving only the family surnames. The aim of the task is for pupils to match the family portraits with the information and them **without** looking at each other's sheets, and so to establish, for example, that *Familie 1* is called *Meyer*.

Divide the class into pairs. Give one partner in each pair Worksheet 5A and the other partner Worksheet 5B. Using one pair as an example, explain what they have in front of them in German, or in English, as necessary.

> *T: So. Robert, du hast zehn Familienfotos.* (Hold up his worksheet so people with the other sheet can get a quick impression of what it looks like.)
> *Du weißt auch, wie die Familien heißen: Kleber, Schmidt, Hoffmann und so weiter. Du, David, hast Informationen über diese*

Familien. (Hold up other worksheet). *Du weißt, Familie Nummer eins hat zwei Kinder. Wie heißen die Kinder?*
P1: *Marion und Sandra.*
T: *Und wie alt sind sie?*
P1: *Marion ist 5 und Sandra ist 4.*
T: *Und haben sie eine Mutter und einen Vater?*
P1: *Ja.*
T: *Gut. Nun, David. Hast du ein Foto von dieser Familie?* (Point out if necessary).
P2: *Ja.*
T: *Wie heißt die Familie?*
P2: *Meyer.*
T: *Gut. Also, Familie I heißt Meyer. Schreibt das auf.* (Write on board). *Und jetzt macht ihr weiter.*

Solution:

	Familie			
	1	Meyer	6	Akkaya
	2	Schmidt	7	Hoffmann
	3	Schiller	8	Kirchner
	4	Strauß	9	Lebert
	5	Rossini	10	Vogel

2 Area 2

● **Numbers 21–100**

L, S, R, W

22
(1A 22)

Wieviel Grad ist es?

Tell pupils to look at the small outline map of Europe and then listen to the 'weather forecast'. They must write the name of the capital and the temperature.

> *T: Seht euch die Karte an. Hier sind die Hauptstädte London, Paris usw. Wieviel Grad ist es* (point to thermometer in book) *in London? Zwanzig, fünfundzwanzig, dreißig? Was ist dreißig?*
> *P: Thirty.*
> *T: Gut, richtig. Hört jetzt gut zu.* (Play no. 1): *Ihr schreibt: London, 21 Grad.*

Wieviel Grad ist es?

1	— London: 2l Grad.	6	— Wien: 28 Grad.
2	— Paris: 24 Grad.	7	— Bern: 29 Grad.
3	— Berlin: 25 Grad.	8	— Bonn: 26 Grad.
4	— Rom: 32 Grad.	9	— Madrid: 30 Grad.
5	— Brüssel: 23 Grad.	10	— Warschau: 18 Grad.

22 (1A 22) Der Bus nach Schenefeld kommt

L, S, R

Further practice of numbers in a useful context.

T: Hier ist eine Bushaltestelle, und hier kommt der Bus nach Schenefeld. Das ist die Linie ... ? Und der Bus nach Pinneberg? Das ist die Linie ... ?

Pupils could practise this in pairs later.

---

23 (1A 23) Wer gewinnt?

L, S, R, W

The results of two winter sports events. Tell pupils to listen to the recordings and decide who wins each event and the distance each managed to achieve.

T: Seht euch die Namen an und hört gut zu. Schreibt auf, wieviel Meter Becker springt. (Play first example). Schreibt Becker in euer Heft. Wieviel Meter springt er?
P: Neunzig.
T: Richtig. Neunzig.

Wer gewinnt?
— Hier ist das Resultat:

Georg Becker, Bundesrepublik Deutschland 90 Meter.
Rudi Schubert, Österreich 94 Meter.
Werner Schmidt, Deutsche Demokratische Republik 95 Meter.
David Spong, Kanada 92 Meter
Richard Street, Großbritannien 91 Meter
Nikki Keller, Schweiz 89 Meter
Serge Truffaut, Frankreich 85 Meter
Jean Blanc, Belgien 97 Meter
Norbert Timm, Liechtenstein 99 Meter
Pedro Hidalgo, Spanien 78 Meter.

— Hier ist das Resultat:

Sari Sinkkonen, Finnland 3 Minuten, 54 Sekunden
Rachel Roberts, Großbritannien 3 Minuten, 28 Sekunden
Dorit Stegemann, Bundesrepublik 3 Minuten, 56 Sekunden
Solange Maillet, Frankreich 3 Minuten, 26 Sekunden
Uschi Koydl, Österreich 3 Minuten, 48 Sekunden
Donna Wilkins, Kanada ist gestürzt
Marie Herrgott, Schweiz 3 Minuten, 3l Sekunden
Gisela Rohwedder, Bundesrepublik 3 Minuten, 57 Sekunden
Ulrike Tank, Deutsche Demokratische Republik 3 Minuten, 39 Sekunden
Margaret Agsteribbe, USA 3 Minuten, 44 Sekunden

---

22 (1A 22) Kennst du die Zahlen?

L, R

Tell pupils to familiarise themselves with the visuals. Then tell them to listen for the numbers in the recording and match them to the visuals. Go through the first dialogue with the whole class as an example.

Schlagt die Bücher auf Seite 22 auf. Seht euch die Bilder an.
Jetzt hört gut zu.
Könnt ihr eine Zahl hören?
75? oder l00? oder 50? (Play first dialogue).
Richtig, 40. Also, das ist Bild 'g'. (Write lg on the board)
Jetzt hört wieder gut zu. Was kommt jetzt?

Kennst du die Zahlen?
1 — Ich gehe jetzt ins Kino. Kommst du mit?
— Läuft denn ein guter Film?
— Ja, Ali Baba und die 40 Räuber.

2 — Du, morgen kommt ein alter Film im Kino.
— Ja? Wie heißt er?
— In 80 Tagen um die Welt.

3 — Macht die Bücher auf. Seite 54.

4 — Du, die Lampe ist kaputt.
— Versuch mal 'ne neue Birne! Hier, diese hat 75 Watt.

5 — Wo wohnst du?
— Frankfurter Straße 81.

6 — Ist der Film lang?
— Nein, nur 90 Minuten.

7 — Ist das ein schnelles Auto?
— Und ob! Es beschleunigt von 0 auf 100 in 6 Sekunden.

8 — Kannst du 50 Mark wechseln?

9 — Fahr nicht so schnell! Hier darfst du nur 60 Stundenkilometer fahren.

10 — Stop! Dreiunddreißig, nicht fünfundvierzig!

Solution:	1 g	2 e	3 f	4 a	5 c
	6 h	7 b	8 d	9 i	10 j

---

24 (1A 24) Telefonnummern und Adressen

L, S, R

Ask pupils to look at the address book and then listen to the short items. Practise the question forms *Wo wohnt ... ? Wie ist die Telefonnummer?* and the replies. The digits may be given singly or in groups of two, e.g. (65577) *sechs-fünf-fünf-sieben-sieben,* or *sechs-fünfundfünfzig-siebenundsiebzig.*

Seht die Adressen und Telefonnummern an. Hört jetzt gut zu!

Telefonnummern und Adressen

1 — Ich heiße Siegrid Blömeke. Ich wohne in Pinneberg. Meine Adresse ist Jappopweide 4, und meine Telefonnummer ist 65 57 7. Die Vorwahl ist 04101.

2 — Ich heiße Maria Feyerabend. Ich wohne in Moorrege. Meine Adresse ist Klinkerstraße 88, und meine Telefonnummer ist 81 27 3. Die Vorwahl ist 04122.

3 — Ich heiße Bernd Goerke. Ich wohne in Norderstedt. Meine Adresse ist Am Stadtpark 4, und meine Telefonnummer ist 52 27 04 0.
Die Vorwahl ist 040.

4 — Ich heiße Elke Hauschildt. Ich wohne in Klein Nordende. Meine Adresse ist Am Redder 22. Meine Telefonnummer ist 94 96 8. Die Vorwahl ist 04121.

5 — Ich heiße Ingeborg Heinrich. Ich wohne in Pinneberg. Meine Adresse ist Memeler Straße 6a. Meine Telefonnummer ist 61 20 5. Die Vorwahl ist 04101.

6 — Mein Name ist Annkatrin Holbach. Ich wohne in Elmshorn. Meine Adresse ist Waldweg 22, und meine Telefonnummer ist 83 21 1. Die Vorwahl ist 04121.

7 — Ich heiße Barbara Kulpe. Ich wohne in Halstenbek. Meine Adresse ist Papenmoorweg 29, und meine Telefonnummer ist 45 91 7. Die Vorwahl ist 04101.

8 — Ich heiße Annelies Lakaw-Dörsel. Ich wohne in Quickborn. Meine Adresse ist Rotdornweg 39, und meine Telefonnummer 69 23 1. Die Vorwahl ist 04106.

9 — Ich heiße Jürgen Meyer. Ich wohne in Itzehoe/Kreis Steinburg. Meine Adresse ist Geschwister-Scholl-Allee 96, und meine Telefonnummer ist 44 46.
Die Vorwahl ist 04821.

10 — Ich heiße Hans-Heinrich Möller. Ich wohne in Uetersen. Meine Adresse ist Heidweg 32, und meine Telefonnummer ist 43 21 4. Die Vorwahl ist 04122.

N.B. **Addresses:** Tell pupils in English that each German town and village has its own numerical postcode. Refer them to the envelopes on page 24 . Tell them also about the practice of writing *Absender (Abs.)* plus the sender's address on the back of the envelope. Practise the codes as follows:

T: *Was ist die Postleitzahl von Quickborn?*
P: *Zwei-null-acht-fünf* (or: *zwanzig-fünfundachtzig).*

Telephone numbers: Explain that each town/village has a dialling code *(Vorwahl)*, then ask pupils to answer a few questions. Follow the same procedure as for post codes.

T: *Wie läutet/Welches ist die Vorwahl von Elmshorn?*
P: *Null-vier-eins-zwei-eins* (or *null-einundvierzig-einundzwanzig).*

L, R, W

24
(1A 24)

Wie alt sind sie?

Tell pupils to look at their book and listen to the recording. Ask them to find out how old the relatives are.

Buch, Seite 24. Schreibt alles in euer Heft. Wie alt ist er? Wie alt ist sie? (Hold up book and point).
Jürgens Mutter - wie alt ist sie? 36? 38? 72? Hört gut zu. Was paßt zu wem?

Wie alt sind sie?

1 — Wie alt ist deine Mutter?
  — 38.
2 — Wie alt ist dein Großvater?
  — 72.
3 — Wie alt ist deine Großmutter?
  — Ich weiß nicht genau. Ich glaube, sie ist 70 Jahre alt.
4 — Wie alt ist dein Vater?
  — Er ist vierzig, glaube ich.
5 — Wie alt ist deine Tante Liesel?
  — Ah, ich weiß nicht. Vielleicht 36.
6 — Wie alt ist dein Onkel Kurt?
  — Moment mal. Er muß 42 sein.

L, S, R, W

24
(1A 25)

Familie Bromma

Ask pupils to pretend they are one of the Bromma's children and then answer the questions in German. Pupils' answers will differ, depending on the identity they have chosen.

T: *Seht euch die Familie Bromma an. Gillian, das ist die Familie Bromma, und das ist deine Familie* (point to pupil). *Wie heißt du? (Helga? Anne? Brigitte? ...)*
P: *Annika.*
T: *Wie alt bist du?*
Schreibt alles in euer Heft.

25
(1A 25)

Wer bin ich?

L, S, R

Both partners should first of all read the 10 descriptions and look at the photographs in silence. Then partner A chooses one of the photographs without telling B and gives a clue as to who he is pretending to be. e.g. *Ich bin 18 Jahre alt. Wer bin ich?* If B does not know or makes an incorrect guess, partner A gives another clue etc.

T: *Und jetzt folgt Partnerarbeit. Seht euch die zehn Fotos an, und lest den Text unter jedem Foto still durch, d.h. ohne dabei zu sprechen.*
Partner A, jetzt denkst du an eine Person und du sagst: Ich bin 18 Jahre alt. Wer bin ich?

Writing about your own family

W

Tell pupils to make up their own (real or imaginary) family tree with photographs or drawings and write about them as in the previous activity. This could then form part of a wall display or class book.

Und jetzt schreibt ‚Meine Familie'. Bringt Fotos mit oder zeichnet Bilder. Schreibt alles auf. Zum Beispiel (draw family tree then write):
1 Dies ist meine Mutter. Sie heißt …

2 Area 3

- Talking about pets
- Using the accusative *(einen, eine, ein)*
- Using the nominative *(der, die, das/ ein, eine, ein)*

L, S

1-10

Pets

Ask pupils if they have various pets. Cue meanings by the flashcards.

T: *Hast du eine Katze? Ja oder nein?*
P: *Ja.*
See also
T: *Hast du einen Hund?*

6

Encourage pupils to take over the teacher's role as soon as possible.

Hast du ein Haustier?

L

Write five names on the board: Oliver, Martin, Maria, Jürgen and Bernd. Tell pupils to listen to the recording to find out what pets each person has.

Hört gut zu. Hat Oliver einen Hund? Hat Bernd eine Katze? Schreibt die Namen auf Englisch.

Hast du ein Haustier?

1 — Hast du ein Haustier, Oliver?
   — Ja, ich habe einen Hund und eine Katze.

2 — Martin, hast du ein Haustier?
   — Ja, einen Wellensittich.

3 — Hast du ein Haustier, Maria?
   — Ja, ein Pferd und eine Maus.

4 — Jürgen, hast du ein Haustier?
   — Ja, ich habe ein Meerschweinchen und einen Hamster.

5 — Hast du ein Haustier, Bernd?
   — Ja, einen Goldfisch und ein Kaninchen.

L, S, R, W

Tiere

6

This Worksheet can be used in a variety of ways: as reinforcement or as a possible homework activity, especially for the less able; as an OHP master, providing an alternative way of presenting and practising animals, or cut up into cards to play various word games.

Genders

L, S, R

1-10

Use the flashcards to revise the pets as above. Collate the answers under three gender columns on the board.

Ask pupils: *Hast du einen Hund?*
                eine Katze?
                ein Pferd? etc.

Pupils reply: *Ja/Nein.*

Then practise *einen/eine/ein* in the above question in the following way:

T: *Hast du einen Hund?*
Hast du _____ Hund? (Indicate the gap by tapping on the desk or snapping fingers, thus encouraging pupils to reproduce the question. Just *einen* will do as a first response, but then use mime to elicit the full question:)
P: *Hast du einen Hund?*

Continue similarly with other **masculine** animals. When pupils consistently produce *einen*, write *Hast du ...* on the board and *einen* above the column of masculine pets.

Follow the same procedure for the the other genders. Clear articulation of the articles is important, but teachers should be careful not to distort the natural flow of speech by undue emphasis.

The final layout on the board should look like this:

Hast du ...?

einen	eine	ein
Hund	Katze	Pferd
Hamster	Schildkröte	Meerschweinchen
Goldfisch	Maus	Kaninchen
Wellensittich		

(from above) **L, S**

Tell pupils to ask the question *,Hast du ... ?'* using the board for reference (see previous activity). Practise in a chain game. Then remove the names of the animals from the columns and continue.

L, S, R, W

26
(1A 26) **Hast du einen Hund? /Tierquiz**

Use *Tierquiz* in the Pupil's Book to cue oral consolidation, in pairs of *einen/eine/ein*. Check pair-work carefully as a class activity before written consolidation.

N.B. The drawings in the book are in three columns according to gender.

Additional pets:

ein	eine
Papagei *(parrot)*	Ratte *(rat)*
	Wüstenspringmaus *(gerbil)*
	Schlange *(snake)*
	Stabheuschrecke *(stick insect)*

26
(1A 26)

L, S, R

Tierquiz

Ask pupils to look at the pictures of animals. Notice that the presentation of genders is now in the Nominative Case.

Schlagt die Bücher auf Seite 26 auf. Seht euch die Tiere an.

Then present the following in one go:

Schnuffel ist ein Hund.
Max ist ein Hamster.
Hansi ist ein Wellensittich.
Goldi ist ein Goldfisch.
Poldi ist ein Igel.
Fipsi ist eine Maus.
Elsa ist eine Schildkröte.
Mitzi ist eine Katze.
Stupsi ist ein Kaninchen.
Amanda ist ein Meerschweinchen.
Rex ist ein Pferd.

Then ask pupils:

T: *Wie heißt der Hund?*
P: *Schnuffel.*
T: *Richtig! Der Hund heißt Schnuffel.* (If an incorrect answer is given, ask the question again later.)

Divide the board/OHP into three columns. Write/display *Hund* in the first column. Continue asking the names of other pets and enter them in the appropriate columns. Then practise *der/die/das* in the same way as *einen/eine/ein*. Repetition of the same procedure should emphasise the concept and link the forms.

The final layout on the board:

Wie heißt

der	die	das
Hund	Maus	Kaninchen?

L, S

Ask pupils to ask the questions *,Wie heißt ...?'* using the board/OHP for reference. Later remove the names of the animals from the three columns and continue.

Jetzt seid ihr dran. Susan, du fragst: ,Wie heißt ...?'

26
(1A 26)

L, S, R

Was ist Max? /Tierquiz

This is a variant of the *Tierquiz* requiring productive use of the indefinite article + animal.

T: *Was ist Max?*
P: *Ein Hamster.*
T: *Richtig!*

If the wrong animal is given:

T: *Nein, Max ist kein ...*

If the wrong article is used, repeat in a questioning tone:

T: *Eine?*

asking pupil to thereby supply correct form.

---

nem 2

228
(1A 106)

S/W

Was ist das?

A guessing game based on incomplete visuals of animals.

---

nem 3

228
(1A 106)

R, W

Was ist das für ein Tier?

Written consolidation of *ein/eine* and *der/die/das*. This is quite a complicated activity and will require careful oral preparation.

---

nem 4

229
(1A 107)

(L, S), R, W

Was für Tiere haben sie?

Written consolidation of *einen/eine/ein*. Practise orally first, if required. Refer pupils to the *Tip des Tages*.

26-27
(1A 26-27)

R

Suche die Tiere

This is a genuine reading activity with questions in English, which encourages pupils to look for specific items/information in texts which they cannot possibly understand in detail.

---

nem 5

229
(1A 107)

R, W

Graf Draculas Familie

Practice of *mein/meine* with both people and animals.

---

2 Area 4

● Using *kein*

28
(1A 28)

R

Hast du kein Haustier?

The concept of *kein* has already been briefly introduced in *keine Geschwister*. It should thus not cause any comprehension problems, nor should some colloquial expressions used in the text, like *aber, mehr, auch*, which are not intended for productive use at this stage.

29
(1A 29)

R

Achtung, Tollwut!

Rabies poster as a brief introduction to the following activity.

28
(1A 28)

(L), (S), R

Haben Sie etwas zu verzollen?

Cartoon practising *kein*. The dialogue could be practised in pairs and later performed in front of the class.

30
(1A 30)

L, S/R

Eine typische Klasse?

Cartoon practising classroom vocabulary with *kein*. This can be further practised as an 'everyday' activity.

L, S, R, W

Umfrage

Some pupils could carry out a class survey of pets and design a chart to display the results.

P1: *Hast du ein Haustier?*
P2: *Nein/Ja, (ich habe) einen/eine/ein ...*
     Ich habe keinen/keine/kein ...

2 Area 5

● Describing in more detail where you live (location, accommodation)

Use flashcards to introduce and practise *Wohnung, Reihenhaus, Doppelhaus, Einfamilienhaus, Bungalow.*

Dies ist ...

L

Ich wohne in ...

Tell the pupils where you live and talk about the environment.

Ich wohne in Eastbourne.
Eastbourne ist eine Stadt in Südengland.
Ich wohne in der Stadtmitte.
Der Supermarkt Tesco ist auch in der Stadtmitte.

Draw a simple outline of the town on the board to illustrate the meaning of *Stadtmitte,* e.g.:

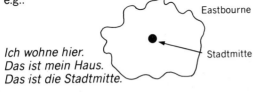

Ich wohne hier.
Das ist mein Haus.
Das ist die Stadtmitte.

Herr/Frau (name of other teacher) wohnt auch in Eastbourne.
Aber nicht in der Stadtmitte.
Er/Sie hat ein Haus am Stadtrand, in Willingdon.
Herr/Frau (...) wohnt in Alfriston.
Alfriston ist ein Dorf in der Nähe von Eastbourne.

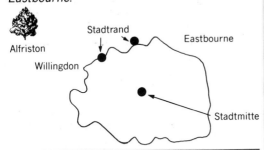

L, S

Practise the vocabulary just introduced using other local towns and villages as cues to prepare for the following activity.

L, S

Wohnst du in der Stadtmitte?

Ask individual pupils where they live, to elicit:

Ich wohne in Eastbourne, in der Stadtmitte.
Ich wohne in Willingdon, am Stadtrand.
Ich wohne in Alfriston. Das ist ein Dorf in der Nähe von Eastbourne.

Wo wohnen sie?

Eight people describing where they live. The symbols on the grid will also appear later in Area 6, in the communicative activity *Wo wohne ich?*. Pupils should become familiar with them as soon as possible. Ask pupils to listen to the recording and complete the grid by marking with a cross in the appropriate columns.

The gap-filling exercise can be used as further written consolidation of the vocabulary if required. This is a possible homework activity.

Hört gut zu. Macht Kreuze in die richtigen Spalten. Schreibt Nord, Süd, Ost oder West und das Land.

Wo wohnen sie?

1 — Ich wohne in Gauting in der Bundesrepublik. Das ist ein Dorf in der Nähe von München im Süden. Ich habe ein Haus am Marktplatz.

2 — Ich wohne in Kassel in der Bundesrepublik. Das ist eine Stadt im Norden. Ich habe ein Haus am Stadtrand.

3 — Ich wohne in Braunau in Österreich. Das ist eine Stadt im Norden. Ich habe eine Wohnung in der Stadtmitte.

4 — Ich wohne in Rostock in der DDR. Das ist eine große Stadt im Norden. Ich wohne in der Stadtmitte. Ich habe eine kleine Wohnung.

5 — Ich wohne in Krempe in Deutschland. Das ist eine kleine Stadt im Norden. Ich habe ein Reihenhaus am Stadtrand.

6 — Ich wohne in Worms in der Bundesrepublik. Das ist eine Stadt im Westen. Ich habe eine Wohnung in der Stadtmitte.

7 — Ich wohne in Zermatt in der Schweiz. Das Dorf ist im Süden. Ich habe ein Haus am Marktplatz.

8 — Ich wohne in Lübeck in der BRD. Das ist eine Hafenstadt im Nordosten. Ich habe eine Wohnung am Stadtrand.

Solution:

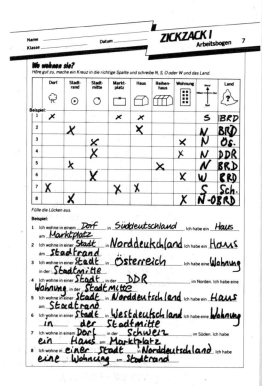

Wo wohnen sie?
Höre gut zu, mache ein Kreuz in die richtige Spalte und schreibe N, S, O oder W und das Land.

	Dorf	Stadt-rand	Stadt-mitte	Markt-platz	Haus	Reihen-haus	Wohnung		Land
Beispiel:		⊙	○	*					?
1	X			X	X			S	BRD
2		X			X			N	BRD
3			X			X		N	Ös.
4			X			X		N	DDR
5		X				X		N	BRD
6	X	X				X		W	BRD
7	X			X	X			S	Sch.
8		X					X	N-O	BRD

Fülle die Lücken aus.

Beispiel:
1 Ich wohne in einem _Dorf_ in _Süddeutschland_ . Ich habe ein _Haus_ am _Marktplatz_ .
2 Ich wohne in einer _Stadt_ in _Norddeutschland_ Ich habe ein _Haus_ am _Stadtrand_ .
3 Ich wohne in einer _Stadt_ in _Österreich_ . Ich habe eine _Wohnung_ in der _Stadtmitte_ .
4 Ich wohne in einer _Stadt_ in der _DDR_ im Norden. Ich habe eine _Wohnung_ in der _Stadtmitte_ .
5 Ich wohne in einer _Stadt_ in _Norddeutschland_ Ich habe ein _Haus_ am _Stadtrand_ .
6 Ich wohne in einer _Stadt_ in _Westdeutschland_ Ich habe eine _Wohnung_ in der _Stadtmitte_ .
7 Ich wohne in einem _Dorf_ in der _Schweiz_ im Süden. Ich habe ein _Haus_ am _Marktplatz_ .
8 Ich wohne in einer _Stadt_ in _Norddeutschland_ Ich habe eine _Wohnung_ am _Stadtrand_ .

R, W

8

Welches Zimmer ist das?
Make an OHP transparency of the Worksheet (8) to present the rooms of a house. A worksheet can also be produced for pupils to label and stick in exercise books (possibly for homework).

If an OHP is not available, the drawings can be reproduced simply on the board.

R

31
(1A 31)

Brieffreunde
Two letters describing where people live, including the rooms of a house/flat.

R

32
(1A 32)

Wer wohnt hier?
Exploitation of the above letters by means of symbols.

Solution:
a Andy's father
b Andy + mother
c Andy's grandparents
d Jürgen + parents
e Margaret
f Sylvia

L, S, R, (W)

Ich habe ein Wohnzimmer
Practise the rooms of a house by talking about your own accommodation. Refer pupils to *Tip des Tages* for the language required and to the OHP transparency of the rooms.

66 99 *Ich habe ein Wohnzimmer* (point to the room), *drei Schlafzimmer, usw.*

Encourage pupils to take over the teacher's role.

This could also be practised in the 3rd person. Pupils could interview each other and report back orally or in writing.

66 99 *Macht jetzt Interviews. Fragt: ,Wie ist dein Haus?' oder ,Wie ist deine Wohnung?' und dann macht Notizen. Dann sagt ihr: ,Er/sie hat eine Wohnung. Die Wohnung ist ..'*

R, W

33
(1A 33)

Der Immobilien-Markt
A matching exercise based on house and flat advertisements. If pupils comment on the dative plural *mit ... zwei Schlafzimmern*, they could be referred to the Grammar survey*. No exploitation is intended at this stage.

Solution: A 9   D 5
           B 4/3 E 6
           C 2   F 1

* Pupil's Book, page 263.

L, S, R, W

9

Was sind die Unterschiede?
Cut the worksheet in half. Tell pupils to work in pairs, (give part A to one partner and part B to the other), in order to find out the different locations of the houses and flats and

the number and types of rooms in each one. Work through the first example with one pair and write the answers on the board.

T: *Jetzt Partnerarbeit.* (To Partner A). *Stell die Frage Nummer 1* (point to question 1).
Partner A: *Wo wohnst du?*
Partner B: *Ich wohne in Köln.*
T: (To A:) *Du schreibst hier unten* (pointing to bottom of sheet): *B Köln.*

Repeat the formula for questions 2-5, if necessary, then tell pupils to continue in pairs and make a note of the details. When pupils have finished, collate the information on the board in writing, or in symbols.

e.g. **1 A** Appen - Dorf - am Marktplatz - Reihenhaus - 2 Schlafzimmer, 1 Badezimmer oben - Küche, Wohnzimmer unten.

   B Köln - Stadt - am Stadtrand - Wohnung, 3 Schlafzimmer, Badezimmer, Küche, Wohnzimmer, Eßzimmer.

   C ...

---

nem 6

229
(1A 107)

R, W

Mein Hund heißt Rowdy

A completion exercise practising the use of *er/sie/es*.

---

2 Area 6

● Consolidation

10

L, S, R

Wo wohne ich?

A game of logic.

Tell pupils to look at the map on their worksheet. Revise *im Norden, im Süden, im Osten* and *im Westen* in the following way:

T: *Wo ist Bonn?*
P: *In Deutschland.*

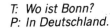

T: *Im Norden? Im Süden? Im Osten? Im Westen?*
P: *Im Westen.*

Provide further examples, if required.

Write on the board *Fragen* with the numbers 1 to 10. Call a pupil to the front and whisper *Du wohnst in Bonn.* Now begin the guessing game in the following sequence:

T: *Wohnst du in Österreich?*
P: *Nein.* (Teacher puts a line through number 1 on board)
T: *Wohnst du in der Schweiz?*
P: *Nein.* (Line through number 2)
T: *Wohnst du in Deutschland?*
P: *Ja.* (Line through number 3)
T: *Wohnst du im Norden?*
P: *Nein.* (Line through number 4)
T: *Wohnst du im Süden?*
P: *Nein.* (Line through number 5)
T: *Wohnst du im Westen?*
P: *Ja.* (Line through number 6)
T: *Wohnst du in einem Dorf?*
P: *Nein.* (Line through number 7)
T: *Wohnst du in einem Reihenhaus?*
P: *Nein.* (Line through number 8)
T: *Du wohnst in einem Haus in Bonn.*
P: *Ja.* (Pointing at board).
T: *Wieviel Fragen waren das?*
P: *Acht.*
T: *So, und jetzt eine Partnerarbeit.*

Tell pupils in English to take it in turns to choose a 'home' shown on the map, and to get their partner to work out in the same way where they live, using the questions and symbols printed below the map. Tell them to note the number of questions they each ask.

R

nem 7

230
(1A 108)

Komm zu uns!

This activity consolidates in written form the main elements of the area. There is some unknown vocabulary. Pupils should be encouraged to guess meanings in context. Try to elicit similarities between English and German, e.g. *lernst*/learn; *kommst*/come; *kannst*/can.

Practise pronunciation of unknown items.

nem 8

230
(1A 108)

R, W

Verstanden?

Five open-ended questions and five multiple choice items to test reading comprehension of *Komm zu uns!* It may be necessary to spend some time going through the questions before pupils tackle this activity. This could be done as a class activity asking pupils to find the relevant part of a letter to support a particular answer.

The questions in English (n.e.m. no. 7) could be answered in addition or as an alternative to the above activity.

nem 9

230
(1A 108)

(R), W

Schreibe einen Brief an einen Freund in Deutschland

Ask pupils to write a letter describing their own house using *Komm zu uns!* and the *Tip des Tages* as a model. This may need quite a lot of preparation for less able pupils.

L, R, S/W

34 (1A 34) Computerliste

Tell pupils to look at the computer program, *Elsafreund*, on page 34, to listen to the tape and spot the mistakes.

Schlagt euer Buch auf Seite 34 auf. Lest den Text 'Computerliste'. Hört gut zu! Was sind die Tippfehler?

Computerliste

1 Elsa: — Schau mal. Stimmt das alles?
  Anne: — Nein. Anne schreibt man mit 'E', nicht mit 'A',... und meine Telefonnummer ist 4404, nicht 4403.
  Elsa: — Danke, Anne. Ist sonst alles in Ordnung?
  Anne: — Ja.

2 Elsa: — Ist da alles richtig, Peter?
  Peter: — Nein, nein, ich bin jetzt sechzehn.
  Elsa: — Ach ja, du hattest am Montag Geburtstag.
  Peter: — Genau. Und wir haben leider keine Katze mehr.

3 Elsa: — Na, Klaus. Stimmt das alles?
  Klaus: — Moment mal ... Vorname Klaus, stimmt, ... Adresse ... ja, die Straße ist richtig, aber die Nummer nicht.
  Elsa: — Wie ist die Nummer denn?
  Klaus: — Ich wohne Poststraße 32.

4 Elsa: — Du, Barbara. Ist das alles hier richtig?
  Barbara: — Moment. Ich gucke mir das mal an: Vorname, richtig ... Alter, Adresse, Telefonnummer, alles richtig. Ja, ich glaube, das stimmt!
  Elsa: — Toll!

5 Monika: — Du, Elsa, du weißt, ja, ich wohne nicht mehr in Ellerbek. Wir sind nämlich umgezogen.
  Elsa: — Wie ist deine neue Adresse?
  Monika: — Wir wohnen Dorfstraße 13, in Borstel-Hohenraden.
  Elsa: — Also, Dorfstraße 13, und B - O - R - S - T - E - L - Borstel H - O - H - E - N - R - A - D - E - N, Hohenraden?
  Monika: — Richtig.
  Elsa: — Und die Telefonnummer?
  Monika: — Die ist 73756.
  Elsa: — Also, 04l0l-73756. Klar.

L, S, R

34 (1A 34) Die erste Stunde fällt aus!

Divide the class into pairs and, at random, give each pair two telephone numbers.

If the class contains more than 15 pairs, invent more numbers to replace 15 and go up to the required amount.
e.g. for 34 pupils: 15a 72201
  b _____
  16a _____ } to
  b _____ } invent
  17a _____
  (15)b 207625

If there are fewer pairs than 15, the numbers can be reduced by cutting out the last few pairs from the solution.
e.g. for 11 pairs: 5a 26924
  (omit 5b, 12, 13, 14, 15a)
  (15)b 207625

Tell them, in English, that sometimes in Germany school starts late if a teacher is absent, and that it would be impossible for the school to phone everybody, so they have a chain system. The school (here, the teacher), phones the first person on the list, who then phones the next person listed to say that there is no first lesson! Tell pupils that they are going to do the same thing in class. For each pair a) is the incoming call and b) is the number of the next person on the list.

Jetzt Partnerarbeit. Seht euch die Telefonnummern an. Du, John. Die erste Nummer a) (point to appropriate number in Pupil's Book) *ist deine Nummer zu Hause. Die Nummer b) mußt du wählen* (mime dialling). Start the game by ringing John.

66 99 T (dials): *Zwei-null-sieben-sechs-zwei-fünf.*
John: *Hallo.*
T: *Du, John. Die erste Stunde fällt aus.*
John: *Oh, danke. Tschüs! (John dials:) sechs-drei-eins-acht.*
P2: *Hallo. ...*

Solution· Correct running order:
1-11-4-9-6-2-10-8-3-7-5-12-14-13-15-1.
If when number 15 is completed and number 1 is dialled, intervene and explain: *,Ja, ,sie wissen schon Bescheid!'*

Vocabulary

der Absender(-) *sender (letter)*
abwaschen *to wash up*
die Achtung *attention*
　*! beware! look out!
der Altbau *old building*
　andere(r/s) *other*
　angucken *to look at*
die Antwort(en) *answer*
　April *April*
　auch *also*
　aufmachen *to open*
　aufschreiben *to write down*
　ausfallen *to drop out, not take place*
　die Stunde fällt aus *the lesson isn't taking place*
　aussuchen *to choose*
das Bad(⁼er) *bath*
　bald *soon*
der Balkon(e) *balcony*
　beantworten *to answer*
　befehlen *to advise; order*
　bei + Dat *with, by*
　Bescheid wissen *to know*
　beschleunigen *to accelerate*
　beste(r,s) *best*
das Bett(en) *bed*
das Bier *beer*
　bieten *to offer*
der Bleistift(e) *pencil*
der Brief(e) *letter*
der Brieffreund(e) *pen-friend (m)*
die Brieffreundin(nen) *pen-friend (f)*
　bringen *to bring, take*
der Bungalow(s) *bungalow*
der Bruder(⁼) *brother*
der Bus(se) *bus*
der Computer(-) *computer*
die Couch *sofa*
　dabei *with it*
der Dachboden(-) *attic*
die Dame(n) *lady*
　Dezember *December*
das Doppelhaus(⁼er) *semi-detached house*
das Dorf(⁼er) *village*
　durch + Acc *through*
　dürfen *to be allowed to*
die Dusche(n) *shower*
die Ecke(n) *corner*
　eigen *own*
das Einfamilienhaus(⁼er) *detached house*
das Einzelkind(er) *only child*
die Eltern *parents*
das Eßzimmer(-) *dining room*
　etwas *something, anything*
　fahren *to drive, go*
der Fahrplan(⁼e) *timetable, (public transport)*

　folgen *to follow*
das Fotoalbum (Fotoalben) *photograph album*
die Frage(n) *question*
　fragen *to ask*
　freistehend *free-standing, detached*
　fressen *to eat (animals)*
der Freund(e) *friend; boyfriend*
die Freundin(nen) *friend; girlfriend*
die Garage(n) *garage*
das Gästezimmer(-) *guest room*
der Geburtstag(e) *birthday*
die Geschwister *brothers and sisters*
der Goldfisch(e) *goldfish*
der Grad *temperature, degree*
　Wieviel * ist es? *What's the temperature?*
die Grippe *flu*
　groß *large, big, tall*
　Großbritannien *Great Britain*
die Großmutter(⁼) *grandmother*
der Großvater(⁼) *grandfather*
der Gruß(⁼e) *greeting*
　haben + Acc *to have*
die Hafenstadt(⁼e) *town with a port*
die Hälfte(n) *half*
der Hamster(-) *hamster*
das Haustier(e) *house pet*
　herzlich *warm, best*
　herzliche Grüße *very best wishes*
das Hobby(s) *hobby*
　hoffen *to hope*
　hoffentlich *hopefully, I hope, we hope, etc.*
das Hotel(s) *hotel*
der Hund(e) *dog*
der Hut(⁼e) *hat*
der Igel(-) *hedgehog*
　jede(r, s) *each, every*
　jung *young*
das Kaninchen(-) *rabbit*
die Katze(n) *cat*
der Keller(-) *cellar*
der Kilometer(-) *kilometer*
das Kind(er) *child*
　klein *small*
　korrigieren *to correct*
　krank *ill*
das Kreuz(e) *cross*
die Küche(n) *kitchen*
der Kugelschreiber(-) (Kuli) *ball-point pen, Biro*
　lang *long*
　leider *unfortunately*
　lernen *to learn*
　Liechtenstein *Liechtenstein*

die Familie(n) *family*
der Fan(s) *fan*
der Fehler(-) *mistake*
die Ferien *holidays*
der Film(e) *film*
　Finnland *Finland*
die Fledermaus(⁼e) *bat*
der Marktplatz(⁼e) *market square*
die Maus(⁼e) *mouse*
das Meerschweinchen(-) *guinea pig*
　mehr *more*
der Meter(-) *meter*
die Milch *milk*
die Minute(n) *minute*
　mitkommen *to come with, go with*
　modern *modern*
　modernisiert *modernised*
der Moment(e) *moment*
　* mal *just a moment*
　Montag *Monday*
　am * *on Monday*
　montags *on Mondays*
　morgen *tomorrow*
　müssen *to have to, must*
die Mutter(⁼) *mother*
　Mutti *mum*
　nämlich **actually**
　nett *nice*
die Notiz(en) *note, item*
　normalerweise *usually*
　nur *only*
　ohne + Acc *without*
die Oma(s) *grandma*
der Onkel(-) *uncle*
der Opa(s) *grandpa*
　in Ordnung sein *to be all right, OK.*
das Ostern *Easter*
　zu * *at Easter*
das Papier(-) *paper*
das Parfüm(s) *perfume*
　passen *to go with*
　Was paßt zu wem? *What goes with what?*
das Pferd(e) *horse*
das Poster(s) *poster*
die Postleitzahl(en) *postal code*
　pünktlich *on the dot*
der Radiergummi(s) *rubber*
die Ratte(n) *rat*
das Reihenhaus(⁼er) *terraced house*
das Resultat(e) *result*
　schauen *to look at*
　schau mal! *look!*
die Schildkröte(n) *tortoise*
　schlafen *to sleep*
der Schlafsack(⁼e) *sleeping bag*
das Schlafzimmer(-) *bedroom*
die Schlange(n) *snake*
　schnell *fast*
　schon *already*
　schön *nice, lovely*
die Schwester(n) *sister*
　sehen *to see*
die Sekunde(n) *second*
　September *September*
　sie *they; them*
das Skispringen(-) *ski jumping*
der Slalom(s) *ski slalom*
der Sommer(-) *summer*
die Spalte(n) *box, column*
　spitze *ace, super*
die Stabheuschrecke(n) *stick insect*
der Stadtrand(⁼er) *outskirts of the town*

das Lineal(e) *ruler*
die Linie(n) *line, bus route*
die Liste(n) *list*
der Liter(-) *litre*
　Lust haben *to want to*
der Luxus *luxury*
　mal *just*
　am * *on the outskirts*
　stehen *to stand*
die Stereoanlage(n) *stereo system*
　still *quiet(ly)*
　stimmen *to be right*
　stinken *to smell, stink*
der Student(en) *student (m)*
die Studentin(nen) *student (f)*
　stürzen *to fall*
die Tante(n) *aunt*
　telefonieren mit *to ring up*
die Telefonnummer(n) *phone number*
der Teller(-) *plate*
der Teppich(e) *carpet*
die Terrasse(n) *terrace, patio*
der Text(e) *text*
das Tier(e) *animal*
die Tollwut *rabies*
　total *completely, totally*
der Trickfilm(e) *cartoon*
　über + Acc/Dat *over, above, more than*
die Umfrage(n) *survey*
　umziehen *to move house*
　und ob! *you bet!*
　unglücklich *unhappy*
　unter + Acc/Dat *under, beneath*
der Unterschied(e) *difference*
der Vater(⁼) *father*
　Vati *dad*
　verkaufen *to sell*
das Verkaufsbüro(s) *sales office*
　versuchen *to try*
　verzollen *to declare (at the customs)*
　viel *many, much*
　voll *full*
die Vorwahl(en) *dialling code*
　wählen *to choose; dial (phone)*
　wann? *when?*
　warten (auf + Acc) *to wait (for)*
　was für? *what sort of?*
das WC *toilet*
　wechseln *to change (money)*
der Wein(e) *wine*
　weiß *white*
der Wellensittich(e) *budgerigar*
die Welt *world*
　wenn *if*
das Wetter *weather*
　wie ist er? *what's he like?*
die Wohnfläche(n) *living area (in house)*
der Wohnort(e) *place/town of residence*
die Wohnung(en) *flat*
das Wohnzimmer(-) *sitting room, lounge*
　worum? *about what?*
die Wüstenmaus(⁼e) *gerbil*
die Zahl(en) *figure (numerical)*
　zeichnen *to draw*
das Ziel(e) *end, destination*
die Zigarre(n) *cigar*
die Zigarette(n) *cigarette*
　zu Hause *at home*

CHAPTER 3 In der Schule

Area 1

- Staying with a German family
- Days of the week
- Revision of Unit 2

36 (1A 36)

Austausch

L, S, R

The photos of the English exchange party and of Veronica Baker together with the short texts, set the scene for what follows. Read the texts with pupils. Ask ‚Wo ist Hamburg?' Elicit ‚In Norddeutschland.' Explain *Austausch*.

> *25 Engländer fahren nach Deutschland und wohnen bei deutschen Familien. Dann kommen die 25 Deutschen nach England und wohnen bei den englischen Familien. Das ist ein* **Austausch.** (Add, if your school has an exchange:) *Diese Schule hat einen Austausch mit -schule in ...*

---

36 (1A 36)

Veronica kommt in Hamburg an

L, S, R

Tell pupils to listen to the conversation in which Veronica meets Kirsten and her family, and to write down the letters **A B C D E F G** in the order in which they hear the phrases. Afterwards, see if pupils can guess the meanings of those that are new.

Solution: **D, F, G, A, C, B, E.**

Veronica kommt in Hamburg an

Kirsten: — Veronica?
Veronica: — Ja. Kirsten?
Kirsten: — Hallo! Wie geht's?
Veronica: — Fein, danke.
Kirsten: — Komm, gib mir deinen Koffer.
Veronica: — Oh, danke.
Kirsten: — Komm. Meine ganze Familie ist da. So, Veronica, das ist meine Mutter ...
Mutter: — Hallo, Veronica.
Kirsten: — ... und mein Vater.
Vater: — Willkommen in Hamburg!
Veronica: — Danke.
Kirsten: — Und das ist mein Bruder, Thomas.
Thomas: — Hallo.
Veronica: — Hallo.
Vater: — Gib mir Veronicas Koffer, Kirsten.
Mutter: — Wie war die Reise?
Veronica: — Ganz gut ... aber lang.
Mutter: — Ja, das stimmt.
Vater: — Kommt. Wir gehen zum Auto.
Kirsten: — Bist du hungrig?
Veronica: — Nicht sehr. Ich habe auf dem Schiff gegessen.
Thomas: — Ich aber!

Mutter: — Ach, der Thomas ist immer hungrig!
Vater: — So. Hier ist das Auto.

---

36 (1A 36)

Richtig oder falsch?

L, W

Play the recording again and ask pupils to write down as they listen whether the statements are true or false.

Solution: Richtig, Falsch, Richtig, Falsch, Richtig, Richtig.

---

37 (1A 37)

Du kommst an

L, S, R

Using the phrases **A-G** (*Veronica kommt in Hamburg an*), reconstruct a conversation similar to the one with Veronica. Get pupils to practise their own in groups.

The visuals can then be drawn on the board or OHP and used as cues for the conversations they have worked out. At this point pupils will have to produce all of the elements of the dialogue themselves, such as ‚Hallo, wie geht's?' and ‚Wie war die Reise?'

Bei Kirsten zu Hause

L

Tell the pupils to listen to the conversation and answer questions in English. Much of this conversation is revision of language introduced in Chapters 1 and 2.

Bei Kirsten zu Hause

Vater: — Na, jetzt sind wir zu Hause.
Mutter: — So, Veronica, komm herein. Ich nehme deinen Anorak.
Veronica: — Danke.
Mutter: — Du bist müde, nicht?
Veronica: — Ja, ein bißchen.
Mutter: — Ja, also setz dich. Fühl dich hier ganz wie zu Hause, Veronica.
Veronica: — Danke.
Kirsten: — Willst du 'was trinken? Cola? Oder Tee?
Veronica: — Ja, Tee bitte.
Kirsten: — Du auch Mutti?
Mutter: — Ja, bitte. Aber das kann ich doch machen.
....
Vater: — So, Veronica. Bist du zum ersten Mal in Deutschland?
Veronica: — Nein, ich war schon einmal hier.
Vater: — In Hamburg?
Veronica: — Nein, in Süddeutschland. In der Nähe von Freiburg.
Vater: — Ach so. Du sprichst aber sehr gut Deutsch!
Thomas: — Wo wohnst du in England?
Veronica: — In Plymouth.
Thomas: — Ist das ein Dorf?

Kirsten:	—	Ach nee! Plymouth ist doch eine große Stadt.
Vater:	—	Aber nicht so groß wie Hamburg, oder?
Veronica:	—	Nein, nicht so groß wie Hamburg.
Mutter:	—	Na, Veronica. Was möchtest du jetzt machen?
Veronica:	—	Ich möchte mich waschen.
Mutter:	—	Ja, natürlich. Kirsten, zeig Veronica, wo das Badezimmer ist.
Kirsten:	—	Ja, OK. Komm, ich zeige dir auch schnell dein Zimmer.
Veronica:	—	Ja, gut. Dann nehme ich meinen Koffer mit.
Kirsten:	—	So, hier ist dein Zimmer. Gefällt's dir?
Veronica:	—	Ja, das ist prima.
Kirsten:	—	Da ist eine Lampe. Und hier ist ein Kleiderschrank für deine Sachen. Und das Badezimmer ist nebenan.
Veronica:	—	Gut, danke. Ich komme gleich nach unten.
Mutter:	—	So. Veronica. Hier ist dein Tee.
Veronica:	—	Oh, schön. Vielen Dank. Ich habe auch etwas für Sie. Nur ein kleines Geschenk aus England.
Mutter:	—	Oh, das ist aber lieb von dir! Danke schön.

R, W

nem 1

231
(1A 109)

Wie sagt man das auf Deutsch?

The phrases pupils are required to identify are not all identical to those in the taped conversation *Bei Kirsten zu Hause*. They are, however, chosen for their usefulness as productive language for pupils to remember.

L, S, R

Die Woche

Teach the days of the week, *heute* and *morgen*. Practise by saying *Heute ist Montag. Morgen ist ...?* and so on. Refer pupils to *Tip des Tages* for written forms or write on the board. It is also important that pupils recognise the abbreviations on the diary page in the next activity.

L, S, R

37
(1A 37)

Pläne für die Woche

A taped dialogue and related diary page.

Tell pupils to look at the diary page as they listen to the conversation. Ask pupils to recount what they have understood of the conversation. The diary page should help. End by drawing attention to the phrases *Gute Nacht* and *Schlaf gut*.

Pläne für die Woche

Kirsten:	—	Also, morgen ist Schule, nicht? Mittwoch auch. Am Mittwoch spiele ich immer Volleyball. Spielst du auch Volleyball?
Veronica:	—	Ja, aber nicht gut.
Kirsten:	—	Dann kommst du mit!
Veronica:	—	Gut.
Kirsten:	—	Am Donnerstag fahren wir nach Lübeck.
Veronica:	—	Wo ist das?
Thomas:	—	Lübeck, das ist eine Stadt im Norden, eine sehr alte Stadt.
Kirsten:	—	Freitag und Samstag ist dann wieder Schule.
Veronica:	—	Samstag auch?
Kirsten:	—	In Deutschland schon, aber nur am Morgen. Und dann fahren wir mit der Familie zum Tierpark, OK?
Veronica:	—	Ja, gut.*(yawns)*
Mutter:	—	Guck mal, Veronica ist schon müde.
Kirsten:	—	Ja. Gehen wir ins Bett? Morgen ist Schule.
Veronica:	—	Ja, gern. Wann stehen wir auf?
Kirsten:	—	Um sieben.
Veronica:	—	Sieben!
Mutter:	—	Ganz schön früh, nicht?
Veronica:	—	Oh, dann gehe ich jetzt ins Bett. Gute Nacht.
Alle:	—	Gute Nacht.
Mutter:	—	Schlaf gut.

R, W

nem 2

231
(1A 109)

Veronicas Tagebuch

Reading comprehension based on the materials in Area 1.

3 Area 2

- **Telling the time (hours, half and quarter hours)**
- **Use of *sie* plural**

38
(1A 38)

Hamburg wacht auf

This series of photos sets the scene for the topic 'Telling the time'.

11

Die Uhrzeit

Make an OHP transparency of Worksheet 11. Cut out the hands of the clock and fix them to the clock with a round headed staple through the holes. This can be used throughout the course for presentation and revision of the times. 24-hour times can also be written in the digital box below the clock face.

If preferred, make a copy of the Worksheet (OHP) and stick it on card for use in the same way. It will last longer if it is laminated.

L, S

Wie spät ist es?

Teach the time - hours only, using a clockface and eliciting answers to the question *Wie spät ist es?*. Now tell pupils to look at the six drawings of clock faces in the book, lettered **A-F**. Read out the following times and tell pupils to write down the letters **A-F** in the order in which they hear them.

  1 Es ist zehn Uhr
  2 Es ist fünf Uhr
  3 Es ist zwölf Uhr
  4 Es ist drei Uhr
  5 Es ist zwei Uhr
  6 Es ist acht Uhr

Solution: **1** D **2** B **3** F **4** C **5** A **6** E

Now teach the half hours.
Repeat the procedure for photos **G-L**, marking the order.

  7 Es ist halb zwei
  8 Es ist halb sieben
  9 Es ist halb fünf
  10 Es ist halb eins
  11 Es ist halb acht
  12 Es ist halb elf

Solution: **7** H **8** J **9** G **10** L **11** K **12** I

L

Wieviel Uhr ist es?

Play the dialogues and ask pupils to write down what time is mentioned in each case.

Höre gut zu, und schreibe die Zeiten in dein Heft.

Wieviel Uhr ist es?

1 — Entschuldigen Sie, bitte. Wieviel Uhr ist es?
  — Es ist ... halb sechs.
  — Vielen Dank.
  — Bitte.

2 — He, Birgit, wieviel Uhr ist es?
  — Es ist ... neun Uhr.
  — Neun Uhr schon?

3 — Entschuldigen Sie, bitte.
  — Ja?
  — Wie spät ist es, bitte?
  — Drei Uhr, genau.
  — Danke schön.
  — Bitte.

4 — Wann kommt Martin morgen an?
  — Um halb zwölf. Kommst du mit?
  — Halb zwölf? Ja gut, dann komm' ich.

5 — Wieviel Uhr ist es?
  — Ich weiß nicht genau. So gegen halb eins, glaub' ich.

6 — Wie spät ist es, Katrin?
  — Halb vier. Warum?
  — Ich bin hungrig.

7 — Wann ist Musikbox, Ralf?
  — Um halb acht, oder?
  — Ach ja, natürlich.

8 — Komm, Werner. Es ist sieben Uhr.
  — Jaa, Mutti. *(With a groan)*
  — Also komm schon! Du mußt in die Schule.

L, S, W

Wecker!

Teach the quarter hours using the clockface or a drawing of one. Dictate some times and ask pupils to write them down. A good way of getting pupils to practise these is to play *Wecker*. Divide the class into groups, each one sitting in a circle. 'Set' the alarm clocks by writing a time (say 8.30) on the board. Establish an imaginary starting time, e.g. 10.00 p.m. Nominate one pupil in each group to start by saying *,Es ist zehn Uhr'*. Members then take it in turns to go up quarter of an hour at a time until they reach the time 'set', at which point the alarm goes off. This can be made more or less competitive as the teacher likes. The cycle ends with the last pupil miming waking up, stretching and yawning.

An alternative is for pupils to write one time (on a quarter hour) in their rough books between 6 am and 8.30 am. The teacher calls times on the quarter hours and pupils answer by saying: *,Tringg! Wecker klingelt!'* when their time is reached. The teacher looks out for the last person (the sleepy head) to give the command *,Aufstehen! Du kommst zu spät in die Schule.'* Pupils should then set the alarm as near as possible to the real time it goes off for them every morning.

Uhren

A series of clock faces showing various times for speaking or writing practice - or both. Invent questions relevant to the times and cue answers:

e.g. **1** — Du wachst auf, John. Wieviel Uhr ist es?
— Acht Uhr. *(Write on the board:)* Ich wache um __ __ auf.
2 — Die Schule ist aus.
3 — Die erste Stunde ist zu Ende.
4 — Du gehst ins Bett. usw.

L, S, R

Ein typischer Schultag

Introduce the five phrases on the left: *ich stehe auf; ich gehe aus dem Haus; der Unterricht beginnt; die Pause; die Schule ist aus.* Get pupils to deduce what they mean from the pictures.

Then go through the five again, giving the times at which they happen, as shown on the right hand side of the page. The teacher should use his/her own school day as an example. Invite pupils to identify the times you mention. Draw pupils' attention to the use of um and write up times for 5/l0/20/25 to/past on the board, if they are needed.

Before being asked to use this language productively, pupils should now do the listening task that follows.

L, R

Was machen Veronica und Kirsten heute?

Tell pupils that they are going to hear Kirsten telling Veronica about her school day. Ask them to note down the times at which:

she gets up	(7.00)
she leaves home	(7.45)
lessons start	(8.00)
they have break	(10.15)
school ends	(12.30)

Was machen Veronica und Kirsten heute?

Kirsten: — Guten Morgen, Veronica!
Veronica: — Guten Morgen. *(yawning)*
Kirsten: — Hast du gut geschlafen?
Veronica: — Ja, danke. Stehst du immer um sieben auf?
Kirsten: — Ja, immer.
Veronica: — Und wann gehst du aus dem Haus?
Kirsten: — Um Viertel vor acht.
Veronica: — Fährst du mit dem Bus?
Kirsten: — Nein, ich gehe zu Fuß.

Veronica: — Wann beginnt denn die Schule?
Kirsten: — Der Unterricht beginnt um acht Uhr.
Veronica: — Und die Pause? Du hast doch eine Pause, oder?
Kirsten: — Ja, um Viertel nach zehn.
Veronica: — Und wann ist die Schule aus?
Kirsten: — Um halb eins.
Veronica: — Halb eins! Das ist nicht schlecht! In England haben wir bis halb vier Schule.

L, S, R, W

Und du?

Get pupils in pairs to ask each other these five questions. The structure for the answers is as in *Ein typischer Schultag.* When they have practised this, mix up the pairs and ask them to ask their new partners the questions in a different order. Aim to get them doing this without referring to their books. To practise the language thoroughly you could write up the phrases and gradually remove some, but not all, of the words.

Finally, it would be useful consolidation to get pupils to write out these questions together with their own answers to them.

3 Area 3

- **Ordinal numbers l-8**
- **Describing the school day**

L, S

In der Schule

The recorded conversations include the excerpts that occur in the reading passages *Schulbeginn, Die zweite Stunde* and *Die Pause.*

Tell pupils to listen to the conversations. Stop the tape after each one and see if they can say what it was about.

In der Schule
Kirsten: — So. Da ist unsere Schule.
Anja: — He, Kirsten!
Kirsten: — Hallo, Anja! Hier, das ist Veronica Baker aus England. Veronica, das ist die Anja aus meiner Klasse.
Anja: — Good morning.
Veronica: — Hallo. Du kannst ruhig Deutsch mit mir sprechen.
Anja: — Du sprichst aber gut Deutsch!
Veronica: — Meine Mutter kommt aus Deutschland, und wir sprechen auch manchmal Deutsch zu Hause.

Anja: — Ach so. Und heute kommst du mit Kirsten in die Klasse?
Veronica: — Ja.
Anja: — Prima.
Kirsten: — So, komm Veronica. Unser Klassenraum ist hier oben.

Questions for aural comprehension:

1 Wie heißt Kirstens deutsche Freundin?
2 Wer spricht gut Deutsch?
3 Ist Veronicas Mutter Engländerin?
4 Spricht Veronica immer Englisch zu Hause?

(Class hubub. The bell rings.)

Veronica: — Was hast du in der ersten Stunde, Kirsten?
Kirsten: — Wir haben Biologie.
Veronica: — Und dann? In der zweiten?
Kirsten: — Dann haben wir Mathe und dann die Pause. Ah, da kommt Herr Bromma schon.
Herr Bromma: — Guten Morgen.
Klasse: — Guten Morgen.
Herr Bromma: — Ja, Kirsten?
Kirsten: — Herr Bromma, wir haben einen Gast. Dies ist Veronica Baker aus England — sie spricht sehr gut Deutsch.
Herr Bromma: — Herzlich willkommen in Deutschland, Veronica.
Veronica: — Danke.
Herr Bromma: — So.

Questions for aural comprehension:
1 Was hat Kirsten in der zweiten Stunde?
2 Wie heißt der Biologielehrer?

R

41
(1A 41)

Schulbeginn - Die zweite Stunde beginnt - Die Pause

This text complements the recorded conversations in *In der Schule*. With the help of the visuals, pupils should be able to understand most of this.

Ask the pupils to read the text. Consolidate comprehension by asking the pupils to explain in English what they have understood. This could be done with the books shut, so that pupils are not induced to follow the text slavishly and translate, but rather produce amongst themselves a gist account of the more important information. Then read out the text for further consolidation. If there are signs that pupils have now understood more, they should be given the chance to report.

Draw pupils' attention to the differences between German and British schools:

— how do pupils address their teachers?
— do the pupils move from room to room?

(S), R, W

nem 3

231
(1A 109)

Wie sagt man das auf Deutsch?

This activity focuses the pupils' attention on the new language items and the spellings. It will also serve as an aid to more detailed comprehension.

Practise pronunciation when pupils read out their answers.

L, S, R, W

12

Welches Fach ist das?

Make an OHP transparency from Worksheet 12 illustrating school subjects, beginning with those already encountered, i.e. *Biologie* and *Mathematik*. As with Flashcards, present them in groups of three or four and ask pupils to repeat individually and chorally. If an OHP is not available, the symbols can be drawn on the board. Individual worksheets can also be made for use in a number of ways.

Pupils could stick the sheet in their exercise books and label it with the full German names for the subjects. Alternatively, cut the sheet up into individual cards to play various games in groups or in pairs, e.g.:

School subject bingo: pupils select five subjects and place the card on the desk. The teacher calls out the various subjects until a pupil has all five subjects. A pupil could then take over.

Pair-work: the set of cards is placed between two pupils. Pupils take it in turns to show a card and ask: *,Was lernst du in der Schule?'* If the partner answers correctly, (s)he keeps the card. The partner with the most cards at the end wins.

Guessing game: pupil A chooses a card but doesn't show it. Pupil B must ask *,Lernst du Mathematik?'* and try to guess using the least number of questions.

Kirstens Stundenplan

42
(1A 42)

Ask pupils to read the timetable and then comment on it in English. This should elicit observations such as:

— the different layout from a British timetable
— length of lessons
— number and length of breaks
— varying number of lessons per day
— similarity in names of some subjects.

L, S, R, W

42
(1A 42)

Ordinal numbers/Kirstens Stundenplan

Draw a blank copy of Kirsten's timetable on the Board/OHP (days and times only). Point to a particular day and lesson and ask pupils to help you fill in the subjects. (Keep your own book closed in order to make this activity more communicative).

T: *Was hat die 7b am Montag in der ersten Stunde?*
P: (subject).

Continue until the timetable is complete.

Without looking at the board, ask the class:

T: *Hat die 7b (subject) am Montag?*
P: *Ja/Nein.*

Help initially with questions like ,... *in der ersten Stunde?'* until pupils can confidently give these answers themselves. Write the ordinal numbers I-8 on the board/OHP for pupils to copy down and use in the next activity.

L, S

Und euer Stundenplan?

Ask pupils about their own timetable.

T: *Hast du montags/am Montag Biologie?*
P: *Ja/Nein.*
T: *Wann?*
P: *In der (ersten usw.) Stunde.*

Other subjects that pupils may wish to know the German for are:

Home economics -
Domestic science - } *Hauswirtschaft*
Child care - *Kinderpflege*
Economics - *Wirtschaftslehre*
Latin - *Latein*
R.E. - *Religion*
Technical drawing - *Technisches Zeichnen*
Needlework - *Handarbeiten*
Woodwork -
Metalwork - } *Werken*
Craft/design/technology -

---

nem 4

231
(1A 109)

R, W

Schulfächer

In addition to being a game, this should help draw pupils' attention to the spelling of the subjects.

Solution: The anagrams are, from left to right:

Physik - Englisch - Geschichte - Erdkunde - Französisch - Mathematik - Deutsch - Biologie

---

R, W

13

Kreuzworträtsel /Stundenplan-Lotto

Solution:

L, (R), W

Stundenplan-Lotto

An additional way of getting pupils used to the names of school subjects. Tell pupils to fill in the timetable along the lines of Kirsten's with the subjects in any order they like.

Now play bingo by calling subject names instead of numbers. The first pupils to cross off a full day's lessons are the winners. If pupils cross out lightly in pencil, this can be rubbed out and played again without having to write out the timetable several times.

L, S, R, W

14

Die Klasse 7c

Cut the worksheets into two and give one timetable A, and one timetable B to each pair. Tell them that they each have part of Class 7c's timetable. They must work in pairs and question each other until they have both completed the full timetable on their sheets.

*Partner(in) A: Was hast du montags in der
ersten Stunde?*
*Partner(in) B: Englisch. Was hast du dienstags
in der ersten Stunde?*

---

3 Area 4

● Expressing likes and dislikes

$\overline{20}$.

43
(1A 43)

L, S, R, W

Sechs Schüler und Schülerinnen

Teach the words *Fach* and *Lieblingsfach* and
the expression *gefällt ... gar nicht*.

*T: Biologie ist ein Fach. Mathe ist auch ein
Fach, und Englisch und Deutsch usw. Wie
heißt 'Fach' auf Englisch?*

*Deutsch ist sehr gut. Deutsch ist mein
Lieblingsfach. Wie heißt das auf Englisch,
Lieblingsfach? ... Französisch ist nicht mein
Lieblingsfach ... Französisch gefällt mir gar
nicht. Wie heißt das ... ?*

*Und dir (to pupil). Gefällt dir Französisch?
Nein? Also, wie gefällt dir Französisch?
(Whisper gar nicht). usw.*

Write the words on the board/OHP, with
appropriate symbols, if necessary. Then tell
pupils to copy the table on p. 43 into their
exercise books and to listen to the six German
pupils discussing their favourite and least
favourite subjects. The word order may need
to be explained.

*T: Seht euch die Tabelle an. 'Lieblingsfach',
das ist ein Fach. 'Lieblingsfächer', das sind
zwei oder drei oder vier Fächer. Na, wie
heißt 'oder' auf Englisch?*
P: Or.
*T: Klar. Hört gut zu. (Complete the first
example with the class.)*

Sechs Schüler und Schülerinnen
1 — Wie heißt du?
  — Susanne Koch.
  — Wie alt bist du?
  — Dreizehn.

3

— Was ist dein Lieblingsfach, Susanne?
— Englisch.
— Und welches Fach gefällt dir gar nicht?
— Geschichte.
— Hast du heute Geschichte?
— Ja, leider.

2 — Wie heißt du?
  — Ich heiße Klaus Genscher.
  — Bist du auch dreizehn?
  — Ja.
  — Klaus, was ist dein Lieblingsfach?
  — Physik.
  — Und welches Fach gefällt dir gar nicht?
  — Kunst.
  — Hast du heute Kunst?
  — Nein. Kunst haben wir nur montags -
    Gott sei Dank!

3

3 — Wie heißt du?
  — Ich heiße Sabine Bauer, und ich bin
    fünfzehn.
  — Was ist dein Lieblingsfach?
  — Sport ... oder Deutsch.
  — Und welches Fach hast du nicht so gern?
  — Naja. Das ist kein Problem. Mathe.
  — Mathe gefällt dir gar nicht?
  — Nein, gar nicht.

4

4 — Wie heißt du?
  — Markus.
  — Und wie alt bist du?
  — Zwölf.
  — Was ist dein Lieblingsfach in der Schule?
  — Tja, ich weiß nicht. Ich mag gern
    Erdkunde. Geschichte ist auch
    interessant.

3

5 — Mein Name ist Katrin Vollmann. Ich bin
    vierzehn. Mein Lieblingsfach ist Biologie.
  — Welches Fach gefällt dir gar nicht?
  — Ooch ... Hauswirtschaft mag ich nicht so
    gern, aber ... es geht.

3

6 — Wie heißt du?
  — Volker Sternberg.
  — Und wie alt bist du?
  — Dreizehn.
  — Dein Lieblingsfach?
  — Mathe, oder vielleicht Musik.
  — Und welches Fach gefällt dir gar nicht?
  — Chemie.
  — Hast du heute Chemie?
  — Ja, nächste Stunde!

4

L, S, R, W

43
(1A 43)

Was ist dein Lieblingsfach?

The short dialogue printed in the Pupil's Book
is part of the first interview from the previous
listening activity. Read through it with the
pupils until they can ask the two questions

themselves, then get them to interview each other. The class results could be recorded in the form of a bar chart on the board/OHP.

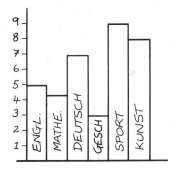

So. Jetzt fragst du deinen Partner. (One pair enacts interview).
Schreibe das Resultat auf.

The teacher could sum up by saying:
Also, was ist beliebt? Mathe? Chemie?
Und was ist nicht so beliebt?

L, S, R

Wie gefällt dir Deutsch?

Using the range of answers shown on the 'meter' in the Pupil's Book, get pupils to ask each other about various school subjects.

T: Jetzt eine Partnerarbeit. Stelle deinem Partner die Frage (point to text): Wie gefällt dir Geschichte? oder Mathe? Hier sind die Antworten (point to text again): Es ist langweilig (yawn); es geht; usw.

L

Eine schlechte Note

Tell the pupils they are going to hear a conversation between Karin and her father. Play the whole conversation once, then ask them to say in general what it was about, i.e. Karin's bad grades. Now play the recording a second time. Depending upon the class, the teacher could either get pupils to work in groups to note down as much as they can about the conversation, or set pupils the individual comprehension questions on it, as listed in the Pupil's Book on page 43.

Eine schlechte Note

Vater:	— So, Karin. Noch eine Fünf in Mathe!
Karin:	— In Musik hab' ich eine Eins gekriegt!
Vater:	— In Musik schon. Aber in Mathe, eine Fünf.
Karin:	— Ich kann nichts dafür - Mathe ist so schwierig.
Vater:	— Ach was! Ich verstehe das nicht. Du hast einen guten Lehrer -
Karin:	— Herr Kohler? Der ist so

langweilig.

Vater:	— Und deine Physiklehrerin, Frau - wie heißt sie? Frau Weiß. Ist die auch langweilig?
Karin:	— Ooch, die geht.
Vater:	— Und was hast du in Physik? 'ne Vier!
Karin:	— Man kann nicht in allen Fächern gut sein.
Vater:	— In allen? In allen, sagst du! Eine Vier in Latein, eine Vier in Geschichte —
Karin:	— Aber Vati —
Vater:	— Eine *Fünf* in Sport! Es ist unverschämt!
Karin:	— Ich habe eine Drei in Deutsch gekriegt.
Vater:	— Oh, wunderbar! Eine Drei in Deutsch. Karin, diese Noten sind nicht gut genug. Du bist vierzehn Jahre alt. Was willst du mit deinem Leben machen?
Karin:	— Ich will Musikerin werden.
Vater:	— Musikerin! OK., du spielst Gitarre. Das ist ein Hobby, schon gut.
Karin:	— Es ist nicht nur ein -
Vater:	— Karin, hör mich an! Das ist durch und durch ein schlechtes Zeugnis. Wenn es so weitergeht, bleibst du nächstes Jahr sitzen! Nun, morgen schreibst du eine Klassenarbeit in Mathe, oder?
Karin:	— Ja, Vati.
Vater:	— Gut. Also jetzt gehst du auf dein Zimmer und lernst dafür. Kapiert?
Karin:	— Ja, Vati.
Vater:	— Und spiel nicht Gitarre!

R, W

nem 5

231
(1A 109)

Fragen und Antworten

Question and answer matching exercise. Some attention to detail is required, e.g. the plural *Lieblingsfächer* - pupils not noticing this may think the answer to this one is *Englisch*.

R, W

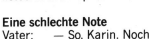

44
(1A 44)

Ein Brief aus England

A letter written by a German pupil about her first experience of an English school, followed by questions. Questions **1-5** are to be answered by *richtig* or *falsch*. Questions **6-10** require English answers for straightforward comprehension. Ease the transition from views expressed on the German system to those expressed on the British system by starting, in English, a brief discussion about how others see us. Chapter I3 *(Internationaler Treff)* will give a fuller picture of the German view of the British, but, for the meantime, the letter gives a first insight.

Solution: **1** R **2** F **3** R **4** F **5** R

England oder Deutschland? R

44
(1A 44)

Pupils have to read the list of statements and decide whether each one was said by an English or a German pupil.

Im Klassenraum R

45
(1A 45)

Labelled picture of a classroom. For information and learning.

Fünf Unterschiede L, S, R, (W)

15

Revise classroom vocabulary already taught, introducing the plurals of all nouns:

ein Heft/2 Hefte
ein Schreiber/kein/keine Schreiber
ein Stuhl/2 Stühle
ein Lineal/2 Lineale

Cut each worksheet into two. Get pupils to work in pairs, giving picture A to one partner and picture B to the other. Explain that there are five differences between pictures A and B. By describing their pictures to each other, pupils have to find out what these differences are.

Solution:

Picture A	Picture B
1 Schreiber (Lehrertisch)	kein Schreiber (Lehrertisch)
2 Lineale	1 Lineal
ein Kassettenrekorder	kein Kassettenrekorder
2 Stühle	1 Stuhl
keine Tafel	1 Tafel

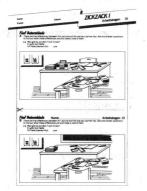

---

3 | Area 5

● **Telling the time (minutes past and to)**
● **Using verbs (all forms)**

Was zeigt deine Uhr? L, S, R, (W)

46
(1A 46)

Revise telling the time, including hours, quarter past, half past, quarter to and numbers to 30. Now ask pupils to look at the five clocks in the Pupil's Book. Alongside are printed the times they show. Ask pupils to try and work out which goes with which. Having checked their answers, ask them to work out how you say 'to' and 'past' in German.

Pupils can then attempt the ten times under the title *Wie spät ist es jetzt?* in *Noch etwas mehr,* some of which are hours, quarters and halves again. These could be written for consolidation.

Wie spät ist es in New York? L, S, / W, R

46
(1A 46)

Using the information about time zones given, pupils have to work out what time it is in various parts of the world when it is a particular time in Germany. Depending upon the class, this can be done as a spoken or a written activity - or both. Teachers may like to introduce this task with some simpler examples, using the 'world clock'.

Solution:

1 12.15	**2** 15.45	**3** 20.05	**4** 8.30
5 9.20	**6** 11.20	**7** 16.57	**8** 00.03
9 6.49	**10** 13.51		

Was machen die Schüler in Deutschland? R, W

47
(1A 47)

Pupils have to decide which of the five things, **A-E,** pupils in Germany would be doing at the times given. Explain the task by doing the first question in front of the class.

Es ist halb zehn morgens in Moskau. Also, wie spät ist es in Deutschland? Ja, es ist halb sieben. Und was machen die Schüler um halb sieben morgens? Richtig, sie stehen auf. Also schreibt ihr:
Nummer eins - A. Und so weiter. Jetzt macht bitte die anderen Aufgaben.

Refer pupils to the visual to avoid confusion over *morgens (vormittags)* and have them copy it into their exercise books to learn by heart.

L

47
(1A 47)

Wann beginnt der Film?

Tell pupils they are going to hear conversations and ask them to try and write down the time that is mentioned in each one.

Wann beginnt der Film?

1 — He, Else, wann beginnt der Film?
— **Zehn nach sieben.**
— Oh, dann müssen wir aber jetzt gehen.

2 — Wann haben wir heute Deutsch?
— Um **Viertel vor neun.** Nach der Pause. Wieso?
— Meine Hausaufgaben sind noch nicht ganz fertig.

3 — Tag, Anja! Heute kommt deine Brieffreundin, nicht?
— Ja, sie kommt um **halb vier** an.
— Hoffentlich ist sie nett!
— Naja, hoffen wir.

4 — Pst! Dieter. Wie spät ist es?
— **Fünf vor elf.**
— Na, Dieter, was ist?
— Nichts, Herr Fuhrmann.

5 — Christine, gehen wir heute zusammen nach Hause?
— Nee, heute ist die Schule für mich um **Viertel nach zwölf** aus.
— Oh, OK. Dann morgen, vielleicht?

6 — Komm doch! Es ist **fünfundzwanzig nach sechs.** Wir kommen zu spät an.
— Ach, was. Wir haben noch Zeit. Ich trinke noch eine Tasse Kaffee.

7 — Brr! Mir ist kalt.
— Mir auch. Wann kommt der Bus?
— Um **zwölf Minuten vor neun.**
— Noch sechs Minuten, also! Mensch! Es ist aber kalt!

8 (Zeitansage)
— (Ton) Beim nächsten Ton ist es achtzehn Uhr, vierundfünfzig Minuten und vierzig Sekunden.
— (Ton) Beim nächsten Ton ist es achtzehn Uhr, vierundfünfzig Minuten und fünfzig Sekunden.

9 — (yawn) Oh, ich bin müde. Ich glaub', ich gehe ins Bett.
— Aber es ist noch früh!
— Ich weiß. Aber morgen steh' ich um **halb sechs** auf.
— Naja. Also, schlaf gut.
— Ja, danke. Gute Nacht.

10 — Was machen wir morgen?
— Ähm ... morgen früh gehen wir in die Schule, nicht?
— Ach ja, natürlich. Auch samstags ist bei euch Schule.
— Aber nur bis **zwanzig nach elf.** Nach dem Mittagessen fahren wir dann zum Tierpark, ja?
— Ja, Klasse.

nem 6

L, S, W

232
(1A 110)

Wie spät ist es jetzt?

This provides further consolidation of times to and past the hour.

nem 7

R, W

232
(1A 110)

Ein geschäftiger Tag

Arno's notebook shows all the things he is doing one day. The pupil's task is to write a short account of his day in sentences. The first sentence is done in the Pupil's Book as a guide. Teachers should draw attention to the note in English below the diary page.

nem 8

R, W

232
(1A 110)

Samstag

A passage of German in which the missing words are all verbs. Pupils will need to pay attention not only to the meaning, but also to the verb endings to make the correct choices.

Solution: **1** kommst   **2** geht   **3** habe   **4** kommen
           5 sind   **6** gehen   **7** haben   **8** gehe
           9 seid   **10** komme

nem 9

R, W

232
(1A 110)

Meine Schwester Birgit wacht um 6.30 auf

A more demanding exercise on the use of separable verbs.

Area 6

● Consolidation

R, W

48
(1A 48)

Unsere Schule

Within the framework given, most pupils should now be able to complete their 'own' letter in German, describing their school day. Pupils should fill the gaps with information appropriate to themselves.

(L), R

Welche Schule?

The aim of the task is for pupils to work out, from what is said, which school each of the ten pupils goes to. A certain amount of detective work and drawing of inferences is needed for some of these.

The timetables could be used for further listening practice, if the teacher invents similar statements for pupils to 'track down'. Alternatively, abler pupils could try devising quotes of their own with which to challenge a partner or a group.

Solution:
Gesamtschule: 3, 6
Gymnasium: 1, 4, 8
Hauptschule: 2, 7, 9
Realschule: 5, 10

Vocabulary

als *than, as, when (in the past)*
anders (als) *different (from)*
anfangen *to begin*
ankommen *to arrive*
der Anorak(s) *anorak*
anschreien *to shout*
die Armee(n) *army*
die Aufgabe(n) *exercise*
aufstehen *to get up*
aufwachen *to wake up*
das Badezimmer(-) *bathroom*
der Beginn *start*
beginnen *to start*
beide *both, two*
das Bett(en) *bed*
　ins * gehen *to go to* *
ein bißchen *a bit*
　Biologie *biology*
der Blick(e) *look, glance*
　auf einen * *at a glance*
　Chemie *chemistry*
die Cola(s) *coca cola*
auf Deutsch *in German*
　Dienstag *Tuesday*
　direkt *direct(ly)*
　doch *however, but, yet*
　Donnerstag *Thursday*
　einmal *once*
　entfernt *distant*
　6 km vom Bahnhof * *6 km from the station*
sich entschuldigen *to apologise*
　Entschuldigen Sie, bitte *excuse me*
　Entschuldigung *sorry*
　Erdkunde *geography*
　essen *to eat*
das Fach(̈-er) *subject*
　fertig *ready; finished*
　Freitag *Friday*
　früh *early*
sich fühlen *to feel*
der Fuß(̈-e) *foot*
　zu * gehen *to walk, go on foot*
　ganz *whole*
　gar *at all*
der Gast(̈-e) *guest, visitor*
das Gedrängel *throng, crowding*
　gefallen + Dat *to like*
　es gefällt mir *I like it*
　gegen + Acc *towards, about (time)*
　genug *enough*
die Gesamtschule(n) *comprehensive school*
　geschäftig *busy*
das Geschenk(e) *present*

Geschichte *history*
die Gitarre(n) *guitar*
　gleich *straightaway, at once*
　grün *green*
die Gruppe(n) *group*
　halb *half*
　es ist * fünf *it's half past four*
　Handarbeiten *needlework*
die Hauptschule(n) *secondary (modern) school*
　Hauswirtschaft *home economics*
　hereinkommen *to come in*
　heute *today*
　hungrig *hungry*
　immer *always*
　interessant *interesting*
der Kaffee(s) *coffee*
　kalt *cold*
　kapieren *to understand (colloquial)*
　kapiert? *understood? Got it?*
　kaputt *broken*
　ich bin *! *I'm worn out*
der Kassettenrekorder(-) *cassette recorder*
　Kinderpflege *child care*
die Klassenarbeit(en) *class test*
der Klassenraum(̈-e) *classroom*
der Kleiderschrank(̈-e) *wardrobe*
　klingeln *to ring*
　kriegen *to get*
　Kunst *art*
　kurz *short(ly)*
　langweilig *boring*
der Lärm *noise, row*
　Latein *Latin*
das Leben(-) *life*
　lieb *nice*
das Lieblingsfach(̈-er) *favourite subject*
　Mai *May*
das Mal(e) *time*
　zum ersten * *for the first time*
　manchmal *sometimes*
　Maschinenschreiben *typewriting*
　Mathe(matik) *maths*
sich melden *to announce one's presence, put one's hand up*
der Mensch(en) *human being*
　*! *Damn!*
der Mittag *midday*

zu * essen *to have lunch*
das Mittagessen(-) *lunch*
　Mitternacht *midnight*
　Mittwoch *Wednesday*
　morgen *tomorrow*
　morgens *every morning, in the morning*
　müde *tired*
die Musik *music*
der Musiker(-) *musician*
　nächste(r, s) *next, nearest*
die Nacht(̈-e) *night*
　gute * *good night*
　nebenan *nearby*
　nehmen *to take*
　nichts *nothing*
die Note(n) *mark, grade*
　oben *at the top, upstairs*
die Pause(n) *break*
　Physik *physics*
　populär *popular*
der Pullover(-) *pullover*
der Raum(̈-e) *room*
die Realschule(n) *secondary school, high school*
die Reihenfolge(n) *sequence, order*
die Reise(n) *journey*
　Religion *religious education*
die Revolution(en) *revolution*
　ruhig *quiet(ly)*
die Sache(n) *thing*
　Samstag *Saturday*
das Schiff(e) *ship, boat*
　schlecht *bad*
　schrecklich *awful, terrible*
die Schule(n) *school*
　die * ist aus *lessons have finished*
der Schüler(-) *pupil (boy)*
die Schülerin(nen) *pupil (girl)*
das Schulfach(̈-er) *school subject*
der Schulhof(̈-e) *playground*
　schwarz *black*
　schwierig *difficult, hard*
das Schwimmbad(̈-er) *swimming pool*
　so *so, thus*
　Sonnabend *Saturday*
　Sonntag *Sunday*
　sowie *just as*
　Sozialkunde *social studies*
　spät *late*
　Sport *P.E., sport*
der Stuhl(̈-e) *chair*
die Stunde(n) *hour; lesson*
der Stundenplan(̈-e) *school timetable*

die Tafel(n) *board*
das Tagebuch(̈-er) *diary*
die Tasse(n) *cup*
　tausend *a thousand*
　technisches Zeichnen *technical drawing*
der Tee *tea*
der Tierpark(e) *zoo*
　tragen *to carry, wear*
　treffen *to meet*
die Treppe(n) *staircase, stairs*
die Uhr(en) *clock; time*
　Wieviel * ist es? *What's the time?*
die Uhrzeit(en) *time*
　unglaublich *unbelievable; incredible*
die Uniform(en) *uniform*
der Unterricht *teaching, lessons*
　der * beginnt *lessons begin*
　unverschämt *disgraceful*
　verbringen *to spend time*
　vielleicht *perhaps*
das Viertel(-) *quarter*
　es ist * nach zwei *it's a quarter past two*
　Volleyball *volleyball*
　vormittags *every morning, in the morning*
sich waschen *to have a wash*
der Wecker(-) *alarm clock*
　weitergehen *to continue, go on*
　Werken *woodwork, metalwork, craft, design and technology (CDT)*
　wieder *again*
　wieso? *for what reason?*
　willkommen! *welcome*
　wohin? *where to?*
　wollen *to want to, wish to*
die Zeit(en) *time*
　ich habe * *I've got time*
das Zeugnis(se) *report*
　zusammen *together*

CHAPTER 4 Die Mahlzeiten

Area 1

- Talking about breakfast
- Revision of times

51
(1A 51)

R

Kann ich mal was fragen?

This provides a short introduction to the next item. It should be easily understood because many of the German words are similar to the English.

51–52
(1A 51–52)

L, R, W

Interviews mit Teenagern

Play the first two dialogues. Tell pupils to listen carefully in order to understand as much as possible. Compare notes in English and then play it again until the new questions *Was ißt du zum Frühstück?', ,Und was trinkst du?'* and *,Und wo ißt du dein Frühstück?'* are understood. Then refer pupils to the text in their books. Play the dialogues again and then ask pupils to do the matching exercise. They should copy the table into their exercise books and write a series of numbers under each person's name,
e.g. Uschi
3
2
3
4
2

Hört gut zu!

Interviews mit Teenagern

1 — Wie heißt du?
— Ich heiße Uschi.
— Wie alt bist du?
— Vierzehn.
— Wann ißt du dein Frühstück?
— Um sieben.
— Was ißt du zum Frühstück?
— Cornflakes mit Milch.
— Und was trinkst du?
— Kaffee mit Milch.
— Und wo ißt du dein Frühstück?
— In der Küche.

2 — Wie heißt du?
— Ich heiße Bernd.
— Wie alt bist du?
— Dreizehn.
— Wann ißt du dein Frühstück?
— Um Viertel nach sieben.
— Und was ißt du?
— Brot mit Marmelade.
— Und was trinkst du?
— Ein Glas Milch.
— Wo ißt du dein Frühstück?
— Im Eßzimmer.

3 — Wie heißt du?
— Ich heiße Oliver.
— Wie alt bist du?
— Zwölf.
— Um wieviel Uhr frühstückst du?
— Um halb acht.
— Was ißt du zum Frühstück?
— Ein Brötchen mit Nutella.
— Was trinkst du?
— Eine Tasse Tee.
— Und wo ißt du dein Frühstück?
— Im Bett.

4 — Guten Tag. Wie heißt du?
— Heidi.
— Wie alt bist du?
— Dreizehn.
— Wann frühstückst du?
— Meistens um Viertel nach sieben.
— Was ißt du zum Frühstück?
— Eine halbe Scheibe Brot mit Honig.
— Und was trinkst du?
— Normalerweise eine Tasse Kakao.
— Und wo ißt du dein Frühstück?
— In der Küche oder (im Sommer) auf dem Balkon.

5 — Wie heißt du?
— Michael.
— Wie alt bist du?
— Fünfzehn.
— Um wieviel Uhr ißt du dein Frühstück?
— Um halb sieben.
— Was ißt du zum Frühstück?
— Toast mit Butter darauf und ein Ei.
— Und was trinkst du?
— Orangensaft.
— Wo frühstückst du?
— In der Küche.

6 — Wie heißt du?
— Ich heiße Udo.
— Wie alt bist du?
— Sechzehn.
— Um wieviel Uhr frühstückst du?
— Normalerweise um Viertel vor acht.
— Was ißt du zum Frühstück?
— Schwarzbrot, Käse und Wurst.
— Und was trinkst du?
— Kakao oder Milch.
— Und wo?
— Unterwegs zur Schule.

7 — Wie heißt du?
— Ich heiße Petra.
— Wie alt bist du?
— Ich bin fünfzehn Jahre alt.
— Wann frühstückst du?
— Um halb acht.
— Was ißt du zum Frühstück?
— Gar nichts.
— Was trinkst du?
— Eine Tasse Tee mit Milch.
— Wo trinkst du den Tee?
— Im Bett.

Note: The word list gives *Balkone* as the plural of *Balkon*. *Balkons* is also possible.

Solution:

A	B	C	D	E	F
Uschi	3	2	3	4	2
Bernd	2	3	4	3	1
Oliver	1	4	1	5	5
Heidi	2	3	7	2	2/3
Michael	4	1	2	1	2
Udo	5	5	6	2/3	4
Petra	4	4	5	6	5

L, S

16-26

Cue similar dialogues with the flashcards to practise food and drink vocabulary

Was ißt du zum Frühstück?

See also | 16

L, S, R

52
(1A 52)

Eine Umfrage in einer Schule in Deutschland

Elicit that the two pie-charts are the result of a survey of the breakfast habits of a German class. It might be interesting to point out that pupils in class 8 would be about 14 years old. Flashcards for new vocabulary (*Quark, Wurst, Käse, Margarine*).

16-26

Use the charts as a cue, e.g.

T: Was ißt du zum Frühstück?
P: Ich esse Brot mit Butter und Honig.
P: Ich esse Brötchen mit Margarine und Käse.
P: Ich esse Brot mit Butter und ein gekochtes Ei.

L, S, R

Was ißt man zum Frühstück?

16

This Worksheet can be used in a variety of ways: as reinforcement or a possible homework activity, expecially for the less able; as an OHP master providing an alternative way of presenting and practising breakfast items; or cut up into cards to play various word games.

L, S, R, W

52
(1A 52)

Statistik

1 Revision of numbers. Practise orally with class, if necessary. Written consolidation e.g. *Sechs Schüler essen ein gekochtes Ei.*

Solution: **a** 6 **b** 13 **c** 1 **d** 1 **e** 4

2 Consolidation of food vocabulary.

Solution:
a) Marmelade
b) ein gekochtes Ei
c) Margarine
d) Butter/Brötchen
e) Honig/Käse/Wurst/Quark

3 *Lückentext*. Consolidation of numbers, verb and drink vocabulary.

Solution:
a 7 Schüler trinken Kakao
b 6 Schüler trinken Milch
c 7 Schüler trinken Saft
d 3 Schüler trinken Kaffee
e 3 Schüler trinken Tee

L, S, R, W

nem
1-5
233
(1A 111)

Mein Frühstück

(Revision of main teaching points)

Activities 1-5. Practise a few examples orally with the class, if necessary. Further practice orally in pairs. Finally ask pupils to answer in written form.

L, S, R, W

17

Zum Frühstück

This provides further practice of breakfast vocabulary and of some question forms as a preparation for Area 2.

Divide the class into pairs, cut the worksheet up and give one half to each partner. Practise the structures first until the procedure is absolutely clear. Selected pupils could report back to the whole class, if desired.

Solution:

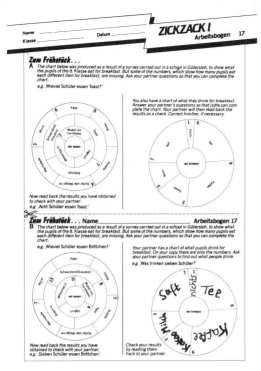

Was ist Großmutters Problem?
— Oma, dies ist mein Freund.
— Was? Was sagst du?
— Mein Freund.
— Ach ja, Freund. Guten Tag. Wie heißt du?
— David.
— Wie?? Wie heißt du?
— David.
— Gut, David. Wie alt bist du?
— Fünfzehn.
— Wie alt?
— Fünfzehn.
— Wo wohnst du?
— In Birmingham in England.
— Wo? In Bingen?
— Nein, Birmingham.
— Wo ist das?
— In England.
— Du bist kein Deutscher?
— Nein, Engländer.
— Hast du Geschwister?
— Ja, eine Schwester.
— Keine Geschwister?
— Nein, ja , nein, doch, eine Schwester.
— Oma, wir gehen jetzt.
— Auf Wiedersehen.
— Auf Wiedersehen.
— Auf Wiedersehen.

Was ist Annas Problem?
— Wie heißt du?
— Ich weiß nicht.
— Heißt du vielleicht Gaby?
— Nein, ich weiß nicht.
— Wo wohnst du?
— Keine Ahnung.
— Hier in Gauting?
— Keine Ahnung.
— Wie alt bist du?
— Ich weiß wirklich nicht.
— Hast du Geschwister?
— Nein ... Ja - ach, ich weiß nicht.
— Wie ist deine Telefonnummer?
— Keine Ahnung.
— Wie ist deine Adresse? Die Straße? Die Nummer?
— Ach, ich habe alles vergessen! Laß mich in Ruhe!

R

Frühstücksposter

As a follow-up activity to this area, provide pupils with German magazines and ask them to look for food pictures and adverts. A selection of these would make an attractive collage for classroom display, or for a project on German food.

4 Area 2

● Asking questions

L, R

54
(1A 54)

Was ist Großmutters Problem?

Two texts to introduce the topic 'Asking questions'. Tell pupils to listen and find out what problems the two people have. No detailed explanation is intended. The visuals in the book provide additional clues.

" T: *Hört gut zu. Was ist Großmutters Problem? Antwortet auf Englisch.*

L, S, R, W

55
(1A 55)

Eine Umfrage in der Klasse

Use the texts and visuals to prepare pupils to conduct their own survey of breakfast habits. Pupils could take it in turn to come to the front of the class. The information can be collated on the board, and the class can make its own pie charts similar to those in the Pupil's Book. If done as posters, these would make an attractive wall display.

55
(1A 55)

Spaghettifragen

This activity focuses pupils' attention on question words. Practise orally at first, if required, then consolidate in writing.

54
(1A 54)

Wie heißt die Frage?

The recordings are in a different sequence from that in the book. Play the recordings and ask pupils to put the visuals in the same order. Then practise framing the questions with the whole class and then in pairs. Consolidate in writing, if required. To reduce the amount of material pupils have to search for at once, numbers **1-8** are answered by a-h and numbers **9-16** are answered by j-p. With some classes it is advisable to pause after each recording.

Wie heißt die Frage?

1 — Was trinkst du zum Frühstück?
— Kaffee.

2 — Bist du Schotte?
— Nein, Engländer.

3 — Wer ist das?
— Das ist mein Bruder, Erich.

4 — Wo ißt du dein Frühstück?
— In der Küche.

5 — Wo wohnst du?
— In Mainz.

6 — Hast du Geschwister?
— Ja, eine Schwester und einen Bruder.

7 — Wie alt bist du?
— Ich bin vierzehn Jahre alt.

8 — Wie ist deine Telefonnummer?
— 22 88 75.

9 — Wie heißt du?
— Karl.

10 — Was ißt du in der Pause?
— Kartoffelchips.

11 — Hast du ein Haustier?
— Ja, eine Katze.

12 — Um wieviel Uhr ißt du das Frühstück?
— Um sieben.

13 — Wieviel Uhr ist es?
— Es ist halb acht.

14 — Wohnst du in der Schweiz?
— Nein, in der DDR.

15 — Was ißt du zum Frühstück?
— Müsli mit Milch.

16 — Wie ist dein Haus?
— Unten sind eine Küche und ein Wohnzimmer. Oben sind drei Schlafzimmer.

Solution:

1 d	5 h	9 k	13 n
2 b	6 c	10 i	14 p
3 e	7 a	11 l	15 j
4 f	8 g	12 m	16 o

4 Area 3

- Describing other meals
- Expressing likes and dislikes

Das Mittagessen. Drei Interviews

Tell pupils that they are going to hear a recording of three teenagers talking about what they like eating and drinking for lunch. Write the names of Sonja, Dorit and Dieter on the board. Tell them to listen carefully and write down in English as many items as they can. The drinks should be well known and some pupils will recognise *Nudeln* and *Pommes frites*.

T: *Ihr hört jetzt ein Interview mit drei Teenagern: Sonja, Dorit und Dieter. Was trinken sie gern? Was essen sie gern?*

Schreibt das auf Englisch in eure Hefte. (Give examples, if necessary).

Das Mittagessen. Drei Interviews

Scott Wilson: — Sonja, was ißt du gern zum Mittagessen?
Sonja: — Gulasch mit Nudeln.
Scott Wilson: — Und was trinkst du gern?
Sonja: — Milch oder Limonade.
Scott Wilson: — Und du, Dorit, was ißt du gern zum Mittagessen?
Dorit: — Hähnchen mit Pommes frites.
Scott Wilson: — Und was trinkst du gern?
Dorit: — Cola oder Saft.
Scott Wilson: — Dieter, was ißt du gern zum Mittagessen?
Dieter: — Frikadellen mit Bratkartoffeln.
Scott Wilson: — Und was trinkst du?
Dieter: — Nichts.

Check that the pupils have understood, and write the items on the board in English next to the names.

L, S, R

56
(1A 56)

Das Mittagessen. Drei Interviews

Ask pupils to look at the dialogues in the Pupil's Book and follow the text as the recording is played. Practise pronunciation of *Was ißt du gern zum Mittagessen? Gulasch mit Nudeln, Hähnchen mit Pommes frites, Frikadellen mit Bratkartoffeln, nichts.*

L, S

27-38

Food and drink vocabulary

The flashcards can be used communicatively to introduce new vocabulary in all of the following ways. It is obviously not intended that all these suggestions should be implemented in one lesson.

a) T: *Trinkst du gern Kaffee?* (Show flashcard)
P: *Ja.*
T: *Ißt du gern Käse?*
P: *Nein.*

b) T: *Ißt du Käse zum Frühstück?*
Trinkst du Kaffee zum Frühstück?

c) T: *Ißt du gern Pommes frites zum Mittagessen?*

d) T: *Du willst Kaffee trinken ja? Was brauchst du? Zum Beispiel, Wasser .... Kaffee ... Milch ... Zucker.*

e) Display flashcards of the ingredients of a meal:

T: *Hier sind die Zutaten für Gulasch: Zwiebeln, Salz, Pfeffer, Paprika, Fleisch und Öl.*

Pupils repeat. Then remove one of the ingredients and ask pupils to guess what is missing.

T: *Was fehlt?*
P: *Salz.*

Repeat for the other meals. Gradually remove more ingredients.

f) T: *Wieviel Scheiben Brot ißt du pro Tag? Eine, zwei, drei, vier? Wieviel Kaffee trinkst du pro Tag?*

g) T: *Willst du Kaffee oder Tee?*
P: *Tee.*

In all the above activities, encourage pupils to ask the questions as soon as possible.

L, S/W, (R)

56
(1A 56)

Drei Rezepte

This provides written consolidation of some of the food vocabulary.

T: *Was sind die Zutaten für Hähnchen mit Pommes frites? usw.*

W

nem 6 Mischmasch

233
(1A 111)

Tell pupils that all the meals are mixed up. Ask them to write out the ingredients.

Was sind die Zutaten für ... ?

R, W

nem 7 Buchstabensalat

234
(1A 112)

Wie ist es richtig?

Written consolidation of ingredients vocabulary.

Ask pupils to re-write the ingredients correctly.

Solution: Nudeln; Gulasch; Frikadellen; Bratkartoffeln; Hähnchen; Pommes frites

L, S, W

57
(1A 57)

Was trinkst du gern? Was ißt du gern?

Both activities require pupils to state their own preference. Practise orally with the whole class first, then divide pupils into pairs or groups. Ask pupils to write down what their partners like and to report back to the class about their partners afterwards, e.g. P: *Er/sie trinkt/ißt gern ...*

This can be consolidated in writing afterwards, both relating to pupils themselves and to their partners.

Jetzt Partnerarbeit. Macht Interviews. Fragt ,Was ißt du gern?' ,Was trinkst du gern?' Dann macht eine Liste.

R

57
(1A 57)

Das Abendessen. Interview mit der Klasse 8b

A simple reading passage. Revision of numbers and food vocabulary.

Statistik - das Abendessen

57 (1A 57)

A simple comprehension check on the number of pupils eating and drinking certain items in the above interview. Pupils should copy the food and drink into their books and write the appropriate numbers next to them.

L, S, R, W

Ißt du gern Süßes?

18

Most of the new vocabulary is for receptive use only at this stage. It should be easily understood in its context, however.

Each partner decides how frequently he or she drinks or eats the various items and marks the boxes with an X. Then partner A questions partner B and marks the appropriate box with a P. Partner B then questions Partner A and marks with a P after each response.

T: Ich esse dreimal am Tag Kuchen. Das ist sehr oft. Schaut mal auf die Tabelle (point to *sehr oft, oft usw.* in the list). *Also, jetzt mache ich hier ein Kreuz* (point to *sehr oft* box on chart).

Continue similarly with other items to illustrate *oft, manchmal, selten, nie.* Now question pupils:

T: Wie oft ißt du Kuchen?, usw. Macht Kreuze in die richtigen Spalten. Jetzt Partnerarbeit. Partner A, du fragst: ‚Wie oft ißt du ...?' ‚Wie oft trinkst du ... ?' Und du schreibst ein P (für deinen Partner/deine Partnerin) in die richtige Spalte. (Demonstrate on board). *Wie ist das Resultat?* (Point to book). *Wie gerne eßt ihr Süßes?*

L, S, R, W

Interviews/Kreuzworträtsel

19

Divide the class into pairs. Each pupil should complete the first part of the chart under *ich*. Pupils are now ready to interview each other. Each partner should note down the responses. The first part of this activity is best done as a homework exercise. After the interviews, pupils can compare charts.

Kreuzworträtsel

Pupils can then complete the crossword about food and drink.

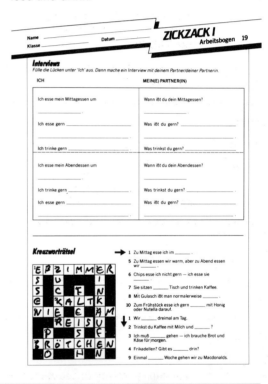

4 Area 4

- Having a meal with a German family
- Choosing a pizza

L, R

Janet Hurst bei Familie Bromma

58 (1A 58)

Tell pupils to listen to the recording and guess what it is about. Then ask them to note down in English what the characters are eating and drinking.

Janet Hurst bei Familie Bromma

Mutter: — Hallo! Kommt bitte! Es ist sechs Uhr. Das Abendessen ist fertig. Zu Tisch, bitte! Janet, setz dich dahin, ja, da. Guten Appetit.
Alle: — Guten Appetit!
Janet: — Kann ich bitte das Brot haben?
Mutter: — Ja, natürlich, hier bitte.
Janet: — Kann ich bitte die Wurst haben?
Vater: — Bitte. Noch etwas zu trinken?
Janet: — Ja, kann ich noch ein Glas Milch haben, bitte?
Mutter: — Noch etwas Brot?
Janet: — Ja, bitte, und etwas Käse.
Vater: — Kann ich die Tomaten haben, bitte?
Mutter: — Noch etwas?
Janet: — Nein, danke, das reicht.
Vater: — Nein, danke. Ich bin wirklich satt.

Then refer pupils to the dialogue and illustration in their book and play the recording again.

Schlagt das Buch auf Seite 58 auf. Hört gut zu und lest den Text.

L, S

16-38

Practise: *Kann ich bitte_____haben? Noch etwas_____?*

Encourage pupils to reply positively and negatively.

L, S, R

58
(1A 58)

Partnerarbeit

Structured pair-work to practise *Kann ich bitte ... haben?*, and *Noch etwas ... ?*

L, S, W

59
(1A 59)

Zu Tisch

A gap-filling activity to consolidate in writing polite language used at the table. Ask pupils to write out the full conversation after oral preparation. A useful homework activity.

L, S, R, W

Playlet

Divide the class into groups of four and ask each group to prepare a playlet based on the above, including references to other food and drink.

59
(1A 59)

(L, S), R, W

In der Pizzeria

Ask pupils to look at the menu and accompanying dialogue, and decide which pizzas Janet and the Brommas order.

Solution: Janet bestellt Pizza 'Margherita' (oder 'Meeresfrüchte') Sabine bestellt Pizza 'Spezial' (oder 'Schinken' oder 'Pilze') Frau Bromma bestellt Pizza 'Spezial' Herr Bromma bestellt Pizza 'Schinken'.

Pupils could then use the menu as a basis for pair-work, asking partners what they like eating and what they would order. Use the prices as number revision.

---

4   Area 5

- **Enquiring about times of meals**
- **Word order**

60-63
(1A 60-63)

L, (S), R, W

Um wieviel Uhr ist die Party?

Tell pupils to look at the visuals in their books and to listen to the recording. The texts in the book contain neither questions nor answers about the times of meals. Pupils should attempt to fill the gaps. This could be practised in pairs afterwards, performed as playlets and consolidated further in writing, if required. The new vocabulary is not intended for active use at this stage, but should be easily understood in context. The missing words are in bold type in the tapescript below.

Hier sind Dialoge: in Hotels, am Telefon, in der Jugendherberge, zu Hause usw. Es gibt einige Lücken im Text: hier, hier und da. Hört gut zu und füllt die Lücken aus.

Um wieviel Uhr ist die Party?

1 — He, du, Heidi. Ich gebe am Sonntag eine Party.
   — Um wieviel **Uhr?**
   — Um **elf.**
   — Das ist zu spät!
   — Nein, das ist eine Frühstücksparty. Im Garten.
   — Ach so! Die Amerikaner sagen ‚Brunch'.

2 — Guten Tag. Kann ich Ihnen helfen?
— Guten Tag. Ich heiße Ziegert. Ich habe ein Zimmer reserviert.
— Ja, Herr Ziegert. Hier bitte. Zimmer Nummer 25.
— Um wieviel Uhr ist das **Abendessen**?
— Das **Abendessen**? Das ist von **sechs** bis **acht**.
— Und das **Frühstück**?
— Von **halb sieben** bis **halb neun**.
— Danke.
— Nichts zu danken.

3 — Wie ist Ihr Name, bitte?
— Rogers.
— Sind Sie Engländer?
— Ja.
— Wollen Sie Vollpension? Also, Frühstück, Mittagessen und Abendessen?
— Ja, **um wieviel Uhr** sind die Mahlzeiten?
— Das **Frühstück** ist von **sechs** bis **neun**. Das Mittagessen ist **um eins**, und das Abendessen ist von **sechs** bis **acht**.
— Danke.

4 — Guten Tag.
— Guten Tag. Mein Name ist Jensen.
— Ach ja, Frau Jensen. Wollen Sie Vollpension?
— Nein, nur das Frühstück und das Abendessen.
— **Um wieviel Uhr** wollen Sie frühstücken?
— Um **Viertel nach acht**. Ist das OK.?
— Ja, kein Problem.
— **Um wieviel Uhr ist das Abendessen?**
— Um **halb sieben**.
— Gut.

5 *(Phone rings)*

— Hallo. Guten Abend. Jugendherberge Bonndorf.
— Guten Abend. Haben Sie Platz am Freitag und am Samstag?
— Ja. Wie heißt du?
— Peter, Peter Schubert.
— Willst du **Abendessen und Frühstück**?
— **Um wieviel Uhr ist das Abendessen?**
— Normalerweise **um sieben**.
— Also, **Frühstück** am Samstag und Sonntag und **Abendessen** am Samstag.
— OK. Tschüs.
— Tschüs.

6 — Ißt du in der Schule in England John?
— Ja, die Schule hat eine Kantine.
— Wie ist das Essen?
— Ach, es geht.
— **Um wieviel Uhr ist das Mittagessen?**
— **Um eins.**

7 — Hallo Dorit.
— Hallo Dieter! Wie geht's?
— Gut danke. Und dir?
— Ja, auch gut.
— Das griechische Restaurant in Eltville? O K.?
— Prima! **Um wieviel Uhr?**
— **Um acht.**
— **Bis um acht, also.** Tschüs!
— Tschüs!

8 — Ist morgen Schule?
— Ja, Jane.
— **Wann** stehst du auf?
— So gegen **Viertel nach sieben.**
— **Wann ist das Frühstück?**
— **Um zwanzig vor acht.**

9 — Guten Tag.
— Guten Tag.
— **Um wieviel Uhr** werden die Tiger gefüttert?
— **Um fünfzehn Uhr.**
— Und die Bären?
— **Um dreizehn Uhr.**

10 — Guten Abend.
— G- Guten Abend. Mein Name ist Timm.
— Ach ja, Timm. Zimmer 13. Hier bitte.
— Danke. **Um wieviel Uhr ist das Abendessen?**
— **Um 12 Uhr.**
— **Mitternacht?**
— Ja.
— **Um wieviel Uhr ist das Frühstück?**
— Wir servieren **kein Frühstück!!**
— Ahh!

60-63
(1A
60-63)

L, S, R, (W)

Um wieviel Uhr ist die Party?

After practising the language of the dialogues pupils could use the pictures as cues and adapt the dialogues by changing some of the information (room numbers, times etc.) Some of these could be performed in front of the class, or written up for homework.

• Consolidation

64 (1A 64)

Briefe aus dem Urlaub   R

In the letters Gaby, Dorit and Peter write about the food they have been having whilst on holiday.

Some of the vocabulary is new, but average and more able pupils should be able to guess much of it, (e.g. *Fisch, Reis, Portionen, Café, Suppe, Hotel, Buffet* etc.). Pupils are asked to write what Gaby, Dorit and Peter say about their holiday food under the headings: breakfast, lunch and evening meal.

65 (1A 65)

Du kannst jetzt eine Postkarte schreiben   R, W

Guided practice on writing a postcard to friends about the food on a summer holiday.

nem 8   L, S, R, W
234
(1A 112)

Kalorienzähler

The calorie counter covers all of the food vocabulary introduced so far. Practise the numbers 1-1000 and briefly teach 200, 300-1200-1300 etc. Pupils should then be able to tackle the following activities both orally and in writing.

1 Work out a menu for a day/week for someone who wants to lose weight (e.g. 1200 - 1400 calories a day).

2 *Was ißt du an einem typischen Tag?*

3 Plan a picnic lunch for four people. How many calories does it have?

64 (1A 64)

Frühstückskarte   R

An authentic menu with questions in English.

65 (1A 65)

Wochenplan   R

A week's menu with questions in English.

nem 9   R, W
235
(1A 113)

Um acht Uhr stehe ich auf

A completion exercise with visuals practising time.

nem 10   R, W
235
(1A 113)

Was machen sie?

A completion exercise practising third person plural present tense forms.

nem 11   R, W
235
(1A 113)

Ich esse gern ...

Pupils write the things they like eating and drinking for breakfast, lunch and evening meal.

Vocabulary

das Abendessen(-) *evening meal*
die Ahnung(en) *notion*
   keine *! no idea!, haven't got a clue!*
   Amerikaner *American person (m)*
   Amerikanerin *American person (f)*
der Apfel(÷) *apple*
der Apfelsaft *apple juice*
die Apfelsine(n) *orange*
der Appetit *appetite*
   guten *! enjoy your meal!*
die Banane(n) *banana*
der Bär(en) *bear*
   belegen *to cover*
   bestellen *to order*
das Bonbon(s) *sweet*
die Bratkartoffeln *fried potatoes*
   brauchen *to need*
das Brot(e) *bread*

das Brötchen(-) *bread roll*
das Büffet(s) *buffet*
die Butter *butter*
die Cornflakes *cornflakes*
   da *there*
der Dialog(e) *dialogue*
die Diät(en) *diet*
   einige *several, some*
der Empfang(÷e) *reception*
die Erbse(n) *pea*
die Erdbeere(n) *strawberry*
   fantastisch *fantastic*
der Fisch(e) *fish*
das Fleisch *meat*
die Frikadelle(n) *rissole*
das Frühstück(e) *breakfast*
   frühstücken *to have breakfast*
der Garten (÷) *garden*
   gebraten *fried*
   gegrillt *grilled*
das Gemüse(-) *vegetables*

das Getränk(e) *drink*
das Glas(÷er) *glass*
   griechisch *Greek*
das Gulasch *goulash*
die Gummibärchen *jelly beans*
das Hackfleisch *minced meat*
das Hähnchen(-) *chicken*
der Hamburger(-) *hamburger*
   heben *to lift*
   helfen + Dat *to help*
der Honig *honey*
der Kakao *hot chocolate*
die Kalorie(n) *calorie*
die Kantine(n) *canteen*
die Karotte(n) *carrot*
die Kartoffel(n) *potato*
die Kartoffelchips *crisps*
der Käse *cheese*
der Keks(e) *biscuit*
die Kirsche(n) *cherry*
der Knoblauch *garlic*
   kosten *to cost*

das Kreuzworträtsel(-) *crossword*
der Kuchen *cake*
   lassen *to let; allow; leave*
   liebe(r) *dear*
die Limonade(n) *lemonade*
der Löffel(-) *spoon*
das Magazin(e) *magazine*
die Mahlzeit(en) *meal*
die Margarine *margarine*
die Marmelade(n) *jam*
die Mayonnaise *mayonnaise, salad cream*
die Meeresfrüchte *seafood*
die Melone(n) *melon*
das Müsli(s) *muesli*
die Nudel(n) *noodle, pasta*
die Nuß(Nüsse) *nut*
das Nutella *chocolate hazelnut spread*
das Obst *fruit*
   oft *often*

das Öl *oil*
die Olive(n) *olive*
der Orangensaft *orange juice*
das Päckchen(-) *packet*
der Paprika *paprika pepper*
der Pfeffer *pepper*
der Pilz(e) *wild mushroom*
die Pizzeria(s) *pizzeria*
der Plan(⁼e) *plan*
die Pommes frites *chips*
die Portion(en) *portion*
die Postkarte(n) *postcard*
    pro *per*
      * Tag *per day*
das Problem(e) *problem*
der Quark *soft curd cheese*
    reichen *to be enough*

    das reicht *that's enough*
der Reis *rice*
das Rezept(e) *recipe*
der Saft(⁼e) *juice*
die Salami(s) *salami*
das Salz *salt*
die Sardelle(n) *anchovy*
    satt *full*
    ich bin * *I've had enough*
    (to eat)
die Schale(n) *bowl*
die Scheibe(n) *slice*
der Schinken(-) *ham*
die Schokolade(n) *chocolate*
der Senf *mustard*
die Soße(n) *sauce*
die Spezialität(en) *speciality*

das Spiegelei(er) *fried egg*
die Statistik *statistics*
das Steak(s) *steak*
das Stück(e) *piece*
der Supermarkt(⁼e)
    supermarket
die Suppe(n) *soup*
    süß *sweet*
die Tafel(n) *bar (of chocolate)*
die Tasse(n) *cup*
die Teenagerin(nen) *teenager*
    (girl)
das Telefon(e) *telephone*
der Tiger(-) *tiger*
der Tisch(e) *table*
    zu * *come to the table*
der Toast(s) *toast*

die Tomate(n) *tomato*
das Tomatenketchup *tomato*
    ketchup
die Torte(n) *tart, cake*
der Urlaub(e) *holiday*
    vergessen *to forget*
die Vollpension *full board*
das Wasser *water*
der Weg(e) *path, way*
    wirklich *really*
der Wunsch(⁼e) *wish*
    auf * *on request*
die Wurst(⁼e) *sausage*
der Zucker *sugar*
die Zutaten *ingredients*
die Zwiebel(n) *onion*

Area 1

- **Talking about leisure time (sports and hobbies)**

L

Interviews about spare time (Was machen sie nach der Schule?)

Tell pupils that they are going to hear interviews with German teenagers. Ask them to guess what they are talking about. This is a genuine listening comprehension activity and although much of the vocabulary is new, most pupils should be able to guess what the dialogues are about. Once the pupils have recognised one or two key words and have guessed the overall context of spare time activities, play the recordings again and ask pupils to listen for more details. *Basketball, Tennis, Schwimmen, Musik, Pony, Hund, Tee* and *Squash* should not prove too difficult to recognise. Encourage pupils to deduce the meanings of unknown words. Exploit in English, if necessary.

Was machen sie nach der Schule?
— Was machst du nach der Schule, Peter?
— Ich esse zuerst, dann mache ich meine Hausaufgaben. Ich gehe zweimal in der Woche zum Basketball. Manchmal fahre ich mit dem Fahrrad in die Stadt. Und ich treffe mich auch oft mit meinen Freunden.
— Was machst du nach der Schule, Anne?
— Nach dem Mittagessen mache ich meine Schularbeiten, dann spiele ich oft Tennis. Manchmal gehe ich in die Stadt einkaufen. Im Sommer gehe ich oft schwimmen. Abends sehe ich fern oder höre Musik.
— Was machst du nach der Schule, Christoph?
— Nach dem Essen muß ich als erstes meine Schulaufgaben machen. Zweimal in der Woche reite ich auf meinem Pony. Und dann gehe ich auch jeden Tag mit meinem Hund spazieren.
— Was machst du nach der Schule, Sabine?
— Nachmittags mache ich meine Schulaufgaben. Oft kommen meine Freundinnen zu mir, und wir trinken Tee und hören Musik. Manchmal gehe ich schwimmen oder Squash spielen.

L

20

Was machen sie nach der Schule?

Play the recording again. Pupils needing more guidance or those who are reluctant to speak out in class may find this detailed listening activity more rewarding than the previous one. Pupils should put a cross in the appropriate box when they recognise a piece of information.

Solution:

Name _____ **Datum** _____   **ZICKZACK I** Arbeitsbogen 20
Klasse _____

Was machen sie nach der Schule?
Listen carefully to the recording of four young people talking about what they do after school. Put a cross in the correct box if you hear them mention any of the items 1–15.

	Peter	Anne	Christoph	Sabine
1 do homework	X	X	X	
2 drink tea				X
3 eat lunch	X	X	X	
4 go for a ride on a bike	X			
5 go horse riding			X	
6 go into town		X		
7 go shopping		X		
8 go swimming		X		X
9 listen to music		X		X
10 meet friends	X			X
11 play basketball	X			
12 play squash				X
13 play tennis		X		
14 take the dog for a walk			X	
15 watch T.V.		X		

L, S

39-58

Present the flashcards singly in the following way:

T: (Displaying tennis flashcard) *Was machst du nach der Schule?... Ich spiele Tennis.*

Practise the reply with a number of pupils before encouraging them to take over the teacher's role.

T: (To pupil) *Stell die Frage: ‚Was ... ?'*
P1: *Was machst du nach der Schule?* (Point to) P2: *Ich spiele Tennis.*
T: *Gut.*

Continue similarly with the remaining flashcards, making sure **not** to present all of the cards which cue *ich spiele* together, as pupils can easily fall into the trap of assuming **all** leisure activities should be prefaced with *ich spiele.*

L, R

67
(1A 67)

Was machst du nach der Schule?

Before allowing pupils to read the texts, tell them to look only at the visuals on the right hand side of the page while you read the answers to them.

Macht eure Bücher auf Seite 67 auf: Was machst du nach der Schule? Nummer eins: deckt den Text mit der Hand zu, so (demonstrate first to the class, then to a number of individual pupils). *Seht euch die Bilder hier* (pointing) *an. Hört zu. Ich bin Birgit. Scott Wilson fragt: ,Was machst du nach der Schule?' Und ich antworte: ,Ich esse um halb zwei und dann .... oft schwimmen.'*

Once you have completed all four sections in this way, tell pupils to read the texts through.

Lest die vier Texte durch.

L, S, R

67
(1A 67)

Was machst du nach der Schule?

In order to elicit the expressions of time employed in the texts, ask the following questions and write the answers on the board once pupils have responded correctly.

1 *Wann ißt Birgit - um halb eins?*
   (Write on board: *Nein, _____ _____*

   P: Um halb zwei. (Fill in gaps on the board).

2 *Wie oft spielt sie Tennis? Einmal in der Woche?* (On board: *Nein, _____ _____ _____ _____.*)

3 *Und wie oft geht sie zum Basketball?* (On board: *_____ _____ _____ _____.*)

4 *Geht sie manchmal im Sommer schwimmen?* (On board: *Nein, _____*)

N.B: if required, a full list of such questions appears in the next activity, in *Noch etwas mehr.*

---

nem 1

R, W

236
(1A 114)

Was machst du nach der Schule?

A written exercise to consolidate the above activity.

---

nem 2

W

236
(1A 114)

Wie sagt man das auf Deutsch?

A simple translation exercise dealing with expressions of time.

L, S, R, W

67
(1A 67)

Lückentext

Complete this gapped activity orally first, then instruct pupils to write out full sentence answers in their exercise books.

L, R, (W)

68
(1A 68)

Richtig oder falsch?

Tell pupils to listen to the series of statements and decide whether or not the table on page 68 has been correctly completed. Tell them to write numbers **1-6** in their exercise books and write *richtig* or *falsch* against the appropriate numbers.

Richtig oder falsch?

1 — Dreimal in der Woche spiele ich Squash.
2 — Jeden Abend spiele ich Fußball.
3 — Zweimal in der Woche gehe ich schwimmen.
4 — Manchmal gehe ich mit dem Hund spazieren.
5 — Oft höre ich Musik.
6 — Dreimal in der Woche spiele ich Basketball.

Solution: **1** richtig **2** richtig **3** falsch
4 richtig **5** richtig **6** falsch.

L, S, R, W

68
(1A 68)

Wann machst du das?

Before asking pupils to write out complete sentences, cue oral responses by using the question forms they have already encountered. *Wann/wie oft spielst du ... gehst du ... fährst du ?*

---

nem 3

R, W

236
(1A 114)

Tennistermine: Was paßt zu wem?

A matching activity designed to focus pupils' attention on expressions of time.

L, S, R, (W)

68-69
(1A 68-69)

Partnerarbeit

Tell pupils to work in pairs in order to find out what others in the class do after school. Encourage them to question five or six different partners each before consolidating either in writing or by means of another *Umfrage* in which you record statistics on the board. The latter will, of course, provide practice in the use of the third person singular verb forms, with which you will need to prompt pupils.

T: *Was macht er zuerst?*
P: *Zuerst spiel ...*
T: *spielt.*
P: *Zuerst spielt er mit dem Computer, und dann ..*

nem 4
236
(1A 114)

W

Was sagt man?

A written activity providing practice in expressions of time and spare time activities.

nem 5
237
(1A 115)

R

Freizeit - Fitness - Sport

A straightforward reading comprehension based on authentic magazine advertisements for sport and leisure activities. Pupils will, no doubt, request assistance with the translation of the motto in question 7c. 'Enjoy an active life' might be suitable.

nem 6
237
(1A 115)

R, W

Brief an Sabine

Start pupils off by pointing out the statement in the printed letter: *Du wolltest wissen, was ich nach der Schule mache* and writing it on the board. Thereafter more able pupils should be able to adapt the letter to fit their own details.

Less able pupils should answer the questions in English before attempting to write a reply. It may be advisable to write key phrases on the board to start each sentence.

L, S, R, (W)

69
(1A 69)

Tip des Tages

Refer pupils to *Tip des Tages* and tell them to ask each other the question and produce replies. This might be best done in a chain activity (and could be consolidated in writing - possible homework).

Continue in pairs.

Once pupils feel confident, encourage them to work independently of the book.

5 Area 2

● **Expressing likes and dislikes**

L, S

16-38

Revise *gern* in the context of food and drink.

T: *Was ißt du gern zum Mittagessen?*
Ißt du gern Brötchen mit Marmelade?
Ich esse nicht gern Fisch. Und du?
Trinkst du gern Kaffee?

L

Interviews mit Teenagern

Tell pupils that they are going to hear some interviews with German teenagers. Play the first few recordings and ask them what the interviewer is asking. Test comprehension after each item, e.g.: *Nummer eins: Was macht sie gern? Sagt es auf Englisch.*

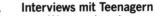

T: *Ihr hört jetzt Interviews mit deutschen Teenagern. Hört gut zu. Was fragt der Reporter? Sagt es auf Englisch.*

Interviews mit Teenagern

1 — Was machst du gern nach der Schule?
  — Nach der Schule ... was ich **gern** mache? Na ja, ich gehe gern schwimmen.

2 — Was machst du gern nach der Schule?
  — Ach, ich spiele sehr gern Tennis. Wir haben eine Tennishalle ganz in der Nähe.

3 — Was machst du gern nach der Schule?
  — Ach, das ist schwer. Ich habe kein festes Hobby. Ich gehe aber gern abends in die Disco.

4 — Was machst du gern nach der Schule?
  — Ich spiele sehr gern Fußball.

5 — Was machst du gern nach der Schule?
  — Ich habe seit einem Jahr einen Computer. Ich spiele gern mit dem Computer in meiner Freizeit.

6 — Was machst du gern nach der Schule?
  — Ich spiele gern Basketball mit meinen Freunden.

7 — Was machst du gern nach der Schule?
  — Ich habe ein neues Fahrrad und fahre gern Rad.

8 — Was machst du gern nach der Schule?
  — Wenn ein guter Film im Kino läuft, gehe ich gern ins Kino.

L, S, R

70-71
(1A 70-71)

Interviews nach der Schule

Tell pupils that you are now going to play the interviews by Scott Wilson, but in a different order from that in their books. Ask them to quote the number of the printed version after hearing a dialogue. The illustrations have been divided into two halves (1-13, 14-26) to reduce the amount of searching that pupils have to do. Ordinal numbers are used incidentally, no exploitation is intended at this stage.

T: *Hier sind Scott Wilsons Interviews.*
   (Play the first interview)
   *Dies ist das erste Interview. Im Buch ist
   es Nummer 3 auf Seite ...
   Könnt ihr das finden? Nummer 3. Hier ist
   das zweite Interview. Welche Nummer hat
   es im Buch?*
P: *Nummer ...*

Interviews nach der Schule

1 — Was machst du gern nach der Schule?
  — Ich spiele gern Tennis.

2 — Was machst du gern nach der Schule?
  — Ich spiele gern Gitarre.

3 — Was machst du gern nach der Schule?
  — Ich lese gern Comics.

4 — Was machst du gern nach der Schule?
  — Ich spiele gern Fußball.

5 — Was machst du gern nach der Schule?
  — Ich höre gern Musik.

6 — Was machst du gern nach der Schule?
  — Ich gehe gern schwimmen.

7 — Was machst du gern nach der Schule?
  — Ich gehe gern mit dem Hund spazieren.

8 — Was machst du gern nach der Schule?
  — Ich gehe gern ins Jugendzentrum.

9 — Was machst du gern nach der Schule?
  — Ich gehe gern in die Disco.

10 — Was machst du gern nach der Schule?
   — Ich spiele gern Basketball.

11 — Was machst du gern nach der Schule?
   — Ich sehe gern fern.

12 — Was machst du gern nach der Schule?
   — Ich reite gern.

13 — Was machst du gern nach der Schule?
   — Ich gehe gern zum Turnen.

14 — Was machst du gern nach der Schule?
   — Ich sortiere gern meine Briefmarken.

15 — Was machst du gern nach der Schule?
   — Ich treffe mich gern mit meinen
     Freunden.

16 — Was machst du gern nach der Schule?
   — Ich gehe gern einkaufen.

17 — Was machst du gern nach der Schule?
   — Ich gehe gern Rollschuh laufen.

18 — Was machst du gern nach der Schule?
   — Ich spiele gern Fußball.

19 — Was machst du gern nach der Schule?
   — Ich fahre gern mit dem Rad.

20 — Was machst du gern nach der Schule?
   — Ich spiele gern mit dem Computer.

21 — Was machst du gern nach der Schule?
   — Ich spiele gern Schach.

22 — Was machst du gern nach der Schule?
   — Ich koche gern.

23 — Was machst du gern nach der Schule?
   — Ich gehe gern spazieren.

24 — Was machst du gern nach der Schule?
   — Ich gehe gern ins Kino.

25 — Was machst du gern nach der Schule?
   — Ich bummle gern in der Stadt.

26 — Was machst du gern nach der Schule?
   — Ich besuche gern meine Großeltern.

Solution:

Interview	Bild	Interview	Bild
1	3	14	23
2	9	15	18
3	11	16	14
4	2	17	24
5	4	18	15
6	12	19	17
7	5	20	16
8	6	21	26
9	13	22	21
10	8	23	25
11	10	24	19
12	1	25	20
13	7	26	22

39-58

L

A class survey of spare time activities

Using the flashcards, ask questions like: *Wer
sieht gern fern? Hebt die Hand.* Count hands,
and tabulate on the board.

L, S, (R)

70-71
(1A
70-71)

Interviews nach der Schule

Ask individual pupils round the class: *‚Was
machst du gern nach der Schule?'* and *‚Was
machst du **nicht** gern?'* Pupils can use
Interviews nach der Schule for their answers.

Form groups of five or six. Tell each member to write down five things they like doing in their spare time. One pupil in each group collects the sheets and reads them out in random order. The others must guess who the person is. Anybody named should reply *ja* or *nein*.

21

L, S

Was machst du gern? Was machst du nicht gern?

Divide pupils into pairs. Ask each partner to indicate by marking with an X five things which (s)he likes doing, and five or six things which (s)he does not like doing. Each partner must then try to discover what the other has written by asking: *,Was machst du gern?'* and *,Was machst du nicht gern?'* They could vary the questions by asking *,Spielst du gern Fußball?'* They should compare sheets afterwards.

Jetzt Partnerarbeit. Jeder Partner bekommt einen Arbeitsbogen. Habt ihr alle einen Bogen? Also gut.

Jetzt, zum Beispiel: Ich spiele gern Fußball. Ich mache also ein Kreuz hier (point). *Ich gehe nicht gern in die Disco, also ich mache ein Kreuz hier. Verstanden? Ihr macht jetzt fünf Kreuze in diese Spalte und fünf oder sechs Kreuze in diese Spalte* (point). *Dann fragst du, Ann: ,Was machst du gern?' und du, Mary, sagst: ,Ich spiele gern Tennis'.*

71
(1A 71)

22

L, R, W

Wer ist dein Computerpartner? Wer ist deine Computerpartnerin?

Ask pupils to look at the pictures of German teenagers and tell them that they are going to be matched to one of them by a computer. They will need the form on Worksheet 22.

L, S, R, W

T: *Schlagt das Buch auf Seite 71 auf. Hier sind zwölf Jungen und Mädchen. Einer oder eine wird euer Computerpartner oder eure Computerpartnerin.*
(Hand out worksheets).
Hier ist ein Fragebogen. Bitte schreibt auf der linken Seite:
Hier: euren Namen,
Hier: macht ein Kreuz für ein Mädchen oder einen Jungen,
Hier: schreibt ihr 5 Hobbys auf, z.B. ,Ich gehe gern schwimmen.'

Once pupils have completed this part of the form, tell them that the computer is going to give them information about the twelve young people.

Hört gut zu.
Der Computer gibt euch jetzt Informationen über die 12 Jungen und Mädchen und ihre Hobbys.
Wer hat eure Hobbys?
Macht Kreuze in die Tabelle.

Demonstrate on the board, if necessary, with a made up example.

Wer ist dein Computerpartner? Wer ist deine Computerpartnerin?
— Guten Tag. Ich bin Compi, der Partnercomputer. Hier sind Informationen über zwölf Partner oder Partnerinnen.

Nummer 1: geht gern schwimmen, faulenzt gern, geht gern in die Disco, spielt gern Fußball, hört gern Musik.

Nummer 2: geht gern einkaufen, spielt gern Basketball, trifft sich gern mit Freunden, geht gern spazieren, spielt gern mit dem Computer.

Nummer 3: spielt gern Gitarre, fährt gern mit dem Rad, besucht gern die Großeltern, geht gern ins Jugendzentrum, sortiert gern Briefmarken.

Nummer 4: geht gern mit dem Hund spazieren, kocht gern, sieht gern fern, hört gern Musik, geht gern schwimmen.

Nummer 5:	liest gern Comics, sieht gern fern, geht gern ins Kino, reitet gern, geht gern spazieren.
Nummer 6:	geht gern in die Disco, hört gern Musik, sieht gern fern, faulenzt gern, bummelt gern in der Stadt.
Nummer 7:	geht gern schwimmen, geht gern spazieren, spielt gern Tennis, spielt gern Basketball, geht gern zum Turnen.
Nummer 8:	spielt gern mit dem Computer, geht gern mit dem Hund spazieren, kocht gern, spielt gern Fußball, geht gern ins Kino.
Nummer 9:	sieht gern fern, trifft sich gern mit Freunden, hört gern Musik, bummelt gern in der Stadt, geht gern Rollschuh laufen.
Nummer 10:	spielt gern Tennis, geht gern schwimmen, hört gern Musik, geht gern mit dem Hund spazieren, geht gern in die Disco.
Nummer 11:	spielt gern Fußball, geht gern ins Jugendzentrum, spielt gern mit dem Computer, hört gern Musik, sieht gern fern.
Nummer 12:	geht gern spazieren, geht gern einkaufen, sieht gern fern, trifft sich gern mit Freunden, hört gern Musik.

Further instructions:

Wieviel Kreuze hat Nummer 1?
Schreibt die Zahl hinter 'Summe'.
(Demonstrate on the board.)
So, jetzt hört wieder gut zu.
Der Computer gibt euch jetzt die Namen.
Schreibt die Namen ganz unten hin.

— Hier ist wieder Compi, euer Partnercomputer.
Hier sind die Namen:

Nummer 1:	Torsten
Nummer 2:	Anne
Nummer 3:	Michael
Nummer 4:	Raphaela
Nummer 5:	Peter
Nummer 6:	Gaby
Nummer 7:	Florian
Nummer 8:	Brigitte
Nummer 9:	Bernd
Nummer 10:	Uschi
Nummer 11:	Christoph
Nummer 12:	Sabine

Pupils can now work out who their partner is. It is possible, of course, that pupils may now have second thoughts concerning their original choice of *Partner/Partnerin*.

R

23

Jugendzentrum Pinneberg

The programme of a youth club detailing the activities on offer during the course of a week. The text is exploited by questions in English.

Solution:
1 On Sundays.
2 Play games, listen to music, dance etc.
3 In the cellar.
4 Two.
5 On Thursdays and Fridays.
6 On Tuesdays.
7 On Mondays.
8 On Tuesdays.
9 Tea bar — moped workshop — table tennis — video group — chess.
10 Every week.
11 Problems — current topics — school.
12 Hamburgers, sausages and chips.
13 Discos, singers etc.
14 On Saturdays.

L

Spielst du ein Instrument?

Ask pupils to listen to the recording and match each dialogue to the visuals in the Pupil's Book.

Schlagt euer Buch auf Seite 72 auf. Hört jetzt gut zu. (Play the first recording). *Welches Bild ist das?* (Once pupils have understood the task, play the remainder of the recording).

Spielst du ein Instrument?

1 — Ich spiele ein bißchen Klavier. Zu Hause aber — nicht in einer Gruppe.

2 — Ich spiele kein Instrument, aber ich singe — einmal in der Woche, in einem Chor.

3 — Ich bin in einer Rockgruppe und spiele die Gitarre. Die Gruppe heißt 'No chance'.

4 — Ich spiele Geige in einem Orchester.

5 — Seit sechs Wochen spiele ich Flöte. Ich spiele aber nicht sehr gut, und mein Bruder schimpft immer. Er sagt: ‚Das ist viel zu laut'.

6 — Ich habe Blockflöte in der Schule gelernt, aber jetzt spiele ich nicht mehr so oft.

7 — Ich spiele Klavier und Klarinette. Ich möchte später Musik auf der Universität studieren.

8 — Ich spiele Mundharmonika in einer Band.

9 — Ich spiele Trompete in einem Blasorchester.

10 — Ich spiele seit zwei Jahren Schlagzeug in einer Gruppe.

Solution: **1**A, **2**J, **3**G, **4**H, **5**I, **6**E, **7**C, **8**D, **9**F, **10**B

---

5 Area 3

- **Talking about music and playing musical instruments**
- **How to say the date**

L, S, R, W

24

Was spielst du?

Introduce the musical instruments by means of OHP.

T: *Wer spielt hier Blockflöte? Hebt die Hand. Du, John, du spielst doch Blockflöte, oder?*
P: *Ja.*
T: *Gut. Jetzt wiederhole: ‚Ich spiele Blockflöte.'*
P: *Ich spiele Blockflöte.*
T: *Spielst du Klavier?*
P: *Nein.*
T: *Spielt deine Schwester Klavier?*
P: *Ja.*
T: *Was spielt … ?* (Name of a popstar).

This worksheet could then be used in a variety of ways: as reinforcement or a possible homework activity, especially for the less able; as an OHP Master providing an alternative way of presenting and practising musical instruments; or cut up into cards to play various word games.

---

nem 7

R, W

238
(1A 116)

Welches Instrument?

A series of incomplete visuals. Pupils have to decide which instrument is being played and then write the complete sentence.

Solution: **1** Klavier **2** Blockflöte **3** Querflöte **4** Geige **5** Mundharmonika **6** Trompete **7** Gitarre **8** Schlagzeug **9** Kein Instrument

Welches Instrument ist das?

Ask pupils to listen to the recording of various instruments and say what they are. This provides an opportunity to practise saying the names of the instruments with the indefinite article.

Welches Instrument ist das? Eine Klarinette, eine Flöte, eine Blockflöte?

Collate the instruments on the board under gender headings:

F	N
eine	ein
Geige	Klavier
Trompete	Schlagzeug
Klarinette	(Chor)
Gitarre	
Blockflöte	
Flöte	
Mundharmonika	

Welches Instrument ist das?

1 Piano
2 Trumpet
3 Drum solo
4 Clarinet
5 Harmonica
6 Rock guitar
7 Classical guitar
8 Recorder
9 Flute
10 Violin
11 Unaccompanied choir

Solution:
1 Klavier
2 Trompete
3 Schlagzeug
4 Klarinette
5 Mundharmonika
6 Rockgitarre
7 Klassische Gitarre
8 Blockflöte
9 Flöte
10 Geige
11 Kein Instrument — das war ein Chor

L, S, R

73 (1A 73) Hörst du gern Musik?

A short text which serves as a model for the following pair-work. Practise the questions with a few pupils first until they are sure of the pattern and the possible answers.

R

73 (1A 73) Statistik

A short text about the popularity of musical instruments. Pupils could conduct a similar survey in their own school.

L, S

73 (1A 73) Partnerarbeit

Ask pupils to make up and practise similar dialogues, possibly as part of a wider class survey.

R

73 (1A 73) Wie oft übst du in der Woche?

A short introductory text to prepare pupils for the following listening activity. This text introduces *üben* and revises expressions of time.

L, R, W

73 (1A 73)

Wie oft üben sie?

Tell pupils to copy the chart into their books. After each interview they should write the correct instrument in the appropriate column.

T: *Tragt die Tabelle in euer Heft ein. Hört jetzt gut zu. Nummer eins. Was spielt Susi?*
P: *Klavier.*
T: *Gut. Wie oft spielt sie Klavier? Jeden Tag, jeden Abend, einmal in der Woche, zweimal in der Woche ...?*
P: *Jeden Abend.*
T: *Gut. Ihr schreibt also Klavier hier unter 'jeden Abend'. (Demonstrate).*

Wie oft üben sie?

1 Scott Wilson: — Hallo, wie heißt du?
  Susi: — Susi.
  Scott Wilson: — Grüß dich. Mein Name ist Scott. Scott Wilson. Welches Instrument spielst du?
  Susi: — Klavier.
  Scott Wilson: — Wie oft übst du in der Woche?
  Susi: — Jeden Abend — eine Stunde nach dem Essen.

2 Scott Wilson: — Und du, Stefan. Welches Instrument spielst du?
  Stefan: — Im Orchester spiele ich Geige.
  Scott Wilson: — Und wie oft übst du?
  Stefan: — Wenigstens dreimal in der Woche.

3 Scott Wilson: — Grüß dich, Birgit.
Birgit: — Hallo.
Scott Wilson: — Welches Instrument spielst du?
Birgit: — Ich spiele Flöte.
Scott Wilson: — Wie oft übst du?
Birgit: — Ach, zweimal in der Woche, vielleicht.

4 Scott Wilson: — Hallo, Detlev.
Detlev: — Hallo.
Scott Wilson: — Welches Instrument spielst du denn?
Detlev: — Schlagzeug.
Scott Wilson: — Und wie oft übst du?
Detlev: — Jeden Nachmittag gleich nach der Schule.

5 Scott Wilson: — Claudia, welches Instrument spielst du?
Claudia: — Trompete.
Scott Wilson: — Und wie oft übst du in der Woche?
Claudia: — Nicht oft. Vielleicht einmal.

6 Scott Wilson: — Und wie heißt du?
Harald: — Harald.
Scott Wilson: — Und du spielst Klarinette, ja?
Harald: — Ja, richtig.
Scott Wilson: — Wie oft übst du?
Harald: — Jeden Nachmittag.

7 Scott Wilson: — Maria, du spielst Gitarre, oder?
Maria: — Ja, ich spiele Gitarre, aber in einer Band, nicht im Orchester.
Scott Wilson: — Wie oft übst du Gitarre?
Maria: — Jeden Abend, normalerweise.

8 Scott Wilson: — Andrea, welches Instrument spielst du?
Andrea: — Ich spiele Mundharmonika.
Scott Wilson: — Gut, und wie oft übst du?
Andrea: — Meistens am Wochenende. Samstags und sonntags.
Scott Wilson: — Zweimal in der Woche also?
Andrea: — Stimmt.

74-75
(1A
74-75)

Orchester und Bands

A variety of posters and advertisements for various musical events. These are initially exploited by questions in English.

R

74-75
(1A
74-75)

Orchester und Bands

Tell pupils to listen to the recordings of people talking about the posters. Focus their attention on the way the dates are said.

Seht euch das Poster für das Pina Konzert an. Hört gut zu! Wann ist das Konzert?

Orchester und Bands

1 — Willst du zum Pina Konzert gehen?
— Ja, wann ist das?
— Am vierten Mai in der Stadthalle in Altona.

2 — Weißt du, Ede Funk und seine Chaoten sind am dreizehnten Februar in Wiesbaden?
— Ist das ein Samstag?
— Nein, ein Freitag. Das Konzert ist in der Rhein-Main Halle.
— Gut, gehen wir hin, ja?

3 — Kennst du die englische Gruppe 'Fair Play'?
— Ist das die Gruppe mit Andy Watson?
— Ja, die ist am zwölften Dezember in der alten Oper in Bremen.
— Toll!

4 — Evi Bamm kommt am vierzehnten November zum Jugendzentrum in Dortmund.
— Gehen wir hin?
— Nein, ich habe keine Lust. 'Hallo Engel', das ist wirklich nichts für mich.

5 — Die Jazz-Sängerin Tania Elvira kommt nach Hamburg!
— Wann denn?
— Am einunddreißigsten März.
— Starke Sache!

6 — He du! Metall Hammer kommt am zwanzigsten Juli nach Paderborn. Kommst du mit?
— Nee, die Gruppe ist zu laut für mich. Die spielen keine Musik — die machen Krach.

7 — Magst du Chansons?
— Ja, wieso denn?
— Die Musiker von der Musikhochschule in Hamburg geben am 22sten Oktober ein Konzert in der Stadthalle in Fürth.
— Um wieviel Uhr?
— Um 21 Uhr.
— Prima.

8 — Gehen wir am sechsundzwanzigsten
  August zum Unterhaus?
  — Wer spielt?
  — Elvin Farrell mit seiner Jazz Maschine.
  — Geil!

9 — Kommst du mit zur Johannes Passion?
  — Wo denn?
  — In der Marienkirche am sechzehnten
  Mai.
  — Ja, gerne.

10 — Wir gehen am vierten August in die
  kleine Musikhalle.
  — Wer sind die Solisten?
  — Marek Jerie spielt Geige und Ivan
  Klansky spielt Klavier.

5 Area 4

● Saying what you like doing best of all

L, S

Ask individual pupils: *,Was machst du gern in
der Schule?',* eliciting the names of subjects.
Follow on with: *,Und was machst du am
liebsten? Was ist dein Lieblingsfach?',* thus
introducing *am liebsten* through known
vocabulary and in a familiar context.

L, S

Present *am liebsten* in the following sequence:

T: *Ich gehe gern schwimmen.*
  Ich spiele gern Squash.
  Ich koche gern.
  Ich sehe gern fern.
  Ich höre gern Musik.
  Am liebsten höre ich Musik.

Repeat and encourage pupils (by mime!) to
repeat after you:
P: *Ich gehe gern schwimmen usw.*

(With some emphasis on *am liebsten* +
inversion:)
  Am liebsten höre ich Musik.

Go through the same list again in a different
order and transform the last item into *am
liebsten ... .*

Continue until all the expressions have been
inverted.

L, S

22

Discuss Worksheet No. 22: *Wer ist dein
Computerpartner/deine Computerpartnerin?*
(see Area 2) with a pupil in front of the class,
e.g.:

T: *Ann, du gehst gern schwimmen?*
P: *Ja.*
T: *Du siehst gern fern?*
.
.
.
T: *Und was machst du am liebsten?*
P: *Am liebsten spiele ich Tennis.*

Briefly practise the question. Repeat with
other pupils.

L, S

1-58

Distribute a selection of flashcards or other
pictures dealing with school subjects, sport,
hobbies, food and drink, and encourage pupils
to display their cards, in turn, in order to elicit
from other pupils:-

Was _____ du am liebsten?

Once a question has been correctly posed, the
pupil displaying the card should answer:-

Am liebsten _____ ich _____.

T: (To pupil) *Zeige deine Karte* (miming).
T: (To class) *Wie stellt man die Frage? Was
  trinkst du am ...*
P1: *Was trinkst du am liebsten?*
T: *Gut.* (To pupil displaying card). *Na, was
  trinkst du am liebsten?* (pointing to card).
P2: *Am liebsten trinke ich Cola.*
T: *Ausgezeichnet. Du* (pointing to another
  pupil). *Zeige deine Karte jetzt* (miming).

L, R, W

77
(1A 77)

Sonja und Max

Refer pupils to the table on page *77*, and the
accompanying instructions.

Sonja und Max
Scott Wilson: — Was trinkst du gern, Sonja?
Sonja: — Das ist schwer. Zum
  Frühstück trinke ich gern
  Kaffee. In der Pause trinke
  ich gern Milch, aber abends
  trinke ich gern Cola oder Tee.
Scott Wilson: — Was trinkst du abends am
  liebsten?
Sonja: — Na ja, ich glaube, ich trinke
  Tee am liebsten.

Scott Wilson:	— Und was ißt du gern?
Sonja:	— Was ich gern esse? Zum Frühstück esse ich gern Brötchen, ganz frisch und warm und knusprig, mit Butter und Marmelade.
Scott Wilson:	— Was ißt du am liebsten?
Sonja:	— Das ist einfach. Am liebsten esse ich Schokolade.
Scott Wilson:	— Und du, Max. Was trinkst du gern?
Max:	— Ich trinke gern Limonade, Cola und auch Wasser.
Scott Wilson:	— Und was trinkst du am liebsten?
Max:	— Am liebsten trinke ich Limonade.
Scott Wilson:	— Und was ißt du gern?
Max:	— Ich esse gern Steak, Pommes frites, Wurst und Käse.
Scott Wilson:	— Und was ißt du am liebsten?
Max:	— Am liebsten esse ich Steak.
Scott Wilson:	— Vielen Dank, Max.

nem 8
238
(1A 116)

W

Mein bester Freund/meine beste Freundin

A letter practising *gern* and *am liebsten*.

77
(1A 77)

L, R, W

Lieblingsfächer

Tell pupils to listen to the tape and to write down in their exercise books the favourite subject of each of the four interviewees.

Lieblingsfächer

Scott Wilson:	— Sonja, welches Schulfach magst du am liebsten?
Sonja:	— Ich gehe gern zur Schule und finde fast alles interessant, aber ich glaube, am liebsten mag ich Deutsch. Ja, Deutsch ist mein Lieblingsfach.
Scott Wilson:	— Und du, Max. Was magst du am liebsten in der Schule?
Max:	— Was ich am liebsten mag? Das ist wirklich schwer zu sagen. Ich lerne gern Musik und Latein, ja ich glaube, am liebsten lerne ich Latein. Latein finde ich sehr interessant.
Scott Wilson:	— Dorit, was magst du am liebsten in der Schule?
Dorit:	— Am liebsten lerne ich Geschichte. Dieses Jahr ist Herr Hulsen mein Lehrer für Geschichte. Der macht das sehr interessant.

Scott Wilson:	— Und du, Felix. Was magst du am liebsten in der Schule?
Felix:	— Ich habe eine Vier in Mathe, Physik, Englisch und Deutsch und eine Fünf in Erdkunde und Latein. Am liebsten mag ich Turnen. Da habe ich eine Eins.

77
(1A 77)

R

Einige Informationen: Freizeit in Deutschland

A simple chart demonstrating *Freizeit* and a brief accompanying text.

78
(1A 78)

R

Statistik: Jugendliche in der Freizeit

This is a simple reading comprehension showing the overall popularity of out-of-school activities among a sample of one hundred 13 to 14 year olds. Pupils could convert the statistics into block graphs.

nem 9
238
(1A 116)

L, S, R, W

Umfrage: Freizeit

Some pupils could interview the class and draw up a *Freizeit-Statistik der Klasse*.

5 Area 5

- Talking about television
- Revision of times (12 hour and 24 hour clock)

78
(1A 78)

R

Sven und Andrea lesen 'Gong'

Ask pupils to look at the page and guess what it is about. Give them a chance to report on any other details they have understood. Then tell them to work in pairs and find out further details.

T: *Seite 78. Was ist das? Sagt es auf Englisch.*
P: A page from a TV magazine.
T: *Richtig. Jetzt Partnerarbeit.*
Tell the pupils in English to look for details under the following headings:
  programmes for children
  music programmes
  sports programmes
  nature programmes
  news bulletins
  films
  English/American programmes/actors/ groups/singers

Collate the results of the previous pair-work on the board under the following headings:

Kinder Musik Sport Nachrichten Filme
Engl./Am. Tiere/Natur

Habt ihr

Programme für Kinder
Musiksendungen
Sportsendungen
Filme
Natursendungen
englische oder amerikanische Sendungen
            Schauspieler
            Gruppen
            Sänger

gefunden?

etwas gefunden, was auf Englisch 'News' ist?

79
(1A 79)

Kinder und Fernsehen

Establish the relationship between the table and the text. Practise *eine Stunde x Minuten, anderthalb Stunden, zweieinhalb Stunden, montags/am Montag.*

Wie lange siehst du fern?

Die Kinder in der Bundesrepublik sehen pro Woche über l2 Stunden fern.

Demonstrate addition on the board. Use a graph to explain *über* and *unter.*

Ist das zuviel? Wie lange seht ihr fern?
Then, to individual pupils:
Wie lange siehst du fern? Montags? etc.
Invite individual pupils to ask the question.

 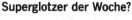

Superglotzer der Woche?

Continue the above activity in pairs. Partners should interview each other, make notes of each other's viewing habits and total the hours for the week. *(Addiert die Stunden für die ganze Woche)* - Demonstrate on the board. Find out who watches television least and most.

Wer sieht über l2 Stunden fern?
Hebt die Hand.
Wer sieht über l3 Stunden fern?
usw.
Wer sieht unter 5 Stunden fern?
usw.

The pupil who watches most TV could be given the title *'Superglotzer(in)'.*

79
(1A 79)

Streit *(Gong extract refers)*

Tell pupils that Sven and Andrea cannot agree about the programmes they want to see. Ask them to listen to the argument and list under the two names the programmes they mention.

Sven und Andrea haben immer Streit.
Sven sagt: ,Ich will die Sportschau sehen.'
Andrea sagt: ,Nein, die Sesamstraße ist besser'.
Sven sagt: ,Ach, das ist doch Quatsch.'
Hört gut zu!
Was will Sven sehen? Was will Andrea sehen?
Schreibt die Programme unter die Namen.

Will should not prove difficult in the context. It is practised in the following activities.

Streit

Sven:	— Ich will die Sportschau sehen.
Andrea:	— Nein, die Sesamstraße ist besser.
Sven:	— Ach, das ist doch Quatsch.
Andrea:	— Ich will Jimmy Conrad sehen.
Sven:	— Nein, Tommys Pop Show ist besser.
Andrea:	— Ach, das ist doch blöd!
Sven:	— Ich will Mafiaboss sehen.
Andrea:	— Nein, die Tagesschau ist besser.
Sven:	— Ach, das ist doch doof!

Check the results of the previous activity.

T: *Was will Andrea sehen? Was will Sven sehen?*
P: *Die Sesamstraße.*
T: *Ja, richtig. Andrea will die Sesamstraße sehen.*
   *Und was will Andrea **noch** sehen?*
P: *Jimmy Conrad.*
   usw.
T: *Es ist fünf Uhr. Was willst du sehen?*
P: *...*

(Noch is incidentally introduced - no exploitation intended. In the second part of the activity, pupils should not be expected to give full sentences.)

L, S, R, W

79
(1A 79)

Was willst du sehen?

Ask pupils to copy the chart from the book. They should fill in the left hand side with the programmes that they would choose from the *Gong* page. In pairs, they should then interview each other and write down their partner's preferences in the other column.

Tragt die Tabelle in euer Heft ein.
Seht euch Seite 79 an.
(Demonstrate) *3 Uhr - was will ich sehen?*
  Ja, was will ich denn sehen?
  Schulfernsehen.
  Ich schreibe hier:
  Schulfernsehen.
  Und so weiter. Bis 8 Uhr.

Und jetzt macht Interviews mit euren Partnern.
Schreibt die Antworten hier hin.

Pupils should be used to comparing notes after an activity of this kind.

---

nem 10   W

238
(1A 116)

Willst du mit dem Rad fahren?

Written practice of the question form: *Willst du ... +* infinitive.

L, S, R

80
(1A 80)

Wie spät ist es?

Read through the examples with the pupils by telling them the times, on the twelve hour clock, and then asking them to repeat the time on the 24 hour clock.

T: Wie spät ist es?
  (To pupil) Du, es ist ein Uhr
  Wie spät ist es?
P: (Es ist) ein Uhr.
T: Ja, oder (pointing to first written example)
  ...
P: Dreizehn Uhr.

Reinforce this activity by referring back to the *Öffnungszeiten* of the *Jugendzentrum,* in Area 2.

(L, S), R, W

80
(1A 80)

Was paßt zu wem?

Tell pupils to match the 12 hour and 24 hour times in their exercise books. Complete one example with pupils, on the board.

T: Also, halb zwölf (drawing clockface, thus:-)

T: Oder ... ?
P: Dreiundzwanzig Uhr dreißig.
T: Richtig. So ... (completing the illustrations and labelling on the board)

23	30

L, S, R

80-81
(1A 80-81)

Der letzte Bus nach Pinneberg

Read through the model dialogues on page 80 with the pupils before telling them to work in pairs, using the eight examples illustrated in the timetable marked *vormittags, nachmittags/abends.* Complete the first dialogue with one pupil.

T: (To pupil:) Nummer eins. Wann fährt der nächste Bus nach Pinneberg, bitte?
P: Um Viertel nach neun.
T: (Whispering to pupil) Guck mal - abends. Also, einundzwanzig Uhr ...
P: Fünfzehn.
T: Richtig. (To class again) Also, hört zu. (To pupil) Wann fährt der nächste Bus nach Pinneberg?
P: Um einundzwanzig Uhr fünfzehn.
T: Danke ... sehr gut. Na, Partnerarbeit!

L, S, R, W

25

Wann ist die Sesamstraße?

An information gap activity designed to provide further practice of times. Tell pupils to complete their TV schedules by questioning their partners. If necessary, complete the answer to the title question with the whole group.

T: Jetzt Partnerarbeit.
  (To pupil with sheet A). Stell die Frage: Wann ist die Sesamstraße?
P: Wann ist die Sesamstraße?
T: (To pupil with sheet B). Na, und ... wann ist die Sesamstraße? Hier, (pointing to the time on the sheet).
P: Um sechzehn Uhr im zweiten Programm.
T: Gut - (writing on board in Sesamstraße slot). 16.00 Sesamstraße, um sechzehn Uhr im zweiten Programm. Und jetzt stellst du (to pupil B) die Frage: ,Wann ist der Bugs Bunny Film?'

R

82
(1A 82)

Einige Informationen:
Schulaufgaben in Deutschland

Brief cartoon text about homework. No detailed exploitation intended.

R

83
(1A 83)

Eine Umfrage über Schulaufgaben

Statistical information about homework as preparation for the following listening activity and later pair-work. Make sure pupils have understood the information and the way it is presented.

L, S, R

26

Dienstag, 18. Februar

Provide pupils with the TV page from a magazine. Ask pairs to plan their evening's viewing, after discussing with them in English the types of programme available. Ask a few comprehension questions in English before attempting any exploitation in German.

L, R, W

82
(1A 82)

Interviews über Schulaufgaben

Tell pupils to listen for 'when', 'how long' and 'where' the German teenagers do their homework, and enter the results on the chart. This is quite a demanding exercise at this stage.

> *Hört gut zu. Ihr hört deutsche Teenager über Schulaufgaben sprechen. Wann machen sie die Aufgaben? Nach dem Essen ... um 6 Uhr ... um 9 Uhr ... ? Schreibt die Antwort auf Deutsch hier unter 'wann' auf usw.*

Interviews über Schulaufgaben

1 —Wann machst du deine Schulaufgaben, Jochen?
—Normalerweise gleich nach dem Mittagessen, so gegen halb drei. Ich arbeite dann bis halb vier oder vier, wenn ich viel aufhabe.
—Du arbeitest also meistens eine Stunde?
—Ja, das stimmt.
—Wo arbeitest du?
—In meinem Zimmer. Dann kann ich nebenbei auch Musik hören.
—Stört das nicht?
—Nee, überhaupt nicht.

2 —Beate, wann machst du deine Hausaufgaben?
—Ich esse zuerst nach der Schule und dann spiele ich Tennis oder gehe schwimmen, oder so. Ich mache meine Hausaufgaben erst abends, so gegen zwanzig Uhr. Ich arbeite dann vielleicht 45 Minuten.

L, S, R

81
(1A 81)

Tip des Tages

Play the three *Streit* dialogues again and ask pupils to listen. Draw their attention to the *Tip des Tages* either before or after this. Ask them to practise similar dialogues in pairs as soon as pronunciation and intonation are satisfactory.

—Und wo machst du deine Hausaufgaben?
—Im Wohnzimmer.
—Geht das?
—Ja, ich sehe auch manchmal ein bißchen fern.

3 —Jens, wann machst du deine Hausaufgaben?
—Am Nachmittag normalerweise. Nicht gleich nach der Schule — so gegen drei Uhr. Ich arbeite dann bis fünf — so zwei Stunden arbeite ich in der Regel für die Schule.
—Und wo machst du deine Hausaufgaben?
—Im Eßzimmer. Nachmittags ist es immer ganz ruhig da. Mein Zimmer ist nämlich ein bißchen klein. Im Eßzimmer ist viel Platz.

4 —Sabine, wann machst du deine Hausaufgaben?
—Meistens spät am Abend. Ich habe keine Lust gleich nach der Schule wieder zu arbeiten. Ich mache meine Schulaufgaben so um 9 Uhr abends. Ich arbeite dann 40 Minuten, dann gehe ich ins Bett.
—Wo arbeitest du?
—In der Küche oder im Eßzimmer.

5 —Wann machst du deine Hausaufgaben, Dietrich?
—Ich arbeite eine halbe Stunde nach dem Mittagessen, also von halb zwei bis zwei und dann nochmals eine halbe Stunde nach dem Frühstück — ganz früh, um 7 Uhr.
—Wo arbeitest du?
—In der Küche oder im Eßzimmer.

6 —Maren, wann machst du deine Hausaufgaben?
—Ich mache sie gleich nach dem Mittagessen. Ich arbeite von zwei bis drei — eine gute Stunde.
—Und wo arbeitest du?
—In meinem Zimmer.

7 —Wann machst du deine Hausaufgaben, Martin?
—Meistens am Abend — von sechs bis halb acht.
—Arbeitest du immer anderthalb Stunden?
—Ja, ich glaube schon.
—Wo arbeitest du?
—In meinem Zimmer.

8 —Claudia, wann machst du deine Schulaufgaben?
—Normalerweise abends. Dann bin ich nicht so müde. So um 19 Uhr.
—Wie lange arbeitest du für die Schule?
—40 Minuten in der Regel.
—Und wo arbeitest du?
—Im Wohnzimmer.

83
(1A 83)

Eine Umfrage über Schulaufgaben

Pupils could do their own homework survey and set out the information about their own homework in a similar way.

27

Hans-Werners Tagebuch

Cut the worksheet in half and give one half to each partner. Partner B must fill in the chart by asking questions. When the chart is complete, Partner B can check the answers by reading them back, or the teacher could collate the results on the board/OHP.

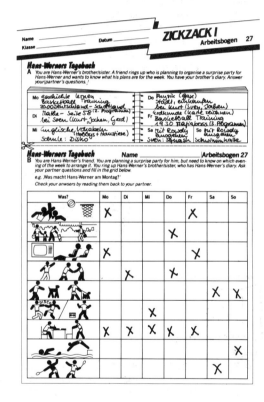

At this point, it might be advantageous to offer a branching programme for further practice/consolidation according to pupils' ability. The following activities are suggested.

a) *Mein Tagebuch*
Some pupils could write their own diary using the worksheet as a model.

b) ... s Tagebuch

Some pupils could write Peter's, Anne's, Christoph's or Sabine's diary, based on the accounts and using the worksheet as a model.

c) Some pupils could write an account in the first person about Hans-Werner's week, using *Tip des Tages* for guidance.

d) Some pupils could do further oral practice using *Tip des Tages* as a model — either in pairs or in a group conducted by the teacher.

The work of groups a and b could be displayed and some pupils in **c** and **d** could perform in front of the class.

R, W

28 Lückentext — Freizeit

A fill-in-the-gap exercise, involving verbs, expressions of time and vocabulary items.

Solution:

Peter	Anne
1 zuerst	1 Mittagessen
2 dann	2 mache
3 gehe	3 spiele
4 Basketball	4 manchmal
5 fahre	5 ich
6 Rad	6 einkaufen
7 Stadt	7 Sommer
8 treffe	8 sehe
	9 höre

Christoph	Sabine
1 erstes	1 nachmittags
2 zweimal	2 Schulaufgaben
3 reite	3 trinken
4 Pony	4 Musik
5 gehe	5 spielen
6 Tag	
7 Hund	

L, S, R, W

29 Gern, nicht gern

Ask pupils to work in pairs and interview each other about their likes and dislikes. Follow the pattern of the dialogue at the top of the sheet. Firstly, each partner should complete the left hand side of the sheet and then each partner should attempt to complete the right hand side by interviewing the other partner. Partners compare sheets afterwards.

T: Jetzt Partnerarbeit. (demonstrate with one pair): *Du füllst es hier aus. Du schreibst:*
Ich esse gern Fisch und Pommes frites
Ich esse nicht gern Frikadellen
Ich trinke gern Cola und Limo
Ich trinke nicht gern Tee
Ich spiele gern ...

This written activity could then be completed as a homework activity. Once each partner has completed his/her section, ask pupils to question each other.

T: Seid ihr fertig? Gut. (Demonstrate with one pair). *Du stellst die Fragen:*
Was ißt du gern?
Was trinkst du gern?
Was ißt du nicht gern?
Was trinkst du nicht gern?

L, R, W

84 (1A 84) Herbert Meyer und Band auf Tournee

Tell pupils to look at the list of Herbert Meyer concerts. Point out that the town is given and the concert hall, but no dates. Ask them to listen to the recording and write in the dates when the band appears in each town.

Herbert Meyer gibt ein Konzert in Hannover.
In der Stadion Sporthalle. Aber wann ist das?
Hört gut zu. Play the first recording and write *Hannover Stadion Sporthalle 20.4.* Explain that 4 = April *(der vierte Monat).*

Herbert Meyer und Band auf Tournee

1 — Herbert Meyer spielt am zwanzigsten April in der Stadion Sporthalle in Hannover.

2 — Am zweiundzwanzigsten April spielt er in der Stadthalle in Bremen.

3 — Am dreiundzwanzigsten April gibt er ein Konzert in der Stadthalle in Osnabrück.

4 — Am zweiten Mai spielt er in Paderborn in der Sporthalle.

5 — Wann ist er in Kiel?
   — Am dritten Mai in der Ostseehalle.

6 — Am dreißigsten Mai kommt er nach Karlsruhe. Er gibt ein Konzert in der Stadthalle.

7 — Und dann am neunten Juni ist er in Hamburg. Das Konzert ist im Stadtpark.

8 — Kommt er nach Kassel?
   — Ja, er spielt am ersten Juli in der Stadthalle.

9 — Wann ist er in Freiburg?
   — Am neunten Juli in der Stadthalle.

10 — Spielt er auch in Luzern?
   — Ja, am achten August im Kunsthaus.

11 — Und auch in Zürich?
   — Ja, am siebzehnten August im Volkshaus.

12 — Spielt er auch in Österreich?
   — Ja, er gibt da zwei Konzerte. Am ersten September spielt er in der Sporthalle in Salzburg, und am zweiten September spielt er in der Kurhalle in Wien.

L

Reporter: — Ich schreibe einen Artikel über die Band. Kann ich ein paar Fragen stellen?

Herbert: — Du hast fünf Minuten. Also los!

Reporter: — Heißt du wirklich Herbert Meyer?

Herbert: — Nein, mein Name ist Sepp. Sepp Dirscherl. Das klingt nicht gut für einen Popstar. Stell' dir vor: Sepp Dirscherl und seine Band. Blöd, nicht?

Reporter: — Ja, stimmt. Wie alt bist du, Herbert?

Herbert: — Dreiundzwanzig.

Reporter: — Hast du eine feste Freundin?

Herbert: — Nein, das geht nicht. Ich bin zu oft auf Tournee. Hier, schau dir das Programm an. Im April, Mai und Juni bin ich im Norden. Juli, August und September bin ich im Süden — in Österreich und in der Schweiz. Ich übe auch jeden Tag Gitarre und lerne jetzt Trompete. Ich habe keine Zeit für eine feste Freundin.

Reporter: — Was für Musik hörst du am liebsten in deiner Freizeit?

Herbert: — Jazz und Popmusik höre ich gern, aber am liebsten höre ich klassische Musik - Bach, Mozart und Beethoven.

Reporter: — Das ist sehr interessant. Klassische Musik. Das ist nicht sehr typisch. Nicht viele Popsänger hören gern klassische Musik.

Herbert: — Du meinst, alle Popstars sind doof, was?

Reporter: — Nein, nein, nein.

Herbert: — Also, die fünf Minuten sind jetzt vorbei. Das Interview ist zu Ende. Ich gehe.

Reporter: — Kann ich noch schnell ein Foto machen?

Herbert: — Nein. Das Interview ist zu Ende, habe ich gesagt.

84
(1A 84)

Ein Interview mit Herbert Meyer

Refer pupils to the visual in the Pupil's Book on page 84, and the questions in English on the interview. Some of the questions are aimed at focusing pupils' attention on the general atmosphere of the text, rather than just factual information.

Ein Interview mit Herbert Meyer

Reporter: — Ich bin Reporter für das Jugendmagazin 'Top'.

Herbert: — Ja und? Was willst du von mir?

R, W

30

Treffpunkt

Tell pupils that they are going to read some adverts for penfriends, and that they should choose both a boy and a girl to write to. Before they start looking, however, tell them that they should decide in advance what they would expect their 'ideal' penfriends to be like.

*Seht euch Arbeitsbogen 30 an. Das sind
Anzeigen für Brieffreunde und
Brieffreundinnen. Lest die Seite und sucht
euch einen Brieffreund und eine Brieffreundin
aus. Aber zuerst sollt ihr entscheiden, was für
Brieffreunde ihr haben wollt. Zum Beispiel:
Wie alt muß er oder sie sein? Dreizehn?
Vierzehn? Fünfzehn? Dreizehn bis fünfzehn?
Was für Hobbys? Fußball, Tennis, Musik?
Zuerst schreibt auf, was ihr sucht:*
Demonstrate on the board.

	Brieffreund	Brieffreundin
Alter	13	12 bis 14
Hobbys	Fußball Kino Radfahren	Schwimmen Tanzen Radfahren

Once pupils have completed the information
about what they are looking for, ask them to
read the advert, and find the most suitable
penfriends.

W

As a follow-up to this activity, ask pupils to
write an advert about themselves for
publication in *'Treffpunkt'*. These would make
a good classroom display. The address is:
BRAVO-Treffpunkt, 8000 München 100.

L

84
(1A 84)

Was machst du am liebsten in der Freizeit?

These ten recordings contain a certain amount
of redundant language, but most pupils
should be able to do the matching exercise.
Refer pupils to page 84 in their books, and
ask them to listen to the tape and match the
recording with a visual.

*Seht euch Seite 84 an und hört gut zu. Was
paßt zu wem?* Play the first recording and
match this as a class activity). *Also Nummer
eins. Was paßt zu Nummer eins? Ja, richtig!*

Was machst du am liebsten in der Freizeit?

1 — Am liebsten höre ich Musik. Zu Hause
in meinem Zimmer mit meinen
Freunden.

2 — Ich sehe am liebsten fern. Meine
Lieblingssendung ist die Sportschau.

3 — Am liebsten treffe ich mich mit meinen
Freunden — in der Stadt, im Park oder
bei mir zu Hause.

4 — Was ich am liebsten mache? Na ja, ich
glaube, am liebsten gehe ich
schwimmen. Wir haben ein schönes
Hallenbad ganz in der Nähe.

5 — Am liebsten spiele ich Fußball in der
Freizeit. Ich bin Mitglied eines
Sportvereins und gehe dreimal in der
Woche zum Fußballtraining.

6 — Am liebsten gehe ich nach der Schule
in die Stadt einkaufen. Ich kaufe
meistens Kleider oder Kassetten.

7 — Ich habe kein festes Hobby, wie zum
Beispiel Fußball oder Briefmarken. Am
liebsten gehe ich in der Stadt bummeln.

8 — Am Sonntag besuche ich am liebsten
meine Großeltern. Es gibt immer
schöne Kuchen mit Sahne. Die haben
auch einen Hund. Wir gehen alle mit
ihm spazieren.

9 — In der Freizeit spiele ich am liebsten
Basketball. Zu Hause haben wir auch
einen Korb im Garten.

10 — Am liebsten gehe ich spazieren —
allein, mit Freunden, oder mit dem
Hund.

Solution: **1** C **2** H **3** E **4** G **5** B
6 D **7** A **8** I **9** J **10** F

Vocabulary

aktuell *current*
allein *alone*
an + Acc/Dat *to, on, at*
anderthalb *one and a half*
arbeiten *to work*
ausgezeichnet *excellent*
die Band(s) *band, group*
Basketball *basketball*
besser *better*
besuchen *to visit*
das Blasorchester(-) *brass band*
die Blockflöte(n) *recorder*
blöd *silly, stupid*
die Briefmarke(n) *stamp*
bummeln *to stroll*
der Chor(⁼e) *choir*
decken *to cover, lay the table*
die Disko(s) *disco*
doof *stupid*
es ist egal *it doesn't matter/doesn't make any difference*
einkaufen *to shop*
der Eintritt *entrance, entry*
entscheiden *to decide*
die Fabrik(en) *factory*
das Fahrrad(⁼er) *bicycle*
fast *almost, nearly*
faulenzen *to be lazy*
der Fernseher(-) *television*
fest *fixed, steady*
das Feuerwerk(e) *firework*
die Flöte(n) *flute*
folkloristisch *folkloric*
die Freizeit *free time*

frisch *fresh; cool*
gastieren *to host*
die Geige(n) *violin*
die Gitarre(n) *guitar*
glotzen *to stare*
die Halle(n) *large hall*
das Hallenbad(⁼er) *indoor swimming pool*
die Hand(⁼e) *hand*
die Hausaufgaben *homework*
das Instrument(e) *musical instrument*
der Jazz *jazz*
die Jugend *youth*
das Jugendzentrum(Jugend-zentren) *youth centre*
Juni *June*
der Kasten(⁼) *box*
die Kirche(n) *church*
die Klarinette(n) *clarinet*
klassisch *classical*
das Klavier(e) *piano*
die Kleider *clothes*
knusprig *crispy*
das Konzert(e) *concert*
der Korb(⁼e) *basket*
der Krach *noise, row*
laut *loud*
links *on the left*
März *March*
der Meister(-) *master*
das Mitglied(er) *member*
die Mundharmonika(s) *mouth organ*
die Muttersprache(n) *mother tongue*

die Nachricht(en) *news*
die Natur *nature*
nebenbei *at the same time*
öffnen *to open*
Oktober *October*
die Oper *opera(house)*
das Orchester(-) *orchestra*
der Park(s) *park*
die Politik *politics*
das Pony(s) *pony*
präsentieren *to present, introduce*
das Programm(e) *TV channel; programme*
das Prozent(e) *per cent*
der Quatsch *rubbish*
  ! rubbish!
die Querflöte(n) *flute*
radfahren *to cycle*
die Regel(n) *rule*
in der * *usually*
reiten *to ride*
der Rollschuh(e) *rollerskate*
das Schach *chess*
der Schauspieler(-) *actor*
schimpfen *to scold, tell off*
das Schlagzeug(e) *percussion*
die Sendung(en) *programme*
singen *to sing*
der Solist(en) *soloist*
sortieren *to sort out*
spazierengehen *to go for a walk*
Squash *squash*
das Stadion(Stadien) *stadium*
stark *strong*

stellen *to put, place*
stelle die Frage *ask the question*
die Stimme(n) *voice*
stören *to disturb*
streiten *to argue*
studieren *to study*
das Symbol(e) *symbol*
die Tagesschau *the News*
tanzen *to dance*
Tennis *tennis*
der Termin(e) *appointment*
Tischtennis *table tennis*
der Titel(-) *title*
die Tournee(n) *tour*
die Trompete(n) *trumpet*
turnen *to do gymnastics*
üben *to practise*
überhaupt *at all*
die Universität(en) *university*
verbinden *to combine, unite*
der Verein(e) *club, society*
der Verkauf(⁼e) *sale*
vorbei *past*
vorstellen *to introduce*
das Wochenende(n) *weekend*
zuerst *first of all*
zuviel *too much*
zwischen + Acc/Dat *between*

CHAPTER 6 Was kostet das?

Area 1

> ● Currency in German-speaking countries

Number spotting

L, S

Revise numbers 1 - 100.

Write a selection of numbers (about 20) at random on the board/OHP. Then read out about 20 numbers of which 5 are on the board. Pupils must call out „Ja' when they hear a number that is written up. If desired, they can be asked to come up and point the number out.

L, S

Reversals

Another game for practising numbers: name a pupil, who has to say any number in German between 10 and 99. That pupil then challenges someone else of their choice to reverse the figures and give the German for that number, e.g.

Pupil A: Vierundzwanzig (24). Sarah.
Pupil B: Zweiundvierzig (42).

Continue with different pupils.

L, S

Write l00 on the board and say *hundert*. Now write 2 on the board and elicit *zwei*. Add two naughts to give 200 and elicit *zweihundert*. Confirm this. Write 300, 400 and so on up to 900.

Finally give *tausend*.

Draw pupils' attention to the absence of an indefinite article — not **a** hundred or **a** thousand.

Build up complex numbers by starting with *vierhunderteins* and counting as pupils did when they first learned numbers in German.

Draw attention to the different position of 'and', e.g.

four hundred and twenty-eight 4 28
vierhundertachtundzwanzig 42 8

The reversals game can be played with these figures too.

Some simple adding or subtracting could be attempted as practice for prices. Dictate the sum and ask for the answers in German.

*Zweihundert minus acht (repeat)
Ist ... ?
or Hundertzwanzig plus sechsundzwanzig (repeat)
Macht ... ?*

(L, S), R

Einige Informationen - Das Geld in der BRD, Österreich, der Schweiz.

Introduce the topic of money:

T: *In Großbritannien haben wir Pounds und Pence.* (Demonstrate). *Dies hier ist das Geld in Großbritannien. Das ist ein Pfund. Das sind zehn Pence.
In Frankreich gibt es Francs und Centimes.
In den USA gibt es Dollars und Cents.*

*Wieviel Cents hat ein Dollar?
Wieviel Pence hat ein englisches Pfund?
Wieviel Centimes hat ein Franc?*

*Wie ist das in der Bundesrepublik? Was gibt es dort?
Wie ist das in Österreich? Was gibt es dort?
Wie ist das in der Schweiz? Was gibt es dort?*

It is likely that some of the currencies will already be known. If not, introduce them orally. Ensure that *Mark* is used, not *Deutschmark*.

L

Wo sind sie?

Give pupils some time to familiarise themselves with the pictures of the coins and notes in *Einige Informationen*. Tell them that they are going to hear people mentioning prices and that they must decide which country they are in.

*Ihr hört gleich einige Leute, die über Geld sprechen.
Sie sagen manchmal ‚Franken' und ‚Rappen' - dann sind sie in der Schweiz.
Manchmal sagen sie ‚Mark' und ‚Pfennig'. Wo sind sie dann?*

So, jetzt hört gut zu. Wo sind die Leute?

Stop after each item and check comprehension orally.

Wo sind sie?

1
— Eine Cola, bitte.
— Hier, bitte schön. 80 Pfennig.

2
— Ein Schokoladeneis, bitte.
— 5 Schilling.
— Ja.
— Danke.

3
— Was kostet das?
— 10 Franken 50 Rappen.

4
— Was macht das?
— 25 Mark.

5
— Hast du Geld dabei?
— Nur 20 Schilling. Wieso?
— Ich möchte noch eine Postkarte kaufen.

6
— Was kostet dieses T-Shirt?
— 12 Franken.
— Nein, danke.
— Bitte schön.

7
— Wieviel Taschengeld kriegst du?
— 10 Mark die Woche. Und du?
— Ich auch.

8
— Guck mal, die LP kostet nur 85 Schilling!
— Mensch, das ist ja billig. Kaufen wir die?
— Natürlich!

(R)

87
(1A 87)

Wechselkurse

The Pupil's Book shows two 'rates of exchange' boards - one from a German bank and one from a British bank. Without turning it into a maths lesson, make sure that pupils understand how to read these in order to make a rough estimate for themselves before changing money. In English, do 2 or 3 examples each way.

nem 1
239
(1A 117)

L, (S)

Wieviel ist das zusammen?

Tell pupils to find the correct combination of coins for the prices you read out. Check the pronunciation of letters before starting.

Ich sage ‚50 Pfennig'. Wo seht ihr das?
Unter ‚a'? - Nein.
Unter ‚b'? - Ja. Ihr schreibt also ‚b'.
Und so weiter.

Nummer 1 - 50 Pfennig
Nummer 2 - 20 Pfennig
Nummer 3 - Eine Mark
Nummer 4 - 5 Pfennig
Nummer 5 - Eine Mark vierzig

Nummer 6 - 60 Pfennig
Nummer 7 - Drei Mark
Nummer 8 - Eine Mark sechzig
Nummer 9 - Zwei Mark
Nummer 10 - 80 Pfennig

Solution: **1b 2c 3a 4d 5f 6h 7i 8j 9e 10g**

L, S

Ask pupils to work in pairs with the same visuals.

Und jetzt Partnerarbeit.
Du sagst ‚c', und du antwortest ‚20 Pfennig'.
Du sagst ‚g'. Wie antwortest du?
Und so weiter.

L, S, (W)

88
(1A 88)

Wieviel Geld hast du dabei?

Introduce the theme by counting some of your money in front of the class and then ask individual pupils how much money they have on them.

T: 50 Pence, ein Pfund ... 2 Pfund dreißig.
Ich habe zwei Pfund dreißig dabei.
Wieviel Geld hast du dabei?
P: 40 Pence.

When pupils are used to the question, tell them to look at the illustration in the Pupil's Book. Depending on the class, this could be done either 'off the cuff' or with some preparation in note form. For each picture ask the question ‚Wieviel Geld hast du dabei?'. These amounts could be written out in words by pupils for consolidation.

Solution: **A** DM 2,80 **B** DM 16,00 **C** DM 24,50
D DM 1,55 **E** DM 41,50 **F** DM 13,25
G DM 62,70 **H** DM 74,00 **I** DM 7,60
J DM 55,30

nem 2
239
(1A 117)

W

Schreibe aus!

A simple activity to consolidate numbers and money.

L, S, (W)

88
(1A 88)

Was bekomme ich zurück?

A matching up task designed to help pupils get used to German money. On the left are 6 priced articles together with the money being handed over for them. On the right is the change being handed back. Which goes with which? Avoid developing language for the full buying-selling transaction at this stage. This is built up later in Areas 4 and 5.

Nummer eins. Du kaufst Schokolade. Das kostet DM 4,75 und du bezahlst mit einem 10 Mark-Schein. Was bekommst du zurück?

Solution: **1**c **2**e **3**a **4**f **5**d **6**b

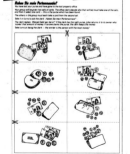

L, S

Haben Sie mein Portemonnaie?

A game to be played in groups of 4 or 5. The worksheets must be cut up into eight equal sized cards. Give each group **two** sets of cards. Explain to pupils in English that they are at the lost property office. One pupil in each group is the clerk, the rest are 'customers'. The clerk keeps one set of cards face down in front of him and chooses one card from this pile. This is the purse that has been found. The other set of cards is spread out, face down, on the table. The rest of the group - the customers - take one card each. These are the purses they have lost.

Pupils take it in turn to ask 'the clerk': *‚Haben Sie mein Portemonnaie?'*
The clerk asks *‚Wieviel Geld war darin?'* and the pupil tells him. If the clerk has the right one, he gives it to the pupil who 'scores' that amount of money. If no one claims the purse with the right amount of money, the clerk keeps the money. Each pupil in the group takes a turn at being the clerk and a running score is kept after each round. The winner is the person with the most money to his credit.

Demonstrate one round with a sample group in front of the class.

(For quick reference, the amounts of money in each purse from left to right are:
35,00, 18,00, 14,00, 21,20, 20,80, 12,25, 45,00, 4,15.)

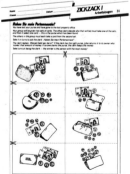

Area 2

● **Changing money and Traveller's Cheques**

89
(1A 89)

(R)

Wo kann ich hier Geld wechseln?

Introduce the topic in English using the photos in the Pupil's Book.

Discuss: where you can change money/traveller's cheques
what times German banks are open
which signs you look for inside the bank *(Wechsel, Auslandsschalter* or *Devisen)*
how you usually go to a special till to collect your money *(die Kasse).*

L

Auf der Bank

Play the recording and tell pupils to write down how much money each customer wants to change. In this way the new vocabulary can be allowed to emerge through further practice in recognising numbers.

Auf der Bank
1 — Guten Tag.
— Guten Tag.
— Ich möchte bitte zehn Pfund in Deutsche Mark **wechseln.**
— Zehn Pfund? Ja, gerne. Bitte schön. Sie bekommen Ihr Geld da rechts an der Kasse.

2 — Guten Morgen. Was kann ich für Sie tun?
— Kann ich hier Geld **wechseln?**
— Ja, sicher. Was möchten Sie wechseln?
— Ich möchte fünfundzwanzig Pfund Sterling in Deutsche Mark umwechseln, bitte.
— So. Moment bitte.

3 — Kann ich hier Pfundnoten gegen D-Mark wechseln, bitte?
— Ja, natürlich. Wieviel wollen Sie wechseln?
— Zweiunddreißig Pfund.
— Danke schön. Fünf, zehn, zwanzig, dreißig, zweiunddreißig. So, Ihre Quittung. Wollen Sie jetzt bitte an die **Kasse** gehen?

4 — Guten Tag. Was darf es sein, bitte?
— Ich möchte gern hundert Pfund in Schweizer Franken **umwechseln**, bitte.
— Ja, gerne. Haben Sie das Geld da?

5 — Kann ich Ihnen helfen?
— Ja, ich möchte etwas Geld wechseln, bitte.
— Ja, gerne. Was möchten Sie wechseln?
— Vierzig Pfund, bitte.
— Danke. So, könnten Sie bitte **unterschreiben?** Danke schön.

6 — Guten Morgen, meine Dame.
— Guten Morgen. Ich möchte diesen Reisescheck **einlösen,** bitte.
— Bitte schön. Das sind fünfzig Pfund, ja?
— Ja.
— So, wollen Sie bitte hier unterschreiben? Und, Ihren Paß bitte.
— Danke schön.

7 — Was kann ich für Sie tun?
— Ich möchte zwei Reiseschecks zu zehn Pfund einlösen, bitte.
— Haben Sie Ihren **Paß** mit?
— Ja, hier.
— Danke. So, gehen Sie bitte zur Kasse drei.

8 — Können Sie mir dreißig Pfund in Schillinge umwechseln, bitte?
— Ja, gerne.
— Wie ist der **Kurs** heute?
— Es gibt heute 4,2 Pence für einen Schilling.

9 — Guten Tag.
— Tag. Kann ich hier Reiseschecks **wechseln,** bitte?
— Ja, sicher. Wieviel möchten Sie?
— Ich möchte einen Scheck zu fünfzig Pfund einlösen.
— Gerne. Wollen Sie bitte den Scheck hier unterschreiben?

10 — Bitte schön?
— Ich möchte diesen Reisescheck **zu** zwanzig Pfund einlösen, bitte.
— Jawohl. Können Sie das bitte unterschreiben? Kann ich bitte Ihren Paß haben?
— Ja, hier ist er.
— Schönen Dank. Bitte sehr. Bitte zur Kasse zwei ...
— Vielen Dank.
— Bitte schön. Wiedersehen.

Solution: **1** 10 **2** 25 **3** 32 **4** 100 **5** 40
6 50 **7** 20 **8** 30 **9** 50 **10** 20

90
(1A 90)

L, S, R

Was sagt man?

Tell pupils to listen to the first dialogue of *Auf der Bank* again, this time looking at sentence number one in the Pupil's Book. Ask them to listen for the missing words - the same in several cases. N.B. This should **not** be used as a writing exercise. The missing words are printed bold in the tapescript above.

*Seht ins Buch, Satz Nummer eins.
,Ich möchte bitte zehn Pfund in Deutsche Mark ... ' - Was sagt man?
Hört gut zu.*

When pupils identify the word *wechseln*, write it up on the board - but **not** the English. Continue with the rest of the ten dialogues, writing the missing words on the board. Immediately after this, pupils could do the matching exercise *Was bedeutet das?* in writing.

---

nem 3

239
(1A 117)

R, W

Was bedeutet das?

This matching exercise consolidates the pupil's knowledge of key words from the dialogues, in preparation for *Partnerarbeit* p. 90 .

90
(1A 90)

L, S, (R)

Partnerarbeit

The diagrams in the Pupil's Book are to be used as cues for role-playing. Build up a dialogue with a sample pair of pupils using diagram A. Pupils can refer to both *Was sagt man?* and *Was bedeutet das?* in preparing their dialogues. Get the class to rehearse their own dialogues about changing money, making sure that each pupil has a go at being both customer and clerk.

Do the same for changing a traveller's cheque, using diagram B.

Finally, ask each pair to prepare a dialogue (A or B) for performance to the rest of the class. Use these dialogues as 'live' listening comprehension, numbering them as you go and asking pupils to fill in a grid as follows:

	Geld?	Scheck?	Wieviel?
1		✓	50
2			
3			

Finally,. check the results together. Good results, of course, reflect as much the speaker's performance as the listener's comprehension.

R, W

90
(1A 90)

Zum Lesen

A slightly longer dialogue on the same topic, with 5 questions in German. Take care with question 4 - he doesn't get any money direct from the clerk at all.

nem 4

R, W

239
(1A 117)

Reisescheck

A jumbled dialogue in a bank for pupils to rewrite in the correct order.

6 Area 3

● Pocket money

91
(1A 91)

L, W

Wieviel Taschengeld bekommst du?

Introduce the word *Taschengeld* visually, by illustrating the meaning of each half of the word, then inviting guesses as to the meaning of the whole.

Tell them they are going to hear ten young people saying how much pocket money they get - or how much they earn themselves. Tell them to copy out the table from the Pupil's Book and complete it whilst listening to the recordings.

N.B. In the title *bekommen* is used as this is the more appropriate word in the written form, but *kriegen* is the commonest expression when speaking.

Ihr hört gleich zehn junge Leute. Wieviel Taschengeld bekommen sie? Oder haben sie einen Job? Wieviel verdienen sie mit ihrem Job? Zuerst, tragt die Tabelle in euer Heft ein.

Wieviel Taschengeld bekommst du?

1 — Beate, wieviel Taschengeld bekommst du?
 — Normalerweise l0 Mark pro Woche.

2 — Und Guido, wieviel Taschengeld bekommst du in der Woche?
 — 15 Mark.

3 — Du, Tanja, wieviel Taschengeld bekommst du?
 — Nur 20 Mark.

4 — Ulla, wieviel Taschengeld bekommst du?
 — Meine Oma gibt mir 10 Mark, und ich bekomme 20 Mark von meinen Eltern. Also 30 Mark pro Woche.

5 — Hans-Jürgen, wieviel Taschengeld kriegst du in der Woche?
 — Ich kriege 25 Mark. Aber samstags habe ich einen Job im Supermarkt und verdiene noch 40 Mark dazu.

6 — Du, Rolf, wie ist das bei dir mit dem Taschengeld?
 — Ich kriege kein Taschengeld, aber ich arbeite nach der Schule in einer Bäckerei. Dafür kriege ich 80 Mark pro Woche.

7 — Rike, bekommst du Taschengeld von deinen Eltern?
 — Ja, meine Eltern geben mir 30 Mark pro Woche.

8 — Fabian, wieviel Taschengeld hast du pro Woche?
 — Normalerweise kriege ich 80 Mark, aber davon muß ich auch den Bus bezahlen.

9 — Und Jens, wieviel kriegst du?
 — Meine Mutter gibt mir 40 Mark Taschengeld.

10 — Anja, bekommst du Taschengeld?
 — Ja, ich kriege l5 Mark von meinen Eltern, und ich verdiene auch noch 30 Mark mit meinem Job.

Solution:

Name	Taschengeld DM	Job DM
Beate	DM 10	—
Guido	DM 15	—
Tanja	DM 20	—
Ulla	DM 30	—
Hans-Jürgen	DM 25	DM 40
Rolf	—	DM 80
Rike	DM 30	—
Fabian	DM 80	—
Jens	DM 40	—
Anja	DM 15	DM 30

L, S

Carry out similar interviews with the pupils in your class. If pupils hesitate, prompt answers by writing amounts on the board to avoid possible embarrassment.

R

91 (1A 91) Stefans und Brittas Taschengeld

Two short reading texts for consolidation and reference. The pictures clarify the meaning of unknown vocabulary, which does not have to be practised, however.

L, S, R

92 (1A 92) Wofür gibst du dein Geld aus?

The diagram is meant to stimulate discussion about what pocket money is spent on. Use it to introduce the question: *Wofür gibst du dein Geld aus?* Go through the various uses named, explaining - in German, if possible - what each one means. Then ask individual pupils what they spend their money on, inviting them to use some of the categories on the diagram.

Pupils could carry out a census, asking a number of fellow pupils what they spend **their** money on. To record the results with a chart or diagram becomes both linguistically and mathematically rather complicated. A simpler way of rounding off this activity is to give pupils a 'selection' summary on the board to which they can add their own findings, e.g.

*In meiner Klasse geben wir sehr viel für ....
und .... aus. Wir geben auch ziemlich viel für
.... aus, aber nur ein wenig für ... und ...*

R, W

92 (1A 92) Wer sagt was?

The first part of the task is to unmuddle what the five people say. Use this to draw attention to the word order with the separable verb *ausgeben*. If wished, the first sentence could be done on the board to indicate the structure. Once pupils have rewritten the five sentences, tell them to read what is written about the five speakers and work out who says what.

Solution:
Anton: ‚Ich gebe ziemlich viel Geld beim Ausgehen aus'
Kirsten: ‚Ich gebe nicht viel aus'
Dieter: ‚Ich gebe mein Geld für meine Hobbys aus'

Barbara: ‚Ich gebe mein Geld meistens für Bücher und Kassetten aus.'
Marga: ‚Ich gebe mein Geld für Kleider und Kosmetika aus'.

L, R, (W)

Acht junge Leute

32

Tell pupils they are going to hear 8 young people talking about their pocket money, or the money they earn.

More able pupils can be asked to record the following information for each one:

*Wieviel Taschengeld bekommen sie?
Verdienen sie etwas?
Wofür geben sie es aus?
Oder sparen sie? Und wofür?*

Less confident pupils can be given Worksheet 32. The three columns show in diagram form:
  i the speakers
  ii how much they get/earn
  iii what they spend it on or what they are saving for.

Tell pupils they must draw lines between the three columns to show **who** has **how much** and **what they use it for**. The first one is filled in as an example.

Acht junge Leute

1   Inga
— Wieviel Taschengeld bekommst du?
— Zehn Mark die Woche.
— Und verdienst du etwas dazu?
— Nein.
— Wofür gibst du dein Geld aus?
— Naja, ich gehe gern weg. Ich gehe immer am Wochenende aus, ins Kino oder so. Und ich kaufe mir auch mal eine Zeitschrift.

2   Omer
— Ich bekomme kein Taschengeld, aber ich verdiene so etwa fünfzig Mark die Woche. Ich arbeite in einem Café in der Stadtmitte.
— Wofür gibst du dein Geld aus?
— Tja, für Kleidung, Sachen für die Schule. Dann brauche ich auch zehn Mark die Woche für den Bus, um zum Café zu kommen, wo ich arbeite!

3   Matthias
— Ich kriege dreißig Mark im Monat.
— Und wofür gibst du das Geld aus?
— Ich gehe in die Disko. Wenn man auch was trinken will, dann ist das Geld schnell alle.
— Hast du auch einen Job?
— Nein.

4 Bianca

— Wieviel Taschengeld bekommst du?
— Vierzig Mark im Monat.
— Verdienst du auch etwas dazu?
— Ja, durch Nachhilfe. Ich gebe Englischstunden.
— Und wieviel verdienst du dabei?
— Fünf Mark die Stunde.
— Gibst du dein Geld aus oder sparst du?
— Ich gebe es aus.
— Wofür?
— Eine ganze Reihe Zeitschriften. Und Schulsachen.
— Auch für Kosmetik?
— Ja, so fünfzehn Mark im Monat für Kosmetik.

5 Cornelia

— Bekommst du Taschengeld?
— Also, ich bekomm' nicht speziell Taschengeld, aber wenn ich was will, dann sage ich es meinen Eltern. Ich sage, ich brauche das und das — und ich krieg's!
— Was, zum Beispiel?
— Ja, Kleider oder :. wenn ich weggehe.
— Hast du einen Job?
— Nee, wir leben auf dem Land. Da gibt's kaum was.

6 Manfred

— Ich kriege dreißig bis vierzig Mark im Monat.
— Hast du auch einen Job?
— Ich hatte mal einen. Aber nicht mehr.
— Wofür gibst du dein Geld aus?
— Für mein Hobby. Das ist Angeln. Ich kauf' mir ziemlich viele Sachen dafür.

7 Susanne

— Wieviel Taschengeld bekommst du?
— Zehn Mark in der Woche, aber ich verdiene mir noch was dazu, durch Babysitten.
— Ja? Wieviel verdienst du dabei?
— Naja, es kommt darauf an. So, fünfzehn, zwanzig Mark.
— Und wofür gibst du das aus?
— Ja, wenn ich abends weggehe, wenn ich zum Beispiel ins Kino gehe ... oder Eis esse.

8 Rainer

— Bekommst du Taschengeld?
— Ich krieg' kein spezielles Taschengeld, nein. Aber wenn ich Geld brauche, gibt mir mein Vater was. Ich verdiene auch nebenbei Geld.
— Was machst du?
— Jeden Sonntag trage ich Zeitungen aus. Dafür kriege ich 20 Mark. Und im Sommer gebe ich auch mal abends eine Tennisstunde. Vielleicht 15 Mark die Stunde.

— Und wofür gibst du das aus?
— Also, das Geld von meinem Vater meist in der Disko und auch für Schulsachen. Aber das Geld, das ich verdiene, das spare ich für ein Motorrad.

Solution:

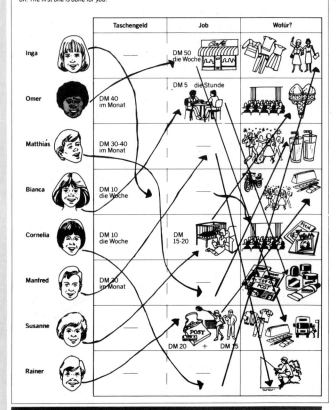

Acht junge Leute

Listen to eight young people talking about their pocket money, or the money they earn.

Draw lines between the three columns to show how much money each speaker gets and what (s)he spends it on. The first one is done for you.

	Taschengeld	Job	Wofür?
Inga		DM 50 die Woche	
Omer	DM 40 im Monat	DM 5 die Stunde	
Matthias	DM 30-40 im Monat		
Bianca	DM 10 die Woche		
Cornelia	DM 10 die Woche	DM 15-20	
Manfred	DM 30 im Monat		
Susanne		DM 20 + DM 15	
Rainer			

6 Area 4

● **Asking and saying what they cost**

L, S, (R)

93 (1A 93)

Was kostet der Film?

Go through the named items first and ask the price.

T: *Was kostet der Film?*
P: *Zehn Mark fünfzig.*
T: *Zehn Mark vierzig?*
P: *Nein, zehn Mark fünfzig.*

Continue similarly in random order with the unnamed items.

Encourage pupils to take on the teacher's role as soon as possible. Insist on correct use of *kostet/kosten*.

Except with very able pupils, it may be best to avoid emphasising the choice of the correct definite article at this stage.

L, S

93
(1A 93)

Was kostet der Film?

Instruct pupils demonstrating with one pair:

T: **Du** legst deine Hand auf den Text.
Dein **Partner** fragt: ,Was kostet der Film?'
Dann antwortest **du**: ,Zehn Mark fünfzig.'
Das ist richtig: ein Punkt. Oder:
,(Ich) weiß nicht.' - kein Punkt.

Dann umgekehrt:
(speaking to the other pupil:)
Du legst deine Hand auf den Text.

While pupils are doing this activity, make sure that they are keeping a score. Check finally by asking ,Wer hat gewonnen?' In the event of a draw, check the score and introduce drei beide, vier beide etc. and/or use unentschieden.

L, S, W

33

Was kostet das?

Tell pupils they are going to fill in the gaps on their worksheets. Choose a pupil to play the part of Schüler(in) B while you assume the role of Schüler(in) A.

T: Also, du bist Schüler(in) B. Ich bin Schüler(in) A.
Was kostet Nummer eins, der Film? Hier (point to DM 10,50, on pupil's worksheet).
P: Zehn Mark fünfzig.
T: Danke. (Write on the board Preis DM 10,50 as you say:) zehn Mark fünfzig. Alles klar? (To whole class) Gut. Jetzt. Partnerarbeit. Nummer zwei, Nummer drei, und so weiter.

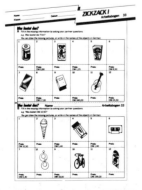

L

93
(1A 93)

Was kaufen die Leute?

Ask pupils to look at the pictures and to write down the letters A-J in the order in which things are bought in the recording.

T: Hört gut zu. Nummer 1 (Play first dialogue).
Was kauft der Mann? (Refer to book) A? B? C?
P. A.
T: Richtig. Schreibt auf: Nummer 1 - A (demonstrate on board).

Was kaufen die Leute?

1 — Was kosten die Postkarten, bitte?
— Die Postkarten? 50 Pfennig das Stück.

2 — Was kostet das Poster, bitte?
— Das da? 8 Mark.
— Oh, danke.

3 — Entschuldigen Sie bitte. Was kosten die Sticker hier vorne?
— Die Sticker kosten alle 1 Mark.

4 — Eine Tafel Schokolade? 3,25 bitte.
— Bitte.
— Danke schön.

5 — Was kosten die Ohrringe?
— Die kleinen? Die kosten 16 Mark.

6 — Ja, bitte?
— Die Notizbücher, was kosten die?
— 2,40.

7 — Was kostet die neue Platte von 'Palace', bitte?
— Moment bitte. Ah ... 29,90.

8 — Eine Flasche Cola, bitte.
— Das macht zwei fünfzig, bitte. Danke schön.

9 — Was kosten die Pommes frites, bitte?
— 3,20 die Portion. Eine Portion?
— Ja, bitte.

10 — Was kostet der Stadtplan, bitte?
— Welcher? Der da?
— Ja.
— Der kostet 6 Mark. Ist aber sehr gut.

Solution: **1**A **2**G **3**J **4**C **5**I **6**E **7**D **8**B **9**H **10**F

L, S

Was kosten die Postkarten, bitte?

Tell pupils to do the true/false activity and play the previous recording *(Was kaufen die Leute)* again.

Buch, Seite 93. Übertragt die Tabelle in euer Heft.
Hört noch einmal zu.
Was kosten die Postkarten? Fünfzig Pfennig.
Was kostet das Poster? Sechs Mark.
Ist das richtig oder falsch?
Macht ein Kreuz in die richtige Spalte.

Afterwards check the results in the following way:

T: *Postkarten 50 Pfennig.*
P: *(Ja,) richtig.*
T: *Poster 6 Mark?*
P: *(Nein,) falsch.*
   usw.

Solution: **1R 2F 3F 4R 5F 6R 7R 8F 9R 10F**

L, S

Wir gehen einkaufen

Four sets of cue-cards for communicative pair-work. Cut up sheets, divide the class into pairs and give each pair a set of two cards. The aim is to generate **natural, adaptable** dialogues. If pupils need further help, refer them to *Tip des Tages*, p.96. When a dialogue has been completed, tell each pair to swap cards with another pair. Pupils who used card A the first time should now use card B.

(Seid ihr) fertig?
Holt euch neue Karten von einem anderen Paar.
A ist jetzt B, und B ist jetzt A.

Eventually each pair should have used all four sets of cards.

Invite a few pairs to perform in front of the class.

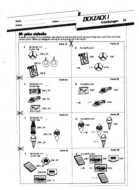

L, S, R

Preissensationen

Practise pronunciation of new vocabulary.

Then ask some pupils: *,Was kaufst du?'*

Draw pupils' attention to the correct use of the articles, using the table in the Pupil's Book (reproduced below).

Ich kaufe	
den einen	die eine
Computer Plattenspieler Stereo-Radio- Rekorder Rechner Kopfhörer Fernsehen	Kamera Videokamera Nähmaschine Gitarre
das ein	die
Radio Fahrrad Fernrohr	Lederhandschuhe Ferngläser Skier

R, W

Wofür sparen sie?

Explain in English that after the word *für* a special form of the words *ein* and *der* is used, the same as they have been practising after *ich kaufe* .... Ask pupils to write out what each person is saving up for, referring them to the table on page 95.

L, S

Zwölf Unterschiede

Divide the class into pairs. One partner has card A, the other card B. By telling each other about the items for sale on their cards, pupils try to identify the twelve differences between cards A and B and make a note of them.

The teacher takes the part of pupil A and chooses someone from the class to be pupil B.

T: *Hast du ein Notizbuch?*
P: *Ja.*
T: *Was kostet das?*
P: *2,50.*
T: *OK. Hast du einen Kopfhörer?*
P: *Ja, er kostet 20,-.*

T: *Hei! Bei mir kostet er 30,-. Das ist ein Unterschied.* (Write *Unterschiede* on the board and make two columns, as below. Write in the first entry *Kopfhörer* as shown.) *Jetzt Partnerarbeit.*

Solution:

A	B
Kopfhörer 30,-	Kopfhörer 20,-
4 Kassetten	3 Kassetten
Radio 95,-	Radio 85,-
Rechner 14,95	Rechner 15,95
Schachspiel 32,50	Schachspiel 36,50
20 Umschläge	40 Umschläge
Taschenmesser 12,75	Taschenmesser 12,25
Kartenspiel 9,90	Kartenspiel 6,90
Briefmarkenalbum 19,-	Briefmarkenalbum 18,-
Keine Ohrringe	Ohrringe 18,-
'Heike' auf dem Becher	'Rudi' auf dem Becher
Tierposter mit Pferd	Tierposter mit Katze

nem 5

240
(1A 118)

R, W

Kostet? Kosten?

A gap-filling activity.

L, S, R

95
(1A 95)

Billig oder teuer?

Tell pupils to look at the pictures.

T: *Seht euch die Bilder und die Preise an. DM 10 für eine Flasche Wein. Ist das zuviel?*
P: *Ja.*
T: *Ja, das ist teuer! Das sind fast vier Pfund.*
150 Mark für ein Fahrrad. Ist das teuer?
P: *Nein.*
T: *Nein, das ist billig.*

Tell pupils that they are going to hear people commenting on the prices of the things shown and that they should listen for other expressions for *billig* and *teuer*. Use the pause button as a signal for repetition. Practise pronunciation of *Wucher*. Refer them to the *Tip des Tages* afterwards.

Billig oder teuer?

1 — 400 Mark für einen Computer. Wie findest du das?
  — Das ist billig.

2 — 10 Mark für eine Flasche Wein. Wie findest du das?
  — Das ist viel zu teuer.

3 — 150 Mark für das Fahrrad! Das ist preiswert!

4 — 3 Mark für die Bonbons. Was meinst du?
  — Tja, ein bißchen teuer.

5 — Guck mal. 2000 Mark für den Ring.
  — Das ist Wucher!

6 — Hier ist eine LP für 9 Mark 50. Wie findest du das?
  — Das ist billig.

7 — Wieviel kostet das?
  — Das T-Shirt? 50 Mark.
  — Nein, das ist viel zu teuer.

8 — Du, nur 2 Mark für die Ohrringe!
  — Mensch, das ist ja sagenhaft billig!

9 — 8 Mark für einen Stadtplan? Ein bißchen teuer.

10 — Eine Stereoanlage für 3000 Mark.
  — Das ist ja Wucher!

11 — 80 Pfennig für ein Eis. Was meinst du?
  — Ja, das ist preiswert.

12 — 150 Mark für Schuhe. Wie findest du das?
  — Das ist ein bißchen teuer.

L, S, (R), W

Tell pupils to make a collage of items from magazines, newspapers etc. for which they know the German and make a separate price list in German currency.
(Homework).

The collages can then be used as prompts for pair-work.

A: (Looking at B's collage):
Was kostet das?
kostet der Computer?
kosten die Ohrringe?

B: *Der Computer? Zweitausend Mark.*
A: *Das ist ein bißchen teuer.*

Monitor the pupils' performance and invite a few pairs to perform in front of the class.

---

nem 6
240
(1A 118)

R, W

He Axel, was kostet ... ?

A gap-filling activity cued by visuals.

R

96
(1A 96)

Auf dem Flohmarkt

A cartoon for comprehension and practice. No exploitation is intended, but point out the practice of pupils buying their own school books in most parts of Germany.

---

nem 7
240
(1A 118)

R, W

Schreibe die Zahlen aus!

Revision of numbers up to one thousand plus.

---

6 Area 5

● Buying things

L, S, R

97
(1A 97)

An der Eisbude

Tell pupils ,*Das ist eine Eisbude. Da kauft man Eis. Nun seht auf die Preisliste'.* Go through the price list, telling them the meaning of all the new words. Then ask them to listen to the first dialogue on the tape.

When they have heard it, say: ,*Ich möchte ein Vanilleeis. Was sage ich?'* Elicit the answer: ,*Einmal Vanille'.*
Repeat for *ein Schokoladeneis*, then play the second dialogue and do the same for *zweimal*.

Finally, read through the transcripts of the dialogue in the Pupil's Book.

An der Eisbude

1 Kunde: — Einmal Vanille und einmal Schokolade, bitte.
Verkäufer: — Mit Sahne?
Kunde: — Nein, danke.
Verkäufer: — Hier, bitte. Eins-vierzig.

2 Kundin: — Zweimal Erdbeer und einmal Schokolade, bitte.
Verkäufer: — Mit Sahne?
Kundin: — Ja, bitte.
Verkäufer: — Drei Mark neunzig.

L

Mit Sahne?

Write the following table (minus the answers) on the board and tell pupils to copy it.

	Eis	Sahne	Preis
1	V S	—	1,40
2	H E	+	2,60
3	Z E	+	2,00
4	S S	+	2,60
5	M V	—	1,40
6	E E H	—	2,10
7	H V	+	2,00
8	M M Z Z	+	5,20

Tell pupils to listen to the recording and make notes of what they can understand. Use S for *Schokolade*, V for *Vanille*, H for *Himbeer* and so on.

Ihr hört einmal Schokolade und ihr schreibt hier ein 'S' hin. Die Kundin oder der Kunde bekommt auch Sahne: ihr schreibt hier ein Pluszeichen. Keine Sahne? Minus. Und hier schreibt ihr den Preis hin.

Mit Sahne?
1 — Einmal Vanille und einmal Schokolade, bitte.
— Mit Sahne?
— Nein, danke.
— Hier, bitte. Eins vierzig.

2 — Einmal Himbeer und einmal Erdbeer, mit Sahne.
— Beide?
— Ja, bitte.
— Zwei Mark sechzig.

3 — Eine Kugel Zitrone und eine Kugel Erdbeer, bitte.
— Mit Sahne?
— Ja, bitte.
— Das macht zwei Mark.

4 — Zweimal Schoko mit Sahne, bitte.
— Zwei sechzig.

5 — Ich hätte gern ein Eis — Mokka und Vanille.
— Möchten Sie auch Sahne?
— Nein, danke.
— Das macht dann eine Mark vierzig.

6 — Zweimal Erdbeer und einmal Himbeer, bitte.
— Mit Sahne?
— Nein, danke.
— Zwei Mark zehn, bitte.

7 — Eine Kugel Himbeer und eine Kugel Vanille, bitte. Mit Sahne.
— Bitt' schön. Zwei Mark.

8 — Zweimal Mokka und zweimal Zitrone, bitte.
— Alle mit Sahne?
— Ja, bitte. Was macht das?
— Fünf Mark zwanzig, bitte.

59-64,
21, 27,
35, 36

See
also

37

L, S

Present the flashcards of other snacks one by one, e.g. *Das ist ein Hamburger*, getting pupils to repeat. After the first three, hold up one of the flashcards and ask *,Was ist das?'* Continue with the next three in the same way, until pupils have seen and said the names of all twelve. Make sure pupils are clear about the meanings of *Chips* and *Pommes frites*.

(der) Hamburger   (das) Schaschlik
(die) Bratwurst   (die) Frikadelle
(das) belegte Brot   (die) Cola
(die) Chips   (der) Apfelsaft
(die) Pommes frites   (die) Limo
(das) Bier

Now tell pupils: *Schreibt eins bis zehn in eure Hefte. Ich halte eine Karte hoch, so,* (hold up *Bratwurst*) *und ich sage ,ein Hamburger'. Stimmt das? Nein! Dann schreibt ihr ,N' für nein. Wenn ,ja', dann schreibt ihr ,J'.*

It is easier to write your list of 1-10 with a mixture of J's and N's **first**, and then to fit your words to the cards accordingly as you go through them. This should be a quick activity, which most pupils will find easy but which nevertheless establishes a confidence in recognising the vocabulary.

Another game for helping pupils to become familiar with the vocabulary: one by one stand the cards in a row with their backs to the class on a table or shelf, naming each one as you position it. Don't work from left to right, but dot them about randomly, filling the gaps with the last ones. (Make sure no pupils are making notes!) Now either divide the class into teams

or choose individuals and ask: *,Wo ist das Schaschlik? Wo sind die Chips?'* etc. The individual or team representative comes up and turns the chosen card, which is removed if he/she is right and replaced if he/she is wrong. If you allow other pupils to call out advice or encouragement this game can be great fun - though noisy!

97
(1A 97)

L, S, R

Hast du Hunger?

Photos of signs, price lists and adverts for reading comprehension.

Give pupils a few minutes to look at the photos, then tell them to look at photo I and ask some simple questions about it, e.g. *,Was kostet hier eine Bratwurst?', ,Kann man hier Chips kaufen?'* Ask similar questions about the other photos. This is best done orally and not with written answers.

Explain in English about the different kinds of sausages as their names occur. Likewise, with *Ketchup* and *Currysoße*.

98
(1A 98)

L, S

Was nimmst du?

Tell pupils to write I to 8 in their books. Explain that they are going to hear eight conversations. The pictures labelled **A-H** show what the people in the conversations are buying. Pupils must write a letter next to each number to show who buys what. Do the first one together as an example.

T: *Ihr hört gleich acht Gespräche. Hier kaufen die Leute etwas zu trinken oder zu essen. Jetzt seht euch das Buch an, Seite 98. Da seht ihr, was die Leute kaufen. Aber wer kauft was? Zum Beispiel, Nummer eins. Hört gut zu!* (Play the first conversation). *Nun, was kaufen sie?*
P: *Eine Cola und zwei Flaschen Bier.*
T: *Richtig. Und wo ist das im Buch?*
P: *Hier. C.*
T: *Gut.* (Write 1C on board) *Und jetzt Nummer 2.*

Was nimmst du?
1 — Was nimmst du, Regina?
— Ich nehme eine Cola.
— Martin?
— Ein Bier, bitte.
— Also, eine Cola und zwei Flaschen Bier, bitte.

2 — Einmal Bratwurst mit Ketchup, bitte.
Und ... was nimmst du?
— Hmm ... Eine Portion Pommes frites für mich.
— Vier achtzig, bitte.

3 — Ja, bitte?
— Zweimal Schaschlik, einmal Bockwurst und ... nee, machen Sie zweimal Bockwurst, bitte.
— So, zweimal Bockwurst und zweimal Schaschlik. Sonst noch etwas?
— Was trinkt ihr denn alle?
— Cola, bitte.
— Ja, ich auch.
— Ich nehme ein Bier.
— Also, drei Cola und ein Bier.
— Das macht neunzehn Mark zusammen.

4 — Ich hätte gern einen Hamburger und eine Bratwurst.
— Mit Ketchup?
— Mit Currysoße, bitte. Und zwei Glas Apfelsaft.
— Bitte sehr.

5 — Zwei belegte Brötchen mit Käse, bitte.
— Etwas zu trinken?
— Nein, danke.
— Das macht vier Mark sechzig.

6 — Du, ich habe Hunger. Essen wir etwas?
— Ja, klar. Guck mal, da ist eine Bude. Was willst du? Pommes frites?
— Ja, gut. Und ich trinke einen Apfelsaft dazu.
— Zwei Portionen Pommes frites, eine Cola und einen Apfelsaft, bitte.

7 — Bitte schön?
— Einmal Schaschlik und ... Karin?
— Zwei Frikadellen, bitte.
— Zwei Frikadellen. Und zweimal Limo. bitte. Was macht das?
— Das macht dreizehn Mark fünfzig, bitte.

8 — Mensch, bin ich durstig! Ich kaufe mir eine Cola. Nimmst du auch etwas?
— Ja, gute Idee.
— Zweimal Cola, bitte.
— Ich glaub', ich kaufe mir auch etwas zu essen.
— Die haben hier nur Chips.
— Wir haben auch Käsestangen.
— Ach ja. Also, zwei, bitte.

Solution: **1C   2F   3B   4H   5A   6D   7G   8E**

---

nem 8   R, W

241
(1A 119)

Du, ich habe Hunger

A gap-filling activity in the form of a dialogue.

L, S

Give instructions for this activity in English.

Divide the class into equal groups. Tell one half they are selling snacks, the other half that they are customers. The best way of organising this is to send the customers out of the room. If not, they must turn away from the board. Write the prices of several snacks/drinks on the board and tell the 'sellers' to make a note of them, e.g.

Bratwurst	1,50
Bockwurst	1,70
Hamburger	2,50
Pommes frites	1,00
Cola	2,10
Apfelsaft	1,40

(N.B. It is important that they have information about more snacks than they will need, so that they really **listen** to the order). When they have copied it down, remove the price list from the board. Now tell the 'customers' (outside the room, if possible), what to order, in English, e.g.

A hamburger, a fried sausage and two apple juices.

Tell them that they must each go to a different stall and order what they have been told. As soon as the seller tells them how much it comes to, they must come to the teacher and say **in English** what they have been charged. If they are right, they have finished. If not, they must go back and go through the transaction again.

When all pairs have finished, change roles and send the other half of the class out. Give the sellers a **different** price list and the customers a different order. Insist that pupils go to a different partner each time.

Most classes will enjoy doing this a number of times. After a while, you could include in the customers' order something that is not on sale. Pupils should be able to cope with *kein, keine* etc.

nem9
241
(1A 119)

Zweimal Cola, bitte

W

An exercise about buying snacks and drinks with the emphasis on accusative forms. Direct pupils' attention to the word list on page 266 (**1A** page 130) for genders.

36

Am Schnellimbiß

R

Pupils read what the customers and stall keepers say and must deduce the prices on the signboard. They can then work out and fill in how much the other four customers will have to pay.

Solution:

Schaschlik	3,20
Bockwurst	2,20
Bratwurst	2,50
Cola	2,00

The customers pay, from left to right, 6,40 14,20 4,50 12,80

37

Was ißt du gern?

(L, S), R, W

This Worksheet can be used in a variety of ways: as reinforcement or a possible homework activity, especially for the less able; as an OHP Master providing an alternative way of presenting and practising different foods; or cut up into cards to play various word games.

---

6 Area 6

- At the fun fair
- Consolidation

L, S, R

100
(1A 100)

Kommst du mit zum Jahrmarkt?

Fun fairs are very common in Germany, especially in spring and autumn. They are very popular with young people.

The visuals introduce the topic and clarify vocabulary, so that pupils should be able to cope with the following questions and give their personal reactions. One-word answers will be adequate in most cases and it is not intended that pupils should be able to produce all the language presented.

— *Gehst du gern zum Jahrmarkt?*
— *Fährst du gern mit dem Riesenrad?*
               der Achterbahn?
               dem Karussell?
               dem Autoscooter?
               der Geisterbahn?
— *Gehst du gern auf die Schiffschaukel?*
— *Macht dir die Geisterbahn*
        eine Schießbude
        eine Losbude   } *Spaß ?*
        eine Wurfbude
        'Haut den Lukas'

If preferred, *Macht dir ... Spaß?* can be used throughout.

L, R, (W)

L, W

99
(1A 99) **Wieviel Geld haben sie dabei?**

Tell pupils to read the text and then listen to
the recording. They should make notes of how
much money each person has.

*Hört gut zu. Wieviel Geld hat David? Wieviel
Geld hat Alison? Ralf? Brigitte?*

Wieviel Geld haben sie dabei?

Alison:	— Brigitte, wieviel Geld hast du dabei?
Brigitte:	— 30 Mark. Meine Oma hat mir 30 Mark gegeben.
Ralf:	— Und wieviel Geld hast du mit, Alison?
Alison:	— 10 Mark. Ist das genug?
Ralf:	— Naja, das geht schon.
David:	— Und du, Ralf? Wieviel Geld hast du dabei?
Ralf:	— Nur 20 Mark.
Brigitte:	— Hast du Geld dabei, David?
David:	— Ja, aber nicht viel. Nur 25 Mark.
Brigitte:	— Naja, das ist nicht schlecht. Fahren wir zuerst mit dem Riesenrad?

R

99
(1A 99) **Fahren wir mit dem Riesenrad?**

This narrative account continues the storyline
of the four young people at the fair. Tell pupils
to answer the questions in English.

nem 10

R, S/W

241
(1A 119) **Wie sagt man das auf Deutsch?**

Tell pupils to find the German in the text for
the five phrases given.

Solution: Fahren wir mit ... ?
gewinnt
Danke für die Fahrt!
Ich spendiere
Es macht ihnen viel Spaß

nem 11

R

241
(1A 119) **Richtig oder falsch?**

True-false questions on the same text.

Solution: **1** richtig **2** richtig **3** falsch
4 richtig **5** falsch

Was gibt es auf dem Jahrmarkt zu essen?

Tell pupils that you are going to play
recordings of dialogues at the fair
ground about what people intend to eat or
drink. Draw the following table (minus the entries)
on the board, and ask pupils to copy it. Teach
Zuckerwatte by means of mime or a drawing.
Tell pupils to fill in the table with the food and
drinks mentioned.

Solution:

	1	2
A	Cola	Apfelsaft
B	Doppelburger	Orangensaft
C	Käsestange	Hamburger
D	Eis	Brötchen
E	Eis	Eis
F	Zuckerwatte	Chips
G	Bratwurst	—
H	Gummibärchen	Eis

Was gibt es auf dem Jahrmarkt zu essen?

A — Ich hab' so einen Durst! Ich kaufe mir
eine Cola.
— Cola trinke ich nicht. Ich kaufe mir einen
Apfelsaft.

B — Mann, habe ich einen Hunger! Ich kaufe
mir einen Doppelburger.
— Ich nicht. Ich trinke nur etwas - einen
Orangensaft.

C — Ich esse eine Käsestange. Und du?
— Nein, ich gehe zur Wurstbude und kaufe
mir einen Hamburger.

D — Gehen wir ein Eis essen?
— Ach nein, ich esse lieber ein Brötchen.

E — Du, ich kaufe mir ein Eis.
— Gute Idee. Ich auch.

F — Die Zuckerwatte da schmeckt gut!
— Nein, die ist mir zu süß. Ich kaufe mir
eine Tüte Chips.

G — Ich esse jetzt eine Bratwurst.
— Ich nicht. Ich hab' keinen Hunger.

H — Ich kaufe mir eine Tüte Gummibärchen.
— Ich hole mir lieber ein Schokoladeneis.

nem 12

R, W

241
(1A 119) **Ich habe Hunger!**

Gap-filling exercise on *einen/eine/ein*.

Auf dem Jahrmarkt

101
(1A 101)

L, S, W

The idea of this activity is for each group of pupils to decide, within a given financial limit but on the basis of their **actual** likes and dislikes, what they are going to eat, drink, ride on or have a go at.

Divide the class into groups of 4 or 5. Tell each group how much they have (allow DM 10 per person).

Now ask pupils to look at the prices on page 101 of the Pupil's Book. Tell them:

Ihr seid auf dem Jahrmarkt. Ihr habt x Mark. Was macht ihr damit? Wofür gebt ihr das Geld aus? (Take someone from one group as an example.) Zum Beispiel, du sagst: ‚Ich kaufe mir eine Bratwurst und eine Cola'. Oder du (choose someone else) sagst: ‚Ich fahre mit dem Riesenrad und ich kaufe mir eine Zuckerwatte.' Aber das muß fair sein! Wenn du sagst ‚Ich kaufe mir ein Schaschlik, ein Schokoladeneis, eine Portion Pommes frites und ein Glas Bier, und ich fahre mit dem Geisterbahn, mit der Achterbahn und mit dem Riesenrad - so ist das nicht fair!

Schreibt auf, was ihr macht!

Go round the class encouraging pupils to discuss it in German, checking that they are keeping an account of what they are spending and ensuring that they use up most of their money. Groups could be asked at the end of the activity to give a short account in German of what they have decided to spend their money on and how much it all comes to.

R, W

38

Die Achterbahn

Part A: Pupils must choose the correct caption to go in each speech bubble, and write them in on the cartoon. This is quite a difficult exercise which could be done in groups.

Part B: A wordsearch based on the *Jahrmarkt* theme.

Solution:

Riesenrad	Apfelsaft	Bier	Chips
Currywurst	Limo	Soße	Erdbeer
Achterbahn	Eis	Sahne	Mokka
Karussell	Cola	Senf	

Cartoon text:

1 Andreas: — Kommst du mit zum Jahrmarkt?
  Sabine: — Ja, gern. Hast du Geld dabei?

2 Andreas: — Zehn Mark.
  Sabine: — Zehn? Na, das geht.

3 Sabine: — Du, ich fahre so gern mit der Achterbahn!

4 Sabine: — Ich habe jetzt Hunger. Essen wir eine Wurst?
  Andreas: — Aber Sabine, ich habe kein Geld mehr.

5 Hanno: — Abend, Sabine! **Ich** kauf' dir was. Diese Schaschliks schmecken prima. Ich hab' schon drei gegessen!

6 Andreas: — Du Schwein!
  Hanno: — Hau ab! Die Sabine geht jetzt mit mir!

7 Andreas: — OK. Aber was Sabine am liebsten macht, ist mit der Achterbahn fahren.

8 Hanno: — So, Süße, fahren wir mit der Achterbahn?

9 Andreas: — Komm, Sabine, ich gehe mit dir nach Hause. Der Jahrmarkt scheint dem Hanno keinen Spaß zu machen!

Solution:

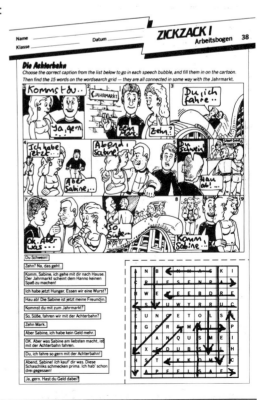

Vocabulary

die Achterbahn(en) *big dipper*
angeln *to fish*
der Angestellte(n) *employee (m)*
die Angestellte(n) *employee (f)*
auslegen *to place on*
aufpassen *to pay attention*
ausfinden *to find out*
ausgeben (für) *to spend money (on)*
ausgehen *to go out*
das Ausland *abroad*
austragen *to deliver*
der Autoscooter(-) *dodgem*
das Babysitten *babysitting*
die Bäckerei(en) *baker's*
die Bank(en) *bank*
bedeuten *to mean, signify*
bekommen *to get*
belegtes Brot *open sandwich*
bezahlen *to pay for*
billig *cheap*
die Bockwurst(⸚e) *sausage*
die Bude(n) *stall, kiosk*
die Currysoße(n) *curry sauce*
die Devisen *(foreign) currency*
das Diagramm(e) *diagram*
die Disko or Disco(s) *disco*
doppel *double*
der Durst *thirst*
durstig *thirsty*
einlösen *to cash in*
das Eis *ice cream*
die Fahrt(en) *journey, trip*
das Fernglas *binoculars*
das Fernrohr(e) *telescope*
die Flasche(n) *bottle*
die Geisterbahn(en) *ghost train*

das Geld *money*
der Groschen *Austrian penny*
das Hähnchen(-) *chicken*
der Handschuh(e) *glove*
'Haut den Lukas' *'Test your strength — ring the bell'*
die Himbeere(n) *raspberry*
hoch *high*
hundert *a hundred*
der Hunger *hunger*
der Imbiß(Imbisse) *snack(bar)*
der Jahrmarkt(⸚e) *funfair*
jawohl *certainly*
der Job(s) *job*
der Jugendklub or Jugendclub(s) *youth club*
das Karussell(s) *roundabout*
die Käsestange(n) *cheese straw*
die Kasse(n) *till*
die Kassette(n) *cassette*
kaufen *to buy*
das Kaugummi *chewing gum*
der Kopfhörer(-) *headphones*
die Kosmetik *cosmetics*
die Kugel(n) *ball*
der Kunde(n) *customer (m)*
die Kundin(nen) *customer (f)*
der Kurs(e) *rate of exchange*
die Leute *people*
die Losbude(n) *lottery stall*
die Mitte(n) *centre*
Mokka *mocca (coffee)*
der Monat(e) *month*
das Motorrad(⸚er) *motorbike*
die Nachhilfe(n) *extra lesson*
die Nähmaschine(n) *sewing machine*
das Notizbuch(⸚er) *notebook*

der Ohrring(e) *earring*
der Paß(Pässe) *passport, identity card*
das Pfund *pound*
die Platte(n) *record*
der Plattenspieler(-) *record player*
das Portemonnaie(s) *purse; wallet*
preiswert *good value*
der Punkt(e) *point; full stop*
der Rappen(-) *Swiss penny*
der Rechner(-) *calculator*
rechts *on the right*
der Reisescheck(s) *traveller's cheque*
das Riesenrad(⸚er) *big wheel*
der Ring(e) *ring*
der Rollschuh(e) *roller skate*
sagenhaft *fabulous*
die Sahne *cream*
der Satz(⸚e) *sentence*
das Schaschlik(s) *kebab*
das Schachspiel(e) *chess game*
der Schalter(-) *counter; switch*
scheinen *to seem, appear; shine*
die Schießbude(n) *shooting gallery, rifle range*
schießen *to shoot*
die Schiffschaukel(n) *swing boat*
schmecken *to taste*
der Schnellimbiß *fast food stall*
die Skier *skis*
die Sonne *sun*
sparen *to save*
die Sparkasse(n) *savings bank*

der Spaß *fun*
spendieren *to buy, get, treat*
speziell *special*
der Stadtplan(⸚e) *streetmap*
der Sticker(-) *badge*
täglich *daily*
das Taschengeld *pocket money*
das Taschenmesser(-) *pocket knife*
teuer *expensive*
tun *to do*
umgekehrt *the other way round*
der Umschlag(⸚e) *envelope*
unentschieden *undecided*
unterschreiben *to sign*
die Vanille *vanilla*
verdienen *to earn*
die Videokamera(s) *video camera*
Wucher! *daylight robbery! a rip-off!*
die Wurfbude(n) *coconut stall*
weggehen *to go out, go away*
wenig *little*
die Zeitschrift(en) *magazine*
die Zeitung(en) *newspaper*
die Zitrone(n) *lemon*
die Zuckerwatte(n) *candy floss*

CHAPTER 7 Willkommen in Osnabrück

Area 1

● Presenting a German town

104-105 (1B 6-7)

Osnabrück - meine Stadt

Tell pupils to listen to the tape while studying, in turn, the places in Osnabrück illustrated on page 104 (**1B** 6).

Macht eure Bücher auf Seite 104 (6) auf: Osnabrück - meine Stadt. Seht euch die Bilder an und hört gut zu.

Osnabrück - meine Stadt

Interviewer: — Wo wohnst du?
Mädchen: — In Osnabrück. Das ist eine Stadt in Nordwestdeutschland. Nicht weit von Hannover.
Interviewer: — Was gibt es da zu sehen?
Mädchen: — Na ja, ich habe hier eine Broschüre über die Stadt, sehen Sie?
(1) Es gibt den Dom. Der Dom ist sehr alt — über 700 Jahre alt, glaube ich.
(2) Osnabrück ist eine alte Stadt. Wir haben eine Mauer rund um die Stadt.
Interviewer: — Und was gibt es sonst für Touristen?
Mädchen: — **(3)** Für Touristen? Es gibt das Rathaus.
(4) Und wir haben auch ein Schloß. Da ist der König Georg der Erste von England gestorben. Heute ist die Universität dort.
Interviewer: — Hat die Stadt viele alte Häuser?
Mädchen: — **(5)** Es gibt das Haus Walhalla in der Bierstraße. Heute ist dort ein Restaurant.
(6) Viel ist aber jetzt modern in der Stadt. Nach dem zweiten Weltkrieg lag Osnabrück in Trümmern.
(7) Die Stadthalle ist auch modern. Hier gibt es manchmal Popkonzerte.
(8) Und hier sehen Sie moderne Einfamilienhäuser in der Weststadt.
Interviewer: — Nicht alle Osnabrücker wohnen in Einfamilienhäusern, oder?

Mädchen: — **(9)** Nein, natürlich nicht. In der Stadtmitte gibt es wenige Einfamilienhäuser. Hier sehen Sie zum Beispiel ein Wohnhochhaus — die meisten Leute wohnen in Wohnungen.
(10) Ja — und was noch? Ach ja, Büros. Es gibt viele neue Büros in der Stadtmitte. Ja, das wäre es.
Interviewer: — Vielen Dank für das Interview.
Mädchen: — Nichts zu danken!

L, S

67-83

In der Stadt

Although *Meine Stadt* has introduced *Es gibt ...*, use the Flashcards initially to present the Nominative Case. Present the places in town in groups of two or three, and refer back to the written text, when appropriate.

T: *Was ist das? ... das ist der Dom.* (To single pupil) *Bitte wiederhol': ,der Dom'.*
P: *Der Dom.*
T: (To p2) *Was ist das?*
P2: *Der Dom.*

Repeat the procedure with five or six pupils before requiring choral repetition. When all cards have been presented, move on to the Accusative, as outlined in the following activity.

L, S, R

67-83

Was gibt es in deiner Stadt zu sehen?

Display the flashcards in turn, presenting the Nominative Case once more, but moving quickly onto the next construction

T: *Das ist der Dom. Was gibt es in deiner Stadt zu sehen? Es gibt den Dom.* (To pupil). *Was gibt es in deiner Stadt zu sehen?*
P1: —
T: *Den Dom. Es gibt den Dom. Was gibt es zu sehen?*
P1: *Es gibt den Dom.*

Use the recording of *Osnabrück- Meine Stadt* to reinforce the point and continue with the presentation until pupils have thoroughly practised the new construction.

Finally, pupils could re-read *Meine Stadt*, numbers 1-5, and answer the question: *,Was gibt es in Osnabrück zu sehen?'* first orally, and then in writing.

103
(1B 5)

Welche Stadt ist das?

Tell pupils to take it in turns to describe one of the towns depicted, without mentioning the name of the town. Partners must work out which town is being described.

T: Also, Seite 103 (5). Welche Stadt ist das? Partnerarbeit. (To Pupil — point unobtrusively to the town you're about to describe). *Also, du. Hör gut zu. Es gibt einen Dom, drei Kinos, einen Bahnhof und ein Freibad. Welche Stadt ist das?*
P: Gütersloh.
T: Richtig. Also, Partnerarbeit.

L, S

---

nem 1

242
(1B 126)

(L, S), R, W

Und deine Stadt?

A simple letter complete with straightforward comprehension questions in German. If necessary, read through the text with the pupils and answer the questions orally before requiring pupils to write out their answers in their exercise books.

---

nem 2

242
(1B 126)

R, W

Lieber Andreas

In this activity, pupils are to answer the letter from the previous section. Tell them to copy out the text, substituting the correct words for the drawings.

---

nem 3

243
(1B 127)

W

Was gibt es in x zu sehen?

Application of the expressions *es gibt ...*, *wir haben*, etc. to pupils' own or nearby town.

---

7 Area 2

● Asking the way

L

Wo ist hier die nächste Post, bitte?

Tell pupils that you are going to play some dialogues and ask them to guess what they are about.

Ihr hört jetzt Dialoge. Worum geht es hier? Antwortet auf Englisch.

Wo ist hier die nächste Post, bitte?

1 — Entschuldigung. Wo ist hier die nächste Post, bitte?
— Hier um die Ecke.
— Danke schön.

2 — Entschuldigung. Wo ist hier wohl das nächste Kino?
— Da drüben.
— Ach ja, danke.

3 — Entschuldigung. Wo ist der Bahnhof, bitte?
— Da hinten.
— Ach ja, danke.

4 — Entschuldigung. Wo ist hier der nächste Parkplatz?
— Hier links.
— Danke.

5 — Entschuldigung. Wo ist das Krankenhaus, bitte?
— Da drüben.
— Ja, danke.

6 — Entschuldigung. Wo ist das Rathaus, bitte?
— Hier rechts, um die Ecke.
— Danke schön.

L, S

Practise the two question forms, (i.e. with and without *nächste*), with known vocabulary, i.e. encourage pupils to repeat after you:

Entschuldigung. Wo ist der Bahnhof, bitte?
          Wo ist die Hauptpost, bitte?
          Wo ist das Krankenhaus, bitte?

This form will usually apply when there is only one such place in a town.

Entschuldigung. Wo ist (hier) das nächste
          Kino (bitte)?
          die nächste
          Disko ?
          der nächste
          Parkplatz?

In these examples, *der/die/das nächste* could be replaced by *ein/eine*, but for the sake of simplicity, the more useful *der/die/das nächste* is taught at this stage.

67-83

L, S

Distribute the Flashcards round the room, either to individual pupils or display them on the wall. Then encourage pupils to ask where various places are.

T: *John, du willst zur Post gehen. Was sagst du?*
P: *Entschuldigung. Wo ist die Post, bitte?*
T: *Da drüben.* (Point).

Continue similarly until pupils have picked up *da drüben, da hinten, hier vorne*. Then ask pupils to take over the teacher's role.

L, S, R

106
(1B 8)

Wer spricht?

Tell pupils to match the drawings and the statements beneath. When they have finished writing, check their answers orally.

Seite 106 (8). Wer spricht? Schreibt 1a oder 1f, zum Beispiel, in euer Heft. (After the written answers have been completed).

T: *Also, Nummer 1.*
P: *C.*
T: *Wo ist ... ?*
P: *Wo ist das Stadion, bitte?*
T: *Gut. Nummer 2 ...*

Solution: **1**c **2**d **3**e **4**a **5**f **6**b

L, S, R

107
(1B 9)

Stadtplan

Tell pupils to study the town map of Osnabrück, on page *107* (**1B** 9), and decide whether the grid references and street names they hear correspond to the places being sought.

T: *Hört gut zu. Ist das richtig oder falsch? Zum Beispiel, ihr hört:*
— Wo ist hier das Verkehrsamt?
— Hier, 5A, in der Martinstraße. (Repeat, then ask:)
Ist das richtig oder falsch?
P: *Falsch.*
T: *Genau. Dann schreibt ihr falsch in euer Heft.* (Write No. 1, *Falsch*, on the board. Then erase it before continuing). *Seid ihr bereit? Gut, hört gut zu.*

Stadtplan
1 — Wo ist hier das Krankenhaus?
   — Hier, eins B, in der Natruperstraße.

2 — Wo ist der Dom?
   — Hier, zwei C — in der Krahnstraße.

3 — Wo ist das Schloß?
   — Hier, sieben B — in der Witterkindstraße.

4 — Wo ist das Museum?
   — Hier, drei A — in der Lotterstraße.

---

5 — Wo ist die Fußgängerzone?
   — Hier, vier D — in der Großen Straße.

6 — Wo ist das Verkehrsamt?
   — Hier, fünf F — in der Witterkindstraße.

7 — Wo ist der Hauptbahnhof?
   — Hier, sieben B — in der Hamburger Straße.

8 — Wo ist der Parkplatz?
   — Hier, acht F — in der Johannisstraße.

Solution: **1** richtig **2** falsch **3** falsch **4** richtig
5 richtig **6** falsch **7** falsch **8** falsch

Once these have been corrected, you may invite pupils to give the correct answers for numbers 2, 3, 6 and 8.

T: *Nr. 2. Ja, das ist falsch. Wie ist es richtig? Nicht zwei C in der Krahnstraße, sondern ... ?*
P: *Zwei D.*

L, S, R

Was ist das?

Tell pupils to take it in turns to refer to the *Stadtplan* and choose a place in town. Then tell them to work out which place in town they have chosen.

T: (To pupil): *Ich bin Partner A, du bist Partner B*
Also, drei A — in der Lotterstraße. Was ist das?
P: *(Das ist) das Museum.*
T: *Richtig. Jetzt bist du dran. Vier F — in der -Straße, usw.*

L, S

106
(1B 8)

Entschuldigung

A series of symbols to cue: *Entschuldigung, wo ist der/die/das ... ?*

T: *Seite 106 (8). ,Entschuldigung'. Partnerarbeit. Nummer eins.* (To pupil). *Stell die Frage hierzu* (pointing to instructions in the Pupil's Book.)
P: *Entschuldigung. Wo ist (hier) der (nächste) Campingplatz, bitte?*
T: (To second pupil). *Bitte, wiederhole: da drüben.*
P2: *Da drüben.*
T: *Gut. Jetzt Partnerarbeit.*

Ich suche das Verkehrsamt

107 (1B 9)

L, S, W

Tell pupils to look at the *Osnabrück Stadtplan* and, following the pattern given in the Pupil's book, say where they want to go using the symbols listed 1—8. Draw pupils' attention to the masculine nouns in particular.

Once this exercise has been successfully completed, invite pupils to produce their own examples, using different places in town and different streets.

Both activities lend themselves to pair-work or classwork.

Ist hier ein Kino in der Nähe?

108 (1B 10)

L, S, R, (W)

A practice activity designed to draw a contrast between the use of the definite article in the previous activity, and the indefinite article in expressions for asking the way. Tell pupils to follow the pattern printed in the Pupil's Book, substituting the underlined words each time with another place in town and the correct street name.

T: *Stell deinem Partner die Frage: ‚Ist hier ein Kino in der Nähe?'*
P1: *Ist hier ein Kino in der Nähe?*
T: *(To P2:) Hier (point to book).*
P2: *Ja. In der Krahnstraße, hier.*
T: *Gut. An die Arbeit. Partnerarbeit.*

The two previous activities could both be consolidated in writing. Certain examples could be juxtaposed. For example: *Ich suche einen Parkplatz. Ist hier ein Parkplatz in der Nähe?*

7 Area 3

• Understanding and giving directions

109 (1B 11)

L, R

Stadtrundfahrt

Ask pupils to look at the visuals in the Pupil's Book and listen to the recording. This presents the basic directions: *links, rechts* and *geradeaus*. The text is not intended for detailed exploitation, but can be tested by questions in English, if required.

T: *Hier ist ein Bus. Die Leute im Bus sind Touristen. Sie besuchen Osnabrück und machen eine Stadtrundfahrt. Der Mann mit dem Mikrofon erklärt alles. Er sagt: Hier links ist der Dom ... usw.*

Stadtrundfahrt

— Guten Morgen, meine Damen und Herren. Mein Name ist Bromma. Herzlich Willkommen in Osnabrück. Wir machen jetzt eine Stadtrundfahrt. Können sie alle gut hören, oder soll ich das Mikrofon ein bißchen lauter stellen? OK? Gut.

Hier links ist der Dom. Der Dom ist aus dem elften Jahrhundert. Hier rechts ist die Stadthalle. Hier gibt es viele Popkonzerte.

— Wo ist das Schloß bitte?

— Das Schloß? Das ist hier geradeaus. Jetzt ist dort die Universität.

Dort links ist das Rathaus. Das Rathaus ist aus dem Jahr 1512.

Hier vorne geradeaus sehen Sie die Stadtmauer. Die Stadtmauer ist aus dem fünfzehnten Jahrhundert.

Hier rechts ist die Altstadt.

Dort links ist die Stadtmitte.

Hier steigen wir aus. Die Stadtrundfahrt ist zu Ende. Auf Wiedersehen. Ich wünsche Ihnen einen schönen Aufenthalt in Osnabrück.

L

Tell pupils that you are going to tell them where certain places are and that they should draw an arrow each time either *links* (←), *rechts* (→) or *geradeaus* (↑).

Hört gut zu.
Die Post ist hier geradeaus. (Draw an arrow on the board.) Der Bahnhof ist da links, usw.

109 (1B 11)

L, S

Straßenschilder

The signs can be used to cue responses such as *hier links, hier rechts* and *hier geradeaus*. Practise with the whole class at first and then continue in pairs.

T: *Wo ist die Post? Hier rechts? Oder hier links? Jetzt Partnerarbeit.*

110
(1B 12)

Wegbeschreibungen

Tell pupils to look at the visuals in their books and listen to the dialogues. Practise the dialogues with the whole class and then continue in pairs.

Seht euch die Bilder an und hört gut zu.
Nummer 1: John, du willst zur Post. Was sagst du?

Wegbeschreibungen

1 — Entschuldigung. Wo ist die nächste Post?
— Die nächste Post? Hier links.
— Danke schön.

2 — Entschuldigung. Wo ist das Freibad?
— Das Freibad ist da rechts.
— Danke schön.

3 — Entschuldigung. Wo ist der Bahnhof?
— Der Bahnhof? Hier geradeaus.
— Danke schön.

4 — Entschuldigung. Wo ist die nächste Disko?
— Hier bis zur Ampel und dann rechts.
— Danke schön.
— Bitte schön.

5 — Entschuldigung. Wo ist das Rathaus, bitte?
— Hier bis zur Kreuzung und dann links.
— Danke schön.
— Bitte schön.

6 — Entschuldigung. Wo ist das Krankenhaus, bitte?
— Hier bis zur Ampel und dann rechts.
— Danke schön.
— Bitte schön.

7 — Entschuldigung. Wo ist das Jugendzentrum, bitte?
— Hier links.
— Danke.
— Bitte.

8 — Entschuldigung. Wo ist die Stadthalle, bitte?
— Hier rechts.
— Danke.
— Bitte.

9 — Entschuldigung. Wo ist die Fußgängerzone, bitte?
— Hier bis zur Ampel und dann rechts.
— Danke schön.
— Bitte schön.

10 — Entschuldigung. Wo ist der Dom, bitte?
— Hier links.
— Danke.
— Bitte.

After practising in pairs, pupils could consolidate in writing, if required.

111
(1B 13)

Erste Straße links

Teach *erste/zweite/dritte Straße links/rechts* by using the visual in the Pupil's Book.

T: *Ich bin hier* (hold up book, or copy on board, and point to x). *Das ist die erste Straße links.* (Hold up book and point) *usw.*
Wo ist der Bahnhof? Die erste Straße links? Die zweite Straße links? Die dritte Straße rechts?
P: *Erste Straße rechts.*
T: *Gut. Und so weiter. Partnerarbeit.*

39

Die Post? Das ist ganz einfach

Tell pupils that they are going to hear dialogues in which people ask the way to various places and that they should mark where each place is on the appropriate street map.

Seht euch die zwei Arbeitsbögen an.
Es sind 8 Ausschnitte aus einem Stadtplan.
Ihr hört jetzt 8 Dialoge.
Ein Mann fragt: ,Wo ist die Post?'
Dann kommt die Antwort: ,Erste Straße links'
und so weiter.
Wo ist die Post? Macht ein Kreuz an die richtige Stelle. (Demonstrate on Board/OHP).

Results are best checked by using an OHP copy of the worksheet plus blank overlay for locations. This can be done either by a pupil or the teacher.

Alternatively, only the acetate copy of the worksheet need be used and individual pupils called upon to mark a location on the overlay. Ask the rest of the class whether they agree or not.

Charles, komm nach vorn.
Mache ein Kreuz an die richtige Stelle.
Ist das richtig?/Stimmt das?/Ist das die Post?

Die Post? Das ist ganz einfach

1 — Entschuldigung. Wo ist hier die Post? Wie komme ich am besten dahin?
— Tja, nehmen Sie die dritte Straße links. Die Post ist auf der rechten Seite.
— Ist das weit von hier?
— Nee, so etwa drei Minuten.
— Danke.
— Bitte.

2 — Entschuldigung. Wie komme ich zum Krankenhaus?
— Zum Krankenhaus? Ja, das ist ganz einfach. Hier geradeaus, dann die erste Straße links rein, auf der linken Seite.
— Also — geradeaus, dann die erste Straße links. Danke schön.
— Bitte sehr.

3 — Entschuldigung. Wo ist hier die nächste Bank, bitte?
— Eine Bank? Ja, gehen Sie hier links, dann geradeaus. Dann biegen Sie rechts ab. Das heißt, die erste Straße rechts. Dann sehen Sie die Bank auf der linken Seite.
— Also, hier links, dann die erste Straße rechts. Schönen Dank.
— Nichts zu danken.

4 — Entschuldigung. Können Sie mir sagen, wo das Sportzentrum ist?
— Das Sportzentrum?
— Ja. Ist das weit von hier?
— Ja, ziemlich weit. So anderthalb Kilometer. Das Sportzentrum ist in der zweiten Straße links nach dem Kino.
— Na — geradeaus, etwa anderthalb Kilometer und dann die zweite Straße links nach dem Kino.
— Genau.
— Danke schön.
— Gern geschehen.

5 — Entschuldigung. Wo ist denn hier die Bushaltestelle?
— Da drüben. Sehen Sie?
— Ach ja. Danke.
— Bitte.

6 — Entschuldigung. Geht's hier zum Dom?
— Zum Dom? Hier geradeaus, an der Post biegen Sie links ab, dann kommen Sie direkt zum Dom.
— Ist das die erste oder die zweite Straße links?
— Ach ja, Entschuldigung. Das wäre die zweite, nein, die dritte Straße links. Alles klar?
— Ja, danke. Auf Wiedersehen.
— Auf Wiedersehen.

7 — Entschuldigung. Können Sie mir den Weg zum Rathaus zeigen?
— Zum Rathaus? Oh — haben Sie ein Auto?
— Nein, ich gehe zu Fuß.
— Also, gehen Sie hier geradeaus bis zum Dom, dann gehen Sie nach rechts, dann etwa 500 Meter geradeaus. Das Rathaus ist dann auf der linken Seite.
— Ist das weit von hier?
— Ja, ziemlich weit. 15 Minuten zu Fuß.
— Ach, das geht schon. Danke.
— Bitte schön.

8 — Entschuldigung. Wo ist der Campingplatz, bitte?
— Der Campingplatz? Sie fahren mit dem Rad?
— Ja.
— Das ist gut. Es ist nämlich ziemlich weit. Also hier geradeaus, ungefähr zweieinhalb Kilometer, dann biegen Sie an der Hauptpost links ab. Den Campingplatz sehen Sie dann auf der rechten Seite, und zwar hinter dem Freibad.
— Also geradeaus, dann biege ich an der Post links ab. Danke sehr.
— Bitte schön.

Solution:

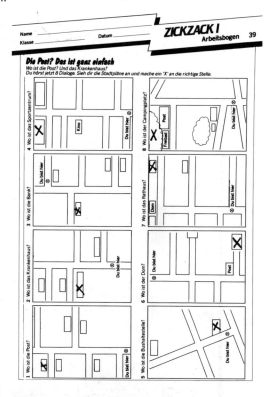

104

Play dialogues 7 and 8 of the previous recording. Stop the tape after ... *auf der linken Seite* in dialogue 7.

T: *Auf der linken Seite? Was ist das auf Englisch?*
P: On the left.
T: *Und auf Deutsch?*
P: *Auf der linken Seite.*

Use the same procedure for *auf der rechten Seite*, dialogue 8.

Practise using the positions where pupils are seated in the classroom.

Wo sitzt David? Auf der linken Seite? Oder auf der rechten Seite?

Ich suche die Post

L

Tell pupils to listen to the dialogues and work out what the destinations represented by **A-H** are.

T: *Hört gut zu. Wo ist die Post?* (Play the first dialogue).
P: *F.*
T: *Richtig.* (Write *die Post* = F on the board). *Jetzt hört zu und schreibt die Antwort in euer Heft.*

Ich suche die Post

1 — Ich suche die Post. Ist das weit von hier?
— Ja, ziemlich weit. Am besten fahren Sie mit dem Bus. Es ist zehn Minuten mit dem Bus.
— Danke.

2 — Ich suche das Freibad. Ist es weit von hier?
— Nein, nur zehn Minuten zu Fuß. Hier geradeaus.
— Danke.
— Bitte.

3 — Entschuldigung. Wo ist bitte das Krankenhaus? Ist es weit von hier?
— Das Krankenhaus? Moment mal. Ja, das ist hier geradeaus. Vielleicht fünf Minuten zu Fuß.
— Danke schön.
— Bitte schön, gern geschehen.

4 — Entschuldigung. Ich suche den Bahnhof.
— Ja, der Bahnhof ist zwei Kilometer von hier.

5 — Ich suche den Sportplatz. Ist es weit von hier?
— Nein, nicht weit. So zwei hundert Meter oder so.

6 — Entschuldigung. Ist der Dom weit von hier?
— Den Dom suchen Sie? Das ist nicht weit. Vielleicht fünfhundert Meter. Hier diese Straße entlang und dann gleich rechts.
— Danke.
— Bitte.

7 — Wo ist die Stadtmauer, bitte? Ist sie weit von hier?
— Nein, nicht weit. Vielleicht ein Kilometer.
— Danke.
— Bitte.

8 — Entschuldigung. Wo ist das nächste Café? Ist es weit von hier?
— Nein, überhaupt nicht. Es ist gleich hinter dem Dom. So hundert Meter entfernt.
— Ach, danke schön.
— Bitte schön.

Solution: **1**F **2**B **3**H **4**C **5**G **6**D **7**A **8**E

Ist es weit von hier?

L, S, R

An information gap activity practising asking how far away somewhere is and understanding distances.

T: *Also, ich suche die Jugendherberge. Partnerarbeit. Stell die Frage* (point to question on worksheet). *Entschuldigung, ich suche die Jugendherberge. Ist es weit von hier? Und die Antwort heißt?*
P: *Ja, ein Kilometer.*
T: *Richtig. Jetzt macht weiter.*

nem 4 Also, du gehst hier geradeaus
243
(1B 127)

An activity practising giving directions in realistic situations.

nem 5 Die Post? Das ist zwei Minuten zu Fuß
243
(1B 127)

An activity practising expressions of distance.

7 Area 4

● Obtaining information from a Tourist Office and finding out what there is to do and see

112
(1B 14)

L, R

Im Verkehrsamt

Play the recording without referring pupils to the visuals on page 112 and ask them, in English, what they think it is about, where it takes place and who might be speaking. Then tell pupils to listen to the recording a second time whilst looking at the visuals.

Im Verkehrsamt

Touristin:	— Guten Tag. Ich bin erst seit gestern hier in Osnabrück. Was für Informationsmaterial haben Sie über die Stadt?
Assistentin:	— Wir haben einen Stadtplan, Broschüren, Posters, Bücher, Hotellisten und Prospekte.
Touristin:	— Also. Ich möchte einen Stadtplan, eine Broschüre, eine Hotelliste und Prospekte über Restaurants und Ausflüge haben, bitte.
Assistentin:	— Ja, also, bitte schön.
Touristin:	— Danke. Was kostet das, bitte?
Assistentin:	— Gar nichts. Das ist alles kostenlos.
Touristin:	— Oh, schön. Vielen Dank.
Assistentin:	— Bitte schön. Auf Wiedersehen.
Touristin:	— Auf Wiedersehen.

Was hat die Frau im Verkehrsamt?

Cue to the use of the Accusative Case by asking pupils to reiterate what is on offer in the *Im Verkehrsamt* on page 112 (**1B** 14). Once they have completed this relatively straightforward exercise, ask them to try and remember what the tourist requests. Re-play the recording, if necessary.

T: *Was hat die Frau im Verkehrsamt? Seht euch die Bilder auf Seite 112 (14) an. Sie hat ...*
...
P1: *... einen Stadtplan.*
T: *Gut. Sie hat einen Stadtplan und ...*
P2: *Broschüren.*
T: *Und jetzt: Was bekommt die Touristin? Sie bekommt ...*
P1: *... einen Stadtplan.*
T: *Gut. Sie bekommt einen Stadtplan und ...*
P2: *... eine Broschüre.*

Finally, collate the information on the board, as follows:

die Frau im Verkehrsamt hat	einen Stadtplan, Broschüren, Posters, Bücher, Prospekte über ... Ausflüge
die Touristin bekommt	einen Stadtplan, eine Broschüre, eine Hotelliste und Prospekte über Restaurants und Ausflüge.

Revise *kein, keine* by asking pupils what the tourist did not request.

T: *Bekommt die Touristin ein Poster?*
P1: *Nein.*
T: *Nein, sie bekommt* (mouth *kein* to P1) *...*
P1: *Kein Poster.*
T: *Bekommt sie Fahrkarten und Prospekte über Konzerte?*
P2: *Nein. Sie bekommt keine Fahrkarte(n) und keine Prospekte über Konzerte.*

Add this information to tables drawn on the board and tell pupils to copy it into their exercise books.

T: *Also. Tragt alles in euer Heft ein. So: 'Im Verkehrsamt'* (write title on board).

L, S

112
(1B 14)

Was kann ich heute nachmittag machen?

Refer pupils to the symbols drawn on the *Stadtplan* on page 107 (**1B** 9), and play the recording of the conversation in the Tourist Information Office. All they could do at this stage is identify the tourist attractions illustrated in the book as they are mentioned on the recording.

Seht euch den Stadtplan auf Seite 107 (9) an. Rechts seht ihr sechs Symbole. Worauf weisen sie hin? Hört gut zu.

Play the recording, pausing after each attraction is mentioned to ask individual pupils to point to the relevant symbol.

T: *'Es gibt den Dom.'*
T: *Welches Symbol weist darauf hin?*
P1:   *Das hier* (pointing to cathedral illustration).
T: *Gut. Was gibt es zu sehen?*
P1:   *Es gibt den Dom.*

Was kann ich heute nachmittag machen?

Tourist:	— Guten Tag. Ich kenne die Stadt überhaupt nicht. Was kann ich heute nachmittag machen? Was gibt es hier zu sehen?
Assistant:	— Es gibt den Dom. Sie können den Dom besichtigen.
Tourist:	— Ach, der Dom interessiert mich überhaupt nicht.
Assistant:	— Es gibt ein modernes Freibad in der Stadt. Sie können schwimmen gehen.
Tourist:	— Nein, lieber nicht. Es ist zu kalt.
Assistant:	— Oder die Stadtmauer und das Schloß. Sie können das Schloß und die alte Stadtmauer besichtigen.
Tourist:	— Ja, vielleicht. Was noch?
Assistant:	— Es gibt Ausflüge. Sie können eine Fahrt auf dem Fluß machen.
Tourist:	— Oh nein. Ich fahre nicht gern mit dem Schiff.
Assistant:	— Na, der Zoo. Es gibt einen Zoo hier.
Tourist:	— Ja gut. Ich kann den Zoo besuchen. Prima.

Solution: **D, A, C, E, F, B**

Was gibt es hier (in ...) zu sehen?

Ask pupils what there is to see either in their own or the nearest sizeable town. Refer them to the previous activity, including the recording, if necessary. When they have practised the new construction sufficiently, move on to the pair-work activity.

41

Was gibt es hier zu sehen?

Consolidation of *es gibt* + Accusative *(den/einen, die/eine, das/ein).*

Jetzt Partnerarbeit. Stelle deinem Partner oder deiner Partnerin die Frage hier (point to the question on the worksheet): *'Was gibt es hier zu sehen?'*

Demonstrate, if necessary, the first example.

Du da hinten

113
(1B 15)

Clarify the meaning of *da hinten, hier vorn, da drüben.*

Point at pupils in various parts of the classroom, e.g.:

Du da hinten, steh auf.
Du da drüben, heb die Hand.
Du hier vorn, halt den Mund.

Then draw a diagram of the classroom on the board and label it as follows:

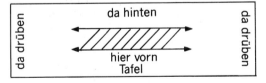

Das hier ist unser Klassenraum.
Dies ist die Tafel. Die Tafel ist vorn.
Das ist hier vorn.
Das ist da hinten.
Das ist da drüben.

Finally, refer pupils to their own copy of the diagram, on page *113*.

113
(**1B** 15)

L, (S), R, W

Wo ist das, bitte?

Tell pupils to listen to the dialogues and to write down in their exercise books where the places mentioned are situated.

T: *Seite 113 (15). ‚Wo ist das, bitte?' Hört gut zu.* (Play the first dialogue). *Also, Haus Walhalla — wo ist das?*
P1: *In der Bierstraße.*
T: *Richtig. Seht ihr hier* (point to *in der* at the front of the page). *In der Bierstraße.* (Write the answer on the board). *Gut. Hört zu!*

Wo ist das, bitte?

1 — Entschuldigung. Ich suche das Haus Walhalla. Wo ist das, bitte?
— In der Bierstraße.

2 — Du, Walter. Wo ist denn nur das Auto?
— Immer mit der Ruhe. Es ist im Parkhaus.
— Ach ja, im Parkhaus, natürlich.

3 — Entschuldigung. Ich suche das Verkehrsamt. Wo ist das, bitte?
— Hinter der Kirche.
— Danke.

4 — Ist hier ein Stadion in der Nähe?
— Ein Stadion? Ja, hinter dem Freibad.
— Ach ja. Da drüben. Danke sehr.
— Bitte sehr.

5 — Wo ist der Parkplatz?
— Da hinten — hinter dem Dom.

6 — Wo hast du geparkt?
— Vor der Stadthalle.
— Wo?
— Vor der Stadthalle.
— Ach so!

7 — Entschuldigung. Wo ist die nächste Bushaltestelle, bitte?
— Da drüben, sehen Sie? Vor dem Bahnhof.
— Danke.

8 — Ich möchte das Schloß besichtigen. Wo ist das, bitte?
— Es ist hinter dem Park.

9 — *(Am Telefon).* Du, hör mal. Ich bin in fünf Minuten da.
— OK. Ich warte an der Bushaltestelle.
— An der Haltestelle?
— Ja.
— Alles klar. Tschüs.
— Tschüs.

10 — Sie können den Dom besichtigen.
— Wo ist das, bitte?
— Am Marktplatz.
— Am Marktplatz. Ist es weit von hier?
— Nein — zwei Minuten.
— Vielen Dank.
— Nichts zu danken.

---

nem 6

243
(**1B** 127)

L, S, R, W

An der Stadthalle, oder?

Tell pupils to practise, in pairs, the use of *in der/im, an der/am, vor der/vor dem, hinter der/hinter dem,* using the visuals on page 243 (**1B** 127). In each instance they have a centrepiece: *Stadthalle, Park, Hallenbad* to use for reference.

When they have completed the pair-work activity, tell them to write out the answers in short form. For each activity complete the first example with a pupil and write the answer on the board.

T: (To pupil). *Du bist mein(e) Partner(in). Stell die Frage. Hier* (point to first question).
P1: *Wo ist die Post?*
T: *Die Post? An der Stadthalle.* (Write answer on the board). *Und jetzt stelle ich dir die nächste Frage: ‚Und das Auto?'* (Wo ist das Auto?)
P1: *Vor der Stadthalle.*
T: *Gut.* (To class). *Also, Partnerarbeit.*

7 Area 5

● **Finding out about the people in a town**

114-115 (1B 16-17)

R

Menschen in Osnabrück

Read through the texts with the pupils after they have studied them in silence. When the readings are complete, prepare pupils for the following listening activity by matching the six shortened dialogues, on page 115 (**1B** 17), to the six people interviewed.

T: Seht euch die zwölf Fotos auf Seite 114-115 (16-17) an und lest die Texte A-F. Jetzt wollen wir die Texte zusammen vorlesen.

(Read the first text in full, then ask pupils to read the replies only of those interviewed. You take the part of the interviewer).
Interviews. Hier sind ein paar Ausschnitte, aus den Interviews auf Seite 114 (16). Wer ist das (read no. 1)?
P1: Ian G.
T: Richtig. Und wer ist das ... ?

115 (1B 17)

L

Wer spricht?

Tell pupils to listen to the recordings of the full interviews and write down, in their exercise books, the names of the interviewees in the order in which they are interviewed.

Seht euch die zwölf Fotos an und hört gut zu. Wer spricht?

Play the first interview and ask pupils to identify the speaker.

T: Also — wer spricht?
P: Hans K.
T: Richtig. Gut. Ihr schreibt: ,Nummer 1, Hans K' (write on board). Verstanden? Gut.

Wer spricht?

1 Interviewer: — Guten Tag. Sind Sie in Osnabrück geboren?
Hans K: — Ja — im Jahre 1919.
Interviewer: — Wie gefällt es Ihnen hier?
Hans K: — Ach, früher war das besser. Jetzt ist alles modern in der Stadtmitte. Es gibt nur ein paar alte Häuser.

2 Interviewer: — Guten Tag.
Kurt Z: — Guten Tag.
Interviewer: — Arbeiten Sie hier in Osnabrück?
Kurt Z: — Ja, ich arbeite bei der Autofirma Karmann.
Interviewer: — Haben Sie Kinder?
Kurt Z: — Ja, einen Sohn und eine Tochter.
Interviewer: — Was sind Ihre Hobbys?
Kurt Z: — Mein großes Hobby ist Fußball.

3 Interviewer: — Hallo, wohnst du in Osnabrück?
Ali T: — Ja, in der Weststadt. Ich bin hier geboren.
Interviewer: — Wie alt bist du?
Ali T: — Vierzehn.
Interviewer: — Wie lange wohnen deine Eltern hier?
Ali T: — Die sind vor sechzehn Jahren aus der Türkei eingewandert.

4 Interviewer: — Hallo.
Ellen M: — Guten Tag.
Interviewer: — Bist du in Osnabrück geboren?
Ellen M: — Nein, wir haben früher in Rheine gewohnt. Wir wohnen erst seit zwei Jahren hier.
Interviewer: — Gehst du noch zur Schule?
Ellen M: — Ja, ich bin erst fünfzehn.
Interviewer: — Wie gefällt dir die Schule?
Ellen M: — Nicht gut.

5 Interviewer: — Guten Tag. Sind Sie in Osnabrück geboren?
Ian G: — Nein, nein. Ich bin Engländer.
Interviewer: — Was machen Sie hier in Osnabrück?
Ian G: — Ich bin Soldat — das heißt, ich bin Major in der Rheinarmee.
Interviewer: — Wohnen Sie hier in der Stadtmitte?
Ian G: — Nein, wir haben ein Haus am Stadtrand, aber meine Frau geht gern bei Hertie und Horten einkaufen.

6 Interviewer: — Sind Sie in Osnabrück geboren?
Theo K: — Nein, ich bin Grieche.
Interviewer: — Wo arbeiten Sie?
Theo K: — Ich habe ein Restaurant hier in der Stadt.
Interviewer: — Aha. Was für ein Restaurant?
Theo K: — Das ist eine Taverne. Meine Frau kocht griechische Spezialitäten. Sehr populär bei den Deutschen.

7 Interviewer: — Guten Tag. Sind Sie hier geboren?
Jochen B: — Ja.
Interviewer: — Arbeiten sie auch in der Stadt?
Jochen B: — Ja, in der Polizeiwache. Ich bin Polizist.
Interviewer: — Gibt es Probleme hier?
Jochen B: — Ganz selten. Nur manchmal mit den Demonstranten oder den Fußballrowdys.

8 Interviewer: — Guten Tag. Wohnen Sie gern in Osnabrück?
Volker S: — Osnabrück ist eine schöne Stadt, aber ich bin nicht so gern hier.
Interviewer: — Warum denn?
Volker S: — Weil ich Soldat bin, und in der Kaserne sind wir zehn Mann in einem Raum.

9 Interviewer: — Hallo. Wie alt bist du?
Laura M: — Sechzehn.
Interviewer: — Hast du einen Job hier?
Laura M: — Ich gehe noch zur Schule, aber abends arbeite ich in der Pizzeria. Ich bin nämlich Italienerin, und mein Vater hat eine Pizzeria.
Interviewer: — Hast du viele deutsche Freunde?
Laura M: — Ja — jede Menge.

10 Interviewer: — Sind Sie in Osnabrück geboren?
Heide L: — Nein. Ich bin Studentin hier.
Interviewer: — Was machen Sie am liebsten in der Freizeit?
Heide L: — Am liebsten bummle ich durch die Fußgängerzone.

11 Interviewer: — Guten Tag. Arbeiten Sie hier in Osnabrück?
Martin F: — Ja. Ich bin Lehrer am Carolinum.
Interviewer: — Das ist eine Schule, oder?
Martin F: — Die älteste Schule in Deutschland.
Interviewer: — Was ist das größte Problem für Ihre Schüler?
Martin F: — Viele junge Leute finden heute keinen Job.

12 Interviewer: — Kennen Sie Osnabrück gut?
Gerd B: — Ja, natürlich.
Interviewer: — Wieso - sind Sie hier geboren?

Gerd B: — Nein, aber ich bin Busfahrer, also ...
Interviewer: — Ach so. Was gefällt Ihnen am besten in der Stadt?
Gerd B: — Die Kneipen in der Innenstadt. Da gibt es saugutes Bier.

Order of interviewees:

1	Hans K	7	Jochen B
2	Kurt Z	8	Volker S
3	Ali T	9	Laura M
4	Ellen M	10	Heide L
5	Ian G	11	Martin F
6	Theo K	12	Gerd B

L, S, R

115
(1B 17)

Wer ist das?

Tell pupils to read the descriptions and short dialogues (A-F) again. They should then work in pairs. Partner A is the interviewer, Partner B is any one of the twelve people from Osnabrück. By asking questions which require yes/no answers, Partner A must decide who the other person is. The roles can then be reversed.

nem 7

244
(1B 128)

(L, S), R, W

Wohnen die Osnabrücker gern in Osnabrück?

Tell pupils to read these extracts from *Wer spricht?*. If necessary, help to elucidate potentially difficult items of vocabulary:

T: *Selten? Das heißt nicht oft.*
Nett? Schön, gut.

Then tell them to copy the table into their exercise books and decide which of the comments are positive and which are negative. Again, if necessary, discuss some of the statements with pupils before they write them up in one or other of the columns.

T: *Viele junge Leute finden heute keinen Job. Ist das positiv oder negativ?*
P: *Negativ.*
T: *Ja, natürlich, negativ. So* (write the sentence up on the board under *Negative Bemerkungen*).

nem 8

244
(1B 128)

W

Und du? Was sagst du über deine Stadt?

For this consolidation activity, pupils can draw directly from the previous activity.

nem 9

244
(1B 128)

W

Menschen in meiner Stadt

Using *Menschen in Osnabrück,* make up similar descriptions of people who live in your town or village.

nem 10

244
(1B 128)

W

Meine Stadt

Tell pupils to design a brochure or a poster advertising their town (in German, of course!).

L, S, R

Ein Quiz: Menschen in Osnabrück

Twelve questions about further details in *Menschen in Osnabrück.* This can be done in various ways. One way would be to split the class into two teams and to ask them questions in turn, and award points for correct answers. Note that some questions apply to more than one person. Sometimes (e.g., with *Wer geht noch zur Schule?),* inference is involved (as Ali is only 14, he should be included).

 (Mime:) *Gruppe A, Gruppe B*

*Wir machen jetzt einen Quiz. A gegen B.
Ich stelle 12 Fragen über die Menschen in Osnabrück.
Seht euch die Texte an.
Für jede richtige Antwort gibt es einen Punkt.
Ich schreibe die Punkte an die Tafel.* (Write A and B on the board).
Los geht's.

Some suggested questions:

1 Wer ist in Großbritannien geboren?
2 Wer ist Studentin?
3 Wer ist nicht Deutsche?
4 Wer geht noch zur Schule?
5 Wer ist sehr alt?
6 Wer hat zwei Kinder?
7 Wer ist Lehrer?
8 Wer ist Fußballfan?
9 Wer ist Soldat?
10 Wer ist fünfundfünfzig Jahre alt?
11 Wer arbeitet in einer Pizzeria?
12 Wer arbeitet in Deutschlands ältester Schule?

116
(1B 18)

R

Einige Informationen: Gastarbeiter in Deutschland

When pupils have read the text and answered the comprehension questions, you may like to expand, in English, on the relatively unfavourable position of the *Gastarbeiter* and on the problems faced by those European countries which recruited a sizeable *Gastarbeiter* workforce, in order to fill the dirtier, less well-paid jobs, only to find that the country's economic situation later led to rising unemployment and, with it, pressure to encourage numbers of *Gastarbeiter* to return to their former homelands (or that of their parents and grandparents).

116
(1B 18)

L, S, R, (W)

Wann bist du geboren?

Tell pupils to look at the cartoons. Practise saying the years, e.g.:

 *Neunzehnhundertdreiunddreißig
Siebzehnhundertsiebzig*

Then ask pupils:
*Wann bist du geboren?
Wann ist dein Bruder geboren?*
etc.

Encourage pupils to ask each other round the class.
This can be consolidated in writing.

---

7 Area 6

● Consolidation

L, S, R

117
(1B 19)

Einige Informationen: Viele Wege führen nach Osnabrück

Geographical information about Osnabrück, such as is found in town brochures.

Verkehrsknotenpunkt should be understood from the dialogues.

 T: *Jetzt lesen wir Informationen über Osnabrück. Wo liegt Osnabrück? Die E8 ist eine Autobahn. Sie führt von Holland nach Hannover und dann weiter nach ... ?*

Wie weit ist es von Osnabrück nach Hamburg mit der Eisenbahn? (Mit dem Zug). Wieviel Meilen sind das? Und auf der Autobahn? Osnabrück hat einen Hafen für Schiffe. Die Elbe ist ein Fluß. Die Elbe fließt von der DDR nach Hamburg. Die Weser ist auch ein Fluß. Wohin fließt die Weser? Es gibt zwei Kanäle in der Nähe von Osnabrück. Wie heißen sie?

R

Ein Brief an David

A letter to an English penfriend describing the exact location of a house. This provides written consolidation of directions. Pupils are required to check the instructions with the map of the town in order to find the house. The date of the letter is 1st April.

R

Wo ist das Hallenbad?

A cartoon practising various forms of asking the way. This could be performed as a playlet.

L, S

Wo ist der Ausgang?

Someone is lost in the centre of a maze. Ask pupils to work in pairs and direct each other out of the maze.

R

Wie ist es richtig?

Four cartoons to illustrate the differences between *Eingang/Einfahrt; Ausgang/Ausfahrt.* Only one of the drawings (no. 2) is correct.

L

Welche Linie ist das?

Ask pupils to listen to the recording and look at the diagram showing the bus routes. They must work out the number of each route.

T: *Seht euch die Buslinien an und hört gut zu.* (Play the first recording). *Welche Linie ist das? Ist das A, B, C? Und was ist die Nummer?*
P: *Das ist A, die Linie 19.*
T: *Ja richtig. A = 19* (write on board).

Jetzt macht weiter.

Welche Linie ist das?

1 —Wohin fährt die Nummer 19, bitte?
   —Die Linie 19? Der Bus fährt von der Stadtmitte nach Schenefeld. Es gibt eine Haltestelle vor der Hauptpost.

2 —Welcher Bus fährt zum Hallenbad, bitte?
   —Das ist die Linie 15. Das ist die nächste Haltestelle nach dem Dom.

3 —Fährt die Nummer 38 bis zum Bahnhof?
   —Ja, der Bahnhof ist die nächste Haltestelle nach dem Jugendzentrum.

4 —Fährt ein Bus zum Campingplatz?
   —Ja, die Nummer 25. Der Bus fährt an dem Kino vorbei, und dann sind es vielleicht noch fünf Minuten bis zum Campingplatz.
   —Ja, gut danke. Welche Linie war das nochmal?
   —Linie 25.

5 —Welche Nummer fährt zum Schloß, bitte?
   —Das ist die Linie 30. Das Schloß ist die nächste Haltestelle nach dem Rathaus.
   —Danke schön.
   —Bitte schön.

6 —Welcher Bus fährt zum Stadion, bitte?
   —Das ist die Linie 5. Fahren Sie bis zur Stadthalle. Das Stadion ist dann die nächste Haltestelle.

7 —Fährt ein Bus zum Freibad?
   —Ja, natürlich.
   —Welche Linie?
   —Linie 14.
   —Ist es weit von hier?
   —Nein, nur fünf Minuten.
   —Das Freibad kommt gleich nach dem Verkehrsamt.
   —Danke.
   —Bitte.

Solution: 19 **A**; 15 **B**; 38 **F**; 25 **G**; 30 **C**; 5 **E**; 14 **D**.

43

Wo ist die Post?

An information-gap activity practising giving directions. Tell pupils in English that they must work out in turn where the next place is located.

Jetzt Partnerarbeit. (Demonstrate with one pair). *Ann, du bist hier. Du fragst: ,Wo ist die Post?' Du, Jane, antwortest: ,Das ist die zweite Straße links auf der linken Seite.' Du* (to Ann) *schreibst: ,Post hier'* (point). *Jetzt seid ihr alle dran.*

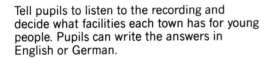

Was gibt's da für junge Leute?

Tell pupils to listen to the recording and decide what facilities each town has for young people. Pupils can write the answers in English or German.

Hört gut zu. Was gibt es in Krempe, in Wedel, in Schenefeld usw. (write on board) *für junge Leute? Schreibt es in euer Heft (auf Deutsch/Englisch).*

Was gibt's da für junge Leute?

1 — Wo wohnst du?
   — In Krempe.
   — Was gibt's in Krempe für junge Leute?
   — Es gibt eine große Sporthalle. Aber das ist alles. Wir haben keine Disko und kein Jugendzentrum. Nichts. Im Winter kann man auf dem See vor der Schule Schlittschuh laufen.

2 — Wo wohnst du?
   — Ich wohne in Wedel.
   — Was gibt's da für junge Leute?
   — Es gibt ein schönes Jugendzentrum und ein Kino.
   — Ja, und was noch?
   — Es gibt auch ein Hallenbad, eine Sporthalle und einen Sportplatz.

3 — Wo wohnst du?
   — Ich wohne in Schenefeld.
   — Was gibt's in Schenefeld für junge Leute?
   — Es gibt nichts da! Absolut nichts. Aber Hamburg ist ganz in der Nähe. Da gibt's alles: Diskos, Kinos, Schwimmhallen, Tennishallen, ein großes Fußballstadion, alles.

4 — Wo wohnst du?
   — In Elmshorn.
   — Was gibt's da für junge Leute?
   — Die Stadt ist ganz gut für junge Leute. Wir haben zwei Kinos. Es gibt ein Jugendzentrum, Squash-und Tennishallen, eine Schwimmhalle, Diskos, Cafés, alles. Ich wohne ganz gern hier.

5 — Wo wohnst du?
   — In Pinneberg.
   — Was gibt's da für junge Leute?
   — Nicht viel. Pinneberg ist eine kleine Stadt. Es gibt zwei Diskos, ein Jugendzentrum, einen Sportplatz, ein Stadion, ein Hallenbad und ein neues Café.

6 — Wo wohnst du?
   — Ich wohne in Tornesch.
   — Was gibt's da für junge Leute?
   — Es gibt eine Sporthalle im Schulzentrum und zwei Tennisplätze. Wir haben kein Jugendzentrum, aber wir haben eine Disko.

7 — Wo wohnst du?
   — In Uetersen.
   — Was gibt's da für junge Leute?
   — Wir haben fünf Sporthallen, eine Schwimmhalle, eine Tennishalle und ein Freibad.

8 — Ich wohne in Quickborn. Es gibt nicht viel da für junge Leute. Es gibt ein Freibad, zwei Sporthallen, eine Disko, ein Jugendzentrum und ein Kino.

105, 114
(1B 7, 16)

Tell pupils to write about the facilities for young people in their own (or a nearby) town. Use the *Tip des Tages* (Areas 1 and 4) for reference.

120
(1B 22)

L

Ist hier ein Tisch frei?

Hört gut zu. Wo sitzen die Leute im Restaurant Zum Adler? Und wie viele Personen sitzen am Tisch?

Ist hier ein Tisch frei?

1 — Guten Tag. Haben Sie einen Tisch frei?
— Ja, für wieviel Personen?
— Zwei.
— Ganz hinten links ist ein Tisch frei.
— Danke schön.

2 — Guten Tag. Haben Sie einen Tisch frei?
— Wieviel Personen sind Sie?
— Fünf.
— Hier in der Mitte ist ein Tisch für fünf Personen.

3 — Ist der Tisch hier vorne am Fenster frei?
— Nein, der ist leider reserviert. Wieviel Personen sind Sie?
— Nur zwei.
— Der Tisch hier links neben den Toiletten ist frei.
— Danke schön. Wie romantisch!

4 — Guten Tag. Haben Sie einen Tisch für sechs Personen?
— Ja, da hinten, rechts.
— Ah, prima! Ein schöner Tisch am Fenster.

5 — Guten Tag. Haben Sie bitte einen Tisch frei?
— Für wieviel Personen?
— Drei.
— Ja, der Tisch hier rechts beim Eingang ist frei.
— Ja, fein. Danke.

6 — Guten Tag. Ich bin allein. Ist ein Tisch frei?
— Ein Tisch für eine Person hier vorne rechts ist frei. Der Tisch neben dem Notausgang.
— Danke.

Solution: **E**2; **A**5; **F**2; **K**6; **C**3; **D**1.

44

L, S

Unsere Stadt

Distribute a worksheet to each pupil. Practise pronunciation of the streets and make sure that the symbols are understood.

Then explain the activity:
Each partner takes it in turn to ask the way to a place indicated beneath the map. For each destination there is a different starting point indicated on the margin. The other pupil decides where the particular place is in the town, and directs his partner accordingly. At this point, both pupils mark the place in their maps. Afterwards, partners can compare maps and, if necessary, correct each other in German by giving the directions again and simultaneously tracing the way on the maps.

If an OHP is available, the procedure can be explained in German (see below). If not, it will be preferable to use English.

(Demonstrate with one pair)

1 *Ihr steht hier* (point to 1 on margin).

(To A): *Du stellst die Frage: ‚Wo ist der Bahnhof'?*
(To B): *Du schreibst ‚1' auf den Stadtplan. Für ‚Bahnhof'. Jetzt sagst du: ‚Erste links, erste rechts', und so weiter. Von ‚Eins' hier* (margin), *zu deiner Eins, dem Bahnhof.*
(To A): *Du hörst gut zu und machst eine Eins an die richtige Stelle.*

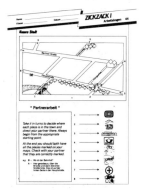

nem 11

R

244
(1B 128)

Urlaubsfreuden in Pfarrkirchen

An extract from a town brochure. Comprehension is tested in English. Pupils have to make a list of the sporting activities on offer.

L, S, R

Stadtrundgang

A 'guided tour' for tourists.

The historic buildings from *Osnabrück - meine Stadt* are presented once more, as they cannot really be omitted on such a tour. Also, it ensures that pupils need not concentrate on taking in new information all the time, but can occasionally go over familiar ground. The material can be exploited in various ways.

a) — Give pupils some time to familiarise themselves with the map and the locations indicated. (Silent reading).
— Announce a *Stadtrundgang*.
— Play part '**a**' of recording and ask pupils to find the location on the map.
Note down results, pupils in their books or on the worksheet, teacher on board or OHP: 'a — 8' or 'a — *Dom*' (or *Domhof*).
— Play next part and continue as before with the other parts of the recording. Briefly practise pronunciation of new places, where appropriate.

b) — Use notes to reconstruct the route of the tour. (Here, an OH projection of the town plan would be helpful.) Get pupils to comment as to whether a sight is familiar to them or not (further practice of new language).
Note down 'new' places on the board.
— Ask pupils to listen again and to try and remember one detail of the spoken commentary in each case. Stop after each part so that pupils can repeat immediately what they remember.

c) — The map could be presented again without the sound and pupils could be encouraged to reproduce as much of the commentary as they can.

d) — As a pair-work activity, pupils could ask each other for directions from the *Verkehrsamt* to various places.

Stadtrundgang

a) — Herzlich willkommen zu unserem Stadtrundgang. Wir stehen hier auf dem Domhof. Der Dom ist aus dem ll. bis l3. Jahrhundert. Hier auf dem Domhof ist jede Woche einmal Markt. Kommen Sie jetzt bitte mit.

b) Hier rechts ist das Verkehrsamt. Hier bekommen Sie Informationen über die Stadt: einen Stadtplan, Hotellisten. Broschüren usw. Die Adresse: Markt 22, 4500 Osnabrück.

c) Diese Kirche ist die Marienkirche aus dem 13. Jahrhundert. Wir gehen jetzt ein paar Schritte über den alten Markt zum Rathaus.

d) So, hier ist also das Rathaus. Es ist über 450 Jahre alt. Der Oberbürgermeister hat hier ein Büro. Die Figuren an dieser Fassade sind verschiedene Kaiser von Deutschland. Folgen Sie mir jetzt bitte in die Bierstraße — hier gleich um die Ecke.

e) Hier in der Bierstraße stehen einige schöne alte Häuser. Dies ist das Haus Walhalla, heute ein Restaurant. Wir gehen jetzt weiter die Bierstraße hinauf.

f) Hier sehen Sie die alte Jugendherberge, jetzt das 'Haus der Jugend', also ein Jugendzentrum.

g) Sehen Sie, wie eng die Straßen hier sind? Dies ist die Altstadt. Hier fahren keine Autos. Es ist eine Fußgängerzone mit ein paar schönen Kneipen.

h) Das ist die zweite Fußgängerzone, die Große Straße. Hier finden Sie Geschäfte, Straßencafés, Kinos.

i) Unser Stadtrundgang geht jetzt noch zum Schloß. Das sind noch gut 10 Minuten zu Fuß. Wer nicht mit will, kann hier vielleicht in ein Café gehen. Guten Appetit und auf Wiedersehen. Die anderen folgen mir bitte zum Schloß.

Solution: **a** - 8; **b** - 5; **c** - 4; **d** - 6; **e** - 7; **f** - 2; **g** - 3; **h** - 1, **i** - 13.

Vocabulary

abbiegen *to turn off (road)*
die Ampel(n) *traffic lights*
angelegt *laid out*
die Anlage(n) *grounds*
die Arbeit(en) *work*
die Aschenbahn(en) *cinder track*
der Aufenthalt(e) *stay*
der Ausflug(⸚e) *excursion*
die Ausfahrt(en) *motorway exit*
der Ausgang(⸚e) *exit, way out*
die Auskunft(⸚e) *information*
der Ausschnitt(e) *extract, cutting*
aussteigen *to get off*
der Bahnhof(⸚e) *station*
die Baustelle(n) *building site*
die Bemerkung(en) *observation*
bereit *ready*
die Beschäftigung(en) *activity, occupation*
die Beschreibung(en) *description*
besichtigen *to visit*
besorgt sein um *to look after*
die Broschüre(n) *brochure*
die Brücke(n) *bridge*
der Bürgermeister(-) *mayor*
das Büro(s) *office*
der Dom(e) *cathedral*
drüben *over there*
die Einfahrt(en) *motorway slip road (for cars)*
der Eingang(⸚e) *entrance, way in (for pedestrians)*
einwandern *to immigrate*
die Eisenbahn(en) *railway*
entlang + Acc *along*
sich erholen *to recover, recuperate*
erklären *to explain*
die Fähre(n) *ferry*

der Fahrer(-) *driver*
die Fahrkarte(n) *ticket*
das Fenster(-) *window*
die Firma(Firmen) *firm, company*
fließen *to flow*
der Fluß(Flüsse) *river*
das Freibad(⸚er) *open-air swimming pool*
die Freude(n) *joy*
früh *early*
führen nach *to lead to*
die Fußgängerzone(n) *pedestrian precinct*
der Gastarbeiter(-) *foreign worker*
das Gasthaus(⸚er) *pub, inn*
geradeaus *straight ahead*
das Geschäft(e) *shop*
geschehen *to happen*
gern *! *not at all!*
Grieche *Greek person (m)*
Griechin *Greek person (f)*
großzügig *generous*
der Hafen(⸚) *docks, port*
die Heimat *home, native country*
sich interessieren für *to be interested in*
das interessiert mich *that interests me*
Jugoslawien *Yugoslavia*
der Kanal(⸚e) *canal, the (English) Channel*
die Kaserne(n) *army barracks*
das Kino(s) *cinema*
die Kneipe(n) *pub, bar*
die Konditorei(en) *confectioner's*
der König(e) *king*
kostenlos *free*

das Krankenhaus(⸚er) *hospital*
sich kreuzen *to cross*
die Kreuzung(en) *crossroads*
lieber *rather*
manchmal *sometimes*
markieren *to mark*
die Mauer(n) *wall*
die Meile(n) *mile*
die Menge(n) *crowd, lot*
das Mikrofon(e) *microphone*
die Million(en) *million*
die Möglichkeit(en) *possibility*
der Mund(⸚er) *mouth*
das Museum(Museen) *museum*
negativ *negative*
neben + Acc/Dat *next to*
der Notausgang(⸚e) *emergency exit*
parken *to park*
die Polizeiwache(n) *Police station*
positiv *positive*
das Privatquartier *private accommodation*
rasch *quick(ly)*
das Rathaus(⸚er) *town hall*
romantisch *romantic*
rudern *to row*
die Rundfahrt(en) *tour*
der Schlittschuh(e) *ice skate*
* laufen *to ice skate*
das Schloß(Schlösser) *castle*
der Schritt(e) *step*
selbstständig *independent*
segeln *to sail*
selten *rare, seldom*
sicher *certainly*
sitzen *to sit*
der Sohn(⸚e) *son*
der Soldat(en) *soldier*
sollen *to be supposed to, ought to*

die Speise(n) *food*
das Sportzentrum (Sportzentren) *sports centre*
das Stadion (Stadien) *stadium*
die Stadthalle(n) *concert hall*
sterben *to die*
das Studentenheim(e) *student's hall of residence*
surfen *to go surfing*
das Theater(-) *theater*
die Tochter(⸚) *daughter*
die Trabrennbahn(en) *pony and trap racecourse*
die Trümmern *ruins*
die Türkei *Turkey*
türkisch *Turkish*
überall *everywhere*
um + Acc *around*
ungefähr *approximately, about*
verboten *forbidden*
verheiratet *married*
das Verkehrsamt *tourist information office*
der Verkehrsknotenpunkt(e) *transport intersection*
verschieden *various*
vervollständigen *to complete*
Vokabeln *vocabulary*
vorgeheizt *heated*
vorlesen *to read out*
sich **vor**stellen *to imagine, introduce oneself*
wandern *to hike, walk*
weit *far*
der Weltkrieg(e) *world war*
der Winter(-) *winter*
das Wohnhochhaus(⸚er) *block of flats*
wunderbar *wonderful*
der Zoo(s) *zoo*

CHAPTER 8 Beim Einkaufen

Area 1

● Names of some shops

84-95

L, S

Welches Geschäft ist das?

Present the shop flashcards beginning with the **feminine** shops (*Bäckerei, Metzgerei, Drogerie, Buchhandlung, Konditorei.*)

Ask pupils to repeat individually (4 or 5 per card), then chorally before pinning the card to the board.

99 66

T: *Welches Geschäft ist das? Das ist die Bäckerei. Die Bäckerei. James, welches Geschäft ist das?*
P: *Die Bäckerei.*
T: *Richtig. Die Bäckerei. usw.*

When all the **feminine** nouns have been presented and attached to one side of the board, write *die* once, next to the column. Follow the same procedure with the **neuter** shops (*Sportgeschäft, Kleidergeschäft, Warenhaus*), then the **masculine** shop (*Supermarkt*), pinning them to the board and writing *das* and *der* next to them.

Practise the names of the shops by concealing a card and inviting pupils to win it by guessing correctly the answer to the question: ,*Welches Geschäft ist das?*'

122
(1B 24)

L

Was kann man hier kaufen?

Refer pupils to the visuals in the Pupil's Book and present the new vocabulary, in preparation for the next activity.

99 66

Macht eure Bücher auf Seite 122 (24) auf: Was kann man hier kaufen?

Hört zu. Nummer eins: Das ist die Bäckerei. Hier kann man Brot und Brötchen kaufen.

Repeat each item once.

At this stage it is not intended that pupils should repeat the new vocabulary: receptive comprehension only is required as attention is to be focused on the shop names.

Was kann man hier kaufen?
1 —Das ist die Bäckerei. Hier kann man Brot und Brötchen kaufen. *(Repeat)*
2 Das ist das Sportgeschäft. Hier kann man Fußbälle, Sportschuhe und so weiter kaufen. *(Repeat)*
3 Das ist die Drogerie. Hier kann man Zahnpasta, Filme, Seife und so weiter kaufen. *(Repeat)*
4 Das ist die Buchhandlung. Hier kann man Zeitschriften *(hold up a magazine)*, zum Beispiel eine Bravo *(display a copy, if available)* und Bücher kaufen. *(Repeat)*
5 Das ist die Metzgerei. Hier kann man Fleisch, Wurst, Schinken und so weiter kaufen. *(Repeat)*
6 Das ist der Markt. Hier kann man Obst, zum Beispiel Bananen, Äpfel und so weiter kaufen. *(Repeat)*

L, S, W

Ingrid geht einkaufen

T: *Hört gut zu. Ingrid geht einkaufen. Wo ist sie jetzt? (Play first dialogue.) Welches Geschäft ist das? Ist das die Metzgerei?*
P: *Nein, die Drogerie.*

99 66

Write '1. *Drogerie*' on the board, and ask pupils to complete the list in their books. Check results orally.

Ingrid geht einkaufen
1 —Guten Tag.
—Guten Tag. Kann ich Ihnen helfen?
—Ja, Zahnpasta, bitte.
—Und sonst noch etwas?
—Einen Schwarzweiß Film.
—So. Das macht 18 Mark, bitte.

2 —Tag.
—Guten Tag.
—Ich möchte ein Landbrot, bitte.
—Ein Kilo?
—Ja, bitte.
—Bitte schön. Sonst noch etwas?
—Nein, danke.
—Also, zwei fünfzig, bitte. Danke schön. Wiedersehen.

3 —Eine Bravo? 3 Mark, bitte.
—Danke.
—Bitte schön.

4 —Ich möchte 200 Gramm Leberwurst.
—Die grobe?
—Ja, gut.
—3 Mark. Sonst noch etwas?
—200 Gramm Schinken, bitte.
—So. Das macht 8 Mark zusammen, bitte.

5 —Guten Tag. Kann ich Ihnen helfen?
—Guten Tag. Was kostet dieser Fußball, bitte?
—Dieser hier? 25 Mark.
—Oh ... Na gut, ich nehme ihn.
—Vielen Dank. Auf Wiedersehen.

6 —Bitte schön?
—Ein Pfund Bananen, bitte.
—2,80. Sonst noch etwas?
—Nein, das ist alles, danke.
—Also, 2,80 bitte.

L, S, R

Wo kauft man das?

Show pupils flashcards of items to be purchased in the shops listed on the board earlier (see *Welches Geschäft ist das?*) Ask the question: ,*Wo kauft man das?*' and answer it yourself at first. Present items which may be purchased in the 'feminine shops' initially.

(Show Flashcard of bread)

T:	*Wo kauft man das ... ? In der Buchhandlung?*
Pupils:	*Nein.*
T:	*In der Metzgerei?*
Pupils:	*Nein.*
T:	*In der Bäckerei?*
Pupils:	*Ja.*
T:	(To one pupil): *Wo kauft man Brot?*
P1:	*In der Bäckerei.*
T:	*Richtig.* (To class:) *Wo kauft man Brot?*
Pupils:	*In der Bäckerei.*

When the 'feminine' list is complete, write up the shop names, as before, in *Welches Geschäft ist das?* and write the question: *Wo kauft man ... ?* above the list. Write *Brot* in the gap, ask the question again, and when it is correctly answered, write *in der* beneath *die*, thus:-

Wo kauft man Brot? *(Fleisch, Zahnpasta, Tabletten, usw.)*

die	⎫	Bäckerei
	⎪	Metzgerei
	⎬	Drogerie
in der	⎪	Apotheke
	⎭	Buchhandlung
		Konditorei

Finally, erase *die* and proceed to the *das* and *der* lists in the same way, ending up with:-

Wo kauft man Fußbälle? *(Schuhe, ...)*

das	⎧	Sportgeschäft
	⎪ im	Schuhgeschäft
	⎨	Kleidergeschäft
	⎪	Warenhaus
der	⎩	Supermarkt

Remember to erase *das* and *der* at the end of the exercise.

Finally, practise the Dative forms, using flashcards.

T:	*Wo kauft man das?* (Showing flashcard of Wurst.)
P1:	*In der Metzgerei.*
T:	*Und das?* (Flashcard of sports equipment)
P2:	*Im Sportgeschäft.*
T:	*Und das ... ?*

123
(1B 25)

L, S, R, W

Wo bist du denn?

Tell pupils to look at the drawings and work out the missing shop names. This also provides further practice of the articles in shops.

T:	*Nummer eins: Was kannst du hier kaufen?*
P:	*Schuhe und Sandalen.*
T:	*Ja, hier kannst du Schuhe und Sandalen kaufen. Wo bist du denn?*
P:	*Im Schuhgeschäft.* (Write answer on the board.)

Encourage pupils to take over the teacher's role as soon as possible.

When the exercise is complete, tell pupils to copy the answers from the board.

T:	*Seht euch die Tafel an. Tragt alles in euer Heft ein.*

123
(1B 25)

L, S

Wo bist du denn?

Tell pupils to take it in turns to choose one of the nine shops and write down, in secret, the corresponding number. The object of the exercise is to guess which one has been chosen. Complete one or two examples with individual pupils.

T:	(To pupil): *Also, wähle ein Geschäft* (point to drawings). *Schreibe die Nummer in dein Heft. Ich gucke nicht. Fertig? Gut. Also, wo bist du denn? In der Konditorei?*
P1:	*Nein. (Ich bin nicht in der Konditorei).*
T:	*Also, in der Drogerie?*
P1:	*Nein.*
T:	*Im Warenhaus?*
P1:	*Ja.*
T:	*Also, was habe ich gesagt: In der Konditorei, ein Punkt, in der Drogerie, zwei Punkte, im Warenhaus, drei Punkte. Du hast drei Punkte.* (Write *3 Punkte* on the board.) *Also, Partnerarbeit.*

R

Ingrid und Franz gehen einkaufen

Tell pupils to read the text in silence, then ask them, in English, what is different about the words before the names of the shops.

Lest den Text, (mime reading), *ohne miteinander zu sprechen.* (Finger on lips) ...

When pupils identify the differences, record them in columns on the board:

in den	in die	ins
Supermarkt	Bäckerei	Sportgeschäft

Then point out the difference in form, as follows, before moving on to the next activity.

T: (Pointing to *in den ...*) *Nicht im, sondern in den ..., nicht in der, sondern in die ..., nicht im, sondern ins. Warum denn?*

L, S

84-95

Wo gehst du hin?

Hand four or five shop flashcards to pupils standing in different parts of the room. Then tell pupils where you're going.

T: *Ich gehe in die Bäckerei ...* (stop before you reach the pupil with the card) *... das heißt, nein, ich gehe ins Schuhgeschäft ... ach nein, ich gehe in den ...*

Then encourage pupils to join in the activity individually, and stop and question them **before** they arrive.

T: *Wo gehst du hin?*
P1: *Ich gehe in die Metzgerei.* (Stop him/her and direct him/her towards another place).
T: *Und jetzt?*
P1: *Ich gehe ins Sportgeschäft.*

Finally, ask pupils, in English, if they have worked out why *in der* has become *in die,* in other words, what has everyone been trying to do in the sketches. Try to elicit 'go **into** a shop' before moving on to the next activity.

L, S

84-95

Wo gehst du hin?

Ask pupils which shop they would go to for the following things:

Film — Brot — Turnschuhe — Schinken — eine Bravo — Äpfel — Zahnpasta — Wurst — Brötchen — Fußball — Bananen — Buch.

T: *Du willst einen Fußball kaufen. Gehst du ins Sportgeschäft oder in die Drogerie?*
P: *Ins Sportgeschäft.*
T: (Showing Flashcard of bread). *Und jetzt? Wo gehst du hin?*

R, W

46

Ausflug/Jörgs Einkaufsliste

Tell pupils to read the text, then fill in the gaps.

Lest den Text 'Ausflug' dann füllt die Lücken aus. Schreibt die Antworten auf, zum Beispiel:
a) in **die** Bäckerei.
b) in **die** Metzgerei.

Solution:
c) ins d) den e) die f) die g) Bäckerei h) ein
i) Brötchen j) in k) die l) Metzgerei m) Gramm
n) 300 o) Schinken p) ins q) Gemüsegeschäft
r) Pfund s) in t) den u) Kekse v) in w) die
x) Apotheke y) Tabletten.

Jörgs Einkaufsliste

This writing activity will focus pupils' attention on Jörg's purchases, thus requiring them to re-read the introductory text *Ausflug.* Although they will not be required, at this stage, to reproduce the full range of vocabulary dealing with provisions, the next activity revises language already introduced and provides advance warning of the language to be presented in Area 3.

(L)

Present a series of visuals showing clearly, in each one, a person inside a shop and a second person about to enter. Stress the imprtance of going **into** and being already **in**. Copy the visuals from the next activity, if necessary.

(Pointing to shop name:) *Das ist die Bäckerei. Das ist Franz in **der** Bäckerei. Und das ist Ingrid — sie geht* (mime walking) *in **die** Bäckerei.*

If necessary, conclude, in English, with: Already **in** = *im* or *in der*; going **into** = *in den*, *in die* or *ins*. Avoid distorting intonation by overstressing *in den, im* etc. Highlight the change in pattern on the board.

L, (S), R

124
(1B 26)

Wo sind sie? Wo gehen sie hin?

Tell pupils to listen to the description of Franz and Ingrid's shopping trip, and choose the correct illustrations from their textbooks. Complete the first answer with them.

T: *Wo sind sie? Wo gehen sie hin? Seht euch die Bilder an und wählt jedes Mal entweder Nummer eins oder Nummer zwei. Zum Beispiel: ihr hört:*

A: *,Es ist Mittwochnachmittag. Franz geht in die Stadt. Zuerst geht er ins Sportgeschäft.'* (Pointing to first illustration, A.) *Ist das Nummer eins oder Nummer zwei? **Ins** Sportgeschäft?*

P1: *Nummer zwei.*

T: *Richtig. Schreibt A2 in euer Heft.* (Write A2 on the board). *Alles klar? Gut. Hört zu.*

Wo sind sie? Wo gehen sie hin?

A: —Es ist Mittwochnachmittag. Franz geht in die Stadt. Zuerst geht er ins Sportgeschäft.

B: Ingrid ist schon in der Bäckerei.

C: Fünf Minuten später geht sie in die Drogerie. Sie will Zahnpasta kaufen.

D: Franz ist jetzt in der Buchhandlung.

E: Ingrid will auch eine Bravo kaufen. sie geht in die Buchhandlung.

F: ... aber Franz ist nicht mehr da. Er ist in der Metzgerei.

G: Schließlich geht er in den Supermarkt.

H: Und wo ist Ingrid jetzt? Im Supermarkt, natürlich. Dort kann man fast alles kaufen.

Solution: **A2 B2 C1 D1 E1 F2 G1 H1**

(L, S), R, W

125
(1B 27)

Was machen Franz und Ingrid?

Tell pupils to put the jumbled sentences in the correct order and write the story in their exercise books. If necessary, go through the text once more orally and refer pupils to *Tip des Tages.*

Correct order: 6, 3, 8, 5, 2, 7, 4, 1.

---

nem 1

245
(1B 129)

W

Die Bäckerei und die ... ?

An exercise focusing on gender.

---

nem 2

245
(1B 129)

W

Wo warst du heute?

An activity practising *im* and *in der* with shops.

---

8 Area 2

● **Expressions of quantity**

L, S

Present the flashcards dealing with weights, measures and containers in groups of 3 or 4, starting with the smaller weights and working upwards, before moving onto different measures.

T: (Showing card for *Wurst 100g,* but covering the individual weight).

P: *Wurst.*

T: *Gut.* (Uncovering.) *Wieviel Wurst? ... Hundert Gramm. Hundert Gramm Wurst.* (To pupil): *Wieviel Wurst? usw.*

Use the same approach for *Liter:*

T: *Das ist Wein. Wieviel Wein? Ein Liter ... wieviel?*

P: *Ein Liter.*

Then use the bottle of wine to switch to **containers:-**

T: *Das ist ein Liter Wein. Oder eine Flasche Wein ... usw.*

R

126
(1B 28)

Wieviel ist das?

The visuals and accompanying explanations are intended to clarify the concept of weights and measures. As for many of the activities in this area, the use of weighing scales to further emphasise the concept of weights and how they can be converted into other everyday measures (glasses, bowls, sandwiches, etc.) cannot be too highly recommended.

Read through the language with the pupils and reinforce with your own examples. Note that a German *Pfund* is exactly 500g, and is, therefore, different from an English pound.

Pupils might practise the concepts by drawing other quantities of food or drink in their exercise books and analysing them, as in the Pupil's Book, in terms of portions, measures per person, etc.

**127
(1B 29)**

L, R

Was kaufen die Leute im Geschäft?

Tell pupils to look at the drawings and to listen to the tape in order to decide which customer buys what in the shop. Play the first two examples and complete them with the group.

*Hier gibt es keinen Supermarkt. Die Leute kaufen in einem kleinen Geschäft ein. Aber **was** kaufen sie? Schreibt eins bis fünfzehn in euer Heft. Hört gut zu und schreibt 1h oder 2s usw. in euer Heft.*

Was kaufen die Leute im Geschäft?

1 — Bitte schön?
— Ein Kilo Käse, bitte.

2 — Bitte schön?
— Einen Becher Margarine, bitte.

3 — Bitte schön?
— Ich möchte eine Dose Tomatensuppe, bitte.

4 — Was darf es sein?
— Eine Dose Heringe, bitte, und eine Dose Cola.

5 — Bitte schön?
— Fünf Kilo Kartoffeln, bitte.
— Sonst noch etwas?
— Nein danke. Das ist alles.

6 — Was darf's sein?
— Dreihundert Gramm Käse, bitte.
— Sonst noch etwas?
— Ja, ich hätte gern eine Schachtel Marzipan.

7 — Bitte schön?
— Einen Liter Milch, bitte.

8 — Was darf's sein?
— Eine Tube Zahnpasta und einen Marsriegel, bitte.
— Sonst noch etwas?
— Ja, eine Tüte Gummibärchen für meine Schwester.

9 — Ja bitte?
— Eine Flasche Apfelsaft.
— So, bitte schön. Sonst noch etwas?
— Ja. Ich möchte auch ein Glas Erdbeerkonfitüre.

10 — Was darf es sein?
— Ich möchte eine Packung Kaffee.
— Jacobs oder Melitta.
— Jacobs, bitte.

11 — Bitte schön?
— Na, ein Glas Honig und einen Becher Heringssalat, bitte.

12 — Sie wünschen?
— Eine Schachtel Marzipan und eine Packung Kekse.
— So, bitte schön. Wünschen Sie noch etwas anderes?
— Ja, ich möchte ein Stück Seife, bitte.

13 — Ja, bitte?
— Ich möchte eine Schachtel Pralinen, bitte.
— Bitte schön.

14 — Guten Tag. Was darf es sein?
— Anderthalb Kilo Käse.
— Anderthalb Kilo Käse. So viel? Darf es sonst noch etwas sein?
— Ja. Eine Kiste Bier.

Solution: **1** h **2** s **3** g **4** r, d **5** b **6** c, m **7** q **8** w, k, x **9** n, e **10** i **11** l, p **12** m, f, t **13** j **14** a, u

---

L, S

**127
(1B 29)**

Follow up *Was kaufen die Leute im Geschäft?* by focusing pupils' attention on the weights and measures relating to the visuals.
Nominate one of the items and see who is first to identify the weight or measure or container.

T: *Secht euch die Bilder auf Seite 127 (29) an. Hört gut zu: ich sage **Kekse**. Ist das eine Tüte Kekse?*
P1: *Nein. Das ist eine Packung.*
T: *Gut. Also, hört gut zu. Hebt die Hand. Kaffee? usw.*

(Continue in pairs, if required.)

Continue until you have covered all the weights and measures before moving on to consolidate in the next activity.

R, W

**127
(1B 29)**

Wie ist das richtig?

A consolidation activity to prepare pupils for the pair-work activity which follows. This is a good homework activity.

127
(1B 29)

Einkaufslisten

Tell pupils to take it in turns to dictate a shopping list to their partner: the pupil dictating may refer to the text, but the pupil writing may not. When they have dictated at **least** five items they may check to see if the right list has been produced. Perform the first dialogue with a pupil.

Partnerarbeit: (To pupil): *Mache dein Buch zu. Schreibe jetzt in dein Heft.* (Now study, in an exaggerated manner, the visuals for *Was kaufen sie im Geschäft?*) *Also, eine Dose Tomatensuppe.* (To pupil): *Schreibe hier, 'eine Dose Tomatensuppe' ... gut ... und 'eine Packung Kekse'.* (Dictate a list of seven or eight items, then allow the pupil to check against *Wie ist das richtig?*)

16-38
59-66

Was wiegt das?

An auctioneer game in which pupils must make intelligent guesses as to the weight either of food nominated by you on flashcards, or of items you have brought into the classroom. Once again, the use of a set of weighing scales makes such an activity come to life. Display the object and allow pupils to discuss, in pairs or in groups, what the weight might be.

T: (Showing loaf of bread or bag of apples). *Was wiegt das?* (Mime weighing with your hand.) *Hundert Gramm? Ein Kilo?*
P1: *Fünfhundert Gramm.*
T: *Fünfhundert Gramm.* (To class): *Stimmt das?*
P2: *Nein.*
T: *Ist das mehr oder weniger? Mehr? Ein Kilo, zwei Kilo? Oder weniger? Dreihundert Gramm?*

Allow pupils to take over the bidding before finally weighing the item to discover the most accurate assessment.

47A
47B

Was kauft ihr für das Picknick?

126
(1B 28)

Divide the class into six groups and distribute Worksheets 47A and 47B to each pupil. Tell pupils to study the price list on Worksheet 47B and decide in their groups how they would like to spend the DM 30,- they have between them to pay for their proposed picnic. They must decide how much of each item they will need to buy to cater for their

own group. Tell them to write down on the worksheet, in the appropriate column, the weights, the individual and total costs. They may refer to *Wieviel ist das?* on page 126 (**1B** 28).

Ihr macht ein Picknick. Ihr habt 30 Mark für die ganze Gruppe, und ihr seid hungrig. Was kauft ihr für das Mittagessen? Schreibt alles auf.

Zum Beispiel, ihr seid fünf, ja? Also, drei Butterbrote pro Person (fünfzehn Butterbrote) mit Wurst (consult Wieviel ist das?). Zweihundert Gramm Wurst ist genug für fünf Butterbrote, also fünfzehn Butterbrote, das macht sechshundert Gramm Wurst. Das kostet ... usw.

Alles klar? Gut. Na, an die Arbeit!

After each group has completed its column on the worksheet, one nominee from each group should read out that group's list and the other pupils in the class should write it down, checking back, if necessary. Results could be collated on an overhead transparency of the worksheet.

Umfrage: make sure that each group has remained within the DM 30 limit, then conduct a survey to establish which foods and drinks are most popular.

Welche Getränke sind am populärsten? Und zum Essen? Wurst, oder Käse, oder ... ?

This activity could also be used in Area 5 or Area 6 to practise reporting back in the Perfect Tense.

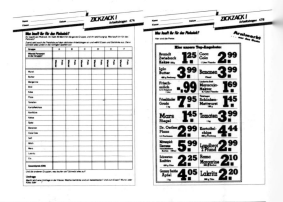

Einige Informationen /Vollautomatik

Read the introductory text with the pupils in preparation for the listening activity, *Vollautomatik*, which follows. Stress again the significance of *wiegen* and use mime and gesture to illustrate the idea of the customer choosing and weighing his own fruit and vegetables.

(Using your own scales, if possible):

Ich bin im Supermarkt. Ich will Obst — Äpfel, Bananen usw. kaufen. Ach, hier sind sie. (Take a bag, mime selecting articles and weigh them in front of the class saying:) *Ich wähle mein Obst und Gemüse, und ich wiege es selbst ab, so.* (Looking at your watch). *Das ist sehr praktisch — es spart viel Zeit, denn es dauert nur ein paar Sekunden.*

For the activity entitled *Vollautomatik*, tell pupils that the usually efficient automatic scales are not printing everything on the receipts, illustrated on page 128 (**1 B** 30). Tell pupils to look at the table of prices for fruit and vegetables and the six incomplete receipts. They should copy the receipts into their exercise books and listen to the tape, in order to be able to fill in the various weights and prices. They will need to use the table for calculations.

'Vollautomatik'— Seite 128 (30). (Pointing to receipts). *Vollautomatisch muß nicht immer gut sein — heute gibt es Probleme. Druckfehler* (auf Englisch heißt das printing errors). *Die Etiketten mit den Gewichten und den Preisen sind nicht immer da. Tragt die Bons in euer Heft ein, seht euch die Preisliste an, hört gut zu und schreibt die richtigen Gewichte und Preise auf die Bons.* (Complete no. 1 with the group by filling in (i) *Tomaten;* (ii) *1 Kg.*

Vollautomatik

1	Erste Kundin:	— Guck mal. Diese Maschine funktioniert nicht gut.
	Zweite Kundin:	— Wieso, denn?
	Erste Kundin:	— Da, der Preis: DM 6,04. Das geht schon. Aber schau mal hier. 500 Gramm. 500 Gramm was?
	Zweite Kundin:	— Tomaten, oder?
	Erste Kundin:	— Ach ja. Tomaten. Aber was für Äpfel habe ich? Für DM 4,05. Stimmt das?

	Zweite Kundin:	— Na, wo ist denn die Tabelle? Hier. (*Liest*) Äpfel — Preis je Kilo ... ja, das stimmt.
2	Kunde:	— Entschuldigung.
	Verkäuferin:	— Ja.
	Kunde:	— Ich habe hier einen Bon für Gemüse, aber der Preis ist nicht darauf und auch nicht alle Gewichte.
	Verkäuferin:	— Also, zwei Kilo hier — was war das?
	Kunde:	— Kartoffeln.
	Verkäuferin:	— Zwei Kilo Kartoffeln. Und wieviel Tomaten?
	Kunde:	— Ein Kilo, glaube ich.
	Verkäuferin:	— Und wieviel Zwiebeln?
	Kunde:	— Das waren 500 Gramm. Was kostet das alles zusammen?
	Verkäuferin:	— Moment mal. Das rechne ich für Sie aus. DM 8,88.
	Kunde:	— Danke.
3	Mutter:	— Schau mal — 750g ... DM 5,40. Was war das?
	Tochter:	— Bananen. Und die Kirschen, zu DM 2,04. Wieviel war das?
	Mutter:	— Tja, 400g. Also, DM 5,40 plus DM 2,04 ... DM 7,44 sollte das sein.
	Tochter:	— Vollautomatik! So was!
4	Kundin:	— Das verstehe ich nicht. Karotten zu DM 2,56. Wieviel war das? Ach ja, 800 Gramm.
	Ihr Mann:	— Und das hier? 600 Gramm?
	Kundin:	— Erbsen.
	Mann:	— Ach ja, die Erbsen. Endpreis DM 11,70. Stimmt das?
	Kundin:	— DM 2,56 für die Karotten, und für die Erbsen DM 3,06, und die Äpfel dazu: anderthalb Kilo. Ja, das stimmt.
5	Erstes Mädchen:	— Guck mal. Wo sind hier auf dem Bon die drei Kilo Kartoffeln?
	Zweites Mädchen:	— Ja, und auch kein Preis. Drei Kilo Kartoffeln, das ist dreimal DM 1,75 ...

das macht DM 5,25.
Und wieviel Bananen?

Erstes Mädchen: — Ein Kilo. Warte mal …
die kosten DM 7,20.
Endpreis DM 12,45.
Stark, diese
Maschine!
Vollautomatik!

6 Junge: — Entschuldigung. Was
soll ich für diese
Karotten, Tomaten
und Erbsen bezahlen?
Verkäufer: — Wo ist der Bon?
Junge: — Hier, bitte schön.
Verkäufer: — Ach so.
Entschuldigung. Die
wiege ich noch einmal
hier. Diesmal wird es
nicht automatisch
sein. Also, die
Karotten … DM 4,80,
die Tomaten … DM
3,98 und die Erbsen
… DM 2,55. Endpreis:
DM 11,33.
Junge: — Vielen Dank.

Solution:

L, S, R, W

Einkaufszettel

Tell pupils they should work in pairs in order
to piece together the torn shopping list. As
they agree on each item on the list, they
should write it out in full on their worksheets,
on the left for *Partner(in) A* and on the right
for *Partner(in) B*.

T: (Tear a piece of paper). *Das Blatt Papier
ist durchgerissen. Ihr habt einen
durchgerissenen Einkaufszettel. Was ist
darauf?* (Speaking to partner B while
pointing to Partner A's page:)
zweihundert Gramm S … ?
P1: *Schinken.*
T: *Danke. Also, ich schreibe es hier auf und
du hier, zweihundert Gramm Schinken.*

(Now write the answer on the board to
reinforce the point). *Zweihundert Gramm,
so, nicht 200g. Alles klar? Gut. Jetzt
Partnerarbeit.*

Collate the results on the board, possibly
inviting pupils to write the answers on the
board themselves.

nem 3
245
(1B 129)
W

Einkäufe am Telefon

An activity practising shop language.

L, S, R

49

Obst- und Gemüsespiele

1 Play bingo using the fruit and vegetable
visuals. Tell pupils to cut out the twenty
items and place nine of them on their
grid. Say the names of the food in any
order. The first pupil to turn over all nine
wins. Encourage pupils to take over the
teacher's role.

2 Pupils work in pairs to play a variation of
noughts and crosses. One pupil has all
the singular items of food, the other has
the plurals. They take it in turns to place
a card on the grid, saying what it is. The
winner is the first one with three
singulars or three plurals in a row.

• Buying provisions

L, S

Revise the food and drink vocabulary from Chapter 4 using the flashcards, then introduce in the usual manner the new items of vocabulary, once again in groups of two or three flashcards.

130
(1B 32)

L, S, R, W

Hanse SB/Beim Einkaufen

In preparation for the listening activity which follows, analyse with the pupils the goods on offer in *Hanse SB*. Read through each item and ask them to decide into which, if any, of the following categories the items fall: *Fleisch, Käse, Wurst, Fisch, Getränke, Waschmittel.*

T: Seht euch Hanse SB an. Also, Schweineschnitzel. Was ist das? Waschmittel?
P1: Nein, Fleisch.
T: Gut. (Write Schweineschnitzel under Fleisch). Und Schnitzelbraten?

Finally, tell pupils to copy the information into their books.

130
(1B 32)

L, (S), R, W

Beim Einkaufen

Tell pupils to look at *Hanse SB* before they listen to the tape. Then tell them to write down in their exercise books the items purchased by Jörg and Frau Jührend and the prices, shown on the till receipt on page 130 (32). Complete the first item with the group. Repeat items whenever necessary.

T: Tragt den Bon in euer Heft ein ... Hört gut zu! Was kaufen Jörg und Frau Jührend? (Play the tape and pause after Na, gut.) Kaufen sie Rouladen?
P: Nein, Schnitzelbraten.
T: Genau. Schnitzelbraten ... 7,99 (Write the information on the board.)

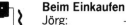

Beim Einkaufen

Jörg:	— Guck mal: Wochenangebote. Was brauchen wir?
Frau Jührend:	— Zuerst brauchen wir Fleisch.
Jörg:	— Hmm, Rouladen. Köstlich. Nur DM 11,99 das Kilo.
Frau Jührend:	— Nein, nehmen wir lieber Schweineschnitzel oder Rinderleber. Was meinst du?
Jörg:	— Rinderleber? Nein danke! Wie wäre es mit Schnitzelbraten? Kostet nur DM 7,99 das Kilo.
Frau Jührend:	— Na gut.
Jörg:	— Brauchen wir Butter? DM 1,94 das halbe Pfund. Das ist billig, oder?
Frau Jührend:	— Ja, aber DM 1,79 für die Margarine ist noch billiger. Hol' mir bitte den Becher Frühstücksmargarine.
Jörg:	— Konfitüre brauchen wir auch.
Frau Jührend:	— Was kostet sie?
Jörg:	— DM 1,99 das Glas.
Frau Jührend:	Gut. Dann hol' mir ein Glas Erdbeerkonfitüre und auch eine — Packung Kekse.
Jörg:	— Welche?
Frau Jührend:	— Prinzenrolle — da, siehst du sie? DM 2,22 die Packung.
Jörg:	— So. Was nun? Wein? Oder Bier?
Frau Jührend:	— Haben sie Meister Pils?
Jörg:	— Nein. Hier ist aber ein Sonderangebot. DM 16,99 die Kiste Flensburger.
Frau Jührend:	— Können wir mal probieren. Hol' mir eine Kiste. Ich gehe mal an die Wurst- und Käsetheke.

An der Wurst- und Käsetheke:

Verkäuferin:	— Was darf's sein?
Frau Jührend:	— Ich möchte 500 Gramm Wilstermarschkäse und 200 Gramm Jagdwurst, bitte.
Verkäuferin:	— Bitte schön. Sonst noch etwas?
Frau Jührend:	— Nein, danke. Das ist alles ... Komm, Jörg. Ich brauche nur noch eine Packung Waschmittel.
Jörg:	— Welches denn?
Frau Jührend:	Persil.
Jörg:	— Ach ja. Das hole ich sofort.
Frau Jührend:	— Danke. Und jetzt zur Kasse!

Solution: **Hanse SB**

Schnitzelbraten	7,99
Rama Frühstücksmargarine	1,79
Konfitüre	1,99
Prinzenrolle (Kekse)	2,22
Flensburger Pilsener	16,99
Wilstermarschkäse	4,95
Jagdwurst	2,58
Persil (Vollwaschmittel)	9,99
Endpreis:	48,50

L, S, R, W

Was darf's sein?

Tell pupils to work in pairs in order to complete the details on their sheets. Partner A begins by asking the lead question. Partner B then asks for the 5 items which are incomplete on his/her list. After each answer (s)he should write the details on the sheet. When the details are complete, partners exchange roles and Partner A completes his/her details in the same way. Complete the first item with a pupil in front of the class.

T: *Jetzt Partnerarbeit. (To a pupil:) Du bist Partner B. Ich bin Partner A. Ich stelle die Frage: ‚Was darf's sein?' Und du antwortest: ‚Ich möchte eine Packung Kekse'. Also: Was darf's sein?*
P: *Ich möchte eine Packung Kekse.*
T: *Brandt Kekse?*
    (Write on board *Brandt Kekse.*)
P: *Ja.*
T: *Du schreibst hier 'Brandt' so, und jetzt stellst du die Frage.*
P: *Was darf's sein?*
T: *Ich möchte l00 Gramm Käse* (point to Pupil's sheet to elicit:)
P: *Berg*käse?
T: *Genau. Jetzt Partnerarbeit.*

(L, S), R, W

In der Stadt: Kreuzworträtsel

The puzzle provides pupils with an opportunity to revise the names of some of the shops and products they have encountered. Follow up with questions on the vocabulary depicted in the clues:

Nr. 1: Was kauft man in der Bäckerei?
     5: Was kauft man in der Drogerie?

Solution:

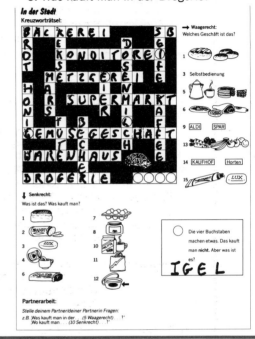

L, R

Wo kommen diese Kisten hin?

Tell pupils to look at the cartoon of an English teenager recently employed to stack the shelves in a German supermarket. Unfortunately he is unfamiliar with the layout of the store and does not recognise where the various boxes should be unpacked and shelved.

Tell pupils to listen to the dialogues and help to identify where each trolley load of boxes should go. Tell them to write the numbers l to l4 in their exercise books and then to listen to the tape, in order to select the correct letter to write next to each number. Complete the first one with the group.

T: *Hier ist ein englischer Teenager in einem Supermarkt in Deutschland. Er muß alle Kisten* (point to the boxes, or to boxes of your own) *in die richtigen Stellen: A, B, C, usw. tragen. (Mime.) Also, schreibt eins bis vierzehn an euer Heft, so etwa:-*

(Demonstrate on the board.) *Na, heißt es 1A oder 1B oder 1C ...? Hört gut zu.* (Play the first dialogue.) *Also, Nummer eins. 'Salami'. Ist das A oder B oder ...*

P1: *C.*

T : *Richtig. Ihr schreibt 1C in euer Heft. Kapiert? Gut. Hört jetzt gut zu!*

Wo kommen diese Kisten hin?

1 Teenager: — Entschuldigung.
Mädchen: — Ja?
Teenager: — Wo kommen diese Kisten hin, bitte?
Mädchen: — Welche?
Teenager: — Diese hier: 'Salami'.
Mädchen: — Salami. Da hinten, siehst du? Da ist Wurst.
Teenager: — Ach ja, danke.

2 Teenager: — Pumpernickel? Was ist denn das?
Und Knäckebrot? Ach ja! Da hinten rechts unter Brot.

3 Direktor: — Bitte, bringen Sie diese Kisten Dosenmilch her!
Teenager: — Gerne, aber wo kommen diese Kisten hin?
Direktor: — Da drüben, sehen Sie? Ganz in der Mitte.

4 Teenager: — So, was nun? Conlei, was ist denn das? Aha, Seife. Muß Waschmittel sein. Hinten rechts.

5 Teenager: — Holsten? Holsten Pils — haben wir auch in England. Wo kommt es denn hin? Da — hinten links. Gut.

6 Teenager: — Entschuldige nochmal! Was ist EG Molkerei?
Mädchen: — Von einer Molkerei bekommt man Milch und Butter, und so weiter.
Teenager: — Ach so. Na, die EG Molkereikisten kommen hier vorne links hin. Danke.
Mädchen: — Nichts zu danken.

7 Teenager: — Butterkekse? Butter von der Molkerei, oder ... ? Ach nein! Blödsinn! Kekse sind das, hinten rechts.

8 Teenager: — Was ist denn das hier? Zwei große Kisten aus Brasilien. Bohnen? Ach ja, Kaffeebohnen. Wo ist denn das ... ja, hinten links. Also, los!

9 Direktor: — Und jetzt die Heringe.
Teenager: — Heringe? Ist das Fleisch?
Direktor: — Aber nein. Fisch. Heringe sind Fische. Da drüben rechts.

10 Teenager: — Also, was nun? Diese Kisten hier: Äpfel und Bananen. Ja, kein Problem. Vorne rechts.

11 Teenager: — Limburger? Was ist denn das? Gouda und Brie — natürlich — Käse. Aber wohin? Da drüben links. Klar.

12 Teenager: — Und jetzt diese Kisten hier. Hmm! riecht ganz frisch. Köstlich. Frisch gebacken, natürlich. Wo kommen die hin? Ach ja, ganz hinten rechts.

13 Kundin: — Entschuldigen Sie, junger Mann.
Teenager: — Ja?
Kundin: — Ich sehe, Sie haben ein paar Kisten Sekt, aber ich brauche keine Kiste — eine Flasche genügt. Wo bekomme ich eine Flasche Sekt?
Teenager: — Ich weiß das leider nicht. Was ist denn Sekt?
Kundin: — Sekt? Wein ist das. Schaumwein.
Teenager: — Ach so. Tja, ganz hinten links, sehen Sie?
Kundin: — Ja. Vielen Dank.
Teenager: — Bitte schön.

14 Teenager: — Schweinefleisch — das ist doch keine Wurst, oder? Hackfleisch, Schweinefleisch. Ach so, ja. Hier vorn, rechts. Gut. Das ist alles.

Solution: **1**C **2**D **3**I **4**E **5**A **6**J **7**D **8**B **9**H **10**F **11**J **12**D **13**A **14**G

131
(1B 33) **Im Supermarkt**

W

Tell pupils, in English, to study the cartoon for *Wo kommen diese Kisten hin?* and ask them if they think the layout of the store is logical. When they have agreed that it is somewhat illogical, tell them to think of their own local supermarket, and draw and label the shelf arrangements, using the Pupil's Book for reference, if required.

Display a number of examples on the classroom wall, where possible.

L, R, (W)

52

Ladendieb!

Tell pupils they are to play the part of assistant store detectives: four customers are being questioned about their purchases and their answers are being checked against their till receipts and the contents of their shopping bags. Pupils must identify who is not telling the whole truth and write his or her name and the stolen article at the bottom of the worksheet, after the questions: *Wer ist der Ladendieb? Was hat er/sie gestohlen?* To help them eliminate suspects, they should cross off purchases on the till recipts, as they are mentioned by the four customers in turn. Pause the tape where indicated and check comprehension so far.

T: *Seht euch das Bild an* (pointing to the visual at the top of the worksheet). *'Ladendieb'. Was ist denn das?*
P1: Shoplifter?
T: *Richtig. Gut. Also, hier seht ihr vier Kassenbons und vier Kunden: Frau Fromm, Herr Ehrlich, Herr Klau und Frau Ernst. Wer ist ein Ladendieb? Ihr seid Detektive. Ihr mußt herausfinden, wer was gestohlen hat. Seht euch die Bons an, hört gut zu und streicht durch die Einkäufe, so.* (Play the first item, and demonstrate by crossing out *'2kg Schweineschnitzel'.*)

Play the tape all the way through, with pauses, then ask: *,Wer ist ein Ladendieb?'* *Schreibt den Namen hier* (point to the bottom of the page). *Und was hat der Dieb gestohlen? Schreibt die Antwort hier* (point to the bottom of the page again).

Ladendieb!

Ladendetektiv: — Guten Tag, meine Damen und Herren. Ich bin Ladendetektiv, und ich muß ihnen leider ein paar Fragen stellen. Wie heißen Sie, bitte?
Frau Fromm: — Fromm. Frau Fromm heiße ich.
Ladendetektiv: — Also, was für Fleisch haben Sie gekauft?
Frau Fromm: — Zwei Kilo Schweineschnitzel.
Ladendetektiv: — Danke. Und Sie, wie ist Ihr Name?
Frau Ernst: — Frau Ernst, junger Mann.

Ladendetektiv: — Also, Frau Ernst. Was für Fleisch haben Sie gekauft?
Frau Ernst: — Ich? Ich habe kein Fleisch gekauft. Nur Wurst.
Ladendetektiv: — Und Sie ... ? Wie heißen Sie bitte?
Herr Klau: — Egon. Egon Klau. Anderthalb Kilo Rouladen.
Ladendetektiv: — Danke. Und Sie? Wie heißen Sie auch, bitte?
Herr Ehrlich: — Ja, ich heiße Herr Ehrlich. Und ich habe ein Kilo Schnitzelbraten und ein Kilo Rinderleber gekauft.
Ladendetektiv: — Und Käse?
Herr Ehrlich: — Ja. Dreihundert Gramm. Das heißt, zwei hundert Gramm Wilstermarschkäse und hundert Gramm französischen Weichkäse.
Ladendetektiv: — Und Sie, Frau Fromm? Was für Käse haben Sie gekauft?
Frau Fromm: — Ich habe keinen Käse gekauft. *(Pause tape.)*
Ladendetektiv: — Frau Ernst?
Frau Ernst: — Tja, Gouda habe ich gekauft — zweihundert Gramm, glaube ich.
Ladendetektiv: — Zweihundert Gramm, danke. Und Sie, Herr Klau?
Herr Klau: — Nein, ich habe keinen Käse gekauft.
Ladendetektiv: — Also, kein Käse für Herrn Klau. Und Wurst?
Herr Klau: — Ja, dreihundert Gramm Salami.
Ladendetektiv: — Frau Ernst?
Frau Ernst: — Hundert Gramm Jagdwurst.
Ladendetektiv: — Herr Ehrlich?
Herr Ehrlich: — Wurst haben Sie gesagt? Nein, ich habe keine Wurst gekauft. *(Pause tape.)*
Ladendetektiv: — Frau Fromm?
Frau Fromm: — Ja, ich habe zweihundert Gramm Leberwurst gekauft.
Ladendetektiv: — Und haben Sie Fisch oder Fischgerichte gekauft?
Frau Fromm: — Fisch? Nein. Keinen Fisch.
Ladendetektiv: — Frau Ernst — Sie haben auch keinen Fisch gekauft?
Frau Ernst: — Doch. Ich habe eine Dose Sardinen gekauft.
Ladendetektiv: — Und Sie, Herr Ehrlich?
Herr Ehrlich: — Ja, ich habe einen Becher Heringssalat gekauft.
Ladendetektiv: — Einen Becher Heringssalat. Danke. Herr Klau?
Herr Klau: — Nein. Ich habe keinen Fisch gekauft.
Ladendetektiv: — Haben Sie Butter oder Margarine gekauft, Herr Klau?
Herr Klau: — Nein — gar keine. *(Pause tape.)*

Ladendetektiv:	— Frau Ernst?
Frau Ernst:	— Butter oder Margarine? Ja, zwei Becher Margarine.
Ladendetektiv:	— Herr Ehrlich?
Herr Ehrlich:	— Ja — eine Packung Molkereibutter.
Ladendetektiv:	— Und Sie, Frau Fromm? Was für Butter oder Margarine haben Sie gekauft?
Frau Fromm:	— Fünfhundert Gramm EG Butter und einen Becher Margarine.
Ladendetektiv:	— Also, Butter **und** Margarine. Haben Sie auch Kekse gekauft?
Frau Fromm:	— Ja.
Ladendetektiv:	— Wieviel?
Frau Fromm:	— Eine Packung.
Ladendetektiv:	— Und Sie, Herr Klau?
Herr Klau:	— Ja, ich auch. Eine Packung Kekse.
Ladendetektiv:	— Herr Ehrlich?
Herr Ehrlich:	— Nein — keine Kekse.
Ladendetektiv:	— Frau Ernst?
Frau Ernst:	— Auch keine Kekse.
Ladendetektiv:	— Na, Frau Ernst, was für Getränke haben Sie gekauft?
Frau Ernst:	— Getränke? Ja, einen Liter Milch, sechs Flaschen Pils und eine Packung Tee.
Ladendetektiv:	— Frau Fromm?
Frau Fromm:	— Drei Flaschen Wein. ،
Ladendetektiv:	— Herr Ehrlich?
Herr Ehrlich:	— Nein. Keine Getränke. *(Pause tape.)*
Ladendetektiv:	— Herr Klau?
Herr Klau:	— Ja, ich habe eine Flasche Sherry und eine Packung Kaffee gekauft.
Ladendetektiv:	— Aa, und haben Sie Waschmittel oder Seife gekauft?
Herr Klau:	— Ja, eine Packung Conlei und ein Stück Seife.
Ladendetektiv:	— Herr Ehrlich?
Herr Ehrlich:	— Ich habe eine Packung Persil gekauft.
Ladendetektiv:	— Frau Fromm?
Frau Fromm:	— Hm, ja, ich habe ein Stück Seife gekauft.
Ladendetektiv:	— Frau Ernst?
Frau Ernst:	— Nein — kein Waschmittel und keine Seife.
Ladendetektiv:	— Ist das alles, Frau Ernst?
Frau Ernst:	— Ja, ich glaube schon.
Ladendetektiv:	— In Ihrer Tasche war auch eine Tafel Schokolade.
Frau Ernst:	— Oh, Entschuldigung. Das ist richtig. Ich habe auch Schokolade gekauft.
Ladendetektiv:	— Danke. Frau Fromm?
Frau Fromm:	— Ja, das ist alles, glaube ich.

Ladendetektiv:	— In Ihrer Tasche war auch ein Liter Milch.
Frau Fromm:	— Ach, ja, Milch. Das habe ich vergessen.
Ladendetektiv:	— Herr Klau — ist das alles?
Herr Klau:	— Ja.
Ladendetektiv:	— In Ihrer Tasche war auch eine Flasche Whisky.
Herr Klau:	— Ach ja, genau.
Ladendetektiv:	— Herr Ehrlich, ist das alles?
Herr Ehrlich:	— Ja, sicher.
Ladendetektiv:	— Danke.

Solution: Wer ist der Ladendieb? Herr Klau. Was hat er gestohlen? Eine Flasche Whisky.

L, S

52

Ladendieb!

Using the four till receipts, ask pupils to play the parts of the four customers and answer the question: ‚*Was hast du gekauft?*' (To be dealt with formally in Area 5). This will afford them practice of *kein*, etc.

T:	*Peter, du bist Herr Ehrlich. Was hast du gekauft?*
Peter:	*Ein Kilo Schnitzelbraten.*
T:	*Und hast du Wein gekauft?*
Peter:	*Nein, ich habe keinen Wein gekauft.*

L, S

52

Wer bin ich? (Ladendieb!)

Pupils could work in pairs, using the four till receipts, and use logic to work out which one of the customers their partner is pretending to be. The following format should be followed, to ensure pupils make full use of their powers of logic: only general questions may be asked and the answers must always be *ja* or *nein*. Write the proposed format on the board.

e.g. **1** Hast du Fleisch gekauft? Ja/nein
2 Hast du Käse gekauft? Ja/nein
3 Hast du Wurst gekauft? Ja/nein usw.

99 66

T: *Seht euch die Kassenbons an.*
Partnerarbeit. Hier (pointing to the board)
seht ihr ein paar Fragen. Antwortet mit ja
oder nein. Machen wir das zusammen.
(To a pupil:) *Wähle einen Namen hier auf*
dem Arbeitsbogen — Frau Fromm, Herr
Ehrlich usw. Sag mir den Namen nicht!
Also, hast du Fleisch gekauft?

P1: *Nein.*

T: *Du bist Frau Ernst!*

P1: *Ja.*

If you're lucky/unlucky enough to guess the
identity so quickly, complete one more
example with another pupil. The winner is the
partner who asks the fewest questions.

---

nem 4   W

245
(1B 129)

Im Geschäft: Partnerarbeit

An activity practising shop language from both
sides of the counter.

---

8   Area 4

● **Buying other items, including stamps,**
mainly in a department store

L, S

Present the new items in groups of 3 or 4, as
usual, calling upon pupils to repeat
individually and chorally. Ask simple, obvious
questions to cue the new vocabulary.

99 66

T: *Ist das eine Postkarte?* (Show box of
chocolates)

P1: *Nein, das ist eine Schachtel Pralinen.*

Conclude this introductory section with the
visual of the department store, thus:

Hier kann man fast alles kaufen — Postkarten,
T-Shirts, Andenken, Fußballschuhe, Blumen,
Pralinen, Schals, Notizblöcke, Schreibpapier,
Portemonnaies, Radiergummis, Bleistifte — ja
*fast alles. Was ist das denn? Das ist **ein***
Warenhaus.

Teach *Warenhaus* before moving onto the next
item.

132
(1B 34)

(L, S), R

Warenhäuser

Bei uns haben wir (name of local department
store). *Das ist ein Warenhaus. Hier seht ihr*
Warenhäuser in Deutschland, Österreich und
in der Schweiz. Practise pronunciation.

133
(1B 35)

(L, S), R

Im Warenhaus

Tell pupils to look at the pictures and to
consult the *Wörterliste* for meanings, if
necessary. Briefly practise pronunciation.

133
(1B 35)

L, R

Wegweiser

Tell pupils that you are going to play them a
few dialogues heard in a *Warenhaus* and ask
them to say, in English, what they are about.

Then tell pupils to look at the *Wegweiser.* Play
the recordings again and use the pause
button after the question. Give pupils time to
find the item on the *Wegweiser,* then play the
answer and ask pupils to repeat it. Continue
similarly with the other dialogues.

Wegweiser

1 — Entschuldigen Sie, bitte. Wo kann ich
hier Schallplatten bekommen?
— Da drüben im Erdgeschoß.

2 — Bitte, wo kann ich hier Topfpflanzen
bekommen?
— Topfpflanzen? Also, das wäre im
Untergeschoß, hinten rechts.

3 — Wo gibt es hier Andenken, bitte?
— Ja, hier im Erdgeschoß.

4 — Entschuldigung, wo haben Sie wohl
Postkarten?
— Im Erdgeschoß . . . bei den
Schreibwaren.
— Danke.

5 — Wo kann ich hier Kassetten bekommen?
— Mal sehen. Ja, da drüben im
Erdgeschoß.
— Vielen Dank.

6 — Wo gibt es hier Pralinen, bitte?
— Unten — im Untergeschoß.
— Danke schön.
— Bitte.

7 — Entschuldigen Sie. Wo kann ich hier Fußballschuhe bekommen?
— Im Erdgeschoß. Die Sportabteilung ist im Erdgeschoß.

8 — Wo kann ich hier einen Schal bekommen?
— Einen Schal? Mal sehen. Das finden Sie im ersten Stock.

9 — Wo gibt es hier Blumen, bitte?
— Im zweiten Stock. Nein, nein — im Untergeschoß.

10 — Wo gibt es hier Schreibpapier und Notizblöcke?
— Tja . . . Schreibwaren — das ist alles im Erdgeschoß.
— Danke.

11 — Wo kann ich hier einen Radiergummi bekommen?
— Einen Radiergummi? Im ersten Stock. In der Kinderabteilung. Hier müssen Sie nach oben.
— So. Danke schön.

12 — Wo kann ich hier ein Portemonnaie bekommen?
— Portemonnaies finden Sie bei den Andenken im Erdgeschoß, oder auch unter Lederwaren.

13 — Wo gibt es hier T-Shirts, bitte?
— Für Herren oder Damen?
— Für Kinder.
— Also, das finden Sie im ersten Stock.

L, S

Wegweiser

Tell pupils to work in pairs and produce dialogues similar to those heard in the recording.

L, S, R, W

53

Wo kann ich das hier bekommen?

Partner A works at the information desk. Partner B makes enquiries about where certain items are to be found and makes a note on his 'shopping list'.

B: *Wo kann ich ... bekommen?*
A: *Im ersten Stock.*

If required, refer pupils to the *Tip des Tages*. Check the results orally as a class activity.

L, R

134
(**1B** 36)

Ich hätte gern ...

Tell pupils you are going to play them some dialogues recorded in different departments of the store. Tell them to match the recordings to the visuals. Look at the visuals carefully, then go through the first dialogue together.

T: *Hört gut zu!* (Play the first dialogue.) *Also, welches Bild ist das?*
P1: *(Bild) A.*
T: *Richtig. Nun, hört zu.*

Ich hätte gern ...

1 Verkäufer: — Darf ich Ihnen helfen?
Junge: — Ja, ich hätte gern einen Schreibblock.
Verkäufer: — Ja, bitte, hier an der Kasse.

2 Mädchen: — Ich möchte ein Portemonnaie, bitte.
Verkäuferin: — Ein Portemonnaie? Ja, also, hier gibt es eine große Auswahl.

3 Junge: — Was kosten die Fußballschuhe, bitte?
Verkäufer: — Fußballschuhe? Ab fünfzig Mark.

4 Junge: — Ich hätte gern eine Topfpflanze.
Verkäuferin: — Ja, was für eine Topfpflanze?
Junge: — Also, sie darf nicht sehr teuer sein.

5 Mädchen: — Ich hätte gern einen Schal.
Verkäuferin: — Welche Farbe? Ein blauer Schal, vielleicht?
Mädchen: — Ja, der blaue Schal gefällt mir gut.

6 Junge: — Kann ich hier Postkarten bekommen?

Verkäufer: — Ja, natürlich. Hier sind sie.

7 Verkäuferin: — Bitte schön?

Junge: — Ich hätte gern ein paar Blumen. Narzissen vielleicht.

8 Mädchen: — Ich hätte gern einen Radiergummi. Einen von diesen hier.

Verkäufer: — Ja, die Tiere. Welches Tier soll es sein? Das Kaninchen oder der Elefant?

Mädchen: — Der Elefant, bitte.

9 Verkäufer: — Was darf es sein, bitte?

Junge: — Eine Schachtel Marzipan, bitte.

Verkäuferin: — Lübecker Marzipan?

Junge: — Ja, bitte.

10 Junge: — Ich möchte ein T-Shirt.

Verkäufer: — Welche Größe?

Junge: — Wie bitte?

Verkäufer: — Ein großes oder ein kleines T-Shirt?

Junge: — Ein kleines, bitte.

11 Mädchen: — Was für Andenken haben Sie?

Verkäufer: — Andenken? Tja, alles — Schlüsselringe, Puppen, Bilder, Postkarten, alles ...

12 Verkäufer: — Bitte schön?

Junge: — Ich hätte gern die neueste Kassette von Evi Bamm.

Verkäufer: — Die Kassetten sind alle ausverkauft, aber wir haben die Platte von Evi Bamm.

Junge: — Danke — ich habe keinen Plattenspieler.

Solution: **1**A, **2**H, **3**D, **4**C, **5**E, **6**B, **7**C, **8**A, **9**H, **10**F, **11**B, **12**G

---

134 (1B 36) Ich hätte gern ... Partnerarbeit

L, S, R

An opportunity to practise the language of the previous exercise and revise *im ersten/zweiten Stock*.

L

Im Warenhaus verkauft man fast alles ... aber keine Briefmarken

Tell pupils to listen to the dialogue then ask them, in English, what has happened.

Hört gut zu! Was passiert hier? (Play the first section of the tape).

Im Warenhaus verkauft man fast alles ... aber keine Briefmarken

Junge: — Entschuldigung.

Verkäuferin: — Ja?

Junge: — Wo bekomme ich hier Briefmarken?

Verkäuferin: — Briefmarken? Im Warenhaus verkauft man fast alles, aber keine Briefmarken.

Junge: — Wo bekomme ich denn Briefmarken?

Verkäuferin: — Auf der Post. Die ist in der Hauptstraße. Gehen Sie hier geradeaus bis zur Ampel dann biegen Sie nach links ab. Die Post ist auf der rechten Seite.

Junge: — Ist es weit von hier?

Verkäuferin: — Nein, so etwa drei Minuten.

Junge: — Danke schön.

Verkäuferin: — Bitte schön.

Ask pupils to tell you what happened and where the Post Office is, then refer them to the Pupil's Book for the dialogues which follow.

L, W

134 (1B 36) Auf der Post

Tell pupils that they are going to hear five dialogues in the Post Office which they should match to the visuals in the Pupils' Book.

T: Jetzt sind wir auf der Post. Seht euch die Briefe und Postkarten an. (Complete no. 1 with the pupils. Play the tape then ask:) *Ist das A, B, C, D oder E?*

P1: A.

T: Richtig. Hört zu!

Auf der Post

1 Junge: — Was kostet ein Brief nach England, bitte?

Dame: — 80 Pfennig.

Junge: — Eine dann, bitte.

Dame: — Eine Briefmarke zu 80. Bitte schön.

2 Mädchen: — Was kostet eine Postkarte nach Frankreich, bitte?

Dame: — 60 Pfennig.

Mädchen: — Und ein Brief?

Dame: — 80 Pfennig.

Mädchen: — Also, eine zu 60 Pfennig und eine zu 80.

3 Dame: — Bitte schön?
Junge: — Eine Postkarte nach Schottland, was kostet das, bitte?
Dame: — 60 Pfennig.
Junge: — Aha, zwei, bitte.
Dame: — DM 1,20 bitte.

4 Mädchen: — Meine Brieffreundin wohnt in Amerika. Was kostet ein Brief nach Amerika, bitte?
Dame: — DM 1,20.
Mädchen: — Danke — und eine Postkarte?
Dame: — DM 70 Pfennig.
Mädchen: — Also, eine Briefmarke zu DM 1,20 und zwei Briefmarken zu DM 70 Pfennig.

5 Junge: — Ein Brief nach Österreich kostet 80 Pfennig, oder?
Dame: — Ja, genau.
Junge: — Also, drei Stück, bitte.
Dame: — Bitte schön. DM 2,40. Mark.

Solution: **1**A, **2**E, **3**B, **4**C, **5**D

Tell pupils to copy the envelopes and postcards into their exercise books and then to write on them the corresponding addresses. Make sure they write the value of the stamps clearly on their versions.

Zeichnet die Umschläge und Postkarten in euer Heft und schreibt die richtigen Adressen (und Briefmarken) darauf, ungefähr so... (point to the example in the text).

L, S, R

Partnerarbeit: Was kostet ein Brief nach Schottland?

Using the visuals now in the pupil's exercise books, practise the transactional language with the pupils before encouraging them to move on to pair-work. For the pair-work activity, refer them to the *Tip des Tages*.

T: *Jetzt seid ihr* (pointing at the group) *auf der Post. Macht Dialoge mit mir* (point to yourself). *Hier, zum Beispiel,* (select a pupil and point to one of the letters or post cards).
     Was kostet ein Brief ...
P1: *Was kostet ein Brief nach Schottland?*
T: *PF. 80.* (Hold up one finger to the pupil and mouth *eine*).
P1: *Eine, bitte.*

Complete several examples in this way before moving on to pair-work.

T: *Partnerarbeit. Seht euch 'Tip des Tages' an und macht Dialoge. Was kostet ein Brief/eine Postkarte nach Spanien, Italien, Nordirland ... ?*

nem 5
245
(1B 129)

W

Im Warenhaus

Consolidation of the language required for transactions in a department store.

8 # Area 5

● **Talking about what you have just bought and who it is for**

L, R

Was hast du heute gekauft?

Tell pupils to listen to the first two recordings and see if they can work out what they are about. Then ask them to look at the visual in the Pupil's Book and listen again in order to find out who bought what.

Hört gut zu! Worum geht es hier? Antwortet auf Englisch. Jetzt seht euch die Bilder an. Wer hat einen Computer gekauft? und eine Kassette?

Was hast du heute gekauft?

1 — Hallo Dorit. Wie geht's?
— Hallo Birgit. Mir geht's gut, danke.
— Wo warst du denn heute?
— In der Stadt. Ich habe ein neues Make-up bei Horten gekauft. Es war ganz billig. Es hat nur DM 4,00 gekostet.
— Mensch, das ist ja sagenhaft billig. Ich gehe auch dorthin. Tschüs!
— Tschüs.

2 — Grüß dich, Peter. Was machst du denn hier in der Fußgängerzone?
— Grüß dich, Bernd. Ich gehe jetzt nach Hause.
— Hast du 'was Interessantes gekauft?
— Ja, einen Computer.
— Einen Computer?? Hast du soviel Geld?
— Nein, aber letzte Woche hatte ich Geburtstag.
— Ach so. Der Computer ist ein Geburtstagsgeschenk, was? War er teuer?
— Ja. DM 900,00.
— Tja, das ist viel Geld!

3 — Hallo, Gaby.
— Hallo, Susi. Gehst du in die Stadt?
— Nein, ich habe kein Geld mehr.
— Wieso denn nicht?
— Ich habe diese Ohrringe gekauft. Die waren wirklich teuer.
— Was haben die gekostet?

— DM 40.
— Das ist viel Geld. Aber die Ohrringe gefallen mir gut.

4 — Hallo, Rachel.
— Hallo, Rebecca. Wie geht's?
— Nicht gut. Ich bin ein bißchen müde. Ich war den ganzen Tag in der Stadt.
— Hast du Lust auf ein Eis? Gehen wir in ein Eiscafe?
— Tolle Idee!

(In the ice cream parlour)

Das Eis schmeckt gut, Rachel.
— Ja, wirklich lecker. Hast du heute viel gekauft?
— Ja und wie! Ich habe diese Hose bei Hertie gekauft.
— Die gefällt mir gut. War sie teuer?
— Nein, es geht ... Ich habe auch diesen Pullover gekauft.
— Der gefällt mir auch gut.
— Hast **du** etwas gekauft, Rachel?
— Ja, eine Kassette von Ede Funk.
— Ede Funk! Der singt so schlecht!
— Nee, mir gefällt er gut.
— Hast du sonst noch etwas gekauft?
— Ja, ein Eis für dich, Rebecca.
— Vielen Dank.

L, S

136 (1B 38)

Was hast du heute gekauft?

Use the visuals in the following way to practise the perfect tense after eliciting the meaning.

T: *Ich habe eine Kassette gekauft. Wie heißt das auf Englisch? John, du bist Peter* (point to visual). *Was hast du heute gekauft?*

L, S

various

Use known flashcards to cue similar dialogues. Encourage pupils to ask the question as soon as possible: *‚Was hast du gekauft?'*

L, S, (W)

136 (1B 38)

Und du? Warst du auch in der Stadt?

Practise with the whole class first of all. Then continue in pairs. Consolidate in writing, if required.

R

136-137 (1B 38-39)

Aldi-Supermarkt

The visuals and text highlight the different tenses: *ist/war; kauft/hat ... gekauft.* Ask pupils to read the text and make observations about the different forms of the verbs (in English).

---

nem 6

245 (1B 129)

L, S, R

Rebecca und Rachel waren heute in der Stadt

This is a transcript with visuals of one of the previous recordings. Detailed comprehension is tested by questions in English. Pupils could practise the dialogue in pairs and then perform it as a playlet. If required, play the recording again.

---

nem 7

246 (1B 130)

R, W

Kannst du einen Satz bilden?

Tell pupils to rewrite the jumbled sentences in the correct order. This activity consolidates further the word order in the Perfect Tense. Go through the first question orally first.

L, S

137 (1B 39)

Was hast du gestern gekauft?

This activity introduces and practises gestern.

T: *Heute ist Mittwoch. Was hast du gestern gekauft?*
P: *Ohrringe.*
T: *Du hast **heute** Ohrringe gekauft, aber was hast du **gestern** gekauft? Was ist gestern auf Englisch? Jetzt Partnerarbeit.* (Once the concept is clear.)

L, S

137 (1B 39)

Wo hat man die Bananen gekauft?

Pupils have to find out which shop the different items were bought in, by referring to the visuals. Practise with the whole class and then in pairs. The suggested language is in the Pupil's Book.

---

nem 8

246 (1B 130)

R, W

Was schreibt man hier?

A word puzzle.

Solution: Warst du in der Stadt? Was hast du gekauft? Einen Pullover, eine Hose und ein Eis.

Einkaufskettenspiel

Divide the class into groups of about eight. The first person must say what he has bought. The second person must repeat the purchase of the first person and then add another, and so on. This activity emphasises the position of *gekauft*.

T: *Ann, du fängst an. Du warst in der Stadt, und du sagst, was du gekauft hast. Du sagst zum Beispiel: ‚Ich war heute in der Stadt und habe eine Hose gekauft.' Du John, du machst dann weiter. Du sagst: ‚Ich war heute in der Stadt und habe eine Hose und einen Pullover gekauft.'*
(Continue until pupils have understood).
Jetzt, Gruppenarbeit!

138
(1B 40)

David kommt nach Hamburg

Read the text with the class and elicit that it is about David giving his German family some presents. Then ask the pupils to listen to the recording and find out what he gives each person. Tell pupils to write their answers in English or German. The suggested language is in the Pupil's Book.

David kommt nach Hamburg

Frau Timm: — Grüß dich, David. Wie war die Reise?
David: — Sehr lang.
Frau Timm: — Bist du müde?
David: — Ja, ein bißchen. Ich habe ein paar Geschenke mitgebracht. Das ist für Sie, Frau Timm.
Frau Timm: — Für mich, David? Oh, wie schön. Eine Packung Tee. Danke schön.
David: — Und Herr Timm, das ist für Sie.
Herr Timm: — Vielen Dank. Eine Flasche Whiskey aus Schottland! Der schmeckt sicher gut. Recht vielen Dank.
David: — Und das ist für dich, Anton.
Anton: — Danke. Was ist denn das? ... Ein T-Shirt. Mensch! Das ist toll!
David: — Für Arko und Mitzi habe ich auch etwas mitgebracht. Einen Gummiknochen für den Hund und Mitzi bekommt ein Foto von meiner Katze in England.

139
(1B 41)

Dialoge

Tell the pupils to work in pairs and produce dialogues similar to the example in their books. The suggested language is in the Pupil's Book.

138
(1B 40)

Was hat David für seine Familie in England gekauft?

Tell pupils to look at the diagram and listen to the recording to find out what David bought for his own family.

T: *Hört gut zu.* (Play the first recording). *Was hat David für seinen Bruder gekauft?*
P: *Ein Popmagazin.*
T: *Ja, richtig. Für seinen Bruder hat er ein Popmagazin gekauft.* (Write on the board). *Hört jetzt gut zu und schreibt die Antwort in euer Heft.*

Was hat David für seine Familie in England gekauft?

— Für meinen Bruder habe ich ein Popmagazin gekauft. Er ist fünfzehn und lernt Deutsch in der Schule. Und für meine kleine Schwester, Tina, habe ich einen Radiergummi gekauft. Schau, ein Kaninchen! Für meine Mutter habe ich diesen Schal gekauft.
— Ist er aus Wolle?
— Nein, Polyester. Für meinen Vater habe ich ein Portemonnaie gekauft. Und für meinen Hund habe ich einen Ball gekauft. Im Garten spielt er gern mit einem Ball. Für meine Katze Bilbo habe ich dieses Spielzeug gekauft.
— Was ist denn das?
— Eine kleine Maus aus Wolle.
— Spitze!

138
(1B 40)

Angela war auch eine Woche bei einer Familie in Deutschland

Presentation of *ihren/ihre*. In the context of the previous activity involving *seinen/seine* this should be easily understood. Practise the examples with the whole class at first and then consolidate in writing.

T: *Was hat Angela für ihren Vater gekauft? Gummibärchen? Einen Ball?*
P: *Nein.*
T: *Briefmarken? Schreibpapier? Ja, vielleicht. Für ihren Vater hat sie vielleicht Schreibpapier gekauft.*
(Continue similarly and then ask pupils to write the answers in their books).

Was hast du gekauft?

An activity to practise *ich habe … gekauft* and *für meine(n) …*

8 Area 6

• Consolidation

140
(1B 42)
R, W

Ich habe den Zettel verloren. Was war darauf?

A type of Kim's game. After reading a shopping list for five minutes, pupils work in pairs to reconstruct the list with their books closed. Suggested language is in the Pupil's Book.

140
(1B 42)
L, S, R, W

Was darf es heute sein?

An open-ended model dialogue to cue simple playlets about shopping for food.

Jetzt Partnerarbeit. Schreibt aber alle zuerst eine Einkaufsliste. Fertig? Gut. Du bist der Verkäufer und du bist der Kunde. Du (shopkeeper) sagst: ‚Guten Tag. Was darf es heute sein?' Und du (customer) sagst: ‚Guten Tag, ich möchte' (start reading from shopping list and stop after three or four items). Also, jetzt macht weiter.

nem 10
246
(1B 130)
L, S, R

Kann man hier Briefmarken kaufen?

Tell pupils to look at the pictures and signs.

T: *Seht euch die Bilder an. Bild Nr. I: Kann man hier Briefmarken kaufen? (Initially:) Ja? Vielleicht? Nein?*
P: *Nein.*
T: *Nein. Auf keinen Fall. Bild Nr. 2: Kann man …*

Encourage pupils to take on the teacher's role as soon as possible. Continue in pairs. Encourage those who can to use the range of variants when replying.

L, S

A variant of the previous activity is to use flashcards as the prompts. Once pupils can do this with confidence, allow them to come to the front of the class, choose a flashcard and frame their own question, e.g.

‚Kann man hier Blumen kaufen?'

54
R, W

Wo kaufst du das?/Zu Weihnachten im Warenhaus

A simple gap-filling activity to consolidate *in der/im* and the names of shops. The suggested language is in the Pupil's Book. The impersonal *man kauft* is more suitable for general statements.

L, R

Zu Weihnachten im Warenhaus

Tell pupils to read the text on their sheets and then listen to the department store announcement to find out what Christmas gifts are on offer for the various groups. Tell them to make notes in English under the headings on their sheets. It is not expected that each pupil will be able to understand all the items, but the class as a whole should be able to piece together the complete picture.

Zu Weihnachten im Warenhaus

— Sehr geehrte Kunden, sehr geehrte Kundinnen. Wir wünschen Ihnen frohe Weihnachten. Im Warenhaus gibt es eine große Auswahl Weihnachtsgeschenke für die ganze Familie. Die Abteilung für kleine Kinder ist im vierten Stock. Hier finden Sie alles für das ein- bis vierjährige Kind. Es gibt Duplo, Stofftiere, Bilderbücher … Alles für das kleine Kind.

Im vierten Stock gibt es auch Geschenke für Kinder zwischen vier und acht. Zum Beispiel Puzzles, Puppen und Bücher. Im dritten Stock sind Geschenke für ältere Kinder zwischen acht und zwölf. Es gibt Fahrräder, Badmintonschläger, Zelte. Alles mögliche.

Im dritten Stock gibt es auch alles für den Teenager. Alles für den Sport ... Sportschuhe, Trainingsanzüge, Tennisschläger. Alles für die Freizeit ... Schallplatten, Kassetten, Jeans, Pullover.

Im zweiten Stock finden Sie alles für Ihren Mann, Ihren Freund, Ihren Onkel oder Ihren Vater. Wir haben Handschuhe, Schals, Rasierapparate, Hosen und so weiter. Das nimmt kein Ende.

Suchen Sie etwas für Ihre Freundin, Ihre Frau, Ihre Mutter oder Ihre Tante? Sie finden alles im ersten Stock. Make-up, Parfum, Büstenhalter, Kleider, Bücher und Schmuck. Sie finden einfach alles!

Wir wünschen Ihnen einen angenehmen Tag bei uns. Wenn Sie hungrig werden, vergessen Sie nicht das Restaurant im Erdgeschoß. Da gibt es eine große Auswahl ... *(fade out)*.

L

141 (1B 43)

Was kaufen sie auf der Post?

A series of short dialogues at the post office. Pupils listen for the number of stamps, the individual price and the total price.

Wieviel Briefmarken kaufen diese Leute? Was kosten die Briefmarken? Was macht das alles zusammen? Hört gut zu! (Play the first dialogue and do the first question on the board with the whole class).

Was kaufen sie auf der Post?

1 —Guten Tag. Zwei Briefmarken zu achtzig Pfennig.
  —Zwei zu achtzig. Eine Mark sechzig, bitte.

2 —Zehn Briefmarken zu sechzig, bitte.
  —Zehn zu sechzig. Das macht DM 6,00.

3 —Acht Briefmarken zu dreißig Pfennig.
  —Das macht DM 2,40. Sonst noch etwas?
  —Nein, danke.

4 —Vier Briefmarken zu fünfzig Pfennig, bitte.
  —Vier zu vierzig?
  —Nein, zu fünfzig.
  —Das macht DM 2,00.
  —Moment, ich habe das klein.
  —Danke.

5 —Ja, bitte?
  —Fünf Briefmarken zu DM 1,00, bitte.
  —Sonst noch etwas?
  —Nein, danke.
  —Also, DM 5,00 bitte.

6 —Eine Briefmarke zu DM 5,00, bitte.
  —Für ein Paket?
  —Ja.
  —Soll ich es wiegen?
  —Nein, das ist nicht nötig.

7 —Zwanzig Briefmarken zu achtzig Pfennig.
  —Zwanzig?
  —Ja.
  —Das macht DM 16,00.
  —Danke schön.

8 —Fünfzehn Briefmarken zu dreißig, bitte.
  —Sonst noch etwas?
  —Zwei Briefmarken zu achtzig.
  —Insgesamt macht das DM 6,10.
  —Danke.

Solution:

1 2 at 80 = DM 1,60
2 10 at 60 = DM 6,00
3 8 at 30 = DM 2,40
4 4 at 50 = DM 2,00
5 5 at DM 1,00 = DM 5,00
6 1 at DM 5,00 = DM 5,00
7 20 at 80 = DM 16,00
8 15 at 30 + 2 at 80 = DM 6,10

R, W

141 (1B 43)

Einige Informationen: Ein Briefkasten

A close-up of a post box giving details of collection times. Questions in English and German.

Solution:

1 Yes.
2 Sunday 8.00.
3 Red dot.
4 Saturday — next collection is 11.30.
5 Yellow; letters in at side; etc.

A gelb
B an der Seite
C am Samstag
D Montagmorgen, 7.00
E zweimal

L, R

140 (1B 42)

Radiorezepte

You know the ingredients for making *Risotto* and *Eintopf*, but you don't know the quantities for *Risotto* for four people and *Eintopf* for six, so you listen to the *Radiorezepte*. The suggested language is in the Pupil's Book. Explain *Zutaten* if necessary, e.g. *Die Zutaten von Risotto sind Champignons, Tomaten, Margarine ...*

Radiorezepte

— Guten Tag, meine Damen und Herren. Es ist 16.00 Uhr. Wir bringen Ihnen 'Radiorezepte für heute'. Heute kochen wir Risotto und Eintopf. Der Risotto ist für vier Personen und der Eintopf für sechs. Haben Sie alle Bleistift und Papier? Ja, dann fangen wir mit den Zutaten an. Zuerst für Risotto für vier Personen. Sie brauchen:

100g Champignons
8 Tomaten
30g (3 Löffel) Margarine
4 Scheiben Schinken
300g Reis
Bouillonwürfel für einen Liter Wasser
200g Hähnchen
100g Karotten
100g Bohnen
150g Krabben
Salz, Pfeffer und Gewürze.

Und jetzt für den Eintopf für sechs Personen brauchen Sie:

30g Mehl
15g Pfeffer
15g Salz
1,5 Kilo Fleisch
2 Kilo Kartoffeln
500g Karotten
500ml Wasser
1 große Zwiebel

Ich wünsche Ihnen guten Appetit!

141
(1B 43)

L

Frank und Erika im Warenhaus

Tell the pupils that they are going to hear a dialogue between Erika and Frank in a department store, and they must decide which of these two people they would rather go shopping with and give their reason.

The text itself is lengthy, and fairly demanding, but the task allows for a variety of individual responses, e.g.: One pupil might prefer to go shopping with Frank because he is interested in records.

Another pupil might prefer to go with Frank because he does not like spending a lot of time in shops.

In discussing the pupils' reasons, it should be possible to build up a fuller picture of the text.

Erika und Frank sind in einem Warenhaus. Hört gut zu.
Wollt ihr mit Erika oder mit Frank einkaufen gehen? Warum?

Frank und Erika im Warenhaus

Erika: — So, wo sind hier die Schuhe?
Frank: — Weiß nicht.
Erika: — Wo ist ein Wegweiser? Ach, da ist einer. Nun, laß mal sehen. Da. Schuhabteilung. Im zweiten Stock. So. Kommst du mit?
Frank: — Was? Schuhe kaufen? Nein, danke!
Erika: — Wartest du dann hier?
Frank: — Wie lange brauchst du denn?
Erika: — Ich weiß nicht. Eine Viertelstunde?
Frank: — Ach, dann gehe ich lieber in die Plattenabteilung.
Erika: — Du, ich will aber auch noch in die Sportabteilung.
Frank: — Und wie lange brauchst du da?
Erika: — Nicht lange. Zwanzig Minuten.
Frank: — Zwanzig Minuten!
Erika: — Ja, und dann komme ich zu dir in die Plattenabteilung. Wo ist die? Platten ... Platten ... Da! Musik, im ersten Stock.
Frank: — Aber nein. Das ist mir viel zu lange. Hier ist es so warm! Ich warte dann lieber draußen.
Erika: — OK. Draußen, am Eiskiosk.
Frank: — In dreißig Minuten.
Erika: — Also, um zwölf. OK. Ich tue mein Bestes. Tschüs!

Vocabulary

ab + Dat *from*
    * 50 Mark *from 50 marks*
die Abteilung(en) *department*
    Amerika *America*
das Andenken(-) *souvenir*
das Angebot(e) *offer*
der Anzug(⁼e) *suit*
die Apfelsine(n) *orange*
die Apotheke(n) *chemist's, pharmacy*
die Aprikose(n) *apricot*
der Arbeitsbogen(⁼) *worksheet*
    ausrechnen *to work out*
    ausverkauft *sold out*
der Badmintonschläger(-) *badminton racquet*
der Ball(⁼e) *ball; dance*
die Banane(n) *banana*
der Becher(-) *tub*
    besorgen *to take care of; get*
die Bettwäsche *bed linen*
    bilden *to form, make*
die Birne(n) *pear*
    blau *blue*
    bloß *simply*
die Bohne(n) *bean*
der Bon(s) *receipt, coupon*
der Bouillonwürfel(-) *stock cube*
    Brasilien *Brazil*
der Briefkasten(⁼) *letterbox*
die Buchhandlung(en) *bookshop*
der Büstenhalter(-) *bra*
das Butterbrot(e) *sandwich*
    daß *that*
    dauern *to last*
der Detektiv(e) *detective*
der Dieb(e) *thief (m)*
die Diebin(nen) *thief (f)*
die Dose(n) *tin*
    draußen *outside*
die Drogerie(n) *chemist's, drugstore*
    durchstreichen *to cross out*
der Einkauf(⁼e) *purchase*
die Einkaufsliste(n) *shopping list*

einstecken *to put in; post; plug in*
der Eintopf *stew, casserole*
der Elefant(en) *elephant*
der Endpreis(e) *total price*
das Erdgeschoß *ground floor*
    im * *on the ground floor*
die Fahrschule(n) *driving school*
die Farbe(n) *colour*
    finden *to find*
    funktionieren *to function, operate*
    gebacken *baked*
    gelb *yellow*
das Gemüsegeschäft(e) *greengrocer's*
    genügen *to suffice, be enough*
das Gericht(e) *dish, meal*
das Gewicht(e) *weight*
das Gewürz(e) *spice*
    grob *rough*
die Gummibärchen *jelly bears*
    Haupt- *main-*
der Hering(e) *herring*
    holen *to fetch*
die Hose(n) *trousers*
    insgesamt *all together*
die Karotte(n) *carrot*
die Kartoffel(n) *potato*
die Kirsche(n) *cherry*
die Kiste(n) *crate*
das Kleidergeschäft(e) *boutique*
das Kleingeld *change (money)*
der Knochen(-) *bone*
die Kondensmilch *evaporated milk*
die Konfitüre(n) *jam*
die Krabbe(n) *shrimp*
die Kreide(n) *chalk*
der Laden(⁼) *shop*
die Leber(n) *liver*
    lecker *tasty, nice*
die Lederwaren *leather goods*
    leeren *to empty*
die Leerung(en) *emptying, collection*
die Linse(n) *lentil*

    los! *come on!*
    Was ist *? *What's up?*
das Make-up *make up*
die Maschine(n) *machine*
die Metzgerei(en) *butcher's*
    miteinander *with one another*
das Möbel *(piece of) furniture*
die Mode(n) *fashion*
    möglich *possible*
die Molkerei(en) *dairy*
    nachher *afterwards*
die Narzisse(n) *daffodil*
der Notizblock(⁼e) *notepad*
    nun *well, now*
die Packung(en) *packet*
das Paket(e) *parcel*
    passieren *to happen, occur*
der Pfirsich(e) *peach*
das Picknick(s) *picnic*
    praktisch *practical*
die Praline(n) *chocolate (in a box)*
der Preis(e) *price*
    probieren *to try, taste*
der Pumpernickel(-) *black bread*
die Puppe(n) *doll*
der Rasierapparat(e) *shaver*
    raten *to guess*
der Riegel(n) *bar (of chocolate, etc.)*
das Rind(er) *beef*
die Rolle(n) *role, part*
    rot *red*
die Roulade(n) *beef olive*
die Sandale(n) *sandal*
die Schachtel(n) *box, packet*
    schade *shame*
    wie *! *what a shame!*
der Schal(s) *scarf*
der Schaumwein(e) *sparkling wine*
    schicken *to send*
    schließlich *finally*
der Schlüsselring(e) *keyring*
der Schmuck *jewelry*
das Schreibpapier *writing paper*

das Schuhgeschäft(e) *shoe shop*
das Schweineschnitzel *pork cutlet*
die Seife *soap*
der Sekt *champagne*
die Selbstbedienung *self-service*
    sofort *at once*
das Sonderangebot(e) *special offer*
    sondern *but, rather*
das Spiel(e) *game*
das Spielzeug(e) *toy*
das Sportgeschäft(e) *sports shop*
    stehlen *to steal*
der Stock(⁼e) *floor, storey*
der Stoff(e) *material, fabric*
der Supermarkt(⁼e) *supermarket*
die Tasche(n) *bag*
die Theke(n) *counter*
die Topfpflanze(n) *potted plant*
die Tube(n) *tube*
das Tuch(⁼er) *cloth, towel, handkerchief*
die Tüte(n) *bag*
die Umfrage(n) *survey*
das Untergeschoß *basement*
der Wegweiser(-) *store guide*
der Verkäufer(-) *sales assistant (m)*
die Verkäuferin(nen) *sales assistant (f)*
    verlieren *to lose*
    vollautomatisch *fully automatic*
das Warenhaus(⁼er) *department store*
das Waschmittel *washing powder/liquid*
    weich *soft*
    Weihnachten *Christmas*
    wiegen *to weigh*
die Wolle(n) *wool*
das Wort(⁼er) *word*
die Zahnpasta *toothpaste*
das Zelt(e) *tent*
der Zettel(-) *note, piece of paper*

Area 1

• Describing means of transport

L, S

Display the transport flashcards and ask pupils how they travel to various places.

T: *Du willst zum Schwimmbad. Wie kommst du dahin?* (Point to flashcards in turn and say:) *Mit dem Zug? Mit dem Wagen? Mit der Straßenbahn? Zu Fuß?*
P: *Zu Fuß.*

T: (Continue similarly with other places, e.g.:) *Du willst zur Disko in ... Wie kommst du dahin? Du willst zum Kino in ...*

Repeat the list of means of transport until pupils are confident to reproduce them without direct prompting.

L, (S)

Wie kommst du dahin?

Ask pupils to look at the pictures on page 144 (**1B** 46). Tell them to listen to the recording and say which picture fits which conversation.

T: *Welches Bild ist das?*
P: *Bild E.*

Wie kommst du dahin?

1 — Wie kommst du zur Schule?
— Ich gehe zu Fuß. Es sind nur zehn Minuten.

2 — Wie kommst du zum Sportplatz?
— Zum Sportplatz fahre ich immer mit dem Rad.

3 — Und wo wohnt deine Freundin?
— In Gütersloh. Das ist 10 Kilometer von hier.
— So weit? Fährst du dann mit dem Bus?
— Nein, mit dem Mofa.

4 — Ich muß morgen nach Köln.
— Und wie kommst du dahin?
— Mit dem Zug. Mein Mofa ist kaputt.

5 — Kommst du heute nachmittag mit zum Hallenbad?
— Gern.
— Fahren wir mit der Straßenbahn?
— Ja, von mir aus.

6 — Du kommst doch heute abend zur Disko? Acht Uhr?
— Acht Uhr? Oh, dann muß ich mit dem Bus fahren.

7 — Kommst du morgen mit dem Moped zu Ullas Party?
— Nein, mein Vater bringt mich mit dem Wagen.

8 — Du fährst nächste Woche nach England?
— Nein, ich fahre nicht, ich fliege.

9 — Was machst du in den Sommerferien?
— Wir fahren nach England.
— Fahrt ihr mit dem Auto? In England muß man links fahren!
— Nein, wir fahren mit dem Zug und mit der Fähre.

Solution: **1E 2G 3B 4F 5C 6A 7D 8I 9H**

L, R, W

Wie kommst du dahin?

A gap-filling exercise. Tell pupils to listen to the previous recording again and to decide whether to write *mit dem, mit der* or *zu* in the gaps.

R, W

144
(1B 46)

Wie fahren sie dahin?

A gap-filling exercise to give written practice of the means of transport. This is followed by pupils writing five sentences about how they get to places.

L, R, W

145
(1B 47)

Gespräche

Two dialogues, in which various means of transport are mentioned. These are exploited by multiple choice exercises. Tell pupils to choose the correct answer each time. Consolidate in written form.

Gespräche

1 — Hallo, Heike!
  — Hallo, Renate. Wie geht's?
  — Danke, gut. Du, hör mal. Ich habe Karten für das Popkonzert am Samstag.
  — Das mit Evi Bamm?
  — Ja, klar!
  — Oh, prima. Dann komme ich also am Samstagnachmittag zu dir nach München. Mit dem Wagen. Meine Mutter bringt mich zu dir.
  — Kommt Heino mit?
  — Nein, der kann nicht so früh, er kommt später mit der Bahn.
  — OK., tschüs. Bis Samstag.

2 — Mutti, meine Klasse plant eine Reise nach London. Darf ich mitfahren?
  — Wie kommt ihr denn nach London? Mit dem Flugzeug?
  — Nein, mit dem Zug nach Ostende und dann mit der Fähre nach Dover. Von da weiter mit der Bahn nach London.
  — Und was kostet das?
  — Nur 800 Mark für 14 Tage.
  — Ich glaube, das ist ein bißchen teuer.

Solution: **1a** Samstag **b** Evi Bamm **c** München
           d Wagen **e** Bahn
           2a London **b** Zug **c** Fähre
           d Bahn **e** DM 800,- ; 14.

---

nem 1

L, S, (R), W

247
(1B 131)

Gruppenarbeit

A class survey of means of travel and transport followed by further written consolidation.

---

nem 2

247
(1B 131)

Zwei Briefe

These two variants are intended to serve as models for pupils' own letters to penfriends in a German-speaking country asking for similar information.

---

nem 3

R, W

247
(1B 131)

Lückentext

Simple, gapped texts on travel and transport.

R

146-147
(1B 48-49)

Einige Informationen: Für junge Leute

Information about modes of transport available to young people. This is not intended necessarily for detailed exploitation. It might, however, be of interest to pupils that there are frequently special *Radwege* for cyclists and that 15-year-olds are allowed to drive certain categories of moped and motorbike.

---

9 Area 2

● **Finding out information, buying tickets and understanding timetables**

L

148
(1B 50)

Entschuldigung ...

A straightforward matching exercise to introduce pupils to the idea of seeking information in a variety of ways and in different situations.

T: *Buchseite 148 (50). Entschuldigung ... Seht euch die Bilder an und hört gut zu. Was paßt zu wem? (Play no. 1) ...*
P: *1E.*
T: *Gut. Ihr schreibt 1E in euer Heft.*

Entschuldigung ...

1 — Entschuldigung. Gibt es hier in der Nähe eine U-Bahnstation?
  — Die U-Bahn ist da drüben, sehen Sie?

2 — Entschuldigung, ich suche den Busbahnhof. Ist das weit von hier?
  — Den Busbahnhof finden Sie hier gerade um die Ecke.

3 — Wo ist der Bahnhof, bitte?
  — Hier geradeaus etwa fünfhundert Meter auf der linken Seite.
  — Danke schön.

4 — Entschuldigung. Ich muß nach Thesdorf
fahren. Wie komme ich am besten dahin?
— Nach Thesdorf — am besten fahren Sie
mit der S-Bahn.

5 — Wo ist die nächste
Straßenbahnhaltestelle, bitte?
— Da drüben, sehen Sie. Vor der
Hauptpost.

Solution: 1E 2A 3B 4D 5C

148
(1B 50)

L, S, R

Ich bin hier fremd

In this activity attention is focused once again
on the questions pupils will need to ask when
seeking information in the street. Tell them to
listen to the recording while looking at the
numbered visuals, in order to work out what
questions are being asked. When they
produce the questions themselves, write them
on the board, in turn, and use the written
forms for individual and choral practice.
Explain, in English, if necessary, that *Ich bin
hier fremd* means 'I'm a stranger here'.

T: *Ihr seid in der Stadt in Deutschland, und
ihr wollt ein paar Fragen stellen. Hört gut
zu — wie sind die Fragen? Nummer eins.
(Play dialogue no. 1) ... Also, wie lautet
die Frage?*
P1: *Wann fährt der nächste Bus?*
T: *Gut. (Repeat with another pupil, then
write the question on the board). Und
wann fährt der nächste Bus?*
P3: *Um 10.57 Uhr.*
T: *Richtig. Also, hört zu!*

Follow the same procedure throughout,
writing the questions on the board. The
questions are underlined in the text.

Ich bin hier fremd

1 — Entschuldigung. Ich bin hier fremd.
Wann fährt der nächste Bus?
— **Wie spät ist es?**
— Halb elf.
— Moment mal. Der nächste Bus fährt um
10.57 Uhr.
— Danke. **Fährt der Bus Richtung
Borstel-Hohenraden?**
— Ja, gleich nach Kummerfeld.
— Vielen Dank.
— Bitte schön.

2 — **Wo kauft man eine Karte, bitte?**
— Im Bus oder am besten am Automaten -
das ist billiger.

---

3 — **Was kostet das, bitte?**
— DM 4,00.
— Ach ja, danke.

4 — **Wie weit ist das?**
— Puh, wie weit ist das? Ungefähr zwanzig
Minuten — tja, acht Kilometer, schätze
ich.

5 — *(Sound of bus drawing up).* Ach, da
kommt der Bus. **Wo steigt man ein?**
— Hier vorn.
— **Und was für Türen sind das in der Mitte?**
— Dort steigt man aus.
— Ach so. Vielen Dank.
— Nichts zu danken.

148
(1B 50)

L, S

Ich bin hier fremd

Tell pupils to use the visuals, on page 148
(**1B** 50), and the questions on the board,
(listed above), in order to produce
dialogues of their own. Practise
pronunciation of places before starting.

*Jetzt Partnerarbeit. Seht euch die Bilder im
Buch und die Fragen hier (an der Tafel/unter
Tip des Tages) an, um Dialoge zu machen.
Zum Beispiel, hört zu.*
(Complete a model dialogue with one pupil).

nem 4

247
(1B 131)

R

Sind Sie hier fremd?

This cartoon provides pupils with the
opportunity to read the new question forms
again. When pupils have read the cartoon, tell
them to answer the questions in English.
Language for buying tickets is introduced here
for recognition only.

R

149
(1B 51)

Einige Informationen: Das 24-Stunden-Ticket + am Automaten

The visuals and text are intended to introduce
the theme of obtaining tickets — principally
bus tickets at this point—by means of the
scheme which operates in Munich. Tell pupils
to read the text and answer the accompanying
questions. Answer questions on vocabulary as
and when they arise, but stress to pupils the
importance of focusing on the information
asked of them in the questions. Either give
explanations briefly in English, or use some of
the suggestions below.

P1: *... beliebig häufig ... ?*
T: *Das heißt, so oft wie du willst - einmal
am Tag, oder zweimal, dreimal, zehnmal*

... so oft wie du willst.

P2: *... Erwachsene ...?*

T: *Männer und Frauen sind **Erwachsene**.
Sie sind keine Kinder.*

P3: *... Stadtgebiet... ?*

T: *Stadtgebiet, das heißt ganz in der Mitte
hier* (point to the centre of the
Tarifschemaplan.)

P4: *... das gesamte Tarifgebiet ... ?*

T: (Pointing to centre again). *Das hier ist
das Stadtgebiet und das alles hier*
(spread your hand over the whole of the
visual) *ist das gesamte Tarifgebiet.*

(L, S), R

150
(1B 52)

Am Bahnhof

An introductory text to present the theme of
railway stations, services, tickets, finding out
information, etc. Read through the text with
the pupils and comment on the visuals of
services available in the larger railway stations
in Germany.

It might be interesting at this point to
compare the facilities available in British
stations, particularly in London.

*Was gibt es in den Endstationen, in den
Bahnhöfen in London? Gaststätten, Cafés,
Geschäfte ...*

L, S, R, W

56

Abfahrt — Ankunft

A straightforward reading comprehension and
pair-work exercise continuing the theme of
information in railway stations. This time the
comprehension questions are in German.

R

151
(1B 53)

Wie heißt das auf Englisch?

For this reading comprehension activity, pupils
should by now have sufficient clues to work
out what all of the signs mean. In preparation
for *Welche Linie ist das?* in Area 3, you could
draw pupils' attention to the two trains, listed
in no. 2:

" *S6 Tutzing: 'S' heißt 'S-Bahn' und sechs, das
ist die Linie — also, Linie sechs fährt nach
Tutzing und Linie 3 nach Maisach.*

L

Zurückbleiben, bitte

These authentic, unscripted recordings are
intended to plunge pupils into the reality of
coping with railway announcements. Gist
comprehension only is required. Tell pupils to
listen to the recordings two or three times in
order to pick out where possible, destinations,
times, and other information. Finally,
tell them that the information office is always
the safest bet and take them on to the next
activity.

Zurückbleiben, bitte

1 — Zurückbleiben, bitte.

2 — In Richtung Bergedorf bitte
zurückbleiben.

3 — Gleis 14 bitte Vorsicht.

4 — Am Gleis 12 bitte einsteigen und Türen
schließen. Vorsicht bei der Abfahrt.

5 — Am Gleis 13 bitte einsteigen. Türen
schließen selbsttätig. Vorsicht bei der
Abfahrt.

6 — Andere Seite aussteigen.

7 — Ein Ausruf. Frau Dorothee Grabo aus
Leipzig. Ich wiederhole, Frau Dorothee
Grabo aus Leipzig, bitte kommen Sie zur
Aufsicht auf diesem Bahnsteig.

8 — Hauptbahnhof. Bitte alle aussteigen, alle
aussteigen bitte. Die Zugfahrt endet
hier. Alle aussteigen, bitte.

9 — Frau Paech wird dringend gebeten, zur
Aufsicht zwischen den Gleisen 11 und
12 zu kommen.

10 — Auf Gleis 13 ab eine Fahrt der IC 79
Enzian nach Zürich, planmäßige
Abfahrtszeit 13.02. Der Zug fährt über
Hannover, Göttingen, Fulda, Frankfurt,
Mannheim, Karlsruhe, Offenburg,
Freiburg und Basel. Für diesen Zug ist
ein IC-Zuschlag erforderlich. Die Wagen
in der 1. Klasse kommen im Abschnitt A
außerhalb der Halle zum Halten. Die
Wagen der 2. Klasse in den Abschnitten
B, C, D und E.

57 Auskunft

Tell pupils to listen to the first four dialogues and decide whether the details on the worksheet are correct. When these have been completed and checked, tell pupils to write up the details for the next five trains. Complete numbers **1** and **5** with pupils, and explain in English the meaning of *Zuschlag* and that it is usually to be paid on Intercity and TEE trains.

Auskunft

1 Woman: — Guten Tag. Wann fährt der nächste Zug nach Hamburg?
Official: — Um 15.30 Uhr. Der Zug hat fünf Minuten Verspätung.
Woman: — Ist das ein Intercity?
Official: — Nein, das ist ein D-Zug: D dreißig, einundsechzig.
Woman: — Muß man Zuschlag bezahlen?
Official: — Nein.
Woman: — Von welchem Gleis fährt der Zug?
Official: — Von Gleis drei.

2 Man: — Wann fährt der nächste Zug nach Verl, bitte?
Official: — Das ist ein Eilzug, und er hat dreißig Minuten Verspätung. Er fährt planmäßig um 16.17 Uhr von Gleis sieben ab.

3 Girl: — Wann fährt der nächste Zug nach Kiel, bitte?
Official: — Um 16.25 Uhr von Gleis zwei.
Girl: — Muß man da Zuschlag bezahlen?
Official: — Ja — sieben Mark. Das ist ein Intercity.

4 Boy: — Fährt der nächste Zug nach Emden um 17.00 Uhr?
Official: — Ja, ein D-Zug von Gleis vier.
Boy: — Muß man Zuschlag bezahlen?
Official: — Nein.

5 Girl: — Guten Tag. Ich fahre nach Bonn — wann fährt der nächste Zug, bitte?
Official: — Um 17.09 haben Sie einen Intercity nach Bonn Hauptbahnhof.
Girl: — Muß man Zuschlag bezahlen?
Official: — Ja, DM 5,50.
Girl: — Von welchem Gleis fährt der Zug?
Official: — Von Gleis acht.

6 Boy: — Wann fährt der nächste Zug nach Köln, bitte?
Official: — Der nächste Zug hat vier Minuten Verspätung und fährt planmäßig um 17.51 von Gleis vier ab.
Boy: — Was für ein Zug ist das — ein Eilzug, oder?
Official: — Das ist ein D-Zug.
Boy: — Muß man Zuschlag bezahlen?
Official: — Nein.

7 Woman: — Wann fährt der Intercity nach München, bitte?
Official: — Um 18.02 Uhr von Gleis eins. Haben Sie schon Ihre Fahrkarte gekauft?
Woman: — Nein, noch nicht.
Official: — Man muß nämlich Zuschlag bezahlen. DM 7,-
Woman: — Ach so, danke.

8 Man: — Von welchem Gleis fährt der Zug nach Tübingen, bitte?
Official: — Der D-Zug, um 19.25 Uhr?
Man: — Ja, ich glaube.
Official: — Gleis zwei. Aber machen Sie schnell. Der Zug hat keine Verspätung, und es ist schon 19.20 Uhr.
Man: — Ja, sicher. Danke.
Official: — Bitte. Gute Reise.

9 Woman: — Wann fährt der nächste Intercity nach Osnabrück?
Official: — Morgen vormittag.
Woman: — Morgen?
Official: — Ja, der nächste Zug nach Osnabrück ist der letzte heute — das ist ein Eilzug. Der fährt erst um 21.00 Uhr von Gleis sechs.
Woman: — Hoffentlich muß man da keinen Zuschlag bezahlen.
Official: — Richtig — gar keinen.
Woman: — Danke schön.

Solution:

1	richtig			
2	richtig			
3	falsch: DM 7,-			
4	falsch: Gleis 4			
5	IC 4332	Bonn Hbf.	17.09	8
		DM 5,50		
6	D 5210	Köln	17.51 4 Minuten	4
7	IC 3782	München	18.02	1
		DM 7,-		
8	D 5963	Tübingen	19.25	2
9	E 3835	Osnabrück	21.10	6

Write the two dialogues on the board when pupils have answered your questions, and practise the dialogues with them, using the models in the Pupil's Book.

Einmal nach Pfarrkirchen, bitte

1 — Einmal nach Pfarrkirchen, bitte.
— Einfach oder hin und zurück?
— Einfach, bitte.
— Einmal einfach nach Pfarrkirchen — DM 27,-.
— Bitte schön.
— Danke.

2 — Einmal nach Pfarrkirchen, bitte.
— Einfach oder hin und zurück?
— Hin und zurück.
— Eine Rückfahrkarte nach Pfarrkirchen — DM 54,-. Bitte schön.

L, S

Auskunft

57

Tell pupils to work in pairs, using the now completed worksheet to practise the various question forms.

'Auskunft'. Partnerarbeit. Stelle Fragen oder beantworte sie mit deinem Partner/deiner Partnerin. (Complete one dialogue with a pupil in front of the class).

R

151
(1B 53)

Fahrkarten

Tell pupils to read the information on the tickets and the text accompanying *Junior-Paß*, then discuss with them in English what they are about and what information is recorded on the tickets. You can mention the different types of ticket — *Tageskarte, Wochenkarte* — and refer to the fact that the *Deutsche Bundesbahn* offers concessions to various age groups, as in England, before concluding that the kind of ticket the pupils are most likely to buy are those illustrated at the start of the activity. The listening activity which follows centres on these two tickets.

L, S, R

151
(1B 53)

Einmal nach Pfarrkirchen, bitte

Tell pupils they are going to hear two dialogues to match the two tickets illustrated at the start of *Fahrkarten*. Once they have heard the recordings, analyse the two tickets and the two dialogues with symbols. Tease out the transactional dialogue.

T: *Seht euch Fahrkarten an, und zwar die zwei Fahrkarten nach Pfarrkirchen. (Point to the two tickets). Hört zu — wir sind auf dem Bahnhof. (Play the two dialogues). Also, wie war das: einmal, zweimal ...*
P1: *Einmal.*
T: *Nach Kiel?*
P2: *Nach Pfarrkirchen.*
T: *Einfach oder hin und zurück?*

L, S, R

nem 5
248
(1B 132)

Zweimal nach Hamburg, bitte

These practice dialogues are intended for **rapid** pair-work. Read through the first dialogue with pupils before telling them to work in pairs. Refer them to *Tip des Tages*, if necessary. Ask a few pairs to perform in front of the class.

9 Area 3

● **Using public transport (bus/underground/train)**

L, R

152-153
(1B 54-55)

Welche Linie ist das?

Tell pupils they are going to hear a series of short dialogues involving people in and around Munich wanting to go out on day trips to tourist attractions. Pupils must look at the map, on page 153 (**1B** 55), and write down in their exercise books which line the tourists must take in order to reach their destination.

Welche Linie ist das? Fahren die Passagiere mit der S-Bahn oder mit der U-Bahn? Hört gut zu und schreibt die Antworten in euer Heft. (Complete Number one with pupils).

Welche Linie ist das?
1 *(Station announcement)*
— München Hauptbahnhof. München Hauptbahnhof.
— Entschuldigung. Ich möchte den Aussichtsturm in Ebersberg besuchen.

145

Fährt dieser Zug nach Ebersberg?
— Ja, der Zug fährt über Eglharting und Kirchseeon nach Ebersberg.
— Schön. Vielen Dank.

2   (Announcement)
— Ebersberg. Ebersberg
— Entschuldigung. Ich muß zum Olympiazentrum. Welche Linie ist das, bitte?
— Sie fahren mit der S4 bis München Hauptbahnhof, dann müssen Sie umsteigen.
— Aha. Welche Linie ist das von München Hauptbahnhof?
— Das weiß ich nicht. Auf jeden Fall fahren Sie mit der U-Bahn weiter.
— Vielen Dank.
— Nichts zu danken.

3   (Station announcement)
— München Hauptbahnhof. München Hauptbahnhof.
— Ich möchte St. Alto besuchen.
— Dann müssen Sie nach Altomünster fahren.
— Muß ich umsteigen?
— Ja, in Dachau. Dann fahren Sie mit dem Bus nach Altomünster weiter.

4   (Station announcement)
— Wolfratshausen. Wolfratshausen.
— Guten Tag. Wir möchten den Kieferngarten besuchen. Fährt dieser Zug durch?
— Nein. Sie fahren mit dieser Linie bis Harras, dann müssen Sie umsteigen und mit der U-Bahn weiterfahren, und zwar bis zum Marienplatz.
— Müssen wir noch einmal am Marienplatz umsteigen?
— Ja, dann kommen Sie direkt zum Kieferngarten.

5   (Station announcement)
— München Hauptbahnhof. München Hauptbahnhof.
— Wie komme ich am besten zum Ammersee, bitte?
— Am besten fahren Sie mit der S-Bahn nach Herrsching.

6   (Station announcement)
— Geltendorf. Geltendorf.
— Entschuldigung. Fährt dieser Zug nach Tutzing? Ich will nämlich den Starnberger See sehen.
— Nein, leider nicht. Sie müssen in Pasing umsteigen.
— Ach so, danke schön.
— Bitte schön.

Solution: **1** S4
2 (S4) - U3/8
3 S2 + Bus
4 S7 - U3 - U6
5 S5
6 S4 - S6

152-153
(1B 54-55)

L, S, R

Welche Linie ist das?

Tell pupils to work in pairs, taking it in turns to find out which route they must take in order to get to the places listed on the table. Read through the example with one pupil in front of the class. When pupils have practised the dialogues sufficiently, ask some of them to perform in front of the class.

154
(1B 56)

L, R

Einige Informationen: Vergessen Sie nicht, Ihre Fahrkarte zu entwerten!

Tell pupils to listen to the recording without referring them to the visual and text in the Pupil's Book. When they have heard the tape, ask them, in English, what they think it is about. Play the tape as often as necessary to elicit some reasonable answers/guesses. Then refer them to the text and visual and read through with them before asking them to answer the questions based on the short extract from an authentic document (beneath the visual).

Vergessen Sie nicht, Ihre Fahrkarte zu entwerten!

Fahrkartenkontrolleur:	— Fahrkarten, bitte.
Reisender:	— Bitte schön.
Fahrkartenkontrolleur:	— Haben Sie diese Fahrkarte heute gekauft?
Reisender:	— Ja, natürlich.
Fahrkartenkontrolleur:	— Sie haben sie aber nicht entwertet.
Reisender:	— Wie bitte?
Fahrkartenkontrolleur:	— Entwertet: hier ist kein Datum auf der Karte.
Reisender:	— Ach so. Entschuldigung. Wo kann man seine Fahrkarte entwerten?
Fahrkartenkontrolleur:	— Am Bahnhof, bevor Sie einsteigen. Sie sind Ausländer, oder?
Reisender:	— Ja, ich bin Engländer.

Fahrkartenkontrolleur:	— Ach, darum. Sie sprechen aber sehr gut Deutsch.
Reisender:	— Danke. Aber was mache ich mit meiner Fahrkarte?
Fahrkartenkontrolleur:	— Entwerten Sie sie, bitte, sobald Sie aussteigen.
Reisender:	— Ja, das mache ich. Danke.
Fahrkartenkontrolleur:	— Bitte.

L, R, W

Zuggespräche

Play the tape section by section and ask pupils to work out what the conversations are about. Wherever possible repeat the new communicative language in order to familiarise pupils with it.

For the second playing tell pupils to look at the drawings on page 154 (**1 B** 56) and to read the gapped text. Then tell them to listen to the tape and complete the missing words in their exercise books. At this stage you should not ask pupils to copy out the complete text. This may be done as a homework once the first two stages have been completed.

Hört zu. Worum geht es hier? (Play the dialogues, one by one, and accept suggestions from pupils in English) ...

Seht euch die Bilder auf Seite 154 (56) an und lest den Lückentext. Jetzt könnt ihr den Text vervollständigen. Hört gut zu und schreibt die Antworten in euer Heft. (Complete the answers with pupils and write them on the board).

Zuggespräche

Junger Mann:	— **Entschuldigung**. Sie sitzen auf meinem **Platz**.
Passagierin:	— Wieso denn?
Junger Mann:	— Ich habe **reserviert**. Sehen Sie mal hier. Und hier ist auch meine **Fahrkarte**.
Passagierin:	— Ach, Entschuldigung. Hier ist kein **Platz** mehr frei ... Kann man im **Zug** essen?
Junger Mann:	— Ja. Vorne gibt es einen **Speisewagen**.
Passagierin:	— Dann gehe ich **zum** Speisewagen.

....

Zugbegleiter:	— Fahrkarten, bitte ... Ist noch jemand **zugestiegen**?

Junger Mann:	— Nein. Wie **weit** sind wir, bitte?
Zugbegleiter:	— In wenigen Minuten **kommen** wir in **Kassel** an.
Junger Mann:	— Danke.

....

Bahnhofansager:	— Zurücktreten, bitte. Bitte **zurücktreten**. Der Zug läuft auf **Gleis** fünf **ein**.

....

Alte Dame:	— Hier steige ich **aus**.
Junger Mann:	— **Kann** ich Ihnen mit Ihrem **Gepäck** helfen?
Alte Dame:	— Gerne. Vielen **Dank**, junger Mann.
Junger Mann:	— **Nichts** zu danken. **Auf Wiedersehen**.
Alte Dame:	— Auf Wiedersehen.

R

Schilder

A straightforward reading comprehension activity using authentic visuals of signs and notices on public transport in Germany.

Solution: 1 D436, Leipzig, DDR **2** No. 4 **3** No. 5 **4** No. 6, do not throw things out **5** Nos. 11, 12 **6** drink the water **7** 2nd class, non-smoking **8** *Waschraum; Fußhebel bedienen; Schwerbehinderte; Gleis 4; bevor der Zug hält; Nichtraucher; Türgriff; nicht öffnen.*

Wer kontrolliert die Fahrkarten?

Tell pupils to look at the drawings and to try and guess which one is the real *Zugbegleiter*. When they have all hazarded a guess, inform them that the guard sometimes wears no uniform.

Wer kontrolliert die Fahrkarten? A? B? ... (Following a number of guesses.) *In Deutschland tragen die Zugbegleiter manchmal keine Uniform.*

Discuss with pupils, in English, the advantages (surprise spot checks) and disadvantages (possible abuse by jokers, etc.) and how pupils might check the identity cards of alleged officials.

e.g. *Kann ich bitte ihren Beamtenausweis sehen?*

Solution:
A = Passenger
B = Soldier in *Bundesgrenzschutz*
C = Passenger
D = *Zugbegleiter*
E = Passenger
F = Soldier in *Bundeswehr*
G = Policeman
H = *Lufthansa* pilot
I = Passenger

9 Area 4

● Planning a journey

R

157 (1B 59)

Das Jugendzentrum Pinneberg plant eine Reise nach Helgoland

The reading passage sets the scene for planning a journey. No detailed exploitation is intended, although pupils will probably be interested in the *Strandkörbe*. Further exploitation of *zollfrei* is in Area 6, if required.

66

99

Seht euch diese Karten an. Wie heißt diese Insel hier? Weißt du was 'Insel' auf Englisch heißt? Ja, richtig, England ist auch eine Insel. Diese Insel hat rote Felsen. Sind die Felsen in Dover auch rot? Und hier gibt es einen Strandkorb. Warum? (Gesture). Ja, im Strandkorb oder in den Dünen ist es nicht so windig.

Was kann man alles auf Helgoland machen? Und abends? Helgoland ist 'autofrei'. Was ist denn das? Die Fußgängerzone in Helgoland ist auch 'autofrei'. Da kann man auch Wein oder Parfüm 'zollfrei' kaufen. Das ist billiger als normal. In einem Flugzeug oder auf einem Schiff kann man auch zollfrei einkaufen.

Seht euch die Karte an. Wie fährt man von Pinneberg nach Helgoland? Mit dem Auto? Mit dem Bus? usw.

Das Jugendzentrum in Pinneberg will eine Reise nach Helgoland machen. Wie kommen sie am besten dahin?

L, R

158 (1B 60)

Wie kommt man nach Helgoland?

Tell pupils to look at the information about flights to Helgoland and listen to the recording. Ask them to make notes in English of any details they understand. Collate these on the board afterwards. You may wish to draw pupils' attention to the use of *mit dem Flugzeug* instead of *ich fliege*. Use the flashcard, if necessary.

66

99

Wollen wir nach Helgoland fliegen? Dann gehen wir zum Reisebüro Mailänder (seht ihr hier ganz unten) und buchen einen Flug. Hört gut zu und macht Notizen auf Englisch in euer Heft.

Wie kommt man nach Helgoland?
(Telefon)
— Reisebüro Mailänder. Guten Tag.
— Ich möchte nach Helgoland fliegen. Kann ich bei Ihnen buchen?
— Ja, natürlich. Wann wollen Sie fliegen?
— Am dritten April.
— Das ist kein Problem. Das ist die Vorsaison.
— Was kostet ein Flug — hin und zurück, bitte?
— Wenn sie an einem Tag hin- und zurückfliegen kostet es DM 270. Der normale Hin- und Rückflug kostet aber DM 296.
— Ist das ein Charterflug?
— Nein, Linienflug.
— Ah gut.
— Um wieviel Uhr ist der erste Abflug von Hamburg?
— Um 08.15. Der fliegt non-stop nach Helgoland und kommt um 8.55 an.
— Das ist nicht lang!
— Nein, der Flug dauert nur 40 Minuten.

(L, S), R, (W)

158 (1B 60)

Mit dem Flugzeug?

Tell pupils to extract information from the *Sommerflugplan* by answering the questions in English. This could be followed by oral and written exploitation in German.

1 Wann beginnt die Vorsaison?
2 Ist der fünfte Juli in der Hauptsaison?
3 Wann ist der erste Flug von Helgoland nach Hamburg?
4 Was kostet eine Rückflugkarte nach Helgoland?
5 Wie ist die Telefonnummer vom Reisebüro Mailänder? *usw.*

R

159 (1B 61)

Mit dem Schiff? Oder mit der Bahn und mit dem Schiff?

Tell pupils to study the details of rail and sea travel.

66

99

Seht euch die Karte nochmal an. Von Cuxhaven kann man auch mit dem Schiff nach Helgoland fahren. Von Hamburg kann man mit dem Zug (mit der Bahn) nach Cuxhaven fahren. Seht euch jetzt diese Informationen über das Schiff und die Bahn an. Beantwortet die Fragen auf Englisch.

**157
(1 B 59)**

Wie fahren wir dorthin?

Tell pupils to look at the speech bubbles and listen to the young people discussing how they want to travel to Helgoland. They have to decide who is talking each time. Point out that they won't always know who everybody is in each conversation. This is quite a difficult task that needs to be taken slowly and carefully.

Jetzt hören wir die jungen Leute vom Jugendzentrum. Sie haben alle Informationen über die Bahn, das Schiff und das Flugzeug gelesen und jetzt diskutieren sie, wie sie dorthin fahren sollen. Hört gut zu und schreibt, wer spricht. (Play the first recording and demonstrate on the board.) *Nummer 1 - das war Dorit. Jetzt hört gut zu und macht weiter.*

Wie fahren wir dorthin?

1 — Wieviel Stunden fährt man mit dem Schiff? Weißt du das?
— Ja, ich glaube zwei Stunden. Genau, das stimmt.

2 — Das Flugzeug ist viel zu teuer. Es kostet über DM 300.
— Nein, das stimmt nicht. Der Flug kostet nur DM 296.

3 — Bekommen wir Gruppenermäßigung?
— Nein, mit dem Schiff nicht. Wir sind nur zwanzig Mann. Mit dem Schiff gibt es Ermäßigung erst ab 25 Personen. Aber mit der Bahn schon. Da gibt es eine sogenannte Minigruppenkarte.

4 — Am besten fliegen wir. Das geht viel schneller.
— Ja, das stimmt. Das Flugzeug ist schneller. Aber es kostet viel mehr. Mit dem Schiff ist es viel billiger.
— Ich will aber nicht fliegen. Ich habe immer Flugangst.

5 — Was kostet der Flug nach Helgoland?
— Hin und zurück, fast DM 300.
— Mann, das ist aber teuer!

6 — Wir fahren am besten mit dem Bus nach Cuxhaven und dann direkt mit dem Schiff nach Helgoland.
— Ach nein! Ich werde immer seekrank!

7 — Ich fliege lieber!
— Ich nicht! Ich fahre lieber mit dem Schiff.

8 — Wieviel Stunden fliegt man?
— Nur 40 Minuten.

9 — Ist das ein Linienflug oder Charter?
— Keine Ahnung! Wirklich.

10 — Schluß jetzt. Ruhe bitte. Ich habe eine gute Idee. Wir fahren mit der S-Bahn nach Hamburg, dann mit dem Zug nach Cuxhaven und mit dem Bus zum Schiff. Mit dem Schiff nach Helgoland. Wir fliegen dann zurück und fahren vom Flugplatz nach Pinneberg mit dem Bus. Martin, du nimmst Tabletten gegen Seekrankheit und du Volker fährst allein mit dem Schiff zurück. OK.?
— Ja, OK.

Solution: **1** Dorit **2** Kirsten **3** Stefan und Anja
4 Bernd, Volker und Gaby **5** Peter
6 Monika und Martin **7** Birgit und Andrea
8 Ralf **9** Dietrich **10** Herr Timm

58

Was paßt am besten?

A matching exercise to practise the new vocabulary and structures. Do the activity orally with the class and then consolidate in writing.

Solution: **1**H **2**F **3**G **4**A **5**E **6**C **7**B **8**D **9**I

Und du!

Tell pupils to produce their own written account of a discussion about various means of transport. They must decide where they are going to travel to.

**160
(1 B 62)**

Mir geht's nicht gut

Two cartoons to consolidate *Ich habe Flugangst* and *Ich bin seekrank*.

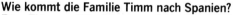

L, (S), R

160 (1B 62) Wie kommt die Familie Timm nach Spanien?

Tell pupils to look at the outline map and then go through the multiple choice items with the class. Then tell them to listen to the recording and make a note of the means of transport used for each part of the journey.

Die Familie Timm verbringt zwei Wochen in Südspanien in Malaga. Die Familie fährt zum Flughafen und fliegt direkt nach Malaga. Aber wie kommt sie zum Flughafen? Mit der S-Bahn? Und wie fliegt sie — Charter oder Linienflug? Hört gut zu.

Wie kommt die Familie Timm nach Spanien?
Frau Timm: — Wie kommen wir am besten zum Flughafen? Was meinst du?
Herr Timm: — Mit dem Wagen wäre es ganz praktisch. Aber es kostet so viel am Flughafen zu parken. Ich glaube, es kostet zehn Mark pro Tag.
Frau Timm: — Das ist eine Menge Geld. Fahren wir vielleicht mit dem Bus oder mit der S-Bahn?
Herr Timm: — Nein, ich will nicht. Wir haben zu viel Gepäck. Ich glaube, am besten fahren wir mit dem Taxi dorthin.
Frau Timm: — Wir sind dann in zweieinhalb Stunden in Malaga. Toll, nicht?
Herr Timm: — Was für eine Maschine ist es eigentlich? Weißt du's?
Frau Timm: — Nee. Aber es ist ein normaler Flug. Kein Charter.
Herr Timm: — Wie kommen wir vom Flugplatz in Malaga zum Hotel? Was hat die Frau im Reisebüro gesagt?
Frau Timm: — Das ist alles ganz einfach. Wir werden mit einem kleinen Bus abgeholt.
Herr Timm: — Hast du auch ein paar Rundfahrten gebucht?
Frau Timm: — Nein, es lohnt sich nicht. Am besten organisieren wir das, wenn wir dort unten sind. Die Frau meint, am besten macht man eine Tour mit dem Zug. Das soll viel billiger sein als mit dem Bus.
Herr Timm: — Ich möchte auch Nordafrika besuchen. Wie kommen wir am besten dahin?
Frau Timm: — Mit dem Flugzeug geht es am schnellsten, aber es kostet sehr viel.
Die Fahrt mit dem Schiff dauert nur ein paar Stunden und soll sehr schön sein.

Herr Timm: — Na gut, dann fahren wir mit dem Schiff.

Solution: **1B 2B 3C 4D 5A**

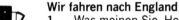

L, R

161 (1B 63) Wir fahren nach England

Tell pupils that they have to decide which route each of the four teachers prefers from Pinneberg to Bristol. The suggested language is in the Pupil's Book.

Wir fahren nach England
1 — Was meinen Sie, Herr Ziegert?
 — Ich glaube, am besten fahren wir mit dem Bus nach Ostende. Das ist alles Autobahn. Und dann mit der Fähre nach Dover. Das sind nur vier Stunden auf dem Schiff. Und von Dover können wir dann direkt mit dem Bus nach Bristol fahren. Es gibt eine Autobahn um London herum — die M25 und dann die Autobahn nach Bristol — die M4, glaube ich.

2 — Und Sie, Frau Heinemann? Was meinen Sie?
 — Am besten fliegen wir. Das geht viel schneller. Und ein Charterflug kostet auch nicht viel. Der Flug dauert nur anderthalb Stunden nach London. Also, ich schlage vor, wir fahren mit der S-Bahn zum Flugplatz in Hamburg. In London gibt's auch eine U-Bahn zur Stadtmitte. Wir fahren also mit der U-Bahn in die Innenstadt und dann weiter mit einem Intercityzug nach Bristol.

3 — Was meinen Sie, Herr Gerecht?
 — Am besten fahren wir mit dem Schiff nach Harwich. Es ist zwar eine lange Überfahrt — so zwanzig Stunden — aber es gibt eine Disko und ein Kino an Bord. Das ist bestimmt viel besser für die Schüler, als acht Stunden im Bus zu sitzen. Also, ich meine, wir fahren mit dem Bus nach Hamburg, mit dem Schiff nach Harwich. Dann wieder mit dem Bus nach London. Von London nach Bristol würde ich lieber mit dem Zug fahren. Das geht nämlich viel schneller.

4 — Und Sie, Herr Fichte?
 — Ich fliege auch lieber. Aber nicht Charter. Am besten fliegen wir also Lufthansa Hamburg-Heathrow. Und es ist viel besser, wenn die Eltern ihre Kinder mit dem Wagen zum Flugplatz bringen. Von Heathrow nach Bristol kann man dann mit dem Bus fahren. Es gibt eine Autobahn.

Solution: **A** Frau Heinemann
B Herr Ziegert
C Herr Gerecht
D Herr Fichte

9 Area 5

- **Describing a journey in the past**

162
(1B 64)

Telefongespräch

L, (S), R

Tell pupils to listen to the recording and work out what it is about. Play the recording in sections and collate the information on the board/OHP. Then refer pupils to the dialogue in the Pupil's Book.

Wie telefoniert man von England nach Deutschland? Was wählt man zuerst (mime) und dann? Wo lebt Davids Mutter jetzt? Wo hat sie früher in Deutschland gelebt? Wie war die Fahrt von Deutschland nach England? Wie war es auf dem Schiff? Wie ist Gerold nach London gefahren? Wie ist er von London nach Bristol gefahren?

Telefongespräch
Gerold ist mit der Schule in Bristol. Es ist sechs Uhr abends, und er ist bei seiner englischen Familie. Er will seine Familie in Deutschland anrufen.

Gerold: — Darf ich meine Familie anrufen?
Mrs. X: — Ja, natürlich. Weißt du die Nummer von England nach Deutschland?
Gerold: — Ja, ich wähle 010 und dann 49 und dann meine Telefonnummer ohne die Null.
Mrs. X: — Ja, richtig.
Gerold: — *(Wählt)* ... Hallo Mutti, Ich bin's.
Mutter: — Ja, wie geht's dir denn? Alles in Ordnung?
Gerold: — Ja, klar. Mir geht's gut. Die Familie ist sehr nett. Davids Mutter spricht gut Deutsch. Sie hat zwei Jahre in Bonn gewohnt.
Mutter: — Ja wirklich? Das wußte ich gar nicht. Wie war denn die Reise?
Gerold: — Die Fahrt mit der Bahn war ganz gut, aber die vier Stunden auf der Fähre waren fürchterlich. Die See war so stürmisch und wir waren alle seekrank. Ich habe dann im Bus nach London geschlafen.
Mutter: — Seid ihr nicht mit dem Zug gefahren?
Gerold: — Doch, von London nach Bristol — mit einem Intercity ... Mutti, jetzt

bin ich aber saumüde. Ich gehe sofort ins Bett. Tschüs. Schöne Grüße zu Hause.
Mutter: — Tschüs. Bis bald. Mach's gut!

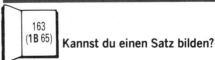
162
(1B 64)
R

Ich bin gut angekommen

Two postcards about a journey to England for gist comprehension. Tell pupils to make notes in English about the two journeys.

163
(1B 65)
R, W

Kannst du einen Satz bilden?

Tell pupils to refer to their books and put the jumbled words in the correct order. Collate on the board afterwards and see if they can provide the rule for word order. Check that pupils understand that the sentences all relate to events in the past.

163
(1B 65)
R, W

Was paßt zu wem?

Tell pupils to work in pairs and match the English and German.

Er hat im Zug geschlafen. Wie heißt das auf Englisch?

59

Was hast du gemacht?

Read pupils a series of statements. Tell them to draw lines either from the circle or the square to the appropriate past participles.

1 Ich bin um 6 Uhr aufgestanden.
2 Ich habe nichts zum Frühstück gegessen.
3 Ich bin mit meinem Vater zur Schule gefahren.
4 Wir sind um halb acht angekommen.
5 Ich habe bis halb neun geschlafen.
6 Wir haben im Restaurant gegessen.
7 Wir sind mit dem Auto in die Stadt gefahren.
8 Ich habe 3 Jahre in Hamburg gewohnt.
9 Wir haben Karten gespielt.
10 Wir haben Dallas im Fernsehen gesehen.
11 Ich habe eine Flasche Cola getrunken.
12 Ich bin zu Fuß in die Schule gekommen.

At the end of this activity tell pupils to cross out the past participles in both halves of the page which are not connected to the circle or the square, in anticipation of the presentation of the Perfect Tense in the *Tip des Tages*.

151

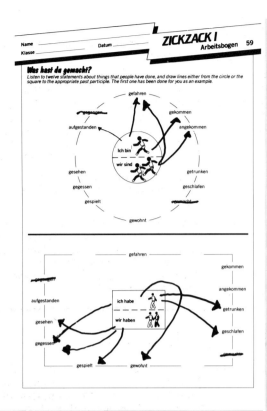

Name _____ Datum _____ **ZICKZACK I** Arbeitsbogen 59

Was hast du gemacht?
Listen to twelve statements about things that people have done, and draw lines either from the circle or the square to the appropriate past participle. The first one has been done for you as an example.

16-38
59-66

Consolidation of meaning of Perfect Tense

L, S

Use food and drink flashcards to cue *Ich esse ...; Ich trinke ...* Then follow by *Ich habe ... gegessen; Ich habe getrunken* (mime patting stomach).

L, S, R, W

163
(1B 65)

Wie war die Reise?

The length of journey, means of transport and what it was like are cued. Practise orally with the whole class first of all, then consolidate in writing. Pupils could make up their own clues and continue the activity in pairs, if required.

nem 6

248
(1B 132)

R, W

Heino ist mit dem Rad zum Schwimmbad gefahren

An activity practising the Perfect Tense with means of transport.

9

Area 6

● Consolidation

R

164
(1B 66)

Zollfrei

Consolidation of the concept *zollfrei*. The text is exploited by questions in English.

R

164
(1B 66)

Schüleraustausch mit England

Tell pupils to read the article about the school exchange and discuss the content.

L, R, W

60

Jens-Peters Tagebuch

Jens-Peter's diary is incomplete. Tell pupils to listen to him talking to his friend Dieter about their stay in England and ask them to fill in the gaps on the worksheet.

Jens-Peters Tagebuch

Jens-Peter: — Wir sind am Montagvormittag in die Schule gegangen, nicht?

Dieter: — Ja, und nach dem Essen haben wir Tennis gespielt.

Jens-Peter: — Was haben wir am Abend gemacht?

Dieter: — Ich bin mit dem Bus zu einem Jugendzentrum gefahren, aber du bist zu Fuß ins Kino gegangen.

Jens-Peter: — Ja, richtig. Ich habe einen Kung Fu Film gesehen. Und dann am Dienstag sind wir alle mit dem Zug nach London gefahren.

Dieter: — Am Mittwoch waren wir alle in Brighton. Erinnerst du dich, wie schlecht die Fahrt war? Mit dem alten Bus?

Jens-Peter: — Ja, ja. Und am Abend? Was haben wir dann gemacht?

Dieter: — Wir sind spät in Hailsham angekommen. Ich glaube, im Bus haben wir Karten gespielt.

Jens-Peter: — Was haben wir am Donnerstag gemacht?

Dieter: — Keine Ahnung! Moment mal ... ich glaube, ja richtig ... wir sind zur Schule gegangen — von neun bis vier. Das war ein langer Tag!

Jens-Peter: — Ja, richtig. Und am Abend sind wir mit dem Zug zu einem

Jugendzentrum in Eastbourne gefahren. Zur Grillparty.

Dieter: — Am Freitag haben wir Sport getrieben. Zuerst haben wir Tennis gespielt, und dann sind wir zum Schwimmbad gefahren. Ja, und am Abend hast du mit Debbie in der Schuldisko getanzt.

Jens-Peter: — Am Samstagvormittag bin ich zu Fuß in die Stadt gegangen und am Nachmittag habe ich eine Kassette gekauft. Um acht Uhr bin ich dann mit meinem Partner zu einer Party gegangen.

Dieter: — Was hast du am Sonntag gemacht?

Jens-Peter: — Wir sind alle mit der Bahn nach Windsor gefahren. Ja, und Montag? Das ist einfach. Wir sind um 9 Uhr nach Harwich gefahren, und um 16.30 sind wir mit der Fähre nach Hamburg gefahren.

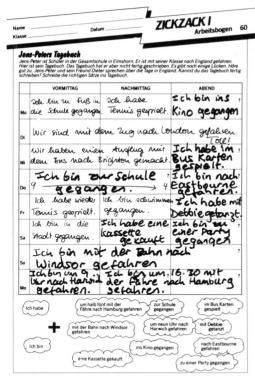

ZICKZACK I
Arbeitsbogen 60

Name ____ Datum ____
Klasse ____

Jens-Peters Tagebuch

Jens-Peter ist Schüler in der Gesamtschule in Elmshorn. Er ist mit seiner Klasse nach England gefahren. Hier ist sein Tagebuch. Das Tagebuch hat er aber nicht fertig geschrieben. Es gibt noch einige Lücken. Höre gut zu: Jens-Peter und sein Freund Dieter sprechen über die Tage in England. Kannst du das Tagebuch fertig schreiben? Schreibe die richtigen Sätze ins Tagebuch.

Wann fährt der nächste Zug nach Elmshorn, bitte?

165 (1B 67)

Tell pupils to work in groups of three (or more), using the Pinneberg Railway Timetable on page 165 (1B 67), to produce dialogues at a railway station: the first dialogue will take place in the information office and the second will follow immediately at the ticket office.

Read through the first example with pupils. Again, pupils may refer to the *Tip des Tages* if necessary.

(To a group of three pupils): *Du bist bei der Auskunft und willst nach Elmshorn fahren. Du bist Partner(in) A. Du bist Partner(in) B und du arbeitest bei der Auskunft. Und du bist Partner(in) C — du verkaufst die Fahrkarten. Also, Gruppenarbeit.*

Was bedeutet das?

165 (1B 67)

R

Further exploitation of the timetable from Pinneberg. Pupils may need some of the symbols explaining first, but others will provide good revision and practice.

nem 8
249 (1B 133)

R

Sicherer Schulweg

Comprehension questions in English on a text about cycle lanes.

Bus-Schiffsreise nach London

166 (1B 68)

R

A straightforward reading comprehension activity based on an authentic travel company advertisement.

nem 9
249 (1B 133)

R, (W)

Was paßt am besten?

A matching activity in which pupils must draw conclusions from statements about reasons for not liking certain means of travel.

nem 7
248 (1B 132)

R, W

Was paßt zu wem?

Consolidation of the difference between the Present Tense and the Perfect Tense.

Solution: 1H 2E 3G 4J 5B 6D 7K 8A 9F 10L 11C 12I

nem 10
249 (1B 133)

R, W

Lieber Kurt

An incomplete letter focusing on verb forms in the past.

153

Vocabulary

die Abfahrt(en) *departure*
der Abfall(⁼e) *rubbish, litter*
der Abflug(⁼e) *departure (plane)*
abholen *to collect, pick up*
die Abteilung(en) *department*
allgemein *general*
der Alkohol *alcohol*
die Angst(⁼e) *fear*
ich habe * davor *I'm frightened of it*
die Ankunft(⁼e) *arrival*
anrufen *to ring up*
anschließend *following, afterwards*
der Aussichtsturm(⁼e) *observation/lookout tower*
außer + Dat *apart from, except*
der Ausweis(e) *identity card, pass*
der Auszug(⁼e) *extract*
die Autobahn(en) *motorway*
der Automat(en) *dispenser (tickets, drinks, etc.)*
der Beamte *civil servant*
beliebig *any, as you like*
* häufig *as often as you like*
das Benzin *petrol*
benutzen *to use*
besetzt *engaged*
bevor *before*
buchen *to book*
der Charterflug(⁼e) *charter flight*
das Datum *date*
drücken *to push, press*
die Düne(n) *dune*
eigentlich *actually*
eine einfache Fahrkarte *a single ticket*
der Einklang *harmony*

einlaufen *to arrive, come in (transport)*
einschließlich *including*
einsteigen *to get in*
das Einzelzimmer(-) *single room*
entwerten *to date stamp*
erforderlich *necessary, required*
die Ermäßigung(en) *reduction*
erreichen *to reach*
der Erwachsene(n) *adult*
das Erzeugnis(se) *product*
die Essenz *essence*
das Fahrzeug(e) *vehicle, means of transport*
der Fall(⁼e) *case, instance*
auf jeden * *in any case*
faul *lazy*
der Felsen(-) *cliff*
finden *to find*
fliegen *to fly*
der Flug(⁼e) *flight*
der Flugplatz(⁼e) *airport*
freihalten *to keep free/clear*
fremd *strange, foreign*
fürchterlich *awful*
das Gepäck *luggage*
gesamt *total*
gesperrt *closed*
die Grillparty(s) *barbecue party*
halten *to stop*
häufig *frequently*
die Hauptsaison(s) *peak season*
herum *around*
hin und zurück *return (of ticket)*
hinauslehnen *to lean out*
ideal *ideal*
die Insel(n) *island*
Japan *Japan*
kennzeichnen *to mark, label*
der Kofferkuli(s) *luggage trolley*

kombiniert *combined*
der Kontrolleur *inspector*
kontrollieren *to control, check*
das Krankenhaus(⁼er) *hospital*
lenken *to steer*
letzte(r, s) *last*
der Linienflug(⁼e) *scheduled flight*
der Liegewagen(-) *couchette*
sich lohnen *to be worth it*
mach's gut! *all the best!*
mindestens *at least*
das Mofa(s) *small moped*
das Moped(s) *moped*
die Nachsaison(s) *after the peak season*
Nordafrika *North Africa*
normal *normal, usual*
Norwegen *Norway*
organisieren *to organise*
der Passagier(e) *passenger*
planen *to plan*
planmäßig *as planned*
das Reisebüro(s) *travel agent's*
reisen *to travel*
die Richtung(en) *direction*
der Sand *sand*
schätzen *to estimate*
das Schema(Schemen) *scheme, diagram*
schnell *quick(ly), fast*
schwarz fahren *to travel without paying*
Schweden *Sweden*
schwerbehindert *severely handicapped*
die See(n) *sea*
seekrank *seasick*
senkrecht *vertical, down*
sich sonnen *to sunbathe*
sogenannt *so-called*

der Speisewagen(-) *restaurant car*
stammen aus *to come from, originate from*
der Strandkorb (⁼e) *wicker beach chair*
die Straßenbahn(en) *tram*
stürmisch *stormy*
der Tabak *tobacco*
die Tablette(n) *tablet*
das Tarifgebiet(e) *fare-zone*
das Taxi(Taxen) *taxi*
die Überfahrt(en) *crossing*
umsteigen *to change (transport)*
unabhängig *independent*
unerfahren *inexperienced*
der Verbrauch *consumption, use*
verbrauchen *to consume, use*
die Verfügung *disposal*
vernünftig *sensible, reasonable*
die Verspätung(en) *delay*
vollenden *to complete*
die Vorsaison *before peak season*
vorwärts *forwards*
waagerecht *horizontal, across*
der Wagen(-) *car, carriage*
werfen *to throw*
windig *windy*
das Zeichen(-) *sign*
die Zeitung(en) *newspaper*
zollfrei *duty free*
der Zug(⁼e) *train*
der Zugbegleiter(-) *train guard*
zurücktreten *to step back*
der Zuschlag(⁼e) *supplement*

CHAPTER 10 Wir feiern

Area 1

| • Dates and birthdays |

168-169
(1B 70-71)

L, S, R

Was ist in Hamburg los?

Tell pupils to look at the selection of adverts on pages 168-169 (1B70-71).

Use the adverts to revise ordinals 1-31. Remind pupils of the pattern *am ersten Juli* etc. by saying ,*Am ersten Juli läuft 'Dumbo' im Kinderkino. Am siebten ...'* etc. Name a pupil to read out the next event, correcting his/her date as necessary. The teacher could write key ordinals on the board as they arise. Check pupils' grasp of the ordinals by asking ,*Wann läuft 'Lucky Luke?'* etc.

nem 1

250
(1B 134)

S, W

Wann war das?

An oral or written activity to revise ordinal numbers and dates.

168
(1B 70)

R, W

Was fehlt?

A quick written check of pupils' grasp of ordinal numbers. Gaps are in a simple arithmetical progression. Check the spelling of the answers on the board:

1 neunten, dreiundzwanzigsten.
2 zwölften, sechsundzwanzigsten.
3 vierundzwanzigsten, einunddreißigsten.

L

Wann ist es?

Tell pupils they are going to hear 10 short dialogues. They must try to write down the date mentioned in each.

Wann ist es?
1 — Du, wann ist das Konzert in Köln?
  — **Am dritten Juni,** nicht?
  — Ja, ich glaube, das stimmt. Am dritten.

2 — Guck mal, Alex. **Am zwanzigsten November** spielt Mönchen-Gladbach in Hannover.
  — Ja? Da möchte ich hin!

3 — Sag mal, wann ist Ostern dieses Jahr?
  — Moment mal, ich schau' nach. Ostern ist ... **am elften April.**

4 — Welches Sternzeichen ist Andreas?
  — Skorpion, glaub' ich.
  — Nee, das kann's nicht sein. Skorpion beginnt **am fünfundzwanzigsten Oktober.**

5 — Wann fährst du nach England?
  — Wir fahren **am einunddreißigsten März** ab. In fünf Wochen.

6 — Hast du gehört? **Am ersten Februar** macht eine neue Disko in der Stadt auf.
  — Ja? Wie heißt sie?
  — Top Ten.

7 — Oh, schau mal. Der neue Film von Werner Herzog.
  — Wann kommt der?
  — **Am siebzehnten August** im Metropolis-Kino. Toll, nicht?

8 — Esther, vergiß nicht, du mußt **am vierzehnten Januar** wieder ins Krankenhaus.
  — Ja, ich weiß. Ach, dieser blöde Arm!

9 — Also, ihr lest bis zum Ende des Kapitels, und dann **am zweiten Juli,** also nächsten Donnerstag, schreiben wir eine Klassenarbeit. OK.? Alles klar?
  — *(Several voices:)* Ja.

10 — Du, wann ist Jörgs Party?
  — **Am dreiundzwanzigsten,** glaub' ich.
  — **September?**
  — Ja, klar.
  — Ist das ein Sonnabend?
  — Ich glaube schon.

L

Wann hast du Geburtstag?

Tell pupils they are going to hear ten young Germans saying when their birthdays are. Write the ten names on the board and ask pupils to copy them down. Tell them to write the date of each person's birthday next to the name.

Wann hast du Geburtstag?
Sonja: — Ich heiße Sonja. Ich habe **am 3. August** Geburtstag.
Michael: — Ich heiße Michael Müller. Ich habe **am 11. Juli** Geburtstag. Wann hast du Geburtstag, Bernd?
Bernd: — **Am 16. Mai.**
Sabine: — Mein Name ist Sabine Roth. Ich habe **am 30. September** Geburtstag.

Miriam:	— Ich heiße Miriam, und ich habe **am 7. April** Geburtstag. Gerd, wann hast du Geburtstag?
Gerd:	— **Am 24. September.**
Jutta:	— Ich heiße Jutta Weigle. Ich habe **am 17. Juni** Geburtstag. Wann hast du Geburtstag, Kai?
Kai:	— **Am 21. Januar.**
Nicole:	— Ich heiße Nicole. Ich bin 14, und ich habe **am 15. November** Geburtstag. Wie heißt du?
Uwe:	— Uwe Fischer.
Nicole:	— Und wann hast du Geburtstag?
Uwe:	— **Am 29. Februar.**
Nicole:	— Also, einmal in vier Jahren!
Uwe:	— Ja.

L, S, R

Geburtstagsumfrage

See if pupils can remember from the previous recording how to ask the question ‚*Wann hast du Geburtstag?*' Then give each pupil a blank calendar and tell them to ask the others, one by one, when their birthdays are and to write in their names on the appropriate date. The teacher may like to pose the questions (and write them on the board).

‚*In welchen Monat fallen die meisten Geburtstage?*'
‚*Wer hat als nächster nach dir Geburtstag?*'

The first should, of course, be answered by everyone, provided enough time is given to ask every other member of the class.

The teacher could ask a selection of pupils for their individual answers to the second question.

R, W

168-169
(1B 70-71)

Was ist in Hamburg los?

A selection of adverts and notices for reading comprehension with statements to complete in German.

Solution: **1** Montag **2** DM12 **3** 6. Juli **4** DM 3,90; Bistro Eichenhof **5** 9. Juli **6** Sport- und Freizeitzentrum Eichenhof; Leichtathletik-Länderkampf **7** 291 88 38 84 **8** Auto-Kino **9** 16 **10** Operettenhaus Hamburg.

R

170
(1B 72)

Das Jahr in Deutschland

A personal account of the main events in the year by a young German, with comprehension questions in English.

Solution: **1** reports **2** 3 weeks **3** bonfires; Easter eggs **4** go on outings **5** end of June **6** 24th December **7** bells and fireworks at midnight.

---

10 Area 2

● Invitations

L, S

Kommst du?

Tell pupils to listen to the recording and guess what is being asked. Play the invitations one at a time and ask pupils to say what they think each one is about before continuing. After each one, ask pupils to produce the words used in the invitation itself *(kommst du/kommst du mit)*.

Kommst du?
1 — Ich gebe morgen eine Party. Kommst du?

2 — Wir gehen heute schwimmen. Kommst du mit?

3 — Ich gehe am Samstag ins Kino. Kommst du mit?

4 — Werner gibt nächsten Mittwoch eine Party. Kommst du mit?

5 — Morgen nachmittag gehen wir alle Rollschuh laufen. Kommst du mit?

6 — Anja und ich gehen heute abend in die Disko. Kommst du mit?

L, R, W

171
(1B 73)

Anjas Tagebuch

Tell pupils to copy the page from Anja's diary into their books. Play the whole conversations from which these lines were taken and ask pupils to fill in Anja's diary with the phrases given in the Pupil's Book.

Most classes will need to hear this twice.

The completed diary should look like this:

11 Mo	18 Mo
12 Di	19 Di
13 Mi Pfadfinderinnen	20 Mi *Party bei Werner* *Pfadfinderinnen*
14 Do *(heute)* Schwimmen	21 Do
15 Fr *Rollschuh laufen* *Sonjas Party*	22 Fr
16 Sa *Kino mit Frank*	23 Sa *Opas Geburtstag*
17 So	24 So

Anjas Tagebuch

1 — Hallo, Ute!
— Hallo, Anja! Du, Sonja gibt morgen eine Party. Kommst du mit?
— Ja, prima. Danke. Um wieviel Uhr?
— So ... gegen acht.
— Toll. Also, bis morgen. Tschüs!

2 — He, Anja, warte mal!
— Was denn?
— Was machst du heute nachmittag?
— Nichts. Warum?
— Wir gehen heute schwimmen. Kommst du mit?
— Ja, gerne. Wer kommt denn noch?
— Heinz, Stephanie, Brigitte, Jens — eine ganze Menge.
— Prima. Also, bis dann!

3 — Anja.
— Ja?
— Ich meinte ... Ich gehe am Samstag ins Kino. Kommst du mit?
— Was läuft denn?
— 'Walhalla'.
— Was ist das denn?
— Ein Rockmusical. Soll gut sein.
— OK.
— Gut. Wo wohnst du? Ich hol' dich ab.
— Semperstraße 14.
— Fein. Bis dann!

4 — Du, Anja. Werner gibt nächsten Mittwoch eine Party. Kommst du mit?
— Nächsten Mittwoch, sagst du?
— Ja. Geht das?
— Ja, sicher. Danke.

5 — Ach, da bist du ja, Anja. Hör mal. Morgen nachmittag gehen wir gehen alle Rollschuh laufen. Kommst du mit?
— Ja, prima. Kommt Gabi auch?
— Ja, die kommt auch.
— Wo treffen wir uns?
— An der U-Bahn. Um halb zwei.
— OK. Bis morgen. Tschüs!

L, S, (R)

171
(1B 73)

Wie sagt man das auf Deutsch?

Play conversations again, one at a time. Ask pupils to spot the German for the phrases listed in the Pupil's Book. Write on the Board/OHP as they are given, practising pronunciation at the same time.

The phrases are:

1 Um wieviel Uhr?
2 Wer kommt denn noch? }
 Also, bis dann!
3 Was läuft denn? }
 Wo wohnst du?
4 Geht das?
5 Kommt Gabi auch? }
 Wo treffen wir uns?

L, S

39-58

Talking about tomorrow afternoon

In preparation for the following activity, practise the structure:

Ich spiele morgen nachmittag Tennis.

Use leisure time flashcards as prompts.

L, S

171
(1B 73)

Morgen nachmittag

(Pointing:)

***Du** machst das Buch auf Seite 171 (73) auf. Du siehst dir **diese** Bilder an.* (Point at left column.)
Du sagst: ,Ich gehe morgen nachmittag ins Kino. Kommst du mit?'

(To other partner:)
Was sagst du? (If necessary, prompt:)
,Ja, gerne'/,Ja, prima'.

When both partners have practised both roles, familiarise pupils with the cues in column B (from *Wie sagt man das auf Deutsch?*, above) and go over the *Beispiel*. Continue with the extended pair-work.

Pupils should be encouraged to develop their exchanges further, if possible.

W

nem 2

250
(1B 134)

Kommst du mit?

Written consolidation of the dialogues practised in *Morgen nachmittag*.

171 (1B 73)   R, (W)

Welche Antwort paßt?

A matching exercise to consolidate previous activities.

Solution: 1d 2h 3e 4g 5c 6a 7b 8f.

172 (1B 74)   R, W

So viele Einladungen!

A reading comprehension based on three party invitations, requiring simple sorting of material. Pupils should copy the gapped dialogue and complete it with information from the invitations.

Solution:
1 vierten November	4 Kleestraße
2 Ingeborg	5 Berlinerstraße 60
3 acht	6 Flasche

nem 3
250 (1B 134)   W

Eine Einladung

Ask pupils to design invitations to a party, using the models in their books as a guide. These could be used for a classroom display.

172-173 (1B 74-75)   R

Wir gehen aus

A selection of adverts and invitations for reading comprehension with questions in English.

Solution: 1 Chris Rea 2 29/11-30/11 3 Sat and Sun, 29/11-20/12 4 5/12 5 313 70 07 6 fireworks 7 1st 8 Sömmeringsporthalle 9 VfL Hannover 10 cycle racing 11 1/11 12 Schwanensee 13 30/11; 6/12 14 Hamburg 15 end of December.

62   L, S, R, W

So eine Woche!

Cut the worksheets in two. Pupils A and B in each pair take turns at inviting each other to various events/functions. The first two events for each pupil are cued simply, with a minimum of information, whilst subsequent events are cued with fuller materials, some of which are authentic, from which pupils will have to extract the information needed. Each pupil should fill in the blanks on his/her worksheet as the information is supplied.

Diary page:

Completed entries:

So: (heute) 17	Tennisturnier 9.30 Uhr
Mo. 18.	nachmittag - Schwimmen am Freibad Film „Psycho' 20 Uhr
Di. 19.	15 Uhr - Rollschuhlaufen - Sportzentrum
Mit. 20.	Party bei Jutta 20 Uhr
Do. 21.	Feier bei Uschi u. Bernd 16.30 Uhr
Fr. 22.	19 Uhr - Jahrmarkt - am Marktplatz
Sa. 23.	21 Uhr - „Heiße Zeiten' Disko

More able pupils may be able to use their completed worksheets from the previous activity to write up their diary at greater length — perhaps as a letter to a penfriend.

Telephone game   L, S

Divide the class into equal groups of five or six. Each group then stands or sits in a line. Tell message 1 (see below) to the first pupil in each line. When the signal is given, this pupil makes an imaginary phone call to the next pupil in order to pass on the invitation. That pupil then 'phones the next and so on, to the last in line.

1-2-3-4-5 Gruppe A, hier (placing them in a line.)
Du-du-du-du und du — Gruppe B, dort
Diese Reihe hier, Gruppe C
Ihr fünf — Gruppe D, da drüben.

The game can be made competitive by timing the teams, perhaps on a second message once they are familiar with the usage.

The last pupil in each group is asked to report the received message either:

a) back to the class/after all the groups have finished
or
b) directly to the teacher, if it is being timed.

Messages:

a) Party — Samstag, 12. März — bei Völker — 8 Uhr.
b) Grillparty — bei Annette — Mittwoch, 1. August — ab 7 Uhr.
c) Klassendisko — Samstag, 20. Juni — in der Schule — halb acht.
d) Schwimmen — Freibad — 3 Uhr — Freitag

10 Area 3

● Accepting and turning down invitations

L

Telefongespräch

Tell pupils to listen to the recording and say what it is about. Then play the recording again and tell pupils to listen for the way Dieter answers the phone. Explain the convention of answering the phone using your surname.

Dieters Telefon klingelt. Was sagt er? (Sagt er ,Hallo'?)

Telefongespräch
— Müller
— Hallo Dieter! Hier ist Gisela.
— Na, wie geht's?
— Gut, danke — hör mal, Freitag habe ich Geburtstag, und ich gebe eine Party. Kommst du?
— Ja, gerne. Vielen Dank.
— Nichts zu danken. Gegen halb acht, OK?
— Prima.
— Also, bis dann. Tschüs.
— Tschüs.

174
(**1B** 76)

L, S

Tut mir leid

Six telephone conversations in which invitations are turned down. Play the first two and ask pupils to decide what they have in common, i.e. that the invitations are declined. Then tell pupils to look at the list of possible reasons for invitations not being accepted on page 174 (**1B** 76) of the Pupil's Book. Tell them you are going to play again the two conservations they have just heard, plus four others. Ask them to decide which reason is given in each conversation. Check orally after each one.

Tut mir leid
1 — Mehde.
— Ucki?
— Ja. Ist das Jens?
— Ja. Hör mal. Morgen geb' ich 'ne Party bei uns im Keller. Kannst du kommen?
— Ja, gern. Oh — aber Moment mal. Morgen haben wir Familienbesuch.
— Ach nein.
— Doch. Ich kann nicht weg. Es ist meine Tante aus Goslar.
— Kannst du nicht später kommen?
— Das geht auch nicht. Wir essen zusammen. Zu Schade.
— Also nein?
— Tja. Tut mir wirklich leid. Aber viel Spaß.
— Danke. Naja denn — tschüs.
— Tschüs.

2 — Seifert.
— Hallo Holger. Hier Wolf. Am Freitag habe ich Geburtstag und gebe eine Party. Kannst du kommen?
— Danke. Aber — du, es geht mir momentan nicht so gut.
— Oh — was ist?
— Tja, ich habe Grippe.
— Oh, das tut mir aber leid. Mußt du im Bett liegen?
— Ja.
— Ja, dann gute Besserung.
— Danke, tschüs.
— Tschüs, Holger.

3 — Ahrendt.
— Kann ich bitte Bettina sprechen?
— Sie ist nicht da. Wer ist da denn?
— Ich bin der Rainer. Hat Bettina morgen abend Zeit, können Sie mir das sagen?
— Ich glaube nicht, aber ... am besten ruft sie dich an. Hat sie deine Telefonnummer?
— Ja, sicher.
— Gut. Dann machen wir's so.
— Ja, danke. Also auf Wiederhören.
— Auf Wiederhören.

4 — Hier bei Schäfer.
— Wer ist da?
— Anthony.
— Ach so. Ist Jürgen da?
— Nein, er ist weg.
— Also, paß auf. Morgen gehen wir schwimmen. Kommt ihr mit?
— Nein, morgen können wir nicht. Wir gehen aus.
— OK., ein anderes Mal vielleicht.
— Ja gut.
— Tschüs dann.
— Tschüs.

5 — Krämer.
— Kathrin?
— Ja. Birgit?
— Ja, wie geht's?
— Gut.
— Ich gehe heute abend ins Kino. Kommst du mit?
— Ich kann leider nicht.
— Was machst du denn? Gehst du aus?
— Nein ... aber ich kann nicht. Ich hab' kein Geld, du.
— Oh, schade.
— Ja, tut mir leid.
— Naja — also bis bald.
— Tschüs.

6 — Hier Schmidt.
— Bernd, du?
— Ja. Hallo Ulrich.
— Du, hast du morgen Zeit?
— Morgen? Wann denn?
— Abends. Silke gibt 'ne Party.
— Ach nee.
— Komm doch.
— Nee, wirklich du, ich hab' keine Lust.
— Schade. Na denn ...
— Ja, tschüs.

Solution: 1c 2a 3f 4b 5d 6e

174
(1B 76)

L, S, R

Nein, ich kann nicht

Tell the pupils that you are going to play the last two dialogues again and ask them to listen for what is missing in the printed version in their book.

(Ich kann leider nicht — Tut mir leid — Ich hab' keine Lust)

Practise these phrases. Then ask pupils to practise the complete dialogues in pairs.

63

L, S, R

Wann denn?

Divide the class into groups of four or (preferably) five. Cut up Worksheet 63 and give a different diary page to each member of the group. Explain in English that the task is for them to decide on a date and time when they are all free in order to go and see a film together. Give pupils the following information on the board or OHP:

Film (or give a topical title) beginnt um 15.00 Uhr, 17.30 Uhr und 20.00 Uhr.

Pupils should not only tell each other when they are and are not free, but should give their reasons too if a date is unacceptable. Emphasise that they must not **see** each other's diaries. Each group should tell the teacher when they have found a suitable date and time. Selected groups could be asked to reenact the discussion in front of the class.

Solution: For groups of five the only possible solution is *Donnerstag, den 17. Mai um 17.30 Uhr.* More solutions will be possible with groups of less than five.

174-175
(1B
76-77)

R, W

Niemand kommt!

In this activity pupils have to match up the speech bubbles with the explanations in the box by filling in the appropriate names. Through doing this activity pupils will see the written forms of some of the phrases they have heard in the previous dialogue.

174-175
(1B
76-77)

L, S, R, (W)

Hallo Inge!

Tell pupils to imagine that they are Inge who receives a number of invitations. They must consult their diary in order to decide whether they can accept or not. Practise orally first and consolidate in writing, if required.

175
(1B 77)

Hast du Lust?

Pupils have already met the phrases *Ich habe Lust, Tut mir Leid* and *Ich kann nicht.*

Read through the first dialogue and get pupils to guess at the meaning of *Hast du Lust?*. Get pupils to practise the dialogue briefly in pairs.

Read through the second dialogue, drawing attention to the way the sentence continues **after** *Hast du Lust?*. Again, get pairs to practise this.

Do the same with the third and fourth dialogues. Finally, ask pupils to construct and practise their own short dialogues based on the summary chart.

nem 4

250
(1B 134)

Hast du Lust?

An activity to consolidate work on offering and accepting invitations.

Solution: **Reginas Tagebuch**

FR	
SA	nachmittag - arbeiten 8.00 Giselas Party
SO	
MO	Kino mit Katja
DI	
MI	2.30 Tenis mit Robert ? abend - Babysitting für Nachbarn
DO	2.00 Klavierstunde
FR	Tennisturnier ?
SA	

176
(1B 78)

Wenn, wenn, wenn

Before drawing pupils' attention to the related item in the Pupil's Book, play the first conversation and ask if they can comment on it. Elicit the observation that it is neither an acceptance or rejection as such, but that it depends on something else — that there is an 'if' involved. See whether (on a second

playing, if necessary), pupils can actually identify the German word for 'if'. Write the *wenn* clause on the board. Now tell pupils to look at the item in the Pupil's Book and read through the list with them. Ask which condition applies to the conversation they have just heard. Play the next conversation (twice, if necessary), and again ask pupils to identify the condition mentioned. See if they can repeat the German used. As before, write the *wenn* clause on the board. Continue in the same way with all ten conversations.

N.B. It is important that the correct answer is established after **each** conversation. Pupils should **not** be asked to listen to the dialogues one after the other and record their answers on paper to be checked afterwards.

Solution: **1B 2G 3D 4J 5H 6E 7A 8C 9I 10F**

Wenn, wenn, wenn

1 — Du, wir gehen am Sonnabend zum Konzert von China Crisis. Kommst du mit?
— Naja, was kostet das?
— Weiß ich nicht. Aber hast du Lust?
— Ja gern, **wenn es nicht zu teuer ist.**

2 — Julia, kommst du morgen abend mit in die Disko?
— Ja, **wenn ich mit meiner Schularbeit fertig bin.** Mittwoch schreibe ich eine Klassenarbeit in Mathe.
— Jedenfalls treffen wir uns um acht vor der Schule, OK.?

3 — Morgen nachmittag gehe ich schwimmen. Hast du Lust mitzukommen?
— Im Freibad, meinst du?
— Ja.
— Na gut, **wenn es morgen warm genug ist,** dann komme ich mit.

4 — Günther und ich fahren am Donnerstag zum Wildpark. Willst du mit? Wir nehmen ein Picknick mit.
— Ich weiß nicht. Donnerstag oder Freitag muß ich wegfahren.
— Naja, also **wenn du Lust hast** ...
— Ja, danke. **Wenn ich nicht nach Frankfurt fahre,** dann komme ich gerne mit.

5 — Also, kommst du am Wochenende oder nicht?
— Du, ich weiß noch nicht. **Wenn meine Eltern ja sagen,** gibt's kein Problem.

6 — Kommst du heute mit zum Flohmarkt?
— Nee, du, ich hab' keine Lust.
— Wirklich? Der Peter kommt aber mit!

— Oh. Also in dem Fall, **wenn der Peter hingeht,** komme ich doch mit!

7 *(Telefon klingelt)*
— Andersen.
— Jürgen? Hier ist Christian. Hör mal, hast du Lust, morgen eine Radtour zu machen?
— Ja, wohin denn?
— Ich weiß nicht. Ins Silbertal vielleicht?
— Ja, OK. Ich komme also gegen 10 zu dir — **wenn es nicht regnet!**

8 — Du, Kirsten — ich gebe am 2l. eine Party. Kommst du?
— Das ist ein Freitag, oder?
— Ja, geht das?
— Ja, ich würde gerne kommen. Das Problem ist immer, wie komme ich nach Hause? Ich muß nachschauen. **Wenn ein Bus fährt,** dann komme ich gerne. Vielen Dank!

9 — Paß auf! Wir treffen uns morgen um halb drei im Fischercafé. Kommst du auch hin?
— Hmmm ... morgen nachmittag hab' ich so viel zu tun. Ich kann jetzt nicht sagen. Aber ich komme gern, **wenn ich Zeit habe.**
— OK. Also, bis dann vielleicht.

10 — Da bist du ja, Erwin. Ich habe dich heute morgen schon zweimal angerufen, aber du warst nicht da.
— Ja, ich war nicht zu Hause.
— Wir gehen heute abend in 'ne Disko. Hast du Lust?
— Ja, wer geht denn noch?
— Der Idris, der Ali ...
— Ach der Ali! Den kann ich nicht leiden! **Wenn der geht, dann gehe ich nicht mit.** Aber danke jedenfalls.

R

With the ten wenn clauses now on the Board/OHP, ask pupils if they can see anything unusual about them. Try to let them discover the change in word order for themselves. It is not meant at this stage that they should become expert at manipulating the word order after *wenn*, but rather that they should have encountered this pattern and understood it receptively. It may therefore be advisable to do the following exercise, *Probleme,* together with the class.

(L, S), R, W

176
(1B 78) **Probleme**

Five short dialogues in which the *wenn* clause has to be provided, based on visual and verbal cues alongside. Unless pupils have grasped the grammatical structure well, it is probably best to do this activity together in class. Decide first of all which picture goes with which dialogue. The dialogues could then be written up together or by pupils on their own for consolidation.

Solution: **1B 2A 3D 4E 5C**

---

nem 5   **L, S**
251
(1B 135)   **Weitere Probleme!**

Further practice of *wenn* clauses and invitations, to be practised orally in pairs.

R, W

nem 6
251
(1B 135)   **Ja, gerne ...**

A further written activity to consolidate word order in *wenn* clauses.

L, R

176-177
(1B 78-79) **Die Clique am Samstagabend**

This listening comprehension includes conversations both face to face and by telephone. In some the invitation is accepted, in others, it is turned down.

Only gist comprehension is sought, and is checked by means of multiple choice items in German.

Die Clique am Samstagabend
1 — Hallo, Uwe. Was machst du heute abend?
— Ich bin Babysitter bei meiner Schwester.
— Oh, das ist Pech! Lutz gibt nämlich eine Party.

2 *(Telephone rings)*
— Bauer.
— Hallo, Christina! Hier ist Annette. Hör mal, was machst du heute abend?
— Weiß nicht. Ich gucke mir vielleicht was im Fernsehen an. Wieso?
— Tja, einige aus der Clique gehen zum Jugendklub. Hast du auch Lust?
— Oh ja, prima! Wann?
— Wir kommen um sieben bei dir vorbei. OK.?

3
— Tag, Thomas!
— Tag, Renate.
— Wo gehst **du** denn hin?
— Nach Hause, und dann später zum Evi-Bamm-Konzert. Gehst du auch hin?
— Ich weiß nicht. Ich hab' keine Karte.
— Ach, kein Problem. Karten gibt's sicher noch. Komm doch mit.
— Ja gut. Bis heute abend.

4
— Hallo, Detmar!
— Ach du! Wie geht's?
— Gut. Und dir?
— Nicht so gut.
— Was? Aber du kommst doch zu Werners Party?
— Nein, ich gehe ins Bett.
— Schade. Hoffentlich geht's dir morgen besser.
— Danke.

5
— Inge! Kommst du heute mit in die Stadt?
— Leider nicht. Ich arbeite.
— Was machst du denn?
— Ich arbeite im Supermarkt. Am Samstag mache ich das immer.
— Also, Schade. Aber wir sehen uns bald. Tschüs!
— Tschüs!

6 *(Telephone rings)*
— Meyer.
— Hallo, Frauke. Kommst du heute abend zum Jugendklub?
— Ich weiß noch nicht. Warum?
— Ich bringe einen Freund aus Frankreich mit, und du lernst doch Französisch, also ...
— Ist er nett?
— Ich finde, ja.
— Dann komme ich vielleicht doch. Gegen neun?
— Fein. Bis dann. Tschüs.

7 *(Telephone rings)*
— Stefan Fuhrmann.
— Hier ist Jörg. Hast du heute abend schon was vor?
— Nein, ich bleibe zu Hause.
— Willst du bei mir Platten anhören?
— Oh ja, nicht schlecht. Ich bringe ein paar Platten mit.
— Ja, gut. Also, bis dann.
— Tschüs.

8
— He, Trudi! Warte doch mal!
— Salut. Wo willst du denn hin?
— Ich gehe zu Gabis Party. Du auch?
— Moment mal — Gabi?
— Ja, wieso?
— Ich gehe auch zu einer Party. Aber nicht bei Gabi.
— Wo denn?

— Bei Ilse.
— Ach was! Das ist nächste Woche. Heute ist die Party bei Gabi.
— Wirklich? Mensch, gut daß ich dich getroffen hab'.
— Kommst du also mit zu Gabi?
— Ja, natürlich.

Solution: **1**c **2**a **3**b **4**c **5**b **6**b **7**a **8**c

Wer kommt mit zur Party?

Pupils should be able to understand this cartoon without help from the teacher. The crossword puzzle is a simple check on comprehension. (Possible homework.)

● Describing people

L, S, R

Present the following language by using pupils as models, writing the phrases on the board as they occur:

er/sie ist groß, mittelgroß, klein, ziemlich groß/klein
er/sie hat lange, mittellange, kurze, glatte, lockige, braune, blonde, rote, schwarze Haare
er/sie hat braune, blaue, grüne, graue Augen

When the majority of this language has been used, test pupils' understanding of it by taking other members of the class and saying:

„*Nun Simon. Er ist mittelgroß und hat kurze, blonde Haare. Stimmt das oder nicht?'*

Get pupils to try and correct the part that is wrong. Do the same for other members of the class, including a few correct descriptions as well. Make sure pupils are familiar, at least receptively, with this new language before going on to the next activity.

180
(1B 82)

Gruppenfoto

L

Tell pupils that they are going to hear descriptions of the ten people in the photograph and that they must decide who is being talked about each time.

Seht euch die Personen an und hört gut zu.
Welcher Text paßt zu welcher Person?
Schreibt zuerst die Zahlen 1 bis 10 von oben nach unten in euer Heft. (Demonstrate on the board.)

Play the first recording as an example.

Also, Nummer 1 - wer ist das? A? B? C?

Write the correct answer on the board. Then play the other recordings.

Gruppenfoto

1 — Hier im Bild sind meine Klassenkameraden. Anja hat lange, lockige Haare, und sie trägt eine schwarze Lederjacke, einen bunten Pullover und eine hellblaue Hose.

2 — Das ist Peter. Den mag ich nicht sehr. Er hat kurze Haare und trägt eine hellblaue Hose und einen roten Anorak.

3 — Das ist meine Freundin Anke. Sie hat blonde Haare und trägt eine grüne Hose. Ihr Haar ist schulterlang.

4 — Und hier ist Elisabeth. Auch sie trägt eine hellgrüne Hose zu einem blau-weiß gestreiften Pulli und einer weißen Jacke. Sie hat sehr lange, blonde Haare.

5 — Markus ist ein Komiker! Er trägt eine dunkelblaue Hose, weiße Schuhe und einen gelben Pullover zu einer grünen Jacke. Er hat kurze, blonde Haare.

6 — Und hier ist Hans-Ferdinand. Er trägt eine schwarze Lederjacke und ein weißes Hemd, eine graue Hose und weiße Schuhe. Er hat eine Brille auf. Ich finde ihn sehr sympathisch.

7 — Wer noch? Ach ja, die Ute. Sie hat kurze, blonde Haare und trägt einen schwarzen Pullover und ein blaues Hemd. Dazu trägt sie einen blauen Rock, schwarze Socken und gelbe Schuhe.

8 — Astrid ist auch eine Freundin von mir. Hier im Bild trägt sie eine rote Bluse und eine blaue Jacke. Sie hat kurze dunkelbraune Haare.

9 — Hasan finde ich toll! Er hat kurze Haare und trägt eine Jacke und Jeans. Ja, und er hat ein schwarzes T-Shirt an.

10 — Der Carlos ist auch ein toller Typ! Er trägt Jeans und ein weißes T-Shirt. Seine hellblaue Jacke finde ich schön. Er hat kurzes, dunkles Haar.

Solution: 1E 2B 3J 4H 5D 6G 7I 8F 9A 10C

L, S, (R), W

Game

Wer ist das?

Prepare this activity orally in the following way:

Ich bin ziemlich groß.
Ich habe ... Augen und ... Haare.
Und du, Sharon?
Und du, Seamus?

Tell pupils to write down descriptions of themselves with the help of the *Tip des Tages*.

Tell five pupils to come to the front with their written descriptions. Collect the descriptions and read them out in random order. Ask the class to identify each person.

... , kommt nach vorne. Bringt eure Hefte mit.
Stellt euch hier in einer Reihe auf. So.
Ihr anderen — hört gut zu. Wer ist das?

Repeat with other groups.

Haarige Probleme

In this activity one pupil pretends to be one of the people on the page and the partner has to work out who he/she is by asking questions. Demonstrate with one pupil.

Ann, komm nach vorn.
Hier sind viele Leute.
Suche dir eine Person aus. (Mime) OK.? Du bist jetzt diese Person.
Du bist jetzt Jörg oder Trudi oder Dieter ... ja?

So. Bist du ein Junge?
Nein. (Write on board): *Mädchen*
Hast du lange Haare?
Ja. *lange Haare*
Hast du schwarze Haare?
Nein. *nicht schwarz*
Hast du blonde Haare?
Ja. *blond*
Hast du lockige Haare?
Nein *glatt*
Bist du ... Alexandra?
Ja!

6 Fragen

Solution:

			m	f
long	curly	dark	3	16
		blond	15	12
	straight	dark	19	22
		blond	11	7
short	curly	dark	4	24
		blond	6	2
	straight	dark	13	20
		blond	9	18
medium	curly	dark	21	10
		blond	5	8
	straight	dark	23	14
		blond	1	17

So ein Durcheinander!

The aim of the task is to match photographs to forms.

Either set the scene:

Hier sind sechs Fotos, sechs Formulare. Die Schule x hat eine Partnerschule in Irland. Diese Schülerinnen kommen nach Irland. Aber die irische Lehrerin hat ein Problem. Was ist das Problem? Wer kann es auf Englisch erklären?

... or leave it to the pupils to make their own deductions from what they see.

When the pupils start tackling the problem, the teacher should help those in difficulty by pointing to clues on the forms or in the photos.

Solution: Key to correct pairings:

NAME	PHOTO NR.
Bärbel	4
Jutta	2
Anne	1
Marga	5
Bettina	6
Alexandra	3

CLUE ON FORM	CLUE IN PHOTO
Größe 1,94	Clearly a tall girl
Hobbys: Reiten	Riding gear
Bruder 2 Jahre	Little boy on lap
Hobbys: Radfahren	Bike
Hobbys: Gitarre	Guitar
None	None

So ein Durcheinander!

Once pupils have matched the forms with the photos, tell them to write a description of each girl. Possible homework.

Beschreibt die sechs Mädchen.
Zum Beispiel: Bettina ist mittelgroß und hat lange, blonde Haare.
Schreibt es auf.

Use appropriate illustrations (e.g. drawings on the board, reference to members of staff, well-known people) to introduce the remaining descriptive vocabulary. A selection of home-made flashcards will make this more fun. These can be further exploited by asking a pupil to come and choose one, then describe it to the class, who have to guess which one it is.

L, S, R, W

T: *Jetzt wieder auf Deutsch. Peters Anorak ist ...*
P: *Blau.*
T: *Ja, Peter hat einen blauen Anorak an.*

Get pupils to repeat.

Continue with the other masculine nouns:
Helgas Rock
Jans Pullover
Trudis Anorak

Write on the board:

| x hat | einen | blauen gelben grauen grünen | Anorak Rock Pullover | an |

Continue similarly with the feminine nouns:
Birgits Bluse
Norberts Hose
Kurts Krawatte
Ankes Jacke
Trudis Weste   and add the second column
                 on the board

... neuter nouns:
Ralfs Hemd
Kurts T-Shirt
Karins Kleid

... and plural nouns:
Andreas' Schuhe
Trudis Strümpfe

If you wish, the relationship between *einen*
and *blauen*, *eine* and *rote* can be highlighted
like this: *einen   eine*

blauen rote

179 (1B 81)   Wie sieht er denn sonst aus?

Game

Tell pupils to write a description of a member of staff with the help of *Wie sieht er denn sonst aus?*

Ask one pupil at a time to read out his/her description and get the rest of the class to guess who it is.

L

180 (1B 82)   Kleidung (Gruppenfoto)

Tell pupils to look again at the *Gruppenfoto* on page 180 (**1B** 82) and listen to the recording.

Play the first recording and ask pupils to say in English what Anja is wearing. Write the name 'Anja' on the board and add in English what she is wearing. Then write the names of the other people in the order in which they appear in the transcript and ask pupils to copy them. Play the remainder of the recording. (The longer recording *Gruppenfoto* could be used instead.)

Hört gut zu. Was hat Anja an? (Play first recording.)
Auf Englisch? (Write answer on board.)
Hier sind die anderen Namen. Schreibt sie ab. Jetzt hört wieder zu.

Kleidung

— Anja hat eine hellblaue Hose an.
Peter hat einen roten Anorak an.
Anke hat eine grüne Hose an.
Elisabeth hat eine weiße Jacke an.
Markus hat weiße Schuhe an.
Hans-Ferdinand hat ein weißes Hemd an.
Ute hat einen blauen Rock an.
Astrid hat eine rote Bluse an.
Hasan hat ein schwarzes T-Shirt an.
Carlos hat eine hellblaue Jacke an.

L, (S), R

Adjective endings

N.B. With some classes you may prefer to omit this section and just use the adjectives predicatively (see *Kleider machen Leute*, TN page 167, PB page 181/**1B** 83).

Suggested sequence for teaching the adjective endings:

Using the pupils' own notes from the previous activity, reconstruct the German in two stages, e.g.

L, S

65   Zehn Unterschiede

Cut up the worksheets and distribute to pairs.

Tell pupils that they must spot the ten differences and make a note of them.

T: *Partnerarbeit. Jeder Partner hat ein Bild. Auf Bild A sind viele Leute, und auf Bild B sind auch viele Leute. Aber es gibt zehn Unterschiede (das ist auf Englisch differences). Sucht die zehn Unterschiede. Paßt auf: John, gib mir dein Bild.* (To John's partner:) *Links steht eine Frau. Sie hat lockige Haare. Wie ist das bei dir?*
P: *Ja, die Frau hat lockige Haare, und sie trägt eine Brille.*
T: *Ah, bei mir nicht. Das ist ein Unterschied. Macht weiter!*

Solution:

The ten differences are:

The ten differences are:

---

nem 7
251
(1B 135)

Sechs Unterschiede

W

A written version of the previous game, using different pictures. Pupils have to spot and describe the six differences between pictures A and B.

Solution: The differences are:

Bild A	— Das Mädchen hat einen weißen Rock an
Bild B	— Es hat einen schwarzen Rock an
Bild A	— Die Frau hat lange Haare
Bild B	— Sie hat kurze Haare
Bild A	— Der junge Mann trägt ein T-Shirt
Bild B	— Er trägt ein Hemd

Bild A	— Der Mann hat keinen Bart
Bild B	— Er hat einen Bart
Bild A	— Der Mann hat eine Glatze
Bild B	— Er hat keine
Bild A	— Das Kind hat eine kurze Hose an
Bild B	— Es hat eine lange Hose an.

---

181 (1B 83)

Kleider machen Leute

R, W

The clothes five young people are wearing are listed by colours. Pupils have to compile a description of what each of them is wearing. This means finding the right article and adjective ending for each noun. Direct pupils' attention to the *Tip des Tages* on page 181 (**1B** 83).

As a simpler activity pupils could draw the people and colour them in appropriately. They could then form sentences **without** adjective endings.

z.B Margas Bluse ist weiß, ihr Rock ist schwarz und ihre Schuhe sind grau.

Marga:	weiße Bluse, graue Schuhe, schwarzen Rock
Nicola:	weiße Schuhe, gelbe Hose, grüne Jacke, graues T-Shirt
Ralf:	weißes T-Shirt, blaue Hose, blaue Schuhe
Jochen:	gelbes Hemd, rote Jacke, schwarze Hose, braune Schuhe
Gisela:	rotes Hemd, rote Schuhe, grünen Pullover, graue Hose

---

10   Area 5

● **Saying what you did and who you met**

182 (1B 84)

Gestern abend

L

Ask pupils to read through the list of things that the eight people named did yesterday evening. Tell them to copy down the list of names, then, as they hear the people saying what they did, to write down next to each name the letter which goes with that activity. This area introduces the Perfect Tense of a number of common 'strong' verbs

Gestern abend

Scott Wilson: — Was habt ihr gestern abend gemacht?

Sonja: — Gestern hatte ich Geburtstag. Also am Abend habe ich eine Party gegeben.

Scott Wilson:	— Schön. Und du, Michael?
Michael:	— Gestern abend? Ich habe einen Film gesehen.
Scott Wilson:	— Bernd, was hast du gestern abend gemacht?
Bernd:	— Also, ich habe in der Stadt ein paar Freunde getroffen, und wir haben zusammen ein Bier getrunken.
Scott Wilson:	— Sabine, hast du 'was gemacht?
Sabine:	— Ja, ich bin zu Erika gegangen, und wir haben Platten gehört.
Scott Wilson:	— Also. Und Miriam?
Miriam:	— Ich habe gestern abend Tennis gespielt.
Scott Wilson:	— Und was hat der Gerd gemacht?
Gerd:	— Gestern abend hab' ich nur Schularbeiten gemacht. Das ist alles.
Scott Wilson:	— Hast du auch Schularbeiten gemacht, Jutta?
Jutta:	— Ich bin zu einer Party bei einer Freundin gegangen. Das war wirklich gut.
Scott Wilson:	— Und schließlich Kai. Was hast du gestern abend gemacht?
Kai:	— Gestern abend? Naja, nichts besonderes. Ich bin zu Hause geblieben, hab' ferngesehen.

Solution:

Sonja	F
Michael	A
Bernd	H
Sabine	D
Miriam	B
Gerd	C
Jutta	E
Kai	G

R, W

182
(1B 84)

Was hast du gemacht?

Written reinforcement of the structures and vocab. heard in *Gestern abend*. Before asking pupils to tackle this task, the teacher may wish to play the eight statements again, pausing after each example of the Perfect Tense and getting pupils to repeat it. Draw attention to the use of *habe* with certain verbs and *bin* with others by writing on the board as they occur:

Ich habe ... gesehen
Ich bin ... gegangen etc.

R

183
(1B 85)

Liebe Miriam

Reading comprehension including the newly introduced language. The questions do **not**

---

follow the order in which the information occurs in the letter.

R, W

183
(1B 85)

Deine Woche

Pupils should use the week's diary entries to write a letter to a 'penfriend' describing what they have been doing each day and what they are going to do for the rest of the weekend. For help with the beginning, ending and sentence structure, pupils should be redirected to the letter *Liebe Miriam*.

---

nem 8

251
(1B 135)

R, W

Eine Postkarte

A gap-filling exercise to focus on the use of *habe* and *bin* in the Perfect Tense.

L, R, (W)

66

Geburtstagsfeier

Tell pupils they are going to hear the same eight people interviewed for *Gestern abend* saying what they got for their last birthday. Hand out the worksheet and ask them to put against each name what presents they were given and how they celebrated their birthday. Answers could be in German or English, perhaps in note form to write up later. The second part of the worksheet provides consolidation of the language and could be used as a follow up to the next activity *Was hast du zu deinem Geburtstag bekommen?*

T: *Ihr hört gleich die acht jungen Leute wieder: Sonja, Michael, Bernd, Sabine, Miriam, Gerd, Jutta und Kai. Sie sprechen über ihren letzten Geburtstag. Hört gut zu! Was für Geschenke haben sie bekommen? Ein Radio? Kleider? Geld? Und wie haben sie gefeiert?* (Tell the class, or write up, that *feiern* means to celebrate). *Zum Beispiel:* (play the first recording).

T: *So, was hat Sonja bekommen?*
P: *Kleider.*
T: *Ja, gut.* (Write on the board *Sonja — Kleider*). *Und wie hat sie gefeiert?*
P: *Eine Party.*
T: *Ja, sie hat eine Party gegeben* (write it up). *Jetzt Michael. Hört gut zu und schreibt auf, was ihr hört.*

Geburtstagsfeier
— Was habt ihr zum Geburtstag bekommen?

Sonja
— Zu meinem letzten Geburtstag hab' ich von meinen Eltern Kleider bekommen. Da hab' ich auch eine große Party gegeben — ich habe nämlich im August Geburtstag, und das Wetter war sehr gut.

Michael
— Ich habe ein paar Bücher, ein paar Kassetten bekommen, aber hauptsächlich habe ich Geld bekommen.
— Und hast du eine Party gehabt?
— Ja, aber nicht direkt an meinem Geburtstag. So einige Wochen später.

Bernd
— Als Geschenk von meinen Eltern habe ich einen Printer für meinen Computer bekommen. Am Abend sind wir zusammen in ein Restaurant gegangen, meine Eltern und ich, und haben italienisch gegessen.

Sabine
— Ich habe eine spanische Gitarre bekommen.
— Und wie hast du gefeiert? Hast du eine Party gegeben?
— Na, das war keine richtige Party. Ich habe mit einigen Freunden bei mir zu Hause gefeiert.

Miriam
— Also, zu meinem Geburtstag habe ich einen neuen Tennisschläger, einen Walkman und etwas Geld bekommen. Am Sonnabend vorher habe ich eine Party gegeben.

Gerd
— Also, ich stehe nicht auf Partys. An meinem Geburtstag bin ich ins Theater gegangen.
— Und was für Geschenke hast du bekommen?
— Einen CD-Player, also einen Compakt-Disk Plattenspieler.

Jutta
— Ja, ich habe Geld bekommen. Und am Wochenende habe ich eine kleine Party gegeben, und zwar eine Grillparty. Ich hab' ja im Juni Geburtstag und wir haben mit dem Wetter Glück gehabt.

Kai
— Mal sehen, was habe ich bekommen? Geld von meinem Onkel, einen Rucksack von meinem Vater, eine Platte von meiner Schwester und noch ein paar andere Kleinigkeiten dazu.
— Hast du eine Party gegeben?
— Nein, unsere Wohnung ist viel zu klein. Ich bin in die Disko gegangen.

Solution:

Geburtstagsfeier
Diese acht jungen Leute sprechen über ihren Geburtstag. Höre gut zu und schreibe die passende Antwort in den richtigen Kasten.

Name	Wie hat er/sie gefeiert?	Wann?	Was hat er/sie bekommen?	Von wem?
Sonja	Party	August	Kleider	Eltern
Michael	Party	einige Wochen später	Bücher, Kassetten, CdD	—
Bernd	Restaurant	am Abend	Printer	Eltern
Sabine	Freunde eingeladen	—	spanische Gitarre	—
Miriam	Party	Sonnabend vorher	Tennisschläge, Walkman..	—
Gerd	Theater	—	CD-Player	—
Jutta	Grillparty	Juni	Geld	—
Kai	Disko	—	Geld, Rucksack, Platte	Onkel, Vater, Schwester

Und du?

● Wie hast du gefeiert?
_____
_____

● Was hast du zu deinem Geburtstag bekommen?
_____
_____

L, S

Was hast du zu deinem Geburtstag bekommen?

A cumulative game to practise the verb *bekommen* and to draw attention to the position of the past participle in a German sentence. Present the question ‚*Was hast du zu deinem Geburtstag bekommen?*' Quote two or three of the answers from the previous listening activity, *Geburtstagsfeier*, e.g. ‚*Ich habe eine Gitarre bekommen*' or ‚*Ich habe Geld bekommen*'.

Now get five or six pupils to stand in line at the front of the class. Ask the first person: ‚*Was hast du zu deinem Geburtstag bekommen?*' Encourage them to give any other answer they can, but correct it if necessary and get them to repeat it. Now ask the second person the same question and begin their answer for them: ‚*Ich habe eine Gitarre und ...?*' so they get the idea that they must **add** to what has gone before. When the last person has recited the whole list so far (remembering to put *bekommen* at the end!) return to the first who must add yet another present, and so on.

It is for the teacher to decide whether
a) to make the game competitive by eliminating those who forget an item;
b) to correct the indefinite articles used, which are likely to be wrong sometimes.

It is a good idea to make sure before the game begins that the rest of the class have put down their pens — a tempting tactic for resourceful participants!

Was paßt zu wem?

i) Tell pupils to look at the group photograph and listen to Petra talking about the people in it. Play the recording, then ask pupils what they think Petra was saying. When the theme of giving opinions about people has been identified, write up the list of comments (from *toll* to *fies*) on the board, and go through it, making the meanings clear through gestures and facial expressions.

" *Seht euch das Foto an. Das sind Mädchen und Jungen aus Petras Klasse. Jetzt hört gut zu. Was sagt Petra?* (Play recording — discuss content in English).

ii) Tell pupils that they are going to listen again to what Petra said about each person. Ask them to copy *Was paßt zu wem?* so that they can link the comments to the names. Then play the recording a second time. Pupils may also be able to link the correct name to the correct picture.

" *Gleich hört ihr Petra noch einmal. Schreibt 'Was paßt zu wem?' in eure Hefte. Zieht Linien zwischen den Namen und dem Kasten.*

Demonstrate on the board. Pupils can later complete the display on the board to look like this:

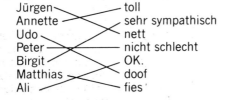

Jürgen — toll
Annette — sehr sympathisch
Udo — nett
Peter — nicht schlecht
Birgit — OK.
Matthias — doof
Ali — fies

N.B. This 'ranking' of adjectives is meant as a rough guide only. The meaning of some of the words will, of course, change according to intonation. It may be worth illustrating this with some English examples, e.g. 'not bad'.

Was paßt zu wem?

— Das sind einige Jungen und Mädchen aus meiner Klasse. Dies hier in der Mitte ist der Jürgen — der ist nett. Und links von ihm steht Annette — die ist toll. Das ist Udo, hier vorn. Der ist doof. Peter ist aber nicht schlecht. Da ist er. Birgit kennst du, ja. Ich finde sie sehr sympathisch. Ach ja, und das da ist Matthias. Der ist fies. Aber der Ali, da ganz rechts, ist OK.

Was hältst du von Elke?

Tell pupils to copy the chart. Tell them that they are going to hear three people saying what they think of Elke, Hanno, Iris, Pamela and Viktor. They should decide whether the comments are favourable, neutral or unfavourable and indicate this by putting a cross in the appropriate box.

" *Übertragt die Tabelle in euer Heft. Gleich hört ihr drei junge Leute. Sie sagen etwas über Elke, über Hanno und so weiter.*
Ist das gut? Oder ist das schlecht? Oder so in der Mitte?
Macht Kreuze in den richtigen Kasten.
Und jetzt hört gut zu.

If necessary, do the first example with the class.

Solution: The completed chart should look like this:

	☺	⊖	⌒
Elke	X X	X	
Hanno		X	X X
Iris	X	X	X
Pamela	X X X		
Viktor	X X		X

The teacher may wish to draw pupils' attention to some of the variants and new ways of commenting on people who occur in these interviews.

N.B. It is strongly advised that pupils are not encouraged to practise these phrases in relation to each other. The pair-work suggested later in this area is based strictly on **imaginary** characters.

Was hältst du von Elke?
1 — Sag mal, was hältst du von Elke?
— Sie ist nett.
— Und Hanno?
— Hanno? Naja, er ist nicht schlecht.
— Und Iris. Wie findest du Iris?
— Die mag ich nicht.
— Und wie findest du Pamela?
— Die ist toll.
— Und Viktor?
— Ja, der ist auch sehr nett.

2 — Du, findest du Elke nett?
— Nicht besonders. Naja, ziemlich OK.
— Und Hanno?
— Ach, der Idiot —
— Ja, und Iris. Was hältst du von ihr?
— Iris finde ich sehr sympathisch.

— Pamela?
— Ja, die auch. Die ist wirklich sehr nett.
— Und Viktor?
— Ja, das ist ein toller Typ.

3— Wie findest du Elke?
— Ach, ich finde sie unheimlich nett.
— Und Hanno?
— Hanno kann ich nicht leiden. Der ist blöd.
— Nun Iris?
— Na also — Iris ist — ein bißchen
egoistisch, nicht? Aber sie kann auch
ganz nett sein.
— Und Pamela?
— Die ist prima.
— Und dann Viktor?
— Der nervt mich. Der ist richtig fies.

L, S

Practise the questions:
,Was hältst du von ... ?'
,Wie findest du ... ?'
,Wie ist ... ?'

Begin by asking a pupil about a well-
known personality (actor, singer,
politician), not a fellow pupil. Then
encourage them to take over the teacher's
role and ask questions round the class.

L, S, (R)

Interviews

Tell pupils to do another chart like *Was hältst
du von Elke?* putting in five names of well-
known people of their own choice. Then ask
them to interview their fellow pupils and
record their opinions about all five on the
chart. Some pupils may want to use the *Tip
des Tages.*

*Macht noch eine Tabelle wie **Was hältst du von
Elke?***
Schreibt jetzt neue Namen in die Tabelle.
*z.B. (give some examples of television
'personalities', pop or sport stars etc.)*

*Jetzt geht zu den anderen in der Klasse und
fragt sie: ,Was hältst du von ... ?' oder ,Wie
findest du ... ?' Macht Kreuze in den richtigen
Kasten.*

Conclude the activity by asking individuals:

,Wer ist der Star auf deiner Liste?'

184
(1B 86)

Hast du die Berti kennengelernt?

This extended conversation incorporates
physical descriptions, descriptions of clothing

L

and comments about character. It introduces
the Perfect Tenses of *kennenlernen, sprechen,
finden* and *tragen.*

i   Play the conversation through once, as far
as the line marked A. Ask pupils to say
what they have understood of it. Try to
build up a picture of the whole thing. Ask
how they think it might end.

ii Next tell pupils they are going to hear the
same conversation again, but that you are
going to stop the tape at certain points
(in bold in the transcript below) and
that they must look at the ten phrases
listed **A-J** in the Pupil's Book and decide
which is the English equivalent of what
has just been said. Tell them to write 1-10
in their books and be ready, each time the
tape is stopped, to put the correct letter
next to the number you give.

Now play the recording again, stopping the
tape immediately after each bold
section and giving the number in the text. It
may be worthwhile playing the recording a
third time to check the answers. In any case,
the last time you play it, allow pupils to hear
the conversation right through to the end to
see if their predictions were correct.

Solution: **1C 2F 3B 4J 5G 6E 7I 8A 9H 10D**

Hast du die Berti kennengelernt?
Konrad: — Tag, Oliver. Wie geht's dir denn
heute?
Oliver: — Och, nicht so gut. Wie war die
Party?
Konrad: — Toll.
Oliver: — Hast du die Berti kennengelernt?
Konrad: — Berti? Nee, ich glaube nicht. Wieso?
Oliver: — Die ist meine neue Freundin. **Ich
bin sicher, sie war da. (1)**
Konrad: — Ja? Wie sieht sie denn aus?
Oliver: — Sie hat kurze, braune Haare ...
Konrad: — Glatt?
Oliver: — Ja. Hast du sie **kennengelernt? (2)**
Konrad: — Ja, sie war mit Susanne
zusammen. Ich habe mit ihr ein
paar Minuten gesprochen, das ist
alles.
Oliver: — Sie ist nett, nicht?
Konrad: — Naja, **sie war ganz OK. (3)** Aber ...
sie ist ein bißchen groß für dich,
oder?
Oliver: — Groß? Die Berti? Die ist aber gar
nicht groß, du. Sag mal, **was hat
sie getragen (4)**, dieses Mädchen?
Konrad: — Ach, ich weiß nicht mehr. So, einen
Rock —
Oliver: — Nein, Berti trägt immer Jeans.
Konrad: — Und sie hat kurze, braune Haare,
sagst du?

Oliver: — Ja.

Konrad: — Und sie ist nicht groß?

Oliver: — Gar nicht. Sie ist ziemlich klein.

Konrad: — Ach ja! Ich glaub', **ich weiß, wen du meinst (5),** aber ...

Oliver: — Aber was?

Konrad: — **Naja, ich habe sie ein bißchen doof gefunden. (6)**

Oliver: — Die Berti? Ach Quatsch! Doof ist sie nicht.

Konrad: — Ich glaub, **sie hat zuviel Wein getrunken. (7)**

Oliver: — Dann war das bestimmt nicht die Berti. Sie trinkt nicht gern Wein. Naja, **macht nichts. (8)** Mit wem hast du denn getanzt?

Konrad: — Du, ich habe ein tolles Mädchen kennengelernt. **Ich habe mit ihr fast den ganzen Abend getanzt. (9)**

Oliver: — Wie heißt sie?

Konrad: — Tina.

Oliver: — Tina! **Wie sieht sie aus? (10)**

Konrad: — Mittelgroß, dunkelbraune Haare, blaue Augen. Sie ist wirklich toll. Wir gehen morgen aus.

A _____

Oliver: — Du Schwein! Das ist die Berti! Das ist meine Freundin!

Konrad: — Ne, ne. Sie heißt Tina, ganz bestimmt, dieses Mädchen.

Oliver: — Ja! Tina Bertoli heißt sie. Ihre Freunde nennen sie alle Berti! Heraus mit dir.

After the above exercise there are eight more sentences from the conversation. The pattern around the phrases will help pupils to match them up.

Solution: **1**g **2**h **3**e **4**f **5**a **6**b **7**a **8**c

L, S, R

184 (1B 86) Partnerarbeit

Either draw a person on the board, labelling hair or eye colour and one or two clothes colours, or use a homemade colour flashcard of a person. Point to this and ask the question: ,*Hast du Ingrid/Dieter kennengelernt?'* Get the class to repeat the question.

Now ask the question ,*Wie hast du sie/ihn gefunden?'* Suggest several possible answers from the range already learnt, if necessary. Both these questions should be familiar from the previous activity *Hast du die Berti kennengelernt?*

Repeat this procedure with a few other pictures. This time address the questions to a particular individual in the class. Eventually you should be able to hand over the teacher's role to a pupil and get him or her to put the questions to another pupil.

Next, resume the original teacher's role and, without drawing or showing a picture, ask ,*Hast du Karola kennengelernt?'* See if pupils can come up with the question ,*Wie sieht sie aus?'* or ,*Was hat sie getragen?'* If they do not, help them, and get them to repeat it. When you give the information requested, draw or show the picture to reinforce its meaning (e.g. *Sie hat lange, rote Haare/sie hat einen weißen Rock getragen).*

Now ask pupils to look at the dialogue model headed *Partnerarbeit* on page 184 (1B 86) of the Pupil's Book. Get the whole class to practise similar dialogues in pairs. Some or all of these could be performed in front of the class. The teacher could number the dialogues as they are performed and pose a question in English after each one ('What colour was Marga's hair?', 'What did he think of Reinhard?' etc.), which the rest of the class would try to answer in writing. These answers could then be checked together, each one being confirmed by the pair with whom it originated.

67

L, S, R

Wie hast du sie gefunden?

Explain that each partner will be asking the other their opinion about four imaginary people they have met at a party. A asks B about four, then B asks A about a different four. Tell the pupils that they will have to describe the people they are asking about, as their partner may not have found out their names. They should base their conversations on the model they have been practising in *Partnerarbeit.* When their partner has identified who they are talking about and they have asked what their partner thought of that person, they should draw a symbol in the appropriate box to record their partner's opinion. Now distribute the worksheets, cut in half, one per pair. To avoid any possible confusion, instructions are given in English on the worksheet.

The activity can be checked, if the teacher wishes, by drawing symbols on the board for the eight people named. Alternatively, it could be considered finished when pairs have completed it to their own satisfaction.

10 Area 6

● Consolidation

185
(1B 87) **Treff-spezial-Ferien** R

Nine personal ads. in which young people are trying to get in touch with someone they met. Before attempting the questions, pupils should be asked to identify this general theme of the ads. The questions range from the particular to the general. The answers to some are a matter of opinion, and discussion of these should lead to a closer look at the German. The questions in no way follow the order of the advertisements.

nem 9
251 R, W
(1B 135) **Treff-spezial**

Pupils invent their own personal ad. based on those in *Treff-spezial-Ferien* on page 185 (**1B** 87) of the Pupil's Book. These could make an interesting and amusing classroom display.

186
(1B 88) **Teenager** L

Eight dialogues for listening comprehension with questions in English.

Ihr hört jetzt acht Gespräche. Hört gut zu und beantwortet die Fragen auf Englisch.

Teenager
1 Petra: — Kommst du heute abend zur Party?
Gerd: — Ja, und ich bringe meinen englischen Brieffreund mit.
Petra: — Oh, ist er nett?
Gerd: — Ja, sehr. Spricht auch gut Deutsch.

2 Rolf: — Kommst du am Sonnabend schwimmen?
Werner: — Wer kommt denn alles?
Rolf: — Torsten, Christof —
Werner: — Ach Christof?
Rolf: — Ja, wieso?
Werner: — Ach, den finde ich nicht so toll.
Rolf: — Also, kommst du oder nicht?
Werner: — Doch, doch, ich komme.

3 Franz: — He, Uwe. Was machst du morgen abend?
Uwe: — Nichts Besonderes. Wieso?
Franz: — Da ist 'ne Party in Kirchheim.

Uwe: — Bei wem?
Franz: — Sie heißt Andrea, glaube ich.
Uwe: — Moment mal. Kennst du die etwa gar nicht?
Franz: — Doch, doch. Sie ist nett. Ich glaube, du kennst sie auch. Glatte, schwarze Haare, schlank.
Uwe: — Ach ja, ich glaube schon. Aber geht das, wenn ich auch komme?
Franz: — Ganz bestimmt. Kein Problem.

4 Ruth: — He, Inge! Wir fahren Dienstag zum Hansaland. Kommst du mit?
Inge: — Gern. Wer kommt denn noch?
Ruth: — Die Sabine — Jutta — Karola.
Inge: — Wer?
Ruth: — Karola. Sabines Freundin.
Inge: — Kenne ich die? Wie sieht sie aus?
Ruth: — Sie hat kurze Haare — blond. Sie ist ziemlich klein.
Inge: — Nee, kenne ich nicht.
Ruth: — Sie ist recht nett.
Inge: — Also Dienstag. Und wann?
Ruth: — Wir treffen uns um halb zehn am Bahnhof.
Inge: — Prima! Ich komme mit.

5 *(Musik. Auf einer Party)*
Hans: — Du, wer ist das Mädchen da drüben, bei Regina?
Peter: — Wer, die große blonde?
Hans: — Nein, die links, mit dem schwarzen Rock.
Peter: — Das ist Daniela.
Hans: — Sie sieht nett aus.
Peter: — Na ja, ganz OK. Ich find' sie aber blöd.
Hans: — Mal sehen *(Walks across)* Willst du tanzen?

6 *(Auf einer Party)*
Simone: — Sag, mal, Karin, was hältst du eigentlich von Martin?
Karin: — Ganz sympathisch.
Simone: — Findest du, er sieht gut aus?
Karin: — Mmm, nicht schlecht. Warum fragst du?
Simone: — Sein langes Haar finde ich schön. Und er hat tolle dunkelbraune Augen!
Karin: — Und er tanzt mit Anja.

7 *(Auf einer Party)*
Kurt: — Setzen wir uns? ‚ne kleine Pause?
Maike: — Ja, gerne.

Kurt	— Hm, das war gut. Du, ich will morgen ins Kino. Hast du Lust, mitzukommen?
Maike:	— Wer kommt denn noch?
Kurt:	— Niemand. Nur ich.
Maike:	— Vielleicht. Was läuft denn?
Kurt:	— Mmm — ich weiß nicht genau. Ich glaube, es ist mit Evi Bamm.
Maike:	— Evi Bamm? Muß das sein?
Kurt:	— Ach, magst du sie nicht?
Maike:	— Schon gut. Ich komme gerne mit.
Kurt:	— Prima! Wollen wir wieder tanzen?

8 Mutti: — So, Sebastian, wer kommt denn alles zu deiner Party?

Sebastian: — Da ist die Liste. Guck sie dir mal an.

Mutti: — Viola? Wer ist das?

Sebastian: — Das ist Roberts Freundin.

Mutti: — Und wie ist sie?

Sebastian: — Sie ist mittelgroß, hat braune Haare, trägt immer Blue Jeans —

Mutti: — Nein, ich meine: ist sie nett?

Sebastian: — Ja, ganz nett.

Mutti: — Und Hanno? Wer ist das?

Sebastian: — Hanno? Das ist — einer aus meiner Klasse.

Mutti: — Ist der neu?

Sebastian: — Ja, ziemlich.

Mutti: — Nett?

Sebastian: — Naja — weiß nicht. Nicht besonders.

Mutti: — Und du willst ihn einladen?

Sebastian: — Naja, also — der hat nächste Woche auch eine Party, und da möchte ich hin.

---

ist für Gespräch Nummer eins. Welche Wörter hört ihr im Gespräch?
Hört ihr das Wort ,Disko'? Hört ihr das Wort ,Party'? Hört gut zu!

(Play first line of Conversation 1)

Also, sagt sie das Wort ,Disko'?

P: *Nein.*

T: *Sagt sie das Wort ,Party'?*

P: *Ja!*
Dann unterstreich das Wort ,Party' auf der Liste. (Demonstrate underlining on board.) *Und jetzt hört zu.*

Solution: The words spoken in each list are:-

1 Party, Brieffreund, nett, gut
2 schwimmen, nicht so toll, ich komme
3 nichts Besonderes, doch, schwarze, geht das, kein Problem
4 klein, treffen
5 da drüben, Rock, blöd, tanzen
6 sympathisch, gut, warum, schön, tolle
7 kleine, morgen, niemand, läuft, weiß, wieder
8 alles, ganz, neu, möchte

68

Teenager

L, R

Each pupil needs a worksheet.

Tell pupils that they are going to hear the eight conversations again. The task is to decide which of the words listed occur in each conversation.

They should underline a word as they hear it. The words are in the correct order. The number of words varies from one conversation to another.

Play the first conversation as an example, then check the results.

T: *Gleich hört ihr noch einmal die acht Gespräche.*
Auf dem Arbeitsbogen habt ihr acht Listen. Seht euch die Liste eins an. Das

---

R

186
(1B 88)

Lieber Karl-Heinz...

Two postcards for reading comprehension. The teacher could set a small number of broader questions rather than questions which focus on items of detail. For example:

What relationship do you think the writers of these cards have with Karl-Heinz?

Which writer do you think is getting most out of his/her stay abroad?

What does each of them say they have been doing?

L, S, R

69

Austauschpartner

Cut the worksheets in two and give one half to each partner. Tell them that one of each pair plays the part of a British pupil, while the other plays the part of his/her German exchange partner. The British pupil knows the other British pupils on the exchange, but not the Germans.

The 'German' partner knows the other Germans, but not the British.

The aims of the activity are:-

1   by matching what information they have, to find out who is whose partner and fill it in on their charts

2   having established pairings, to decide of which pairs both partners are nice, in order to invite four pairs on an outing.

N.B. Pupils should not look at each other's charts, though even if they do it will not help much as the British are listed in a different order from the Germans.

(Pair 1) *Emma, du kommst aus Großbritannien. Cath, du bist Deutsche. Ihr seid Partner in einem Schulaustausch. Ihr seid **ein** Paar. Es gibt zehn andere Paare. Emma, du kennst natürlich die anderen Briten.*
Und Cath, du kennst die Deutschen. Du weißt auch, wie Christianes Partnerin aussieht. Aber du weißt nicht, wie sie heißt.

Ihr müßt die Namen der Partner finden, und auf die Tabelle schreiben.

Solution:

Correct pairings:		Both partners liked?
Jamie	— Holger	✓
Sharon	— Anne	✗
Andrew	— Rainer	OK
Catherine	— Hedwig	✓
Darren	— Stefan	✗
Joanna	— Kerstin	✗
Lisa	— Christiane	✓
Greg	— Thomas	✓
Linda	— Sabine	OK
Robin	— Bruno	✗

70

Was hast du gesehen?

A visual memory game. Pupils are shown the scene of a crime for a short time, then have to say in German what they can remember about the people in it. The game is probably best done in groups of about four. The teacher should make an OHP slide of drawings A and B on Repromaster no. 70, and colour in the figures in drawing A with a range of felt-tips for whose colours pupils have already learnt the German (see Area 4 of this Chapter).

Divide the class into groups and tell them that they are going to be shown a picture of the inside of a bank for just 20 seconds. They will then have 10 minutes to make notes or a labelled diagram (in German) of everything they can remember about the people in the picture, including who was with whom and whereabouts everyone was standing.

Now show the coloured OHP drawing A for 20 seconds. Give pupils the ten minutes discussion time, then show an OHT slide (or freehand reproduction on the board) of drawing B. Ask one group to give a piece of information about someone who was in the first picture. The teacher may act as 'quizmaster', accepting or rejecting the information offered, or alternatively may allow other groups to challenge it if they disagree. Once a piece of correct information is established, it can be entered on the OHP or board in the form of a drawing. It can be fun to let pupils do this themselves, especially if coloured pens (or chalks) are available.

The teacher then turns to the next group to add something that they have remembered, and the process continues until as full a picture as possible has been built up. The degree of accuracy required in the pupils' spoken German must depend, of course, on the ability of the class. An excess of correction by the teacher will dampen pupils' enjoyment of the game.

When as full a picture as possible has been built up, show the original (drawing A) again. Comments on any disparities or omissions should be made in German too!

Vocabulary

das Abenteuer(-) *adventure*
alles *everything*
anstoßen *to clink glasses*
die Aufnahmegebühr(en) *admission/enrolment fee*
das Auge(n) *eye*
aussehen *to look like*
die Ausstellung(en) *exhibition*
der Ball(⁼e) *dance, ball*
der Bart(⁼e) *beard*
der Bauernhof(⁼e) *farm*
berühmt *famous*
die Bescherung *giving of Christmas gifts*
besessen *possessed*
die Besserung *recovery*
die Bestellung(en) *order*
bestimmt *definitely*
der Bikini(s) *bikini*
blond *blond, fair*
die Bluse(n) *blouse*
die Brille(n) *glasses*
braun *brown*
bunt *colourful*
die Clique(n) *gang, group*
dick *fat*
die Diele(n) *hall; parlour*
dunkel *dark*
egoistisch *selfish*
einladen *to invite*
die Einladung(en) *invitation*
einmalig *unique*
fallen *to fall*
die Feier(n) *celebration, party*

die Kleinigkeit(en) *small thing*
die Krawatte(n) *tie*
das Fest(e) *party, celebration*
feiern *to celebrate*
fies *horrid, unpleasant*
die Gefahr(en) *danger*
der Gegenstand(⁼e) *object*
gestern *yesterday*
glatt *straight, smooth*
die Glatze(n) *bald head*
die Glocke(n) *bell*
das Glück *luck; happiness*
grau *grey*
das Haar(e) *hair*
das Hallenbad(⁼er) *indoor swimming pool*
halten von *to think of, have an opinion of*
hauptsächlich *mainly*
heiß *hot*
hell *light*
das Hemd(en) *shirt*
der Heilige Abend *Christmas Eve*
der Herbst *autumn*
der Idiot(en) *idiot*
die Jacke(n) *jacket*
die Jeans *jeans*
jedenfalls *anyway, in any case*
kegeln *to bowl*
kennen *to know*
kennenlernen *to meet, get to know*

lachen *to laugh*
leiden *to bear, stand; suffer*
ich kann ihn nicht * *I can't stand him*
lockig *curly*
die Meisterschaft(en) *championship*
mittelgroß *medium height*
momentan *at the moment, just now*
der Nachbar(n) *neighbour*
nachschauen *to look up (something)*
nerven *to get on one's nerves, annoy*
neu *new*
niemand *nobody*
Ostern *Easter*
das Pech *hard luck*
der Pfadfinder(-) *pathfinder; scout*
das Pferderennen *horse racing*
Pfingsten *Whitsuntide*
der Printer(-) *printer*
die Reihe(n) *row*
retten *to save*
der Rock(⁼e) *skirt*
rodeln *to sledge*
der Schäferhund(e) *Alsatian dog*
schlank *slim*
der Schluß(Schlüsse) *end, conclusion*
der Schnee *snow*

der Schnurrbart(⁼e) *moustache*
schulterlang *shoulder-length*
schwarz *black*
die Sorge(n) *concern*
das Sternzeichen(-) *sign of the zodiac*
der Strohhut(⁼e) *straw hat*
der Strumpf(⁼e) *sock*
die Süßigkeit(en) *sweet*
Sylvester *New Year's Eve*
sympathisch *nice*
das Tal(⁼er) *valley*
traditionell *traditional*
treiben *to do (sport)*
das T-Shirt(s) *t-shirt*
das Turnier(e) *tournament*
es tut mir leid *I'm sorry*
der Typ(en) *chap; bloke*
unheimlich *sinister; tremendously*
verknallt in *in love with, crazy about*
vermissen *to miss*
verstecken *to hide*
vorgestern *the day before yesterday*
warm *warm*
weg *away*
die Weste(n) *waistcoat*
der Wettbewerb(e) *competition*

CHAPTER 11 Mir ist schlecht

Area 1

● Talking about feeling unwell

188
(1B 90)

L, S, R

Ich habe Kopfschmerzen ... Mein Fuß tut weh

Present the new language in two sections, as in the Pupil's Book, **without** the visuals initially. Using appropriate mimes, tell pupils you are suffering various ailments (**A** to **F**, in the book), then ask them to repeat these ailments individually, then chorally.

T: *Ich habe Kopfschmerzen. Was habe ich?*
P1: *Kopfschmerzen.*
T: *Gut. Ich habe auch Halsschmerzen ...*

For the second set of visuals (**G—J**), continue to use mime but, in order to avoid confusion over *mein/dein,* have the pupils mime the injury before repeating the new language;

T: *Mein Fuß tut weh.* (To pupil). *Du, mach so* (mime) ... *Was fehlt dir?*
    Mein Fuß tut weh.
P: *Mein Fuß tut weh.*

Now tell pupils to complete the matching activity using the visuals, on page 188 (**1B** 90).

Ich habe Kopfschmerzen

(Sound of loud pop music on the radio)

1 — Du, nicht so laut ... Ich habe Kopfschmerzen.
  — Kopfschmerzen? Oh. Entschuldigung.

2 — *(Husky sounding voice)* Ich habe Halsschmerzen.

3 — *(Sound of wailing boy).* Aua, aua. Ich habe Magenschmerzen.

4 — Was? Heute kommst du nicht in die Schule, sagst du? Warum?
  — Ich habe Ohrenschmerzen.
  — Es tut mir leid. Gute Besserung.

5 — Ich habe zu viel getanzt.
  — Wieso?
  — Ich habe Rückenschmerzen.

6 — Soll ich dir eine Tüte Bonbons kaufen?
  — Danke. Ich habe Zahnschmerzen.

Solution: 1A 2F 3C 4E 5D 6B

Mein Fuß tut weh

7 — Ich muß mich hinsetzen. Mein Fuß tut weh.

8 — *(Sound of somebody half shuffling, half hopping across the room before slumping into a chair).* Mein Bein tut weh.

9 — Tennis, sagst du? Leider nicht. Mein Arm tut weh.

10 — Es tut mir leid. Ich kann meine Hausaufgaben nicht machen. Meine Hand tut weh.

Solution: 7I 8H 9J 10G

188
(1B 90)

L, S

Was fehlt dir?

Tell pupils to take it in turns, working in pairs, to describe one of the ailments illustrated **without** mime. Their partners must say which picture corresponds to the ailment described. Complete one or two dialogues with pupils before starting the activity.

L, S, R

188
(1B 90)

Gesundheit!

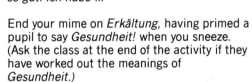

Mime the illnesses and complaints depicted, without referring pupils to the text. Begin with the question *‚Wie geht's?',* asked of you by one of the pupils and answer with: *‚Gut, danke. Ich bin fit und gesund'.* Continue through the other complaints/states of health, using *Nicht so gut. Ich habe ...*

End your mime on *Erkältung,* having primed a pupil to say *Gesundheit!* when you sneeze. (Ask the class at the end of the activity if they have worked out the meanings of *Gesundheit.*)

Now go through the procedure again, without mime, but with the Pupil's Book.

Write on the board the question *Wie geht's?* and *gut/nicht gut,* before practising the new forms with pupils individually.

L, S, R

188
(1B 90)

Gesundheit

Tell pupils to work in pairs, practising both the new forms and the language from the previous activity. As a final activity for the whole class, ask pupils who have not performed as pairs previously to go through model dialogues in front of the class.

189
(1B 91)

Ich kann nicht kommen

Tell pupils they are going to hear some recordings of people who will try any excuse to avoid doing something they don't wish to do. Questions may be answered orally or in exercise books.

Ich kann nicht kommen

1 — *(Telefon klingelt).* Braun.
 — Du, Heino. Ich kann nicht kommen. Ich bin krank.
 — Aber, Frank. Was fehlt dir?
 — Mein Fuß tut weh. Heute kann ich nicht Fußball spielen.
 — Wie schade. Dein Fuß tut weh, sagst du?
 — Ja.
 — Dann kannst du auch nicht tanzen, oder?
 — Tanzen? Natürlich nicht. Warum denn?
 — Heute abend gibt es eine Party bei Jutta.
 — Du, warte mal. Vielleicht kann ich doch Fußball spielen. Wann beginnt die Party?
 — Das Fußballspiel beginnt um drei. Bis dann. Tschüs.

2 — Mutti, heute kann ich nicht in die Schule gehen.
 — Wieso denn?
 — Ich habe Magenschmerzen.
 — Du armes Kind. Ich rufe den Arzt an. Wir bekommen ein Rezept, und ich hole dir Medikamente von der Apotheke.
 — Von der Apotheke?
 — Ja — geh mal ins Bett, mein Schatz.
 — Nein. Weißt du was, Mutti? Mir geht es schon viel besser. Ich gehe doch in die Schule. Tschüs.

3 — Na, Britta und Bernd. Wollen wir im Garten arbeiten?
 — Im Garten? Ach nein, Vati. Ich kann nicht. Ich habe Rückenschmerzen.
 — Ja, ich auch ... und Kopfschmerzen dazu.
 — Rückenschmerzen und Kopfschmerzen? Ach so. Na, Mutti, wir fahren morgen alleine zum Campingplatz, du und ich?
 — *(Beide Kinder).* Zum Campingplatz?
 — Ja, aber wenn ihr Rückenschmerzen und Kopfschmerzen habt, dann geht das nicht. Ihr könnt zu Hause bleiben.
 — Oh nein. Weißt du was, mein Rücken tut nicht mehr weh.
 — Merkwürdig. Mir geht es auch viel besser. Keine Kopfschmerzen mehr.

— Fein. Gehen wir mal im Garten arbeiten.

4 — Aua ... ich kann keine Karotten essen.
 — Warum denn? Was ist mit dir?
 — Ich habe furchtbare Zahnschmerzen.
 — Zahnschmerzen? Dann gebe ich deinem Bruder die Tüte Bonbons.
 — Bonbons? Warte mal ... unglaublich! Ich habe keine Zahnschmerzen mehr. Hmmm, diese Karotten schmecken toll... Wo sind die Bonbons?
 — Ich habe keine.
 — Oh, Papa.
 (Sound of father laughing)

189
(1B 91)

L, S, R

Ich kann nicht ... ich bin krank

Tell pupils to look at the visuals, on page 189 (**1B** 91), and practise giving reasons for not being able to do various things, as a result of illness or injury. Complete one or two dialogues with pupils before starting the pair-work. Refer pupils to *Tip des Tages*, if necessary.

R, W

nem 1
nem 2 Entschuldigungszettel
252
(1B 136)

Tell pupils to read these excuse notes and answer the two sets of questions which follow, in their exercise books. Although introduced here, *wegen* + Genitive is not intended for formal presentation.

Solution: To English questions

1 Moritz Hartenstein
   1 week
   bronchitis

2 Lessons 2, 3 and 4
   at the dentist's

3 Waltraud Edelweis
   (in)flu(enza)

4 Felix Schweiger
   hospital doctor: Dr. Meier
   broken leg

5 Gertraud Vogt

6 3rd, 6th and 10th of the month.
   She'll be absent again with bouts of hay fever

7 Scherenzel family
   December 20th
   December 18th

8 *Entschuldigungszettel*

Area 2

| • Talking about sports-related injuries |

L, S

Was wird hier gespielt?

Tell pupils they are going to hear a series of recordings of various sports being played and that they should identify the sports in turn. Disputes can be resolved by putting the matter to the vote.

T: *Hört gut zu. Was wird hier gespielt?* (Play no. 1.) *Also, spielt man Tennis oder ...*
P1: *Tischtennis.*
T: *Richtig. Tischtennis wird hier gespielt.*

Was wird hier gespielt?
(Sound recordings of ...)
1 table tennis match
2 badminton match
3 basketball match
4 football match
5 swimming
6 skiing
7 tennis
8 volleyball match
9 roller skating
10 ice skating
11 handball match
12 squash match

190
(1B 92)

L, R, W

Die neue Turnhalle

Tell pupils to listen to the conversations of the 'clique' as they enter their new sports hall. Refer them to the visuals on page 190 (**1B** 92), and tell them to write out full sentence answers to questions **1-7** in their exercise books. Complete no. 1 orally with the group.

Suggested language as in Pupil's Book.

Die neue Turnhalle
— Du, hast du die neue Turnhalle schon gesehen? Schön, nicht?
— Ja, klar. Was machst du denn heute abend? Spielst du Basketball, oder ... ?
— Nein. Ich laufe Ski.
— Was?! He, habt ihr das gehört, Jungs? Kurt läuft Ski.
— Warum denn nicht? Es gibt hier eine schöne Piste — hinter der Turnhalle.
— Ach so. Toll!
— Und du, Jens?

— Ich? Ja, ich trainiere ein bißchen Judo mit Heidi.
— Mit Heidi? Ist sie so stark?
— Na, klar. Sie hat schon den braunen Gürtel.
— Den braunen Gürtel! Vorsicht, Jens. Sie ist vielleicht gefährlich.
— Wer spielt Basketball mit uns? Du, Sabine?
— Ja. Und Silvia, Guido und Ralf. Spielst du auch mit, Jutta?
— Danke. Ich gehe zum Fitness-Raum. Wer macht mit? Bernd? Anke?
— Zum Fitness-Raum? Lieber nicht. Anke und ich spielen Badminton.
— Ja, dann gehen wir schwimmen, nicht wahr, Bernd?
— Genau. Das macht fit: Badminton und Schwimmen.
— Guck mal, Robert — Karate!
— Ja, das weiß ich schon. Ich will mal Karate trainieren.
— Und Dirk und ich spielen Volleyball.
— Nee, Handball.
— Du, Dirk. Handball spiele ich nicht so gern.
— OK. Astrid. Dann spielen wir Volleyball.

Answers:

1 Kurt läuft **Ski.**
2 Jens und Heidi trainieren **Judo.**
3 Sabine, Silvia, Guido und Ralf spielen **Basketball.**
4 Jutta geht zum **Fitness-Raum.**
5 Bernd und Anke spielen **Badminton.** Danach gehen sie **schwimmen.**
6 Robert trainiert **Karate.**
7 Dirk und Astrid spielen **Volleyball.**

190
(1B 92)

L, S, R, W

Was sagt Long John Silver?

Complete this light-hearted matching activity orally with the group, then tell pupils to write the answers in their exercise books. Refer pupils to *Tip des Tages*, if required.

L

Sonja sagt

Play a German version of *Simon Says* in order to rehearse parts of the body and classroom commands.

Sonja sagt: Hört zu!
　　　　　Steht auf!
　　　　　Hebt die Hand! (Hände)
　　　　　Hebt den Fuß!
　　　　　Nickt mit dem Kopf!

179

Macht die Augen zu!
Hände 'runter!
Spielt Tennis/Fußball *usw.*
Legt die Hand auf den Rücken!
Legt die Hand auf den Magen!
Faßt das Ohr an, *usw.*

heute.
— Ich rufe ihn an und wünsche ihm gute
Besserung.

Solution: Jens **C**, Heidi **H**, Robert **G**, Anke **A**,
Bernd **E**, Astrid **B**, Sabine **D**,
Kurt **F**

**191
(1B 93)   Im Jugendzentrum**

The day after their visit to the new sports hall,
the 'clique' are sitting in the youth club
nursing various aches and pains. Tell pupils to
listen to the dialogues without the help of the
Pupil's Book visuals and see if they can work
out what the conversations are about. Then
play the recordings a second time and tell
pupils to complete the matching activity.

*Hört zu — worum geht es hier? Antwortet auf
Englisch.*

Im Jugendzentrum

1 — Wie war es beim Judo, Jens?
   — Gut, aber ich habe mir das Fußgelenk
      verstaucht. Ich kann kaum gehen, es tut
      so weh.
   — Und wie geht es Heidi?
   — Ganz gut, natürlich. Wie gesagt, sie hat
      den braunen Gürtel, und ich habe nur
      den weißen.

2 — Wie war es beim Karate, Robert?
   — Meine Hand tut weh, aber es hat viel
      Spaß gemacht.
   — Und Badminton? Wie war das, Bernd?
   — Tja, Anke hat Rückenschmerzen und ich
      habe Muskelkater, aber im Schwimmbad
      wurde es gleich besser.

3 — Na, Astrid, willst du Tischtennis spielen?
   — Du, das kann ich nicht. Gestern abend
      habe ich Volleyball mit Dirk gespielt und
      habe mir das Handgelenk verstaucht.
      Aua, das tut weh.
   — Ach du, es tut mir leid.

4 — Wie geht es dir heute, Sabine?
   — Meine Füße tun weh. Das
      Basketballspiel hat aber viel Spaß
      gemacht.

5 — Wo ist Kurt?
   — Kurt? Hast du nicht gehört?
   — Was?
   — Beim Skilaufen ist er hingestürzt.
   — Na, und was ist passiert?
   — Er hat sich das Bein gebrochen.
   — Oh, der Arme. Wo ist er jetzt — im
      Krankenhaus?
   — Nein, im Moment sitzt er mit seinem
      Gipsbein zu Hause. Ihm geht es besser

**191
(1B 93)   Im Jugendzentrum**

Using the visuals for the previous activity,
practise the new language relating to injuries
incurred whilst playing various sports. Tell
pupils to repeat the new expressions
individually and chorally. Refer them to the
Tip des Tages after they have practised the
language sufficiently.

Seht euch das Bild C an. (Mime playing tennis
and twisting your ankle). *Ich habe mir das
Fußgelenk verstaucht ...*

**190
(1B 92)   Die neue Turnhalle**

Refer pupils to the visuals which accompany
Die neue Turnhalle and tell them to work in
pairs to produce dialogues. The object of the
exercise is to get partners to guess which
sport their partners played, once they have
been told of the injury incurred.

Seht euch Die neue Turnhalle *auf Seite 190 (92)
an. Partnerarbeit: Dein(e) Partner(in) sagt:
‚Ich habe Rückenschmerzen' und du sagst:
‚Hast du Squash gespielt?' ‚Nein? Hast du ...
?'* (Perform one or two dialogues with pupils,
making sure you play the part of 'guesser'.)

71

Wo tut es ihm weh?

A simple gap-filling activity to revise parts of
the body and various illnesses. When they
have completed the exercise, ask pupils if they
can work out the meaning of *Heu* from
Heuschnupfen. Then tell them in English to
try to produce their own grids, along the lines
of the illustration, using the words listed.

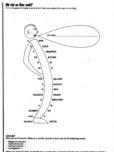

Area 3

11

> ● **Minor ailments, sunburn, allergies, food-poisoning**

192
(1B 94)

In der Imbißstube

Tell pupils to listen to the conversations in the snack bar and to answer the questions which follow the menu in English, in their exercise books. This revision exercise is intended to cue the second activity, which deals with allergies. Do not at this point, over-emphasise the use of *ich darf nicht,* as it will become the central feature of *Ich darf nicht ... ich bin allergisch dagegen.*

The Pupil's Book gives the language to introduce the activity.

In der Imbißstube
— Na, Robert. Was bestellst du?
— Tja, laß mal sehen ... ich glaube, ich hätte gern ein Spiegelei und eine Portion Pommes frites.
— Spiegelei?
— Ja, schmeckt mir gut. Und ich will kein Fleisch essen. Du auch nicht, Jutta, oder?
— Richtig. Ich bin nicht so hungrig. Ich esse Tomatensuppe. Was ißt du, Heidi?
— Hmmm ... ein halbes Hähnchen und eine doppelte Portion Pommes frites. Ich habe einen Bärenhunger. Dazu trinke ich ein Glas Milch. Du bist auch hungrig, Guido, oder?
— Ja, aber Hähnchen schmeckt mir nicht so gut. Ich esse lieber Schnitzel.
— Zigeuner?
— Nee, die Soße ist mir zu scharf. Lieber Jägerschnitzel mit Pommes frites. Und zu trinken? Ich hätte gern Kaffee, aber ich will kein Kännchen bestellen. Kurt, wollen wir zusammen ein Kännchen Kaffee trinken?
— Danke, Guido. Ich trinke aber lieber Cola zu meiner Bratwurst.
— Also, du Jens. Wollen wir ein Kännchen Kaffee bestellen?
— Ich darf keinen Kaffee trinken.
— Wieso?
— Ich bin allergisch dagegen. Ich trinke Milch und esse nichts.
— Tja, also, was trinke ich zu meinem Jägerschnitzel? Ach was, ist egal! Ich bestelle sowieso ein Kännchen Kaffee.

Solution:

1 a Portion of chips.
   b He likes them and he doesn't want to eat meat.

2 a Tomato soup.
   b Not very hungry.

3 a A double portion of chips.
   b She's ravenous.
   c A glass of milk.

4 a Guido.
   b *Jägerschnitzel* and a portion of chips.

5   He prefers coke with his *Bratwurst.*

6 a He's allergic to coffee.
   b Milk and nothing to eat.

7   No-one.

192
(1B 94)

Ich darf nicht ... ich bin allergisch dagegen

This listening activity presents the vocabulary needed to talk about allergies. Pupils should listen to the tape and match the pictures to the text. After each item, check that pupils have found the right answer.

Ich darf nicht ... ich bin allergisch dagegen
1 — Was willst du trinken, Walter? Ein Glas Milch?
   — Danke. Ich darf nicht.
   — Du darfst nicht? Wieso?
   — Ich bin allergisch gegen Milch. Ich darf auch keinen Fisch, keinen Käse, keine Sahne und keine Bananen essen.
   — Mensch, das ist schlimm. Und was passiert, wenn du zum Beispiel Sahne oder Fisch ißt?
   — Ich bekomme Hautausschlag. Das juckt und tut so weh, wenn man sich kratzt. Das sieht auch so häßlich aus. Siehst du meine Hand hier — diese roten Flecken?
   — Ach ja. Was hast du gegessen — Fisch oder Käse oder was?
   — Ich weiß nicht, was das sein kann. Ich habe Kaffee getrunken. Vielleicht darf ich auch keinen Kaffee trinken.
   — Na, Walter. Du hast es schlecht. Darfst du Tee trinken?
   — Ja.
   — Gut. Gehen wir ins Café.

2 — Mutti. Komm her, bitte.
   — Was ist los, Hans?
   — John ist krank.
   — Was fehlt ihm?
   — Er hat Magenschmerzen und Kopfschmerzen.

— Hat er auch Fieber?
— Ich glaube ja.
— Hmm. Wir wollen mal sehen ... Na, John. Was ist mit dir? Kopfschmerzen und Magenschmerzen?
— Ja. Ich weiß nicht, warum ich so krank bin. Das Omelett hat mir geschmeckt!
— Hast du Allergien, John?
— Ja. Ich darf keine Meeresfrüchte essen, also keine Krabben, keine Muscheln.
— Du armer. Das ist es. Im Omelett waren Muscheln.
— Muscheln?
— Ja ... komm, Hans. Rufen wir den Arzt an. Mach dir keine Sorgen, John. Der Arzt kommt gleich.
— Vielen Dank, Frau Klee.

3 — (Sneezing)
— Gesundheit, Karl. Du, kommst du mit? Wir gehen spazieren.
— Danke, aber (sneezes) heute nicht. Am besten bleibe ich zu Hause.
— Warum denn? Es ist schön warm heute. Komm doch mit!
— (Sneezes). Da, siehst du? (Sneezes again.)
— Bist du erkältet?
— Nein. ich habe Heuschnupfen. Bei diesem heißen Wetter ist es immer fürchterlich. (Sneezes again).
— Es tut mir leid. Hoffentlich geht es dir bald besser. Tschüs, Karl.
— Danke, Dieter. Tschüs.

4 — Kopfschmerzen und Halsschmerzen, sagst du? Hier, Aspirin.
— Danke. Ich darf aber kein Aspirin nehmen. Ich bin allergisch gegen solche Tabletten, besonders gegen Aspirin.
— Ach so. Was nimmst du denn, wenn du Kopfschmerzen hast?
— Nichts. Oder vielleicht homöopathische Mittel. Aber überhaupt keine Aspirin.

5 — Jane, kommst du mit? Ich gehe zum Tierarzt. Mein Hund ist krank.
— Ich darf nicht.
— Du darfst nicht mit zum Tierarzt kommen! Du spinnst!
— Nee. Ich bin allergisch gegen Tiere. Ich bin asthmatisch. Wenn ich mit Tieren zusammenkomme, kann ich kaum atmen.
— Unglaublich. Es tut mir leid.
— Ach was. Das macht nichts. Viele Leute sind asthmatisch.

Solution: **1**B **2**C **3**D **4**E **5**A

L, R

Krank im Urlaub

Tell pupils to look at the visuals on page 192 (1B 94) and to listen to the telephone conversation. Their task is simply to identify the correct visuals as they are mentioned during the course of the conversation.

Krank im Urlaub
— Hallo, Torsten!
— Jens. Wo bist du?
— In Spanien auf Urlaub.
— Schön. Du bist nicht alleine, oder?
— Nein. Ich bin mit Sabine, Kurt, Stefan und Britta hierher gekommen.
— Toll. Das muß aber viel Spaß machen.
— Gar nicht.
— Wieso?
— Wir sind alle krank.
— Das tut mir leid. So ein Pech — krank im Urlaub. Was fehlt euch?
— Kurt hat Sonnenbrand. Er hat am ersten Tag fünf Stunden in der Sonne gelegen.
— Das war blöd! Natürlich kriegt man Sonnenbrand, wenn man so lange in der Sonne liegt. Was fehlt Stefan?
— Er hat Magenschmerzen. Eine Lebensmittelvergiftung, meint er.
— Eine Lebensmittelvergiftung? Das ist schlimm. Was hat er gegessen?
— Paella.
— Das ist wirklich Pech. Wenn man nach Spanien fährt, will man selbstverständlich Paella essen.
— Ja.
— Die Sabine ist noch fit und gesund, oder?
— Auch nicht. Wespenstiche.
— Aua. Wespenstiche? Die Arme!
— Und Britta hat Heimweh. Spanien gefällt ihr gar nicht. Sie will sofort wieder nach Deutschland fahren.
— Wie schade. Und du, Jens? Bist du auch krank?
— Eigentlich nicht. Ich bin nur sehr müde. Ich kann nicht schlafen. Mir ist es zu heiß hier. Und dann muß ich mich um Kurt und Sabine und Britta kümmern. Sie können auch nicht schlafen, weil sie alle so krank und unglücklich sind.
— Du Jens, es tut mir ...
— Oh, nein! Ich muß dringend zur Toilette. Tschüs, Torsten.
(Sound of hurried footsteps across hotel floor)

nem 3

R, W

253
(1B 137)

Krankheitspuzzle

A word puzzle to reinforce some vocabulary from the previous activity. Tell pupils to find the full words and write them down.

Was paßt zusammen? Findet die richtigen Wörter und schreibt alles in euer Heft.

R

193
(1B 95)

Grillparty

A brief cartoon commenting light-heartedly on the practice of sunbathing in public. Not intended for detailed exploitation.

L, S, R

193
(1B 95)

Gymnasium Schwarzenberg

An authentic German-English exchange form reproduced here in order to present questions of health, allergies and parental permission for certain activities in context.

Read the document and discuss it with pupils in English. In order to cue the worksheet activity which follows, revise the question forms required to enable pupils to fill in a blank form by discussing the form of Sven Fey.

Wie heißt er?
Wo wohnt er?
Telefonnummer?
Bestehen Allergien?
Darf er schwimmen?
Krankenkasse?
Darf er abends ausgehen?
Darf er zur Disko gehen?
Darf er mit dem Rad fahren?

L, S, R, W

72A
72B

Englandaustausch (Gymnasium Schwarzenberg)

Tell pupils to work in pairs and complete their respective blank forms by asking the questions listed at the end of the previous activity. **Begin** to complete **A** orally with the class before proceeding to pair-work.

T: *Partnerarbeit: Englandaustausch. Stellt und beantwortet Fragen. (To Pupil B): Wie heißt sie?* (pointing to picture.)
P: *Stefanie Peters.*
T: *(To class): Ich schreibe Peters, Stefanie ...* (Write answers on the board, then erase).

W

nem 4

253
(1B 137)

Ich bin allergisch gegen ...

An activity practising the language connected with allergies.

11 Area 4

● **Talking about accidents that have happened in the past**

R

194
(1B 96)

Der Skiball

This passage sets the scene for a skiing accident. *Gipsbein* is introduced in context and can be explained by reference to the visual. No detailed exploitation is intended.

R, W

194
(1B 96)

Wie kommt man nach Interlaken?

This gap-filling activity is based largely on the map of Interlaken (only question **5** requires reference to the text). Draw pupils' attention to Genf and Genève, Roma and Rom, Milano and Milan. This could be expanded to include Basel, Wien, München, Köln, Brüssel, Venedig, Nizza etc.

Auf Deutsch heißt diese Stadt Genf — und auf Französisch? Und auf Englisch?

Solution: **1** Basel **2** Zürich **3** Zürich **4** Genf **5** Autobahnen und Eisenbahnen

L, S, R

195
(1B 97)

Probleme beim Skifahren

Firstly read the text and practise the sentences. Then tell pupils to listen to the recording and decide where at the ski resort each person was injured.

Probleme beim Skifahren

1 — Das ist mir am ersten Tag passiert. Ich wollte das Hotel verlassen, und es war so glatt auf der Treppe. Ich bin gerutscht und habe mir das Handgelenk gebrochen.

2 — Ich fahre immer sehr schnell — so sechzig oder siebzig Stundenkilometer. Letzte Woche bin ich aber gestürzt und habe mir das rechte Bein und das rechte Handgelenk gebrochen.

3 — Ich bin zum ersten Mal hier in Interlaken. Der Ort gefällt mir gut. Ich komme sicher nächstes Jahr wieder. Der Unfall war meine Schuld. Ich bin gegen einen Baum gefahren und habe mir die Schulter gebrochen.

4 — Die ganze Woche haben wir tolles Wetter gehabt. Schnee, Sonne aber keinen Wind. Ich habe keine Sonnencreme mitgebracht und habe Sonnenbrand bekommen. Jetzt tut es aber nicht mehr weh.

5 — Das kann ich kaum glauben. Ich bin die ganze Woche gefahren — sechs Stunden am Tag auf den Pisten und nichts ist passiert. Dann am letzten Abend in der Disko habe ich mir den Fuß verstaucht.

6 — Interlaken gefällt mir gut. Ich komme jedes Jahr hierher. Das ist aber das erste Mal, daß ich einen Unfall beim Skifahren gehabt habe. Es war wirklich doof. Ich bin aus dem Lift gefallen und habe mir den Rücken verletzt.

Solution: **1** Anna D **2** Peter F **3** Jochen A **4** Klaus E **5** Jutta C **6** Andrea B

R, W

195
(1B 97)

Was ist passiert?

A completion activity requiring pupils to 'report' what has happened to Anna, Klaus etc. on their skiing holiday. This simple manipulation from first person singular to third person singular is in preparation for a later communicative activity, when pupils have to report the main points in a letter.

L, R

195-196
(1B 97-98)

Renate ruft ihre Mutter an

Tell pupils to listen to the recording and work out what it is about. Elicit that it is one half of

---

a phone call and that the speaker is distressed. Then read the text in the Pupil's Book.

Renate ruft ihre Mutter an

(Phone rings.)
— Meyer.
— Ach, grüß dich, Renate. Wie geht's denn?
— Was!?
— Ach nein!
— Wie denn?
— Wo war das?
— Wo?
— Wie geht's dir denn jetzt?
— Schreib' mir bitte bald ganz genau drüber.
— Tschüs!

L, R

196
(1B 98)

Interlaken, den 2. Februar

Read the letter from Renate, which gives the details about her accident and then play the recording of the dialogue between her mother and father. The mother has read the letter and is explaining its contents.

Interlaken, den 2. Februar

Vater: — Was schreibt sie?
Mutter: — Es geht ihr jetzt viel besser.
Vater: — Gut, und wie ist das passiert?
Mutter: — Sie ist zu schnell gefahren ... gegen einen Baum.
Vater: — Und was hat sie sich gebrochen?
Mutter: — Die Schulter und das Bein.

Encourage pupils to spot the differences between the letter and the report of its contents. This could include the change in person and shorter version of the incident.

L, S, R, (W)

196-197
(1B 98-99)

Was haben sie sich gebrochen?

Tell pupils to use the visuals in order to produce as many sentences as possible. This activity consolidates: *Ich habe mir/Er hat sich/Sie haben sich ... gebrochen.*

Practise orally with the whole class, continue in pairs and complete in writing, if required.

T: *Was sagt Harald?*
P1: *Ich habe mir die Schulter gebrochen.*
T: *Also, du, was hat er sich gebrochen?*
P2: *Er hat sich die Schulter gebrochen.*

73

L, S, R

Was hat Monika geschrieben?

Divide the class into pairs and ask each partner to read either letter **A** or **B**. Then each pair should take it in turns to inform each other of the 3 or 4 **main points** in each letter. The listener should make notes in English and compare them afterwards with the original text.

196-197
(1B 98-99)

L

Was ist in diesem Haus passiert?

Tell pupils to look at the visuals and listen to the recording in order to find out where each incident took place and what injury was incurred.

Was ist in diesem Haus passiert?

1 — Gestern war ich im Badezimmer und habe, wie üblich, geduscht. Plötzlich bin ich aber hingefallen und habe mich am Kopf verletzt.

2 — Monika hat die Tür schnell zugemacht. Leider waren meine Finger dazwischen. Ich hab' so geschrien! Es hat fünf Minuten lang wahnsinnig weh getan.

3 — Gestern habe ich sehr lange geschlafen — bis neun Uhr. Als ich den Wecker sah, war ich so erschrocken, daß ich aus dem Bett gesprungen bin und mir den Fuß verstaucht habe.

4 — Gestern habe ich den ganzen Tag im Garten gearbeitet. Jetzt tut mein Rücken sehr weh. Ich kann kaum gehen.

5 — Am Samstag habe ich eine Party bei mir in meinem Zimmer gegeben. Es war toll. Wir haben Musik gehört, haben getanzt und sind erst um zwei ins Bett gegangen. Die Musik war wohl etwas zu laut. Jetzt habe ich Kopfschmerzen.

6 — Jede Woche putze ich die Fenster. Letzten Dienstag bin ich aber plötzlich von der Leiter gefallen und habe mir das Bein gebrochen.

7 — Ich bin in die Küche gegangen und habe gefrühstückt. Ich wollte Brot schneiden, aber das Brotmesser war sehr scharf, und ich habe mir in den Finger geschnitten.

8 — Gestern bin ich spät aufgestanden und in der Eile bin ich die Treppe hinuntergefallen. Glücklicherweise ist nichts Ernsthaftes passiert. Ich habe nur ein paar blaue Flecken.

9 — Ich war im Wohnzimmer, und plötzlich ist das Licht ausgegangen. Ich habe eine Birne geholt und bin auf einen Stuhl gestiegen. Plötzlich bin ich runtergefallen — ich weiß nicht warum — und habe mir das Handgelenk gebrochen.

10 — Ich war im Schlafzimmer und habe die Fenster geputzt. Ich habe ein Fenster zerbrochen, Glas lag überall auf dem Teppich. Ich hatte keine Schuhe an und ja, ja, du kannst raten. Blut war überall. Mein Fuß tut immer noch weh.

Solution: **1** c — injured head **2** g — fingers caught in door **3** d — sprained foot **4** a — injured back **5** e — headache **6** j — broken leg **7** f — cut finger **8** h — bruises **9** i — broken wrist **10** b — cut foot.

---

nem 5
253
(1B 137)

S/W

Ich kann nicht!

In this activity pupils must offer excuses for not doing something.

---

nem 6
253
(1B 137)

W

Ich habe Kopfschmerzen

Further consolidation of the language required to describe illness and injury (Present and Past Tense).

---

nem 7
253
(1B 137)

(W)

Ein Brief an das Verkehrsamt

An authentic writing task intended to produce attractive classroom displays on ski resorts. This could be a class activity.

Area 5

- Visiting a doctor and dentist
- Buying things from a chemist

R, W

197
(1B 99) **Kann ich morgen in die Sprechstunde kommen?**

A series of photographs of signs showing surgery times. Comprehension is tested by questions in English and German. This activity sets the scene for making appointments.

Solution:
1 2 21 31
    Ja
2 Vogler und Puls
3 Dr Maurin
4 Montag (7.00)
5 10-11.30
6 Vogler and Puls
7 he accepts all of them.
8 only for smaller pets.
9 Tuesday evening, Saturday 10.30-11.30
10 **a** Schreck = fright
     b Puls = pulse
     c und nach Vereinbarung

L, R, W

198
(1B 100) **Ist am Freitag noch ein Termin frei?**

Tell pupils to copy the chart into their books and then to listen to the recordings in order to write in the name of the patient and the time of the visit.

Ist am Freitag noch ein Termin frei?

1 — Guten Tag. Hier Frau Fichte. Kann ich morgen in die Sprechstunde kommen?
— Nein. Leider nicht, Frau Fichte.
— Hat Frau Doktor am Freitag noch einen Termin frei?
— Ja, um 14.00.
— Also, gut. Ich komme um 14.00.
— Danke schön. Auf Wiederhören, Frau Fichte. Ihr Termin ist also am Freitag um 14.00.
— Auf Wiederhören.

2 — Guten Tag. Herr Schmidt am Apparat. Hat Herr Doktor am Mittwoch einen Termin frei?
— Ja, Herr Schmidt. Mittwoch um 10.00. Ist das in Ordnung?
— Ja, prima. Mittwoch um 10.00. Auf Wiederhören.
— Auf Wiederhören, Herr Schmidt.

3 — Guten Tag. Mein Name ist Ziegert. Z - I - E - G - E - R - T. Ich habe Grippe. Kann ich am Dienstag in die Sprechstunde kommen?
— Nein, morgen sind keine Termine frei. Aber Mittwoch um 15.00 ist möglich.
— Ja, gut, Mittwoch ... 15.00. Auf Wiederhören.
— Auf Wiederhören, Herr Ziegert.

4 — Guten Tag. Hat Frau Doktor am Freitag noch einen Termin frei?
— Guten Tag. Wie heißen Sie, bitte?
— Timm. ... Frau Timm.
— Am Freitag? Moment mal ... ja, um 11.00, Frau Timm.
— Freitag um elf. Das ist sehr gut. Danke schön.
— Auf Wiederhören, Frau Timm.
— Auf Wiederhören.

5 — Guten Tag. Hat Herr Doktor am Samstag einen Termin frei?
— Nein, am Wochenende ist die Praxis nicht offen. Wie heißen Sie, bitte?
— Bromma ist mein Name. Kann ich am Montag in die Sprechstunde kommen, bitte?
— Ja ... um halb zehn ist ein Termin frei.
— Montag — 9.30. Gut. Auf Wiederhören.
— Auf Wiederhören.

6 — Guten Tag. Frau Heinemann am Apparat. Hat Herr Doktor am Donnerstag noch einen Termin frei?
— Ja, um 16.00 oder um 17.00?
— 16.00 wäre mir lieber.
— Gut, Frau Heinemann. Donnerstag ... um 16.00.
— Danke. Auf Wiederhören.
— Auf Wiederhören, Frau Heinemann.

7 — Guten Tag. Mein Name ist Carolus. Kann ich bitte den Arzt sprechen?
— Nein, leider nicht, Herr Carolus. Wollen Sie in die Sprechstunde kommen?
— Ja. Kann ich morgen kommen?
— Moment mal. Ich sehe nach. Ja, Dienstag um 9.00. Ist das in Ordnung, Herr Carolus?
— Ja, also morgen um neun. Auf Wiederhören.
— Auf Wiederhören.

8 — Guten Tag. Ich heiße David Jones. Ich bin Engländer. Ich habe Heuschnupfen. Kann ich in die Sprechstunde kommen?
— Guten Tag, Herr ... ? Wie schreiben Sie das, bitte?
— Jones, J - O - N - E - S.
— Danke schön, Herr Jones. Am besten kommen Sie am Montagnachmittag um 18.00. Verstehen Sie das?

— Ja, Montag um 6.00. Danke schön. Auf Wiederhören.
— Auf Wiederhören, Herr Jones.

9 — Mein Name ist Stegemann. Frau Stegemann. Kann ich heute in die Sprechstunde kommen? Ich habe starke Kopfschmerzen.
— Heute ist das leider überhaupt nicht möglich. Aber morgen um 8.30 hat Herr Doktor einen Termin frei.
— Aber ich habe schwere Migräne.
— Am besten nehmen Sie Aspirintabletten und kommen am Donnerstag um 8.30.
— Ja, OK. Donnerstag um 8.30. Auf Wiederhören.
— Auf Wiederhören, Frau Stegemann.

10 — Guten Tag. Mein Name ist Meyer. M - E - Y - E - R. Hat Herr Doktor heute noch einen Termin frei?
— Nein, Herr Meyer, heute nicht.
— Geht es wirklich nicht heute? Ich habe starke Schmerzen.
— Wo denn?
— Im Magen. Ich habe heute Fisch gegessen und habe jetzt Magenschmerzen.
— Am besten fahren Sie direkt zum Krankenhaus.
— Danke schön. Auf Wiederhören.
— Auf Wiederhören, Herr Meyer. Gute Besserung!

Solution:

	NAME	ZEIT
Mo	Herr Bromma David Jones	9.30 18.00
Di	Herr Carolus	9.00
Mi	Herr Schmidt Herr Ziegert	10.00 15.00
Do	Frau Stegemann Frau Heinemann	8.30 16.00
Fr	Frau Timm Frau Fichte	11.00 14.00

+ Herr Meyer told to go straight to the hospital.

L, S, R

Ist am Freitag noch ein Termin frei?

Encourage pupils to work out their own dialogues in pairs using the two dialogues in the Pupil's Book as models.

198
(1B 100)

L, R

In der Sprechstunde

Ask pupils to look at the visual in the book and then play the recording. Collate as many details as possible, in English, on the board, under the following headings:

Patient	Illness	Treatment
e.g. Frau Timm	headache can't sleep	Tablets for 2 weeks. 3 tablets a day taken before meals Return in 14 days.

Then ask pupils to copy the chart into their books and complete as many details as possible after listening to the remainder of the dialogue. Refer pupils to the dialogue printed in their books afterwards.

In der Sprechstunde

Ärztin: — Guten Tag, Frau Timm. Bitte nehmen Sie Platz. Wie kann ich Ihnen helfen?
Frau Timm: — Ich habe Kopfschmerzen und kann nicht schlafen.
Ärztin: — Ich verschreibe Ihnen diesmal Baldriparan. Nehmen Sie drei Tabletten pro Tag. Eine zwanzig Minuten vor dem Frühstück, eine zwanzig Minuten vor dem Mittagessen und die dritte Tablette vor dem Abendessen. In vierzehn Tagen kommen Sie bitte wieder.
Frau Timm: — Vielen Dank, Frau Doktor. Auf Wiedersehen.
Ärztin: — Auf Wiedersehen, Frau Timm.
— Der Nächste, bitte!

— — — — — — — — — —

Guten Tag, Herr Bromma. Kommen Sie bitte herein. Setzen Sie sich dahin. Was fehlt Ihnen?
Herr Bromma: — Ich bin sehr erkältet. Seit vier Tagen arbeite ich nicht.
Ärztin: — Naja, wollen Sie Tabletten, oder sind Ihnen Tropfen lieber?
Herr Bromma: — Ach wissen Sie, die Tropfen habe ich schon und die helfen gar nicht.
Ärztin: — Gut, dann gebe ich Ihnen jetzt etwas stärkere Tabletten. Die Dosierung

finden Sie auf dem Zettel in der Packung.

Herr Bromma: — Vielen Dank.

Ärztin: — Wenn es in drei Tagen nicht besser ist, kommen Sie bitte wieder.

Herr Bromma: — Ja, klar. Tschüs.

Ärztin: — Auf Wiedersehen.
— Der Nächste, bitte!

———————————

Good morning, Mr. Jones.

Mr. Jones: — Guten Morgen, Frau Doktor. Sie können ruhig Deutsch mit mir sprechen. Ich wohne schon seit 2 Jahren hier in Stuttgart.

Ärztin: — Gut. Und wo brennt es?

Mr. Jones: — Ich habe dieses Jahr einen furchtbaren Heuschnupfen, obwohl ich starke Tropfen aus England habe.

Ärztin: — Aha, es gibt hier ein neues Medikament, aber da müßten Sie fünf Spritzen bekommen.

Mr. Jones: — Ja, das ist schon OK., wenn es hilft.

Ärztin: — Gut, dann gebe ich Ihnen jetzt eine, und dann kommen Sie die nächsten fünf Donnerstage.

Mr. Jones: — Mpf.

Ärztin: — Schon vorbei. Auf Wiedersehen. Bis Donnerstag in einer Woche.

Mr. Jones: — Gut. Bis dann.

Ärztin: — Der Nächste, bitte!

———————————

Ah! Grüß Gott, Herr Carolus. Wie geht es denn mit Ihrem Fuß?

Herr Carolus: — Danke, sehr gut. Ich bin froh, daß der Gips jetzt endlich runterkommt — bei **dem** Wetter!

Ärztin: — Das geht sehr schnell. *(Noises.)* So! Fertig sind wir.

Herr Carolus: — Ah! Das tut gut.

Ärztin: — In einer Woche können Sie wieder normal gehen.

Herr Carolus: — Danke schön. Auf Wiedersehen!

Ärztin: — Auf Wiedersehen!

In der Apotheke

200 (1B 102)

Authentic advertising material for straightforward reading comprehension.

R

L

199 (1B 101)

Haben Sie etwas gegen Kopfschmerzen?

A simple matching activity providing the opportunity to present medicines in different forms. Tell pupils to listen to the tape and match the drawings to the medicines depicted.

Haben Sie etwas gegen Kopfschmerzen?

1 — Guten Morgen.
— Guten Morgen. Haben Sie etwas gegen Kopfschmerzen?
— Ja. Haben Sie Migräne?
— Nein.
— Also, diese Kopfschmerztabletten hier sind gut — nicht zu stark. Das macht DM 4,50.
— Danke schön.

2 — Guten Tag. Haben Sie etwas gegen Magenschmerzen?
— Haben Sie starke Magenschmerzen?
— Nein, das ist nicht so schlimm.
— Also, hier haben Sie einen Saft. Er schmeckt gut und tut gut. Das macht DM 7,00.
— Danke schön.
— Bitte schön.

3 — Guten Morgen. Haben Sie etwas gegen Heuschnupfen?
— Sie brauchen eine Spritze. Sie sollten am besten zu einem Arzt gehen.
— Ich bekomme nicht gern Spritzen. Haben Sie wirklich nichts gegen Heuschnupfen?
— Doch. Diese Kapseln hier. Aber am besten sollten Sie zu einem Arzt gehen.
— Danke, aber ich glaube, ich nehme lieber die Kapseln.

4 — Bitte schön?
— Ich brauche etwas gegen Ohrenschmerzen.
— Gegen Ohrenschmerzen? Diese Tropfen hier sind sehr gut.
— Gut. Die nehme ich.

5 — Ich hätte gern etwas gegen Erkältung.
— Ah, Sie sind erkältet?
— Ja, leider.
— Haben Sie auch Halsschmerzen?
— Ja.
— Dann empfehle ich diese Hustenbonbons.
— Gut. Was kostet die Packung?
— DM 3,00.

6 — *(Young girl.)* Ich habe mir in den Finger geschnitten. Das blutet so und tut weh.
— Haben Sie etwas dagegen?
— Laß mal den Finger sehen ... ja, das ist

nicht so schlimm. Hier Pflaster.
— Danke.

7 — Guten Tag. Ich fahre übermorgen mit
der Fähre von Hamburg nach Harwich.
Haben Sie etwas gegen Seekrankheit?
— Diese Tabletten hier. Aber Vorsicht! Sie
machen müde.
— Das macht doch nichts. Ich schlafe gern
— besonders auf einer Fähre auf der
Nordsee.

Solution: **1**D **2**F **3**A **4**G **5**B **6**C **7**E

L, S, R

199
(**1B** 101)

Haben Sie etwas gegen Kopfschmerzen?

Tell pupils to practise the language of the
previous activity in pairs, using the model
dialogue and/or the *Tip des Tages* as a guide.

---

11 Area 6

• Consolidation

200-201
(**1B** 102-
103)

L

Wundermittel

Tell pupils they are going to hear a series
of advertisements for various medicines.
The illnesses and ailments they claim to
cure are grouped together in the flasks
and bottles, depicted on page 201
(**1B** 103). Pupils should listen to the tape
and match the products to the containers.
Complete no. 1 with the class.

Hört zu: Medikamentewerbung. (Explain in
English: advertising medicines.)
Was paßt zu wem?

Wundermittel

1 — *(Jingle)* ... kaufen Sie 'Heili'
Medikamente, die Wundermittel gegen
alles — Kopfwehtabletten, Saft gegen
Magenschmerzen, Verbände. In allen
Apotheken zu finden. 'Heili'. *(jingle)*.

2 — *(Jingle)* ... 'Zickzack', die allerbesten
Medikamente: Hustenbonbons,
Kopfschmerztabletten, Salbe gegen
Rückenschmerzen und Verbände.
'Zickzack'.

3 — *(Jingle)* ... kaufen Sie 'Mirgehtsbesser',
Wundermittel. Tropfen gegen
Ohrenschmerzen, Salbe gegen
Rückenschmerzen, Tabletten gegen
Zahnschmerzen und Verbände.
'Mirgehtsbesser'. Natürlich.

4 — *(Jingle)* ... 'Schluckundlach': Tropfen
gegen Ohrenschmerzen, Saft gegen
Magenschmerzen, Verbände und
Tabletten gegen Zahnschmerzen.
'Schluckundlach', echte Wundermittel.

5 — *(Jingle)* ... Wenn Sie krank sind, nehmen
Sie 'Medikawohl' — Medikamente gegen
alles. Pillen gegen Magenschmerzen,
Tropfen gegen Ohrenschmerzen und
Verbände. 'Medikawohl' und Sie fühlen
sich wohl.

6 — *(Jingle)* ... 'Fitundfett' Wundermittel.
Haben Sie Halsschmerzen? Kaufen Sie
unsere Hustenbonbons. 'Fitundfett'.
Haben Sie Magenschmerzen? Kaufen
Sie unseren Saft. Haben Sie sich das
Bein oder den Arm verletzt? Kaufen Sie
unsere Verbände. 'Fitundfett'.

7 — *(Jingle)* ... 'Gesundwienie', weil es so
gesund ist. Kaufen Sie unsere
Kopfwehtabletten, unsere Verbände und
unseren Saft gegen Halsschmerzen.
'Gesundwienie'.

8 — *(Jingle)* ... 'Heilkraft', wirkungsvolle
Medikamente: Salbe gegen
Rückenschmerzen, Tropfen gegen
Ohrenschmerzen und Verbände.
'Heilkraft' Wundermittel. 'Heilkraft'.

Solution: **1**A **2**G **3**E **4**C **5**B **6**D **7**H **8**F

L, S, R

201
(**1B** 103)

Partnerarbeit

Tell pupils to play a guessing game in pairs,
using *Wundermittel* to cue the dialogues.
Pupil A chooses one of the containers **(A-H)**,
without saying which one, and describes the
medecines (s)he's buying, using the language
underneath the illustrations. Pupil B must
guess which container his/her partner has
chosen. By revealing only one medecine
purchased at a time, the game becomes more
interesting, as the ailments recur throughout
the containers. Complete one example in front
of the class.

Suggested language is in the Pupil's Book.

(L, S), W

201
(**1B** 103)

Frank ist krank!

A written activity to consolidate illness and
injuries. Complete the exercise orally first, if
required, before telling pupils to draw and
label their own version of Frank in their
exercise books.

Tragt 'Frank' in euer Heft ein und füllt die Felder aus.

Was fehlt dir?

L, S, R

74

This worksheet practises the question forms relating to illness and injury. Cut the worksheet up into individual cards. One pupil chooses one of the cards without declaring which and the second pupil must work out which one has been chosen by asking the questions on the larger card. Complete one example in front of the class before moving on to pair-work. As a variation, one pupil could take two or three cards at the same time.

The game could also be played in small groups as a kind of 'Happy Families', the winner being the pupil who has all the illnesses! The question card should be placed in the centre for reference.

Was macht die Zähne kaputt?

L, S, R, W

75

Give out one worksheet to each pupil. Tell them to look at the visuals of food and drink and decide which are bad for their teeth. When they decide, they should record the information on the worksheet. Once the activity has been completed by a majority of pupils, conduct your own *Umfrage*, with pupils reporting back on their findings for you to record on the board or OHP. You could agree or disagree with the findings, leading to discussion among the class. (See worksheet for example).

 202 (1B 104)

R

Kannst du das lesen?

Three authentic texts testing comprehension, in English, of material dealing with health and medicine.

Aua!

L, S, R

76

Further pair-work practice of illness and injuries. This time the language provided enables pupils to compare the extent of their injuries depicted in the four visuals they each have.

 202 (1B 104)

L

Was meinen Sie, Herr Doktor Schweiger?

A difficult, 'authentic' listening text designed to help pupils imagine how they might react to finding themselves in a hospital in Germany listening to two doctors diagnosing the illness, without thinking that the patient might be able to understand some of what they are saying.

Tell pupils to listen to the tape and write down, in English, anything they understand in the course of the doctors' conversation, which considers the possibility of use of stomach pump, appendicitis, and observation.

Was meinen Sie, Herr Doktor Schweiger?

— Herr Doktor Schweiger: was ist denn mit diesem Patienten los?
— Frau Doktor Nagel, dieser Patient Michael Smart aus England klagt über Magenschmerzen.
— So, was hat er denn gegessen, so in den letzten Tagen?
— Er sagt, er habe gestern Fisch gegessen, und der Fisch muß wohl schlecht gewesen sein.
— Hat er sich erbrochen?
— Ja, er hat gestern abend und heute früh ziemlich stark brechen müssen.
— Hat er denn Fieber?
— Eigentlich nicht. Er hatte gestern erhöhte Temperatur, aber nicht erwähnenswert.

— Und hat er irgendwo anders noch Schmerzen?
— Nein, eigentlich nicht ... nur im Magenbereich.
— Was meinen Sie, Herr Doktor Schweiger? Sollten wir ihm vielleicht den Magen auspumpen lassen?
— Ja, ich wäre dafür, den Magen auszupumpen, weil es mir eine normale Lebensmittelvergiftung zu sein scheint.
— Oder sollten wir operieren? Ich meine, es könnte der Blinddarm sein. Was halten Sie von Operieren?
— Nein, Frau Doktor Nagel, von einer Operation halte ich überhaupt nichts, denn in diesem Fall ist wohl eine Lebensmittelvergiftung die wahrscheinlichste Ursache der Krankheit.
— Sie mögen Recht haben, aber wir müssen ganz sicher sein.
— Ja, ich möchte den Jungen noch weitere zwei oder drei Tage im Krankenhaus behalten.

— Ja, gut. Wir müssen aber noch seine Gastfamilie anrufen, damit sie Bescheid weiß, und seine Eltern in England ...
— Ja, sehr gut. *(Turning to patient).* Auf Wiedersehen, Michael.

Points raised by doctors:-

(i) (Complaining of) stomach pains
(ii) eaten fish (could have been off)
(iii) vomited previous evening and early that morning
(iv) no particularly high temperature
(v) no pain other than (around) stomach
(vi) use a stomach pump?
(vii) could be (straightforward) food poisoning
(viii) could it be appendicitis (Blinddarm)?
(ix) food poisoning most likely
(x) 2 to 3 days observation in hospital
(xi) host family + parents to be informed (by phone)

Vocabulary

Ade! *Goodbye*
die Allergie(n) *allergy*
allergisch gegen *allergic to*
die Angabe(n) *detail, instruction*
der Apparat(e) *appliance, phone*
  am * *on the phone*
  arm *poor*
der Arm(e) *arm*
  asthmatisch *asthmatic*
  atmen *to breathe*
der Aufenthalt *stay*
das Badminton *badminton*
der Baum(¨e) *tree*
das Begräbnis *funeral, burial*
  behalten *to keep, retain*
das Bein(e) *leg*
der Berg(e) *mountain*
  beruhigen *to calm*
die Beschwerde(n) *hardship, trouble, complaint*
  bestehen *to exist*
die Betreuung(en) *care, looking after*
der Blinddarm *appendix*
das Blut *blood*
  brechen *to break*
  brennen *to burn*
die Chance(n) *chance*
der Dienst(e) *service*
  dringend *urgent(ly)*
  duschen *to have a shower*
  enthalten *to contain*
der Entschuldigungszettel(-) *excuse note*
sich erbrechen *to be sick*
  erkältet sein *to have a cold*
die Erkältung(en) *cold*
  ernsthaft *serious*
die Ersatzkasse(n) *health insurance company*
  erschrocken *shocked*
  erwähnenswert *significant, worth mentioning*
das Faß(Fässer) *barrel*
Was fehlt dir? *What's wrong?*

das Fieber *high temperature, fever*
die Flecke(n) *spot, stain*
  frieren *to freeze, be cold*
das Fußgelenk(e) *ankle*
der Fußpilz(e) *athlete's foot*
  gesund *healthy*
die Gesundheit *health*
  ! Bless you! (when sneezing)
der Gips *plaster (of Paris)*
  glücklicherweise *fortunately*
der Gürtel(-) *belt*
der Hals(¨e) *neck, throat*
die Halsschmerzen *sore throat*
  Handball *handball*
das Handgelenk(e) *wrist*
  häßlich *ugly*
die Haut *skin*
der Hautausschlag(¨e) *rash*
das Heilkraut(¨er) *natural herbal remedy*
das Heimweh *homesickness*
der Heuschnupfen(-) *hay fever*
  husten *to cough*
  hüten *to look after, mind*
  Hochachtungsvoll *Yours faithfully*
  jucken *to itch*
das Judo *judo*
das Kännchen(-) *pot (coffee, tea, etc.)*
die Kapsel(n) *capsule*
das Karate *karate*
  kaum *hardly, scarcely*
  klagen über *to complain about*
der Kopf(¨e) *head*
  Kopfschmerzen *headache*
die Krankenkasse(n) *health insurance company*
die Krankheit(en) *illness*
  kratzen *to scratch*
der Kurs(e) *course*
die Lebensmittel *groceries, food*

die Lebensmittelvergiftung *food poisoning*
die Leiter(n) *ladder*
das Licht(er) *light*
der Magen *stomach*
  Magenschmerzen *stomach ache*
das Medikament(e) *medicament*
die Meinung(en) *opinion*
das Messer(-) *knife*
die Migräne(n) *migraine*
die Muschel(n) *shellfish*
der Muskelkater *aching muscles*
  nachsehen *to check*
  nicken *to nod*
das Ohr(en) *ear*
  Ohrenschmerzen *earache*
das Omelett(e) *omelette*
  operieren *to operate*
der Patient(en) *patient*
das Pflaster(-) *sticking plaster*
der Pickel(-) *spot, acne*
die Piste(n) *ski slope*
  plötzlich *suddenly*
  putzen *to clean*
  rein *pure*
der Rettungsdienst(e) *rescue service*
das Rezept(e) *prescription*
der Rücken(-) *back*
die Rückenschmerzen *backache*
  rutschen *to slip, slide*
die Salbe(n) *ointment*
  scharf *hot (spicy); sharp*
der Schatz(¨e) *treasure*
der Schmerz(en) *pain, ache*
  schneiden *to cut*
der Schnupfen(-) *runny nose, head cold*
  schreien *to yell, cry out*
die Schuld *fault*
die Schulter(n) *shoulder*
  Seekrankheit(en) *seasickness*
die Seilbahn(en) *cable railway*

selbstverständlich *naturally, it goes without saying*
  Ski laufen *to ski*
der Sonnenbrand *sunstroke*
die Sonnencreme(Sonnencrems) *suntan cream*
  sowieso *anyway*
  spinnen *to be mad, talk rubbish*
die Sprechstunde(n) *surgery hours*
die Spritze(n) *injection*
die Störung(en) *disturbance*
  teilnehmen an *to take part in*
der Tierarzt(¨e) *vet*
die Toilette(n) *toilet*
der Tropf(¨e) *drop*
die Turnhalle(n) *gymnasium*
  überall *overall*
der Unfall(¨e) *accident*
die Veranstaltung(en) *event*
der Verband(¨e) *dressing*
  verbinden *to combine, unite*
  verfügen über *to have at one's disposal, be in charge of*
  verletzen *to injure*
  verschreiben *to prescribe*
die Versicherung(en) *insurance*
das Verständnis(se) *understanding*
  verstauchen *to sprain*
die Voranmeldung(en) *appointment*
  Vorsicht! *Be careful!*
  wahrscheinlich *probably*
  wehtun *to hurt*
der Wespenstich(e) *wasp sting*
der Wind(e) *wind*
  wirksam *effective*
der Zahn(¨e) *tooth*
der Zahnarzt(¨e) *dentist*
die Zahnschmerzen *toothache*
  zart *gentle*
  zerbrechen *to break*
  zumachen *to close*

Area 1

> ● Holiday plans

204
(1B 106)

L, R, W

Wo fährst du hin?

A recording of eight young people talking about what they are going to do in the holidays.

Tell pupils to look at page 204 (**1B** 106) in the Pupil's Book. Go through what the eight people are saying. Explain that these are excerpts from what they will hear them saying on the tape. Then tell them that you are going to play the recordings and that they should decide who is speaking. Play the first recording and when the speaker has been identified, write her name on the board. Then play the rest of the recordings, one at a time, to complete the list. Add the following table (without answers) once the list is complete and ask pupils to copy it down.

Name	Wohin?	Mit wem?	Wie lange?
Ulla	Spanien	Eltern	14 Tage
Rudi	Österreich	Freunden	1 Woche
Frauke	Holland	Mutter/Bruder	2 Wochen
Kai	England	—	3 Wochen
Jochen	Alpen?	—	paar Tage
Karola	Dänemark	Freundin	10 Tage
Gina	Mallorca	Eltern	2 Wochen
Udo	Bodensee	Familie	14 Tage

Now tell pupils to listen to the recordings again and fill in the details on the grid.

Seht euch Seite 204 (106) an. Wie heißen die jungen Leute? Was sagen sie? Jetzt hört gut zu. Wer ist das? Rudi? Frauke? (Play first recording.) *Richtig, es ist Ulla.* (Write on board and continue.) *Schreibt jetzt diese Tabelle in eure Hefte. Ihr hört jetzt alles noch einmal. Hört gut zu: Wohin? Mit wem? Wie lange? Zuerst Ulla.* (Play the first recording again and complete the first line as an example, if required. Continue.) Collate results on the board.

Wo fährst du hin?

1 — Meine Eltern und ich fliegen nach Spanien. Wir bleiben da 14 Tage in einem Hotel an der See.

2 — Ich fahre mit ein paar Freunden für eine Woche nach Österreich. Wir nehmen unsere Zelte mit. Hoffentlich regnet es nicht.

3 — Meine Mutter hat ein Ferienhaus in Holland gebucht. Direkt an der See. Für zwei Wochen. Mein Bruder kommt auch mit.

4 — Ich fahre nach England und wohne drei Wochen bei meinem Brieffreund Tom in Leeds. Ich war letztes Jahr auch da.

5 — Wir fahren nicht weg. Vielleicht kann ich aber ein paar Tage zu meinen Großeltern in die Alpen fahren.

6 — Meine Freundin und ich machen eine Radtour durch Dänemark. Wir übernachten in Jugendherbergen. Wir wollen in 10 Tagen 600 Kilometer fahren.

7 — Ich muß mit meinen Eltern nach Mallorca. Jedes Jahr dasselbe! Zwei Wochen ohne Computer!

8 — Wir mieten dieses Jahr einen Caravan am Bodensee. Meine Schwester und ich schwimmen gern, und unsere Eltern fahren gern in die Berge. Leider sind es nur 14 Tage.

204
(1B 106)

L, S, R

Ferienpläne

Ask pupils to look at the pictograms on page 204 (**1B** 106). Practise the four questions:

> Wohin fährst du in den Ferien?
> Wie kommst du dahin?
> Mit wem fährst du?
> Wie lange bleibst du da?

and a selection of possible answers.

T: *Was machen Monika, Claudia, Thomas und Werner? Diana. Du bist Monika. Wohin fährst du in den Ferien? Nach Deutschland? Nach Spanien?*
P: *Nach England.*
T: *Und wie kommst du dahin? Mit dem Zug? Mit dem Schiff?*
P: *Mit dem Schiff.* etc.

Give fewer prompts as pupils become more confident, but help when necessary.

Encourage pupils to ask the questions as soon as possible.

Finish by asking pupils to continue in pairs for two or three minutes.

L, S, R, W

204
(1B 106)

77

Eine Umfrage

Cut up the worksheets and distribute the cue cards. Refer pupils to *Eine Umfrage* in the book for reference.

Tell pupils to interview each other about 'their' holiday plans. Once a pair has interviewed each other, ask them: either to swap cards with another pair, or to break up and find other partners.

Pupils could be asked to keep a record of replies.

" *Hier sind Zettel für die Partnerarbeit. Macht Interviews. (Schreibt die Antworten auf.) Seid ihr fertig? Jetzt geht zu einem anderen Paar und holt euch neue Zettel/interviewt andere Partner.*

L, S, (W)

Interviews

Ask pupils to interview each other about their real holiday plans. Results could be collated, if felt desirable.

(L, S), R

205
(1B 107)

Was paßt zusammen?

Eight extracts about holiday plans for pupils to match to eight photos of those holidays. This could either be talked through together in class or done as an individual activity with the results to be marked afterwards.

Use Susanne's comments to lead into the topic of Area 2.

Solution:

Gisela	7
Anneliese	4
Michael	1
Konstanze	5
Dirk	8
Birgit	2
Stefan	6
Susanne	3

nem 1

R, W

254
(1B 138)

Wie heißt das auf Deutsch?

Pupils refer back to the extracts on page 205 *(Was paßt zusammen?)* and find the German for certain English phrases, identifying who says them. This should increase pupils' scope in the ensuing writing activity.

W

Pupils could write up their own holiday plans in brief. This could be done in the form of a postcard in reply to one from an imaginary German penfriend who has written from his/her holiday. The teacher might start pupils off with something like this:

" *‚Liebe(r) ...!*

Danke für Deine Postkarte aus ... Hier haben wir leider bis zum ... Juli noch Schule. Aber am ... August fahre ich ... ' usw.

12 Area 2

● The 'Bundesrepublik' and the 'DDR'

R

206-207
(1B 108-9)

Einige Informationen: Deutschland geteilt

An explanation in English of how Germany came to be divided and subsequently reunified. It is hoped that the topic is of sufficient interest for pupils to **want** to read it for themselves, though the teacher could set some questions in English on it, if so desired.

Das ‚neue' Deutschland

R

Some statistics and photographs about the reunification of Germany. A map shows the sixteen *Länder*.

208-209
(1B 4 +
120-121)

As with the previous information, teachers may wish to set some questions on the text or base some further research on it, or they may wish pupils to just read it for interest.

These two pages do not appear in Pupil's Book **1B**, but pupils can be referred to the full map on page 4 and to the activity on page 120-121 which describes some of the *Länder*.

Daniels Geschichte

210
(1B 110)

A true account by a young German of his pre-1989 emigration from the former DDR to West Germany with his mother. Ask pupils to summarise what Daniel says about it. Certain headings or cues could be written up to guide them, e.g.:

What did he feel about it when he was first told? How long was it before they heard the result of their application? How long did the authorities give them to get out? How did Daniel feel as they approached the border? What was his mother's reaction to reaching the West? What were **his** first impressions?

---

12 Area 3

● Choosing a holiday

L

Was machst du gern im Urlaub?

Ten young people's answers to the question: *‚Was machst du gern im Urlaub?'* The teacher may like to revise vocabulary for leisure activities using flashcards 39-58, before beginning this activity.

Ask pupils to listen for what the ten young people on the tape say they like doing on holiday. Write up on the board any new phrases or any that pupils have difficulty with.

R

Was machst du gern im Urlaub?

1 — Ich liege gern in der Sonne und lese ein gutes Buch. *2*

2 — Ich schwimme gern in der See. Ich gehe gern am Abend aus ... *2*

3 — Ich besuche gern Sehenswürdigkeiten — aber natürlich nicht jeden Tag. Es gefällt mir auch am Strand. *2*

4 — Ich mache gern Wanderungen, und ich spiele sehr gern mit meinem Vater Tennis. *2*

5 — Ja, ich gehe gern schwimmen — aber in der See; das Schwimmbad gefällt mir nicht. Und dann, wenn es regnet, spiele ich gern Schach oder andere Brettspiele mit meinen Geschwistern. *3*

6 — Also, ich besuche **nicht** gern Kirchen, was meine Eltern so gerne machen. Aber ich sehe mich ziemlich gern in alten Städten um. Ich gucke mir die Geschäfte gern an. *2*

7 — Schwimmen. Eis essen. Mädchen ansprechen. In der Sonne liegen. Und abends in die Disko. Das ist's. *5*

8 — Ich verbringe gern den ganzen Tag am Strand. Von Morgen bis zum Abend. Ab und zu schwimmen gehen und dazwischen Musik hören, auf meinem Walkman. *3*

9 — Es kommt darauf an. Wenn wir ans Meer fahren, dann schwimme ich bloß und sonne mich. Aber wenn wir woanders hinfahren, dann besuche ich gern Schlösser und so weiter. Ich reite auch sehr gern. *4*

10 — Ich mache gern Picknicks, besonders an einem Fluß oder so. Der Strand gefällt mir gut, aber nicht, wenn es zuviel Leute gibt. Ich esse auch gern im Hotelrestaurant. *3*

R

Meine Art Urlaub

211
(1B 111)

Comments by seven young people about what they like and dislike doing on holiday. The accompanying true/false questions in German often deliberately use paraphrase and, in some cases, require inferences to be drawn from the actual texts.

Solution:
1 True   2 False   3 True   4 False   5 False
6 True   7 False   8 True   9 True   10 False

194

L, S, R, W

Tell pupils to prepare (using notes, if necessary), a short statement about what they like (or dislike) doing on holiday. When these are ready, tell them to find a partner and in German exchange their views about holidays. Each should note down the main points in English as they hear them.

When everyone has done this, tell them all to change partners and repeat the procedure with their new partner, again making notes in English about what they are told. Get each pupil to do this with at least five different partners.

This activity will, in itself, provide good speaking and listening practice. With a good class, however, one of the following forms of exploitation could be attempted.

i) Ask pupils to select one of the people they interviewed and from their notes on them, write a short summary of what that person said. They may find the true/false statements on page 211 (**1B** 111) of the Pupil's Book useful to refer to. When these summaries are ready, ask a pupil to read his/hers out, and see if some other pupils can identify whose it is. (At least four other pupils will have interviewed the same person).

ii) A simpler conclusion is to ask pupils which of the people they interviewed has a taste in holidays closest to their own.

78

R, W

Der ideale Urlaub

The worksheet, to be completed by pupils individually, is in two parts. The key to both parts is printed below the tables on the worksheet, but the method of calculation for the results is not. This is given below and is for the teacher to explain to pupils when they have completed the charts.

Pupils will probably need help with certain phrases, particularly in the small results section at the bottom of the worksheet. Having thought about the task, however, they should prove sufficiently motivated to want to understand the conclusions!

Section 1
Pupils answer the ten questions about holidays, using the code *Ja = 3, Nein = 2, Egal = 1.* When they have completed this, write the following instructions on the board.

If explanation is needed, it will probably be safest to give this in English.

Resultat =
$(c + d + e + f + h) - (a + b + g + i + j)$

The result will be either a plus or a minus number. Its meaning is given on the worksheet.

Section 2
Prioritäten!

Tell pupils that 'most important' is *am wichtigsten.* Read out the instructions given on the sheet. Against the figure 1, they fill in what is most important for them from the list on the left. Against the figure 10, what is least important. It may be a good idea to use pencil at first, until they have definitely decided on the order. When everyone is ready, tell them to write down these values against the factors they have listed in the box.

Familie 3
Freunde 3
Dauer 1
Sehenswürdigkeiten 1
Einkaufsmöglichkeiten 5
Sportmöglichkeiten 3
Wetter 3
Essen 5
Landschaft 1
Unterbringung 5

Explain that they should now multiply each priority number (i.e. the ones listed **1-10** in the printed column) by the value assigned to the factor they have filled in.

e.g.

1	Freunde	3	1 x 3 = 3
2	Wetter	3	2 x 3 = 6
3	Sehenswürdigkeiten	1	3 x 1 = 3
4			

The product of all ten columns should then be added together to give a total, whose meaning can be read off the bottom of the worksheet.

212
(1B 112)

(L, S), R

Ferienpuzzle

Six advertisements for different types of
holidays accompanied by statements about
what some people expect from their holidays.
Pupils have to match up adverts and
statements. Check orally. No further
exploitation of the material is intended.

*Hier sind 6 Sachen aus einer Ferien-
Broschüre. Und hier sind 6 Leute.
Sie sagen, was sie in den Ferien machen
wollen. Was paßt zu wem? Wohin fährt ... ?*

L, S, R

79

Im Reisebüro

Cut the Worksheets as indicated. Give sheet X
to one partner in each pair and one of the
cards on Worksheet Y to the other partner.

Tell the first pupil that (s)he has information
about 16 different holidays. Tell the second
that their card explains what kind of holiday
they are looking for.

The aim is for one partner to help the other to
find a holiday that will fit his/her requirements
— including price.

The activity can be extended by the
'customer' partners exchanging cards, as well
as by each pair exchanging roles and the
'customer' becoming the 'agent'.

T: *Nicola, du hast hier sechzehn
Urlaubsangebote. Angela, du hast Karte
A. Was für einen Urlaub möchtest du
machen? Fährst du alleine hin oder mit
Familie?*
P: *Mit Familie.*
T: *OK. Und wo willst du hin? In die Berge?*
P: *Nein. An die See.*
T: *Gut. Nun, Nicola. Angela will mit der
Familie an die See fahren. Aber für wie
lange? Wie kommt sie hin? Mit dem Zug?
Mit dem Flugzeug? Und was kostet das?
So, du mußt einen Urlaub für Angela
finden.*

The following 'solutions' work well, but pupils
should not be given the idea that there are
'right answers' to this activity. The point is to
get them talking.

Card	Holiday
A	3,5
B	12
C	6
D	16 (15)
E	10, 13
F	15

(L, S), R

80

Was machst du dieses Jahr?

A jumbled-up picture story about a family
arguing about where to go on holiday. Divide
the class into groups of four. Give each group
a worksheet and ask them to cut it up.

Then pupils have to establish the correct
order as given below. A few groups can then
act out their version.

This activity is fairly demanding.

*Jetzt Gruppenarbeit. Immer vier in einer
Gruppe. Hier ist ein Arbeitsbogen. Für jede
Gruppe einer. Schneidet den Bogen in Stücke.
(Demonstrate.)
Welches Bild ist Nummer eins? Welches ist
Nummer 2? Und so weiter.*

Seid ihr fertig? Dann Rollenspiel. Gruppe A?

Solution: E I D B H A G C F

12 Area 4

● Going to a campsite

213
(1B 113)

R

Campingplatz Nürnberg

This is an extract from a campsite brochure giving details of prices and facilities offered at the site.

Tell pupils to read the text and familiarise themselves with the prices. They should also be able to guess some of the facilities offered.

'Campingplatz Nürnberg'. Lest den Text. Seht euch die Preise an: für ein Auto, einen Caravan, ein Zelt. (Pupils' responses in German.) *Und was gibt es alles auf dem Campingplatz? Antwortet auf Englisch.*

213
(1B 113)

L, R

Camping ist billig, oder?

Tell pupils that they are going to hear a number of people booking in to the campsite in Nürnberg. Ask them to copy out the chart and then fill in as many details as possible.

Ihr hört jetzt Leute auf dem Campingplatz Nürnberg. Was wollen sie? Schreibt die Tabelle in euer Heft. Hört gut zu. Was könnt ihr verstehen? Schreibt es in die Tabelle.

Camping ist billig, oder?

1 — Guten Tag. Haben Sie noch Platz frei?
  — Ja. Wie lange wollen Sie bleiben?
  — Eine Nacht.
  — Und wieviel Personen sind Sie?
  — Zwei Erwachsene und zwei Kinder.
  — Wie alt sind die Kinder?
  — Acht und dreizehn.
  — Haben Sie einen Wohnwagen?
  — Nein, wir haben ein Auto und ein Zelt.
  — Also, zwei Erwachsene und zwei Kinder, mit Auto und Zelt für eine Nacht — das macht 19 Mark 50.

2 — Guten Abend. Wir haben nicht reserviert. Ist noch was frei?
  — Wieviel Mann sind Sie?
  — Wir sind zwei, mein Freund und ich.
  — Haben Sie ein Zelt?
  — Nein, einen Wohnwagen.
  — Wie lange wollen Sie bleiben?
  — Eine Nacht.
  — Also, zwei Personen, ein Wohnwagen und das Auto, für eine Nacht — macht 14 Mark 50.

3 — Guten Abend. Mein Name ist Krull. Wir haben eine Reservierung für heute nacht.
  — Wie heißen Sie nochmal?
  — Krull, K - R - U - L - L.
  — Ja, ich hab's schon. Also, das ist für zwei Erwachsene, zwei Kinder, mit Zelt und Auto. Stimmt das?
  — Nein, wir haben drei Kinder.
  — OK., danke schön. das macht dann also — Moment mal — 22 Mark.

4 — Guten Tag.
  — Guten Tag. Kann ich Ihnen helfen?
  — Haben Sie noch Platz für einen Motorcaravan für heute nacht?
  — Ja, es ist viel frei zur Zeit. Bei **dem** Wetter. Wie lange wollen Sie bleiben?
  — Drei Nächte.
  — Ja, gut. Wieviel Personen sind Sie?
  — Meine Frau und ich und die zwei Kinder.
  — Sind die Kinder unter fünfzehn?
  — Ja, die sind erst dreizehn und vierzehn.
  — Also, zwei Erwachsene, zwei Kinder, ein Motorcaravan, für drei Nächte, das macht 58 Mark 50.

5 — Haben Sie noch was frei?
  — Ja, wieviel Mann sind Sie?
  — Nur ich. Ich bin allein.
  — Also, ein Erwachsener mit Zelt und PKW —
  — Ich habe kein Auto. Ich bin mit dem Bus gekommen.
  — Also, ein Erwachsener mit Zelt für eine Nacht. Das kostet 6 Mark 50.

Solution:

	Nächte	Erwachsene	Kinder 3-14	Auto
1	1	2	2	1
2	1	2		1
3	1	2	3	1
4	3	2	2	
5	1	1		

Wohnwagen/ Motorcaravan	Zelt	Preis DM
	1	19,50
1		14,50
	1	22,-
1		58,50
	1	6,50

Camping ist billig, oder?

Ask pupils whether they can remember any of the questions used by the campsite warden or the people booking in. Some pupils might remember some of the questions without prompting. Then play the first dialogue again, so that pupils can reproduce more of the language. Practise each phrase.

R, W

213
(1B 113) ### Bist du ein Genie in Mathe?

Tell pupils to look at the price list of the campsite in Nürnberg and to work out what it would cost for each family (possible homework).

Solution: **1** DM 34 **2** DM 18,50 **3** DM 70,50 **4** DM 58 **5** DM 44

R

213
(1B 113) ### Am Campingplatz

Eight questions to match the eight answers, based closely on the dialogues in *Camping ist billig — oder?* This should familiarise pupils with the kind of questions the warden would ask, ready for the pair-work activity that follows.

Solution: **1**e **2**g **3**a **4**h **5**f **6**b **7**d **8**c

L, S

213
(1B 113)

Pupils should now be able to make their own dialogues using the visuals from *Bist du ein Genie in Mathe?* as cues.

Jetzt Partnerarbeit. Seite 213 (113).
Du *arbeitest auf dem Campingplatz, und* **du** *kommst mit einem Zelt oder einem Caravan.*

Du *sagst: ‚Guten Abend. Haben Sie noch was frei?' Und* **du** *sagst: ‚Ja. Wieviel Personen ...?' und so weiter. OK.? Los geht's.*

nem 2
254
(1B 138)

R, W

Gespräch an einem Campingplatz
A conversation is presented in the wrong order. Pupils have to deduce the correct order and write it down.

R

214
(1B 114) ### Campingplatz Sonneneck

The plan and the description of the *Campingplatz Sonneneck* and two notices are to set the scene for the following activity. Pupils will need time to establish the relationship between the extract from the camp brochure and the plan.

R

214
(1B 114) ### Welcher Campingplatz ist für dich der Beste?

A table with a breakdown of facilities offered by *Campingplatz Nürnberg* and *Campingplatz Sonneneck*.

Pupils could be asked to say which campsite they would most like to visit.

R

215
(1B 115) ### Campingplatz — Regeln

Four rules of a campsite have to be matched with the illustrations. No detailed exploitation intended.

L, S, R, W

81A
81B

Welcher Campingplatz?

There are two worksheets for this activity. No. 81A consists of ten sets of campsite details. These should be cut up and given to ten different pupils, who then take the role of campsite wardens. No. 81B consists of ten sets of requirements **(A-J)** of ten imaginary families or groups of people. Either give **one** of these to each of the remaining pupils (in which case you may need to use each one more than once) and ask them to work individually, or issue one card to a pair of pupils and ask them to go round the campsites together.

Position the ten campsite wardens around the room. Tell the customers to visit each site in turn, and decide which is best suited to their needs. They will need to make notes as they go.

Ihr habt jeder einen Campingplatz. Lest die Details.

Ihr *seid Touristen in Deutschland. Ihr macht einen Campingurlaub. Was erwartet ihr von einem Campingplatz?*

(Tell the wardens where to sit)

So. Jetzt geht ihr zu allen Campingplätzen und fragt, wie sie sind und was sie bieten. Macht Notizen. Welcher Campingplatz ist geeignet für euch?

If further help is needed, explain briefly in English.

Best solution: **A**7 **B**3 **C**6 **D**9 **E**2 **F**5 **G**10 **H**1 **I**4 **J**8

Note that other solutions are possible in many cases, though not as well-suited. Campsites 2, 3 and 4 do not allow dogs and are therefore out of the question for campers D, G and H.

The teacher may like to discuss solutions with the class when the activity is over. It could even be analysed in detail or used as a follow-up written task if every pupil were given a complete copy of both worksheets.

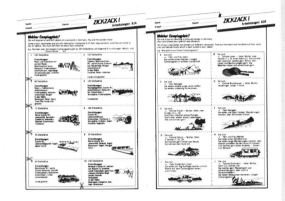

12 Area 5

● On holiday

216
(1B 116)

L

Drei Telefonate aus den Ferien

Three phone calls made by people on holiday to their friends, including comments about the weather. There are questions in English in the Pupil's Book. Check pupils' answers after each conversation.

Drei Telefonate aus den Ferien
1 — Hallo, Evi.
 — Hallo, Birgit! Wo bist **du** denn?
 — An der See. Tolles Wetter haben wir hier. Die Sonne scheint, und heiß ist es!
 — Was machst du denn die ganze Zeit?
 — Ich gehe schwimmen, ich gehe spazieren, und abends gehe ich in die Disko.

 — Prima. Und wann kommst du zurück?
 — Am Samstag. Also, tschüs. Bis dann, ja?
 — Ja, tschüs. Danke für den Anruf.

2 — Bernd, du?
 — Ja. Hallo, Ingrid. Wie geht's dir denn in England?
 — Nicht gut. Das Wetter hier ist schrecklich. Es regnet, und es ist so kalt.
 — Was machst du denn die ganze Zeit?
 — Ich lese, höre Musik und gehe ins Kino.
 — Das kannst du doch auch hier zu Hause machen. Wann kommst du zurück?
 — Montag.
 — Gut. Also, tschüs, dann. Bis Montag.
 — Ja. Tschüs.

3 — Hallo, Martin!
 — Hallo, Michael. Du?! Wo bist du?
 — In Saas Fee, in der Schweiz.
 — Du läufst doch nicht Ski?
 — Doch, ich laufe jetzt Ski. Aber ich gehe auch spazieren, und abends gehe ich in die Disko.
 — Und ist das Wetter gut?
 — Fantastisch. Nachts schneit es, und am Tag scheint die Sonne.
 — Und wann kommst du zurück?
 — Am Freitag.
 — Also, viel Spaß noch.
 — Danke. Tschüs.

216
(1B 116)

R

Schönes Wetter heute!

Three pictures with accompanying texts to illustrate the meanings of comments about the weather. Mainly for reference or revision.

L, S, R, W

82

Wie ist das Wetter?

This Worksheet can be made into an OHP transparency and used to present and practise different kinds of weather. It can also be used as reinforcement or as a possible homework activity, especially for the less able.

216 (1B 116) Partnerarbeit

Verbal and visual cues for pupils to practice conversations similar to those in *Drei Telefonate aus den Ferien*. One partner 'phones' the other. Tell pupils to practise using the first set of cues. Ask one or two pairs to perform it, then change to the second set of cues, exchanging roles too. Again, ask one or two pairs to re-enact their phone call. Continue until all four sets of cues have been practised.

Pupils should now be ready to invent their own holiday details in answer to the four questions. When everyone is ready, choose someone to begin and ask them to select someone else in the class (but not their partner) to phone. The person phoned must ask (at least) the four questions that have been practised. The rest of the class would be asked to note down in table form the answers to the four questions.

The teacher then chooses another pupil to make the next phone call, and so on. Half an hour should be enough time for everyone in a class of 30 to take part, and to check the answers together afterwards.

217 (1B 117) Ferienpostkarten

Ask pupils to read the *Ferienpostkarten* and make notes in English under the following headings: place, weather, what the people are doing, name of towns to which the cards are sent.

Using the three postcards as models, together with the material they have been practising in pair-work, pupils should now be able to compose their own imaginary holiday postcard in German.

nem 3
254 (1B 138) Ferienpostkarten

A gap-filling exercise based on the three holiday postcards on page 217 (**1B** 117), but requiring verbs to be changed into the third person.

nem 4

254 (1B 138) Alles Gute!

Four brief texts to match to the picture postcards on which they were written.

Solution: 1 D
2 C
3 A
4 B

Wie war denn dein Urlaub?

Eight young people saying what they thought of their holiday. The vocabulary is similiar to that used in Areas l and 3, but the verbs are in the Past Tense.

Tell pupils to listen to the recording and decide what the first speaker says about her holiday. Play it again, then discuss it with the class. Continue with the other recordings, discussing each one after it has been heard.

Hört gut zu. Wie war Claudias Urlaub? Gut? Oder nicht so gut? Was sagt sie?

Wie war denn dein Urlaub?

1 Claudia: — Ja, Paris war toll, aber das Wetter war furchtbar. Es hat fast jeden Tag geregnet. Wir haben aber sehr gut gegessen — in Bistros und so. Das war Klasse.

2 Andreas: — Also, das war meine erste Auslandsreise. Es war prima. Und das Wetter war wunderschön.

3 Sabine: — Das Hotel war schön genug, und der Strand auch. Aber ... nach einigen Tagen habe ich das schon ein bißchen langweilig gefunden. Meine Eltern wollten ja nicht viel machen und ... naja, es war OK.

4 Elmar: — Es war ein fantastischer Urlaub. Das Wetter, das Essen, die Gegend — alles. Und die italienischen Mädchen habe ich toll gefunden.

5 Renate: — Er war sehr gut, aber nicht lang genug. Wir waren ja nur zehn Tage lang da. Ich möchte gern nächstes Jahr wieder dorthin fahren.

6 Torsten: — Die erste Woche war nicht so gut. Es war ein bißchen kalt und der Campingplatz war auch nicht sehr schön. Aber die zweite Woche war dann schon viel besser.

7 Annika: — Es hat wirklich Spaß gemacht. Das Wetter war ziemlich gut, es hat nur einmal geregnet. Und die Jugendherbergen waren prima — so schön gelegen, meine ich, und so bequem. Und auch billig, natürlich!

8 Patrick: — Es war eine Katastrophe! Die Pension war miserabel, das Essen war furchtbar. Wir haben am Ende meistens in Restaurants gegessen. Das war OK., aber sehr teuer, nicht? Und es war kalt. Wir haben die Sonne nicht sehr oft gesehen. Aber die Rückreise habe ich toll gefunden.

R, W

216-217
(1B 116-7)

Wer hat was gesagt?

A selection of separate sentences, which pupils have to organise into 3 coherent statements about 3 quite different holidays.

The 'intended' solutions are as follows, though ingenious pupils may find others.

Solution: ‚Das Wetter war toll. Jeden Tag Sonne. Aber das Hotel war nicht so gut. Es stand direkt an der Hauptstraße, und es war ein bißchen laut.‘

‚Ich habe Irland toll gefunden. Die Campingplätze waren sehr schön. Die Leute waren alle sehr freundlich. Und das Wetter war auch nicht schlecht.‘

‚Wir waren auf einer Nordseeinsel. Da haben wir ein Ferienhaus gemietet. Das Haus war OK., aber das Wetter war furchtbar. Es hat jeden Tag geregnet.‘

nem 5

254
(1B 138)

(R), W

Mein letzter Urlaub

Pupils should now be able to write a short account of their last holiday, entitled *Mein letzter Urlaub,* using the *Tip des Tages* for guidance.

---

12 Area 6

● Consolidation

218
(1B 118)

L

Treffen im Urlaub

Four conversations in which young German people get to know each other on holiday. Comprehension is tested by a different form of question in each case. Give pupils time to read through the questions for each section before playing the tape. Play each recording twice.

Solution:

A: Am Strand
1b 2a 3b 4a 5b

B: In der Jugendherberge
1 False 2 False 3 True 4 True 5 False

C: Am Campingplatz
1 Even in the holidays the dog wakes up at school time
2 Slept badly — ground was too hard.
3 Because she has a comfortable caravan to sleep in.
4 Her younger brother.
5 Quarter to six.

D: Am Berliner Flughafen
1a 2a 3a 4c 5c

Treffen im Urlaub
1 Am Strand

Junge: — Bist du hier auf Urlaub?
Mädchen: — Ja, und du?
Junge: — Ja, ich auch. Bist du zum ersten Mal hier?
Mädchen: — Nee, wir waren auch letztes Jahr da. Gefällt es dir?
Junge: — Ja, schon. Den Strand find' ich toll. Oder?
Mädchen: — Doch, doch. Der Strand ist schön.
Junge: — Die Stadt ist ein bißchen zu ruhig, nicht viel los, aber ...
Mädchen: — Hast du die Copacabana entdeckt?
Junge: — Nee, was ist das?
Mädchen: — So eine Disko. Kennst du den Marktplatz?
Junge: — Ja.
Mädchen: — Da ist sie ganz in der Nähe. Nur, man sieht das nicht sehr leicht von der Straße. Sie ist einem Schuhgeschäft gegenüber.
Junge: — Und sie ist gut, meinst du?
Mädchen: — Ja, sie ist nicht schlecht. Vielleicht sehen wir uns da.

	Wann fährst du ab?
Junge:	— Nächsten Samstag, leider. Und du?
Mädchen:	— Ich bleibe noch zwei Wochen hier.
Junge:	— Ja? Du hast aber Glück! ... Hast du morgen abend was vor?
Mädchen:	— Du, ich weiß noch nicht.
Spanier:	— Kirrrrsten! Hola! Wirr geh schwiemen. Komm!
Junge:	— Du heißt also Kirsten? Ich heiße Andreas.
Mädchen:	— Ja? Also, bis bald, Andreas.

2 In der Jugendherberge

Junge 1:	— Du siehst müde aus. Hast du eine lange Wanderung hinter dir?
Junge 2:	— Nicht weit, aber ... es ging bergauf bergab.
Junge 1:	— Ja, ich weiß, was du meinst. Wir sind gestern auch nur 10 Kilometer gegangen, aber Mensch, war ich kaputt!
Junge 2:	— Naja, wenigstens ist das Wetter zum Wandern jetzt besser.
Junge 1:	— Ja, das stimmt. Gestern war es wirklich zu heiß... woher kommst du?
Junge 2:	— Aus der Nähe von Braunschweig. Und du?
Junge 1:	— Ich komme aus Dortmund. Bist du mit einer Schulgruppe da?
Junge 2:	— Mit meinem Bruder. Er spielt jetzt draußen Fußball. Dazu hatte ich keine Lust.
Junge 1:	— Spielst du gern Karten?
Junge 2:	— Ja, sicher.
Junge 1:	— Also, nach dem Abendessen können wir vielleicht Skat spielen, oder so?
Junge 2:	— Ja, prima. Wie spät ist es denn jetzt?
Junge 1:	— Zehn vor sieben. Das Abendessen ist um sieben, oder?
Junge 2:	— Weiß ich nicht. Wir kochen immer selbst. Ich bin aber sehr hungrig. Ich glaube, ich gehe meinen Bruder holen. Bis bald, denn.
Junge 1:	— Ja, tschüs!

3 Am Campingplatz

Mädchen 1:	— Morgen!
Mädchen 2:	— Salut! Ist das dein Hund?
Mädchen 1:	— Ja. Er heißt Mickey.
Mädchen 2:	— Gehst du immer so früh mit ihm spazieren?
Mädchen 1:	— Ja, weißt du, wenn Schule ist, steht er immer mit mir auf. Leider macht er das aber in

	den Ferien auch. Und du, du stehst aber auch schön früh auf.
Mädchen 2:	— Tja, also, ehrlich gesagt hab' ich nicht sehr gut geschlafen. Wir zelten ja.
Mädchen 1:	— Was war's denn? War dir kalt?
Mädchen 2:	— Nee nee. Ich habe einen guten Schlafsack. Nur der Boden ist ein bißchen hart. Und du, bist du auch mit der Familie da?
Mädchen 1:	— Ja, in dem blau-weißen Wohnwagen da drüben.
Madchen 2:	— Oh, toll. Du hast also kein Problem mit dem Boden!
Mädchen 1:	— Nein, ich habe nur ein Problem mit meinem kleinen Bruder — und mit dem Hund. Naja, ich muß ihn jetzt laufen lassen, sonst kriegen wir heute keine Ruhe.
Mädchen 2:	— Gehst du weit?
Mädchen 1:	— Och, so ein paar Kilometer. Hast du Lust, mitzukommen?
Mädchen 2:	— Warum nicht? Es ist ja erst — ach du lieber Gott! Viertel vor sechs!

4 Am Berliner Flughafen

Junge:	— Hallo.
Mädchen:	— Hallo ...
Junge:	— Entschuldige, aber ... ich glaube, ich kenne dich.
Mädchen:	— Kann sein. Woher kommst du?
Junge:	— Aus Berlin.
Mädchen:	— Nein. Dann kann's nicht sein. Ich bin hier nur zu Besuch, auf Urlaub.
Junge:	— Ach so. Du wartest auf jemanden?
Mädchen:	— Ja, mein Cousin holt mich ab. Ich bin gerade angekommen. Holst du auch jemanden ab?
Junge:	— Nee nee. Ich fliege nach Hamburg.
Mädchen:	— Ja? Wohin denn? Ich komme nämlich selbst aus Hamburg.
Junge:	— Ja, ich habe Freunde in Harburg.
Mädchen:	— Das glaub' ich nicht! Dort wohne ich selber! Wie heißen denn deine Freunde?
Junge:	— Hugo Fischer —
Mädchen:	— Du spinnst!
Junge:	— Wieso? Kennst du ihn?
Mädchen:	— Ich gehe mit ihm auf die Schule. Er wohnt ganz in meiner Nähe.
Junge:	— Dann hab' ich bestimmt recht. Ich habe dich doch schon gesehen. Wahrscheinlich zu Ostern letztes Jahr.

Lautsprecher: Passagiere für den
Lufthansaflug Nummer 702
nach Hamburg werden gebeten,
sich jetzt zu Tor Nummer 3
zu begeben.

Junge: — Das bin ich. Paß auf, wie lange
bleibst du denn in Berlin?

Mädchen: — Ich fliege am siebten zurück.

Junge: — Oh, schade. Ich bleibe ja auch
zwei Wochen in Hamburg.

Mädchen: — Naja, dann treffen wir uns am
Flughafen vielleicht wieder?

Junge: — Ja, hoffentlich. Also, tschüs.

Mädchen: — Tschüs. Gute Reise.

L, R, W

83

Treffen im Urlaub

Worksheet with reading/listening tasks in
German to go with the same four
conversations. All four activities, though
different, are designed to focus attention on
the actual German words and phrases used. It
will depend on the class whether pupils need
to hear each conversation once or twice. In
either case, pupils will need time (and
possibly help) to read through the task before
hearing the recording.

Section 1
Requires them to listen for specific words and
write them into gaps in the printed sentences.

Solution:
1 zum ersten Mal hier
2 toll
3 der Straße
4 nicht schlecht
5 Glück
6 noch nicht

Section 2
Involves listening for the order in which six
questions occur in the conversation, and
numbering them accordingly.

Solution:
4
5
2
1
6
3

Section 3
Requires pupils to spot which of two ways of
saying the same thing are actually used in the
conversation.

Solution:
1 (b)
2 (a)
3 (a)
4 (b)

Section 4
Consists of a list of phrases, only **some** of
which occur in the conversation. Pupils have
to underline the ones they hear. To develop
their listening discrimination, some of the
printed phrases are deliberately **similar** to
those in the recording. So emphasise that they
must only underline those which are exactly
the same. The phrases are listed in the order
in which they are spoken.

Solution: Phrases used: Dann kann's nicht sein
Ich bin gerade angekommen
Dann hab' ich bestimmt recht
Ich fliege am siebten zurück
Gute Reise!

W

219
(1B 119)

Sabines Ferienfotos

A selection of holiday photos. Pupils have to
devise a caption to show what the people are
saying. There is plenty of room for humour
here!

This and the following activity lend
themselves readily to revision of previous
chapters in the book.

L, S, R, W

84

Ferienkrimskrams

Three collections of tickets, receipts,
brochures etc. from three different holidays,
from which can be inferred where the people
went, what they did and so on. These can be
used either for discussion in English, for
discussion in German or for guided
composition in German — or for any
combination of these.

Prepared packs of loose, authentic 'remains'
of a similar kind provide marvellous stimuli for
oral as well as for written work. Remember
that even receipts and tickets in English can
do the job — Germans do come to Britain as
well!

218
(1B 118) **Wo die Deutschen Urlaub machen/ Lieblingsländer der Touristen**

It is hoped that these statistics will be of interest in themselves. There are a few questions in the Pupil's Book, but teachers could well extend discussion of the facts and figures in the classroom.

nem 6   R
255
(1B 139) **Nur für Superhirne!**

A dialogue accompanied by a map of Europe indicating various holiday locations.

By careful examination of text and map it is possible to deduce where the people mentioned are going on holiday. This is a more complex problem-solving activity, probably not for everybody.

Solution:
Brigitte — Bern
Jürgen — Neapel
Ulla — Nizza
Petra — Lourdes
Karl — Tarragona
Werner — Sylt
Kirsten — Mittenwald
Anke — Loch Ness (by final deduction — no clue given)
Georg — Graz

R

220-221
(1B 120-
121) **Urlaub in Deutschland!**

Eight of the German *Länder* described for what is attractive about them, rather than factually. Using simple geographical clues in the texts together with visual clues from the photos, pupils have to match the texts to the photos.

Solution: **1** Hessen **2** Schleswig-Holstein **3** Rheinland-Pfalz **4** Baden-Württemberg **5** Das Saarland **6** Nordrhein-Westfalen **7** Niedersachsen **8** Bayern.

Vocabulary

aktiv *active*
alles Gute *all the best*
die Alpen *the Alps*
der Antrag(⁻e) *application*
die Art(en) *sort, kind*
aufnehmen *to receive, admit*
aufregend *exciting*
die Ausbildung *education*
ausbrechen *to break out*
ausreisen *to emigrate*
außerdem *moreover*
bauen *to build*
Bayern *Bavaria*
bedeckt *cloudy; covered*
sich begeben *to undergo, undertake*
die Behörde(n) *authority*
bequem *comfortable*
bewachen *to guard*
es blitzt *there is lightning*
der Boden *floor*
das Brettspiel(e) *board game*
der Caravan(s) *estate car; caravan*
chinesisch *Chinese*
der Cousin(s) *cousin(m)*
der Dialekt(e) *dialect*
das Ding(e) *thing*
donnern *to thunder*
ehrlich *honest(ly)*
der Eindruck(⁻e) *impression*
die Einrichtung(en) *equipment, furnishing*
einerseits *on one hand*
empfangen *to receive*
die Erfrischung(en) *refreshment*

die Erlaubnis *permission*
erst(r/s) *not until*
die erste Stunde *the first lesson*
an ersten Mai *on 1st May*
erwarten *to expect*
erzählen *to tell, relate*
Federball *badminton*
das Ferienhaus(⁻er) *holiday home*
das Fernsehen *television*
die Freiheit *freedom*
sich freuen auf + Acc *to look forward to*
frostig *frosty*
die Galerie(n) *gallery (art)*
das Gebirge(-) *mountains*
die Gebühr(en) *charge, fee*
das Gefühl(e) *feeling*
das Gehöft(e) *farmstead*
gemütlich *cosy*
genehmigen *to allow, give permission for*
gepflegt *looked after*
die Geschichte(n) *story; history*
gestattet *allowed, permitted*
geteilt *divided*
das Gewehr(e) *rifle*
die Giraffe(n) *giraffe*
die Grenze(n) *border*
Griechenland *Greece*
der Güterzug(⁻e) *goods train*
Halbpension *half-board*
die Hektik *hectic rush*
die Herde(n) *herd*
der Himmel *sky*
die Industrie *industry*

innerhalb *within*
inzwischen *in the meantime*
irgendwo *somewhere, anywhere*
die Katastrophe(n) *catastrophe*
das Kinderschwimmbecken(-) *children's swimming pool*
das Klima *climate*
komisch *odd, funny*
der Kontinent(e) *continent*
der Krimskrams *bits and pieces*
kühl *cool, chilly*
die Küste(n) *coast*
leicht *easy, light*
der Löwe(n) *lion*
das Meer(e) *sea*
merken *to notice, perceive*
mieten *to rent, hire*
mild *mild*
nebelig *foggy*
der Palast(⁻e) *palace*
persönlich *personally*
regelmäßig *regular(ly)*
regnen *to rain*
reiselustig *enjoying travel*
riesig *great(ly), enormous(ly)*
schießen *to shoot*
Schweden *Sweden*
die Sehenswürdigkeit(en) *place of interest*
der Skat *card game (skat)*
das Sperrgebiet(e) *forbidden area*
springen *to jump*
spüren *to feel, sense*
staatlich *of the state*

der Stacheldrahtzaun(⁻e) *barbed wire fence*
der Stierkampf(⁻e) *bullfight*
der Strand(⁻e) *beach*
der Straßenübergang *crossing*
das Stück(e) *piece*
stundenlang *for hours (on end)*
stürmisch *stormy*
das Superhirn(e) *superbrain*
das Telefonat(e) *telephone call*
das Tor(e) *gate*
traurig *sad(ly)*
trocknen *to dry*
überfüllt *overcrowded*
übernachten *to spend the night*
die Übersiedlung(en) *emigration*
unwohl *uneasy*
vergehen *to go by (of time)*
versprechen *to promise*
sich verstehen mit *to get on with*
die Verwandten *relatives*
das Volk(⁻er) *people, nation*
Vollpension *full-board*
die Wanderung(en) *hike, walk*
die Waschmaschine(n) *washing machine*
wetten *to bet*
wolkig *cloudy*
der Wohnwagen(-) *caravan*
der Zaun(⁻e) *fence*

INTERNATIONALER TREFF

This section can be used at various stages of the book and is intended to:
- promote discussion of differences and similarities.
- break down barriers and promote greater understanding.

221
(1B 121)

Inhalt

General introduction and contents of this section.

What some Germans think about school in the UK

L

Die Schule in Großbritannien

Play part of the recording of German pupils talking about their impressions of school life in Great Britain and ask pupils to decide what they are talking about.

Then play the whole recording stopping after each statement. Ask pupils to give as many details as they can.

Die Schule in Großbritannien
1 — Die Schule fängt um Viertel vor neun an und ist erst um vier Uhr aus.
2 — Man hat immer acht Stunden am Tag. Man muß den ganzen Tag in der Schule bleiben. Man darf nicht nach Hause gehen.
3 — Die Pause dauert 20 Minuten am Vormittag und 10 Minuten am Nachmittag.
4 — Die Mittagspause ist von halb eins bis zwei.
5 — Der Schultag ist zu lang. Es gibt zu viele lange Pausen.
6 — Sie gehen länger zur Schule am Tag und haben nur den späten Nachmittag und den Abend frei.
7 — Die haben samstags keine Schule. Das finde ich toll.
8 — Nachmittags Schule? Ich finde das nicht gut.
9 — Die Freizeit ist zu kurz.
10 — Ich kann länger schlafen als in Deutschland.
11 — Der Lehrer ist der große Boß in Großbritannien. Er macht mit den Schülern, was er will.
12 — Die Schulen sind sehr streng. Man muß ‚Yes, Sir' oder ‚Yes, Miss' sagen.
13 — Viele kommen mit dem Schulbus zur Schule. Der Schulbus ist sehr komfortabel. Er hat gepolsterte Sitze. Es gibt sehr laute Popmusik im Bus.

222
(1B 122)

R

Ist das an deiner Schule auch so?

Ask pupils to decide whether or not the views expressed by some Germans about schools in the UK apply to their school.

Afterwards it might be useful to discuss briefly the way in which a visitor to a foreign country can easily gain a false picture or make generalisations from insufficient information.

222
(1B 122)

R

Die Schule in Großbritannien

This printed display provides every pupil with a record of what they have previously heard.

In addition, some pupils might find it rewarding to do the reading comprehension activity in *Noch etwas mehr.*

nem 1
255
(1B 139)

R

Die Schule in Großbritannien

This is not a demanding activity. It should be of particular help to slower pupils.

What some Germans think about houses in the UK

222-223
(1B 122-3)

R

Häuser und Wohnungen

Ask pupils to look at page 222 (**1B** 122) and discover what some Germans think about houses in Great Britain. They can then read *Mein Problem in England* (page 223 (**1B** 123)).

223
(1B 123)

L, S, R

Wie ist das bei dir?

Ask pupils to work in pairs to decide whether or not the opinions expressed by some Germans apply to them. Check results orally round the class.

Some views about English clothes and make-up

L, S, R, W

224
(1B 124)

Kleidung und Make-up

Ask pupils to listen to the recording and find out what is being talked about.

Play the recording again, making frequent use of the pause button, and ask pupils to match the split-up sentences. Check orally. Pupils can then write down the complete summary for consolidation and as a basis for the following exploitation.

Kleidung und Make-up

1 — Sie tragen alle eine Schuluniform am Tage. Die Farben sind ganz dunkel: dunkelblau, dunkelgrau und schwarz. Das sieht sehr traurig aus und gefällt mir gar nicht. Abends tragen die Mädchen ganz ausgeflippte Kleider, vielleicht als Kontrast zur Uniform.

2 — Die Kleidung für Jungen und Mädchen ist sehr extravagant. Mädchen tragen zum Beispiel knallgelbe Schuhe und einen rosa Rock mit einem grünen T-Shirt. Die Mädchen tragen viel mehr Röcke. Meine Freundinnen und ich tragen fast immer Hosen oder Blue Jeans.

3 — Die Mädchen sind sehr toll geschminkt, und die Schminke ist oft ganz dick. Manchmal ist der Lippenstift purpur oder grau. Einige Jungen tragen auch Make-up, und Ohrringe für Jungen sind viel populärer als in Deutschland.

Solution: 1f 2h 3a 4e(b) 5c(g) 6d 7g 8b(e/g)

L, S, R, W

224
(1B 124) **Ein Fragebogen**

Practise the questions. Revise ways of answering questions 1 and 2. Refer pupils to the *Tip des Tages* in Chapter 10, page 181 (**1B** 83). Ask pupils to interview each other in pairs and to take notes.

Pupils should now be in a position to evaluate the comments made by the Germans about clothes.

Read out items at random from *Was paßt zusammen?* and ask pupils to say whether they agree with them on the basis of their interviews.

,Britische Schüler tragen eine Schuluniform. Ist das richtig?'

Some comments about spare time in the UK

R

223
(1B 123) **Freizeit**

This is a collection of quotations about spare time in the UK, followed by some correct and incorrect inferences in German about spare time in Germany.

Ask pupils to read the quotations and then decide whether the comments are correct. Possible homework.

Solution:

Richtig	Falsch
	✓
✓	
	✓
	✓
✓	

R

223
(1B 123) **Ein Aufenthalt in England**

This is a young girl's account of her impressions during an exchange visit. It is intended for private reading. Pupils can, of course, use the *Wörterliste.*

Some German views about radio and television

L, (S), R

224
(1B 124) **Radio und Fernsehen in Großbritannien**

Play the recording of the comments about viewing and listening habits or read the text in the Pupil's Book.

These comments may be provocative enough to stimulate spontaneous reactions from pupils. At the same time, pupils can draw on the language presented to make their own statements, e.g.:

*Nein, der Fernseher ist **nicht** den ganzen Tag an.*

Unser Fernseher läuft nur von sieben bis elf.

Radio und Fernsehen in Großbritannien
— Der Fernseher ist den ganzen Tag an.
— Sie haben ein Radio im Badezimmer.
— Die Familie sitzt von sieben bis elf vorm Fernseher.
— In der Küche steht ein Fernseher.
— Der Fernseher läuft rund um die Uhr.
— Sie gucken fern zum Frühstück.

— Das Radio in der Küche läuft
  ununterbrochen.
— Der Fernseher läuft fast den ganzen Tag.
— Auch im Eßzimmer gibt es einen Fernseher.
— Sie sehen fern im Bett.

L, S, R, W

224
(1B 124) **Fragebogen zu Radio und Fernsehen**

A questionnaire to elicit information about
radio and viewing habits. This will provide
pupils with written evidence on which to base
their comments on the views expressed by
Germans.

Practise some of the questions, if required.

Ask pupils to interview each other in pairs and
to take notes.

Partnerarbeit.
Hier ist ein Fragebogen.
Fragt eure Partner und schreibt die Antworten
auf.

---

nem 2
R
255
(1B 139) **Radio und Fernsehen**

Some pupils might find it useful to summarise
and evaluate the German comments in
English.

R, W

224
(1B 124) **Das Fernsehprogramm**

Several comments about television
programmes.

Ask pupils to sort the comments into three
columns under the headings:

positiv +   neutral   negativ -

Hier sind einige Meinungen von Deutschen
über unser Fernsehen. Macht drei Listen: Was
ist positiv? Was ist neutral? Was ist negativ?
(Demonstrate on the board.)
'Es gibt viele Sendungen für junge Leute' —
Ist das positiv oder negativ?

The list into which pupils put some comments
will largely be a matter of personal opinion.
This could lead to some interesting discussion.

R, (W)

224
(1B 124) **Diese Woche im Fernsehen**

Pupils are given instructions in German for a
project about television programmes, which
should provide them with more data so that
they can evaluate the German comments
more competently.

Comments on traffic in
the UK

R

225
(1B 125) **Straßen und Verkehr**

Only the texts under the heading *Ist
Linksfahren ein Problem?* are intended for
exploitation.

Ask pupils to read both texts and comment on
the different attitudes towards driving on the
left. Ask for an explanation of Jutta's attitude.

What some Germans think
about English food

L, R

225
(1B 125) **Deutsche Teenager auf Urlaub in
Großbritannien**

Tell pupils that you are going to play a
cassette of German teenagers talking about
food in England. Tell them to look in their
books and decide who is talking.

**Deutsche Teenager auf Urlaub in
Großbritannien**
1 — Bonbons, Kekse und Schokolade
    schmecken toll. Die Kuchen schmecken
    nicht so gut, finde ich.

2 — Das Frühstück schmeckt gut. Das Essen
    in der Schule ist fürchterlich! Die
    englischen Kuchen schmecken prima.

3 — Das Essen in den Pubs schmeckt immer
    gut. Fisch mit Pommes frites ist
    fantastisch!

4 — Das Toastbrot zum Frühstück schmeckt
    nicht. Die Marmelade schmeckt aber
    gut. Die Cornflakes schmecken auch
    gut.

5 — Ja, das Essen geht, aber ich kriege nicht
    genug. Nach dem Abendessen bin ich
    immer noch hungrig und gehe zu
    McDonalds.

6 — Es ist immer so ein Berg auf meinem Teller — acht Kartoffeln, dann noch Gemüse, Fleisch und Soße!

7 — Das englische Brot schmeckt überhaupt nicht. Der Tee schmeckt gut, aber der Kaffee ist grauenvoll!

Solution: **1** Birgit **2** Jens **3** Wiebke **4** Jürgen **5** Harald
6 Sabine **7** Sonja

---

nem 3   R
225
(1B 139)
Deutscher Teenager auf Urlaub

For this task pupils can be referred to *Deutsche Teenager auf Urlaub in Großbritannien.*

                                                                          R

Findet Jürgen das Essen gut?

85

Tell pupils to read *Deutsche Teenager auf Urlaub in Großbritannien* and mark the table on the Worksheet with a plus or a minus according to whether the people like or dislike the food. There is an extra column for pupils to record their own likes and dislikes. They could then complete the questions in English. The gap-filling is intended partly as revision of *gern/nicht gern.*

                                                                          R, W

86

Kreuzworträtsel

A crossword puzzle to consolidate some of the vocabulary of this magazine section. Possible homework.

                                                                          (W)

Ein Brief an Michael

87

Encourage pupils to consider the issues raised in this magazine section, and to put their ideas in writing (preferably in German, but some pupils may prefer to do this in English). It is hoped that this exercise will reduce some misconceptions and promote discussion. All letters will be answered!

Vocabulary

ähnlich wie *similar to*
altmodisch *old-fashioned*
amerikanisch *American*
sich **an**ziehen *to get dressed*
ausgeflippt *outrageous, freaky*
der Bericht(e) *report*
der Boß(Bosse) *boss*
einarmig *one-armed*
Eis laufen *to skate*

die Eisbahn(en) *ice rink*
extravagant *extravagant*
gepolstert *sprung, upholstered*
geschminkt *made-up (with cosmetics)*
grauenvoll *dreadful*
im Hintergrund *in the background*
sich kleiden *to dress*

der Kohleofen(⸚) *coal stove (fire)*
die Komödie(n) *comedy*
der Kontrast(e) *contrast*
die Kurve(n) *bend*
der Lippenstift(e) *lipstick*
purpur *purple*
sauber *clean*
die Schnecke(n) *snail*
die Serie(n) *series*

der Sitz(e) *seat*
staunen *to be amazed*
der Streik(s) *strike*
streng *strict*
stricken *to knit*
die Telefonzelle(n) *phone box*
veröffentlichen *to publish*
verrückt *crazy, mad*
die Werbung(en) *advertising*